To the End of the Earth

To the End of the Earth

A HISTORY OF THE CRYPTO-JEWS OF NEW MEXICO

Stanley M. Hordes

COLUMBIA UNIVERSITY PRESS
NEW YORK

Columbia University Press
Publishers Since 1893
New York Chichester, West Sussex

Library of Congress Cataloging-in-Publication Data
Hordes, Stanley M.
To the end of the earth : a history of the crypto-Jews of New Mexico / Stanley M. Hordes.
p. cm.
Includes bibliographical references and index.
ISBN 0-231-12936-X (cloth : alk. paper)
1. Jews—New Mexico—History. 2. Marranos—New Mexico—History. 3. Sephardim—New Mexico—History. 4. Marranos—Social life and customs. 5. Jews—Cultural assimilation. 6. Jews—Identity. 7. New Mexico—Ethnic relations. I. Title.

F805.J5H67 2005
978.9'004924—dc22 2005045455

∞ Columbia University Press books are printed on permanent and durable acid-free paper.
Printed in the United States of America
c 10 9 8 7 6 5

Dedicated to my mother and to the memory of my father, with gratitude for their support and encouragement

With deep appreciation to the Estate of Eva Feld for its generosity in providing the support necessary to complete the research and writing of this book

Contents

Foreword

The academic study of crypto-Judaism has been developing over the past few years in several important directions. Two related avenues of research have opened up: the historical and the more broadly social scientific, especially in the fields of sociology, anthropology, and folklore. To a great extent, the social scientific approaches have looked at modern aspects of crypto-Jewish practice and culture, making attempts to develop some historical arguments. But up to this point, in-depth professional historical analysis has not been readily available. On a different level, there are two main clusters of approaches: the proponents of the first, including Stanley M. Hordes and me, argue for the significance, historicity, and authenticity of crypto-Judaism in the American Southwest (and beyond), while supporters of the second reject the authenticity of crypto-Judaism. Although several academics and nonacademics have written in support of this self-styled revisionist approach, their work draws on that of Judith Neulander, who comes to the material from the academic discipline of folklore. The questions raised by both approaches depend on detailed historical analysis. This book provides both the data and the analysis that enable the resolution of these significant academic questions.

Academics working in the social sciences have largely been assessing the current practices and identity of crypto-Jews. To the extent that their studies have asked questions of authenticity or historical origin, they have largely depended on the analysis of oral histories and individuals' self-understanding. Very little work has been done by these scholars in the detailed textual investigation necessary to probe the history of the movement of people and thereby the ideas, identities, and practices that characterize modern crypto-Judaism. In this volume, Hordes presents a detailed and documented historical analysis that conclusively demonstrates the movement of individuals descended from Jewish families from Spain and Portugal to Mexico and, subsequently, New Mexico and other parts of the New World. In doing so, his work lays the foundation for the anthropological and sociological research that is also under way. It allows us to examine the arguments regarding the development of crypto-Jewish culture and thus to assess the proper application of these arguments to different crypto-Jewish sociocultural contexts, be it families or communities, and to different geographic contexts, exploring various issues that relate to the distinct parts of New Mexico.

Although from an anthropological perspective, historical authenticity is not a primary question—anthropologists tend to be more interested in how people see and understand themselves—the historical work provides an invaluable basis from which to evaluate these processes and to understand the nature of practice and its transformation and the relationship between memory and identity construction. This foundation also allows the social scientist to judge the nature of the symbols and practices deployed by crypto-Jews, providing the basis for examining the way symbols and practices are taken up and the social and cultural contexts through which they are transformed. Thus Hordes's groundbreaking work also allows us indirectly to trace the movement of ideas through different cultural contexts. His analysis forces the social scientist to recognize that the movement of communities to New Mexico was a complex process, bringing together different individual choices and cultural contexts. This complexity is no doubt the hallmark of current crypto-Judaism; it challenges any approach that seeks pure "Jewish" forms. From an anthropological perspective, it provides a significant case study for the development and transformation of cultural practices.

This important historical analysis also allows us to both contextualize and analyze the processes through which people choose to identify with the crypto-Jewish aspects of their identity today; it may be that this is the place in which economic and past religious choice play a part. Such an analysis can now, on the basis of Hordes's work, take the claims and interpretations seriously.

It is important to also address the academic debate within the broad field of crypto-Judaic studies. Although the two broad clusters seem to be diametrically opposed, each establishes the challenges that the other must address. Judith Neulander challenges those of us studying crypto-Judaism to examine a range of issues that may have played only a secondary role in our research projects. Her questions should be seen as both historical and ethnographic. On the level of history, Neulander raises important questions about the chain of continuity between the Jewish communities of Spain and Portugal and the crypto-Jews of present-day New Mexico. She asks if there are sources other than fifteenth-century Spanish Jews for the apparently Jewish practices found in New Mexico; her primary contention is that these rituals arose from Judaizing messianic groups that she believes flourished in New Mexico in the early part of the twentieth century. On the ethnographic level, she raises important questions about the interpretation of data both by crypto-Jews and by ethnographers—charging, in effect, that both are skewing the data toward their preferred interpretation.

In this book, Hordes takes up the gauntlet flung down by Neulander. Perhaps the primary issue addressed is that of continuity. Given the nature of the easily available data, there has been a problem in linking the families that were forcibly or voluntarily converted between 1390 and 1492 (*conversos*) to their possible descendants in the twenty-first century. An additional puzzle is the sense of identity of those in succeeding generations of *converso* families from the fifteenth to the twenty-first century. Does their Jewish origin imply continuing Jewish identity? In relation to the first issue, Hordes's research in both the Americas and Europe conclusively demonstrates the historical connections between the families and individuals claiming crypto-Jewish origin in the twenty-first century and the *conversos* of the fifteenth century. The link in Jewish identity between those two poles is clearly harder to establish. It relies on data that includes Inquisition documents, marriage patterns, and current practices. While each of these sources is problematic on its own, when they are viewed together, as Hordes demonstrates, they provide a strong argument for the persistence of both Jewish practice and Jewish identity.

Hordes also examines the role of messianic Christianity in shaping identity and practice among today's Hispano community. Neulander's argument relies on a significant number of conversions from Catholicism to various forms of Protestantism, particularly Seventh-Day Adventism and messianic groups. It also relies on the willful or unwillful forgetting of this conversion in a family's history. The first of these presuppositions is a historical question; the second is ethnographic. Hordes's data suggest that the penetration of New Mexico by messianic and other sectarian Protestant groups in the periods significant to crypto-Judaism was not as significant or as widespread as required by Neulander's hypothesis. Most of the families whose history he traces back to Spain—families that both embrace a significant repertoire of practices that they identity as crypto-Judaic and have a clear and articulated identity as being of Jewish origin—experienced little or no conversion to messianic Protestantism, either remaining within the Catholic Church or converting to such mainstream Protestant denominations as Methodism and Presbyterianism. In regard to the ethnographic aspect of Neulander's hypothesis, I would strongly argue that ethnographic practice or experience does not support it. While individuals and groups do reinterpret their past, often unconsciously, they do not usually forget significant aspects of their family's recent past, especially, as in this case, events that would have occurred within almost living memory. If we assume that they are willfully forgetting or lying, this must be based on the presupposition that they make a connection (or believe that we might make a connection) between their Christian associations and their crypto-Jewish practices. Given the range of people interviewed, most of whom are not aware of the academic debates or problems, it is unlikely that this connection would be foremost in their minds or that they would regard one form of Christian past as more or less favorable than another.

Stanley Hordes's book thus works on several significant levels. It provides a link with the social scientific work and serves as the essential foundation for the ethnographic studies that seek to understand how crypto-Jews understand themselves and construct models of identity for the future built on those of the past. In terms of academic debate, it also presents a pivotal response to the challenges posed by the revisionists, taking their arguments seriously and addressing the issues they raise. In my view, the volume conclusively demonstrates the historical origins of modern crypto-Jews, descending from families converted from Judaism to Catholicism in Spain and Portugal. It thus forces us to take the debate to a new level, no longer examining issues of authenticity, but processes of transmission and transformation.

Seth D. Kunin
School of Divinity
University of Aberdeen

Preface

As I was changing planes on a snowy afternoon recently, I struck up a conversation with one of the other passengers waiting in the gate area. He, too, was from Santa Fe, New Mexico, and we soon found ourselves discussing topics of local interest, such as the current drought, challenges faced by the public schools, and the progress of the Santa Fe High School basketball program. Predictably, the conversation turned to the topic of our respective occupations. I told him that I was writing a book about the history of a group of Hispanos[1] in New Mexico who traced their roots back to people who were forced to convert from Judaism to Catholicism in fifteenth-century Spain and Portugal, and who were now exploring their ancestral Jewish roots. My fellow passenger seemed momentarily stunned, and then excitedly told me, "My grandmother always told me that we were Sephardic Jews," and proceeded to describe customs suggestive of a Jewish past practiced by his family in his small, rural village in northern New Mexico.

This was hardly the first time that I found myself the object of such a revelation. For more than two decades, many people from Hispano communities throughout New Mexico had been investigating the possibility that they descended from Iberian crypto-Jews, or secret Jews. Given the long and rich history of crypto-Judaism in Spain, Portugal, Mexico, and the far northern frontier of the Viceroyalty of New Spain,[2] it seemed logical to consider the question of whether there existed a connection between the beliefs expressed and practices followed by twenty-first-century native New Mexicans and those of the *conversos*[3] of fifteenth and sixteenth-century Iberia. It is the purpose of this study to examine the historical development of crypto-Judaism, the secret practice of Judaism, in New Mexico from its inception in the sixteenth century, down to the recent past, when descendants of the original settlers began to emerge from the shadows and assert their Sephardic heritage. But as interesting as is the history of these individuals, the story of how I became aware of their existence is, perhaps, even more intriguing.

In 1980, I completed my doctoral dissertation, "The Crypto-Jewish Community of New Spain, 1620–1649: A Collective Biography," at Tulane University. Drawing on a variety of documentary sources in Spain and Mexico, including Inquisition records, civil and criminal court files, notarial documents, and shipping and immigration records, I was able to reconstruct how the secret Jews of Mexico fit into the political, social, religious, and commercial context of the colony. I was unaware of any later or present-day manifestations of crypto-Judaism in either Mexico or the American Southwest, assuming that, generation by generation, the *conversos* of New Spain had gradually assimilated into the mainstream of Spanish Catholic society, eventually losing any unique ethnic identity.

The following year, I assumed the position of state historian of New Mexico, maintaining my office in the New Mexico State Records Center and Archives in the state capital, Santa Fe. I had not been in my position for more than a few weeks before I began receiving some very unusual visitors to my office. People from within the Hispano community would come in, close the door behind them to make certain that no one could overhear them, and then lean across my desk and whisper, "So-and-so lights candles on Friday nights" or "So-and-so doesn't eat pork." I initially dismissed these people as cranks, but over the succeeding weeks and months the visits continued. Hispanos representing different walks of life, from different parts of New Mexico, felt compelled to relate to me stories of their *comadres* and *compadres* observing customs suggestive of a Jewish background.

Gradually it became clear to me that I should be asking myself some critical questions: Could it be possible that the same phenomenon that I had studied in seventeenth-century Mexico had survived for more than three hundred years—and in a place as remote as New Mexico? Once I formulated the questions, other pieces of information began to fall into place. I began to ask my Hispano friends and colleagues if they had heard of similar accounts of secret Judaism practiced by their families. Several would respond with such answers as "Well, Grandma always said that we were Jews, but we never took her seriously," and "Grandpa told us that eating pork was unhealthy."

My search took me to two colleagues at the University of New Mexico who, from different disciplinary perspectives, had been investigating similar themes. Sociologist Tomás Atencio, who grew up in Dixon, New Mexico, had been aware of crypto-Judaism in his hometown and was interested in how this phenomenon fit into the context of contemporary Hispano culture. Rowena Rivera, of the Department of Spanish, had been studying similarities between the music and literature of present-day Hispano New Mexicans and the same genres of Sephardic culture in fifteenth-century Spain.

As a consequence, in 1987 the three of us initiated an interdisciplinary project, sponsored by the Latin American and Iberian Institute at the University of New Mexico: "The Sephardic Legacy in New Mexico: A History of the Crypto-Jews." Several years later, anthropologist Seth D. Kunin, of the University of Aberdeen in Scotland, and I began a collaboration, with Kunin initiating fieldwork in New Mexico in 1996, which continued over the course of the succeeding seven years.

On the basis of interviews conducted with New Mexico Hispanos, it appears that there does exist in the region a Sephardic legacy—vestiges carried on by descendants of crypto-Jews who emigrated to the area as early as the sixteenth and seventeenth centuries. This cultural remnant spans quite a wide spectrum of society. At one extreme are individuals who are biological descendants of the original fifteenth-century *conversos*, but retain neither an awareness of their ancestral faith nor any vestigial Jewish customs. The other extreme, very few in number, encompasses those who profess a retention of a consciousness of the family's Judaism and continue to observe Jewish practices, either openly as Jews or in secret under the cover of Catholicism or Protestantism. The majority, however, fall in a middle category: those Catholics or Protestants whose families display observances suggestive of Judaism, but without any specific knowledge about why they do so.

The emergence of this group—or at least my becoming aware of their existence—in the last decades of the twentieth century served as the motivation for my undertaking research into the history of the crypto-Jews of New Mexico. This study is designed to examine the nature and extent of *converso* participation in the formation and development of Spanish New Mexican society from the earliest exploration and settlement of the colony in the late sixteenth century until the recent past. It is based principally on a synthesis of the published historical literature and documentary research conducted in archives located in Spain, Portugal, France, Mexico, and New Mexico, supplemented by oral history interviews conducted by me and ethnographic interviews carried out by social scientists. The last served to shed light on possible indications of cultural continuity in the early to mid-twentieth century.

Such a study could not have been accomplished without the assistance of a number of key individuals and institutions. I would particularly like to acknowledge the generous grant awarded by the Estate of Eva Feld, which provided me the opportunity to conduct extensive archival research not only in New Mexico, but in Mexico, Spain, Portugal, and France from 1998 to 2001. Special thanks is extended to William Schneck, executor of the estate, and to Gail Schneck, administrator of the grant, for their confidence in me to see the project through to publication. I am indebted to U.S. Office of Education, Division of International Exchange, for granting me a Fulbright-Hays Dissertation Research Fellowship, thus enabling me to perform research in the archives of Mexico and Spain in the mid-1970s. The doctoral dissertation that resulted from this grant served as the basis for chapters 1 and 2 of this book. I would also like to express my appreciation for the contributions provided by the Albert and Ethel Herzstein Foundation, Hyman and Marjorie Weinberg Foundation, Max and Anna Levinson Foundation, Sidney Stern Memorial Trust, and A. L. H. Foundation.

I deeply appreciate the dedication of my research assistants, Robert Martínez, Richard Salazar, Gerald González, Martina Will, and Janice Martínez, who put in far more hours than could be compensated with money, *tapas*, or *copas de vino tinto*. I owe a debt of thanks to volunteers Andrea Kron, for undertaking the tedious task of extracting names from census and sacramental records; Lorie Baca McNeil, for searching in vain for the student records of Alonso Rael de Aguilar in the archives of the Universidad de Salamanca; and María Manuela Alves, for guiding me through trial records of the Portuguese Inquisition from the Arquivo Nacional da Torre do Tombo in Lisbon.

Anthropologists Seth D. Kunin, David Gradwohl, and Schulamith C. Halevy; folklorist Annette Fromm; and sociologists Tomás Atencio and Abraham Lavender helped immensely by providing me with the opportunity to view the phenomenon of crypto-Judaism from other valuable methodological perspectives. Similarly, Father Thomas Steele, S.J.; Michael Perko; and Manuel Rodríguez kept me on the straight and narrow path with regard to the proper interpretation of Catholic customs and doctrine. Ferenc Szasz, Edmundo Vasquez, and Jane Vasquez contributed constructive guidance relative to the early history of Protestantism in New Mexico. David Gitlitz's *Secrecy and Deceit:*

The Religion of the Crypto-Jews, together with his kind advice over the years, helped significantly to provide a context for understanding *converso* customs in Spain, Portugal, and Mexico. José Antonio Esquibel selflessly gave countless hours of his time and expertise to the project, sharing his vast stores of genealogical information.

My understanding of New Mexican *santos*, *santeros*, and other aspects of material culture was enhanced by the guidance furnished by Charles Carrillo, Paul Rhetts, Ross Frank, Robin Gavin, David H. Snow, David Rasch, and Diana DiSantis. The mysterious world of medical genetics was made slightly less so through the counsel of Dr. Kristine Bordenave, Sharon Graw, Louise G. Chatlynne, David Epstein, and Bennett Greenspan.

I am appreciative of the help, advice, and support generously given by my colleagues Solange Alberro, Nancy Valentine Benavides, Fay Forman Blake, James Boyajian, Susan Califate Boyle, Emilio Coca, Dennis Durán, Estevan Rael Gálvez, Moshe Shaltiel Gracián, Mona Hernández, Louisa Schell Hoberman, Francine Landau, Mercedes López-Wooten, Charles Martínez, Patrick O'Brien, Rowena Rivera, William Robertson, Ramón Salas, Isabelle Medina Sandoval, Amir Shomroni, Suzanne Stamatov, Henry Tobias, Gloria Trujillo, Regina Turner, Patricia Vargas, Seth Ward, and J. Benedict Warren. I would especially like to thank Father Thomas Steele, Orlando Romero, John L. Kessell, and Adrian Bustamante for the crucial role that they have played as "devil's advocates," constantly urging me to exercise care to make certain of the accuracy of my facts, and soundness of my interpretations. If I have wandered too far afield, it is not for their lack of effort to keep me on track.

Special thanks are offered to Cary Herz, whose photographs grace the pages of this volume, for her sensitivity to her subjects and her persistence in documenting the crypto-Jewish experience, from the *camposantos* of New Mexico, to the mountains of Portugal, to the pasture lands of Extremadura, Spain. I also express appreciation for the contributions of Todd Delyea and Javier Fraga, who prepared the maps that complement the text.

Deep appreciation is extended to Irene Pavitt, of Columbia University Press, for her excellent editing skill. Thanks to her efforts, my prose appears much better than it actually is. I am grateful for the work of Senior Executive Editor Wendy Lochner, who guided me through the maze of the publication process.

I would also like to acknowledge the dedicated professional staffs of the archives and libraries in New Mexico, Mexico, Spain, and Portugal who rendered excellent assistance to the research team: Sandra Jaramillo and Daphne Arnaiz de León of the New Mexico State Records Center and Archives, Santa Fe; Nancy Brown and Ann Massman of the Center for Southwest Research, Zimmerman Library, University of New Mexico, Albuquerque; Joseph Sánchez and Jerry Gurulé of the Spanish Colonial Research Center, National Park Service and University of New Mexico, Albuquerque; Tomas Jaehn of the Fray Angelico Chávez History Library, Museum of New Mexico, Santa Fe; Marina Ochoa of the Archives of the Archdiocese of Santa Fe; Walter Brem of the Bancroft Library, University of California, Berkeley; Huntington Library, San Marino, Calif.; Salvador Victoria Hernández and Roberto Beristain of the Archivo General de la Nación, Mexico City; Liborio Villagómez of the Biblioteca Nacional, Mexico City; Archivo General de Notarías, Mexico City; Archivo Histórico del Estado de Querétaro; Archivo Histórico del Estado de Zacatecas; Centro de Información del Estado de Chihuahua; Instituto Tecnológico y de Estudios Superiores de Monterrey, Campus Zacatecas, Guadalupe; Archivo Municipal de Chihuahua; Archivo Histórico Nacional, Madrid; Archivo General de Indias, Seville; Biblioteca Nacional, Madrid; Archivo Provincial de Murcia; Juan Guirao and Eduardo López of the Archivo Histórico Municipal de Lorca; Antonio López Gimeno of the Fondo Cultural Espín, Lorca; Archivo Municipal de Orihuela; Archivo Histórico Provincial de Las Palmas; Archivo Histórico Provincial de Santa Cruz de Tenerife; Archivo-Biblioteca José Pérez Vidal, Santa Cruz de la Palma; Museo Canario, Las Palmas; Archivo Histórico Provincial de Cuenca; Archivo Histórico Provincial de Toledo; Archivo Histórico Provincial de Salamanca; Archivo del Ayuntamiento de Ayamonte; Archivo Histórico Municipal de Jerez de los Caballeros; Archivo Diocesano de Cuenca; Archivo Diocesano de la Laguna de Tenerife; Archivo Diocesano de Canarias; Archivo Diocesano de Salamanca; Archivo Diocesano de Ciudad Rodrigo; Arquivo Nacional da Torre do Tombo, Lisbon; and the dozens of parish priests in church archives in various parts of Mexico, Spain, and France who generously provided me with access to the sacramental records in their custody.

I am also deeply appreciative of the contributions of Theo Crevenna, deputy director of the Latin American and Iberian Institute of the University of New Mexico, and of Vickie Madrid Nelson, senior program manager, who offered their encouragement and support over the past decade and a half.

My greatest professional debt is owed to Richard E. Greenleaf, retired director of the Roger Thayer Stone Center for Latin American Studies, chair of the Department of History, and France Vinton Scholes Professor of Colonial Mexican History at Tulane University. He trained me, as well as the dozens of other graduate students under his tutelage, in the essential skills of objective methodology, archival research, and Spanish colonial paleography. His many publications on the history of the Mexican Inquisition stand as a model of outstanding scholarship and served as an inspiration for my work. I am grateful to him for his mentorship, his collegiality, and his sharp editorial eye.

To my family, there are no words sufficient to express my gratitude. My love of history was instilled by my brother, Don, who read to me from Roger Butterfield's *The American Past* before I was old enough to read on my own, and by my parents, who filled our home with a wide assortment of books. My parents encouraged me at an early age to study the Spanish language, which provided me with the opportunity to gain an appreciation for a culture other than my own. I deeply regret that my father did not survive to see the publication of this book. Melissa and Paul endured their father's long absences necessitated by extended research trips abroad at critical times in their lives. My wife, Helen, stood by me through the painfully long research and writing process and put up with the dry periods before the grants came in and after they ran out. This book is, indeed, as much hers as it is mine.

NOTES

1. I recognize that a preference might be expressed for other terms to describe descendants of Spanish colonists, such as "Latinos," "Chicanos," "Mexicanos," "Indo-Europeans," and "Hispanics." "Hispano" appears to be the word most widely accepted in New Mexico among this group and, consequently, will be used throughout this book.
2. The Viceroyalty of New Spain was the administrative unit that encompassed what is today the American Southwest, Mexico, Central America, and the Philippine Islands.
3. *Conversos* is the Spanish designation for Catholics who had converted from Judaism in the fourteenth and fifteenth centuries. The term was also applied to their descendants. A more extensive discussion of terminology appears in the introduction.

To the End of the Earth

Introduction

At a recent conference, historian Robert Ferry recounted the anguish expressed in May 1642 by Blanca Méndez de Rivera and her daughter María de Rivera from their prison cell. The two women had been arrested just days earlier by the Holy Office of the Inquisition in Mexico City on suspicion of observing the "Dead Law of Moses." Confronted with denunciations by family and neighbors for the secret practice of Jewish observances, Blanca wailed, "Ay, how has so much misery come to me [!] they've just thrown us in here and already we're lost and without honor and no one will look us in the face even though we don't say a thing," to which her daughter responded, "We're lost and we'll have to flee to the ends of the earth."[1]

María did not survive the inquisitorial persecutions of the mid-seventeenth century, dying in her cell within four years after her incarceration. But her plaintive lament epitomized the experiences of crypto-Jews and their descendants throughout the Hispanic world, beginning with the expulsion and forced conversion of the Jews of Spain and Portugal in the 1490s and extending for three centuries thereafter. It was the sad reality of the *conversos* that the farther they fled from the centers of authority, the more secure their existence.

In the sixteenth and seventeenth centuries, the remote frontier province of New Mexico, indeed, represented one of the "ends of the earth." Heading west and north from Mexico City along the Camino Real (Royal Highway), one could not travel any farther and still remain within the range of European "civilization." This book is designed to tell the story of those men and women who left their homes in Spain, Portugal, and Mexico to begin new lives on the periphery of what was then known as the Viceroyalty of New Spain, as well as the ways in which their descendants manifested their cultural values throughout succeeding generations.

STRUCTURE OF THE BOOK

This book begins with contextual discussions of the history of the Jews in Spain and of the crypto-Jews in Iberia (Spain and Portugal) and Mexico after the forced conversions of the fifteenth century. It then follows the narrative of New Mexico history from the initial attempts at exploration and colonization in the early 1590s; through the establishment of the first permanent European colony in 1598, the struggles between civil and religious authorities that characterized the seventeenth century, the reestablishment of Spanish administration after the Pueblo Revolt of 1680, the growth of Spanish New Mexico through the eighteenth century, and the adjustments made by New Mexicans to rule by the Republic of Mexico in the early nineteenth century; to the accommodations made by New Mexicans to governance by the United States in the nineteenth and twentieth centuries.

Within the framework of this background, the text examines the crypto-Jewish origins of the participants in the historical process, the extent to which the *conversos* and their descendants exhibited conduct that may have reflected these origins, and the reaction—or lack thereof—among the general, Old Christian[2] society to these patterns of behavior. These chapters describe and analyze religious customs, encounters with the Holy Office of the Inquisition, tendencies toward endogamy (marriage within the group), occupational patterns, reading habits, and family naming practices from the late sixteenth through the mid-twentieth century.

The last chapter focuses on possible vestiges of crypto-Judaism in New Mexico in the late twentieth and early twenty-first centuries, based largely on the work of scholars in the fields of anthropology, sociology, and folklore. It includes debates among these experts about the validity of the ethnographic evidence supporting a continued crypto-Jewish presence, as well as a discussion of potential expressions of Jewish identity through material culture. The chapter—and, in more detail, the appendix—also analyzes recent developments in genetic research, specifically examining the discovery of a rare autoimmune disease characteristic of Jews, pemphigus vulgaris, among Hispano populations in New Mexico. It concludes with a genealogical investigation of the family histories of nine individuals who, at the end of the twentieth century, either claimed a Jewish heritage or suffered from pemphigus, examining the extent to which these families could be traced back to Jewish and crypto-Jewish families in the colonial period.

CHALLENGES AND CAVEATS

This was a very difficult book to write. The biggest challenge in completing a study of this kind was determining the history of a group of people who for centuries tried desperately to cover their tracks, to leave behind as little evidence as possible, documentary or otherwise, that would jeopardize their security and that of their families. The Inquisition records that survived the vicissitudes of time provide unique windows into the past, through which historians can view the lives of people who ordinarily would have left no other records.[3] These windows offer the opportunity to examine the contributions of crypto-Jews to the society and culture of Spain, Portugal, New Spain, and New Mexico as well as the relationships that they maintained with one another and with non-*conversos*. But these documents relate to only those crypto-Jews who were unfortunate enough to get caught in the inquisitors' web. The vast majority of *conversos* succeeded in evading detection by the authorities and leading anonymous lives within normative Old Christian society. Many were able to escape from Spain and Portugal to Mexico and eventually to remote frontier regions of the hinterland. Thus historians are able to identify only a fraction of those crypto-Jews living in these areas based on Inquisition records.

From its establishment in the 1480s until the late seventeenth century, moreover, the Holy Office of the Inquisition maintained only a sporadic interest in the prosecution of *judaizante* cases,[4] more or less intense, depending on the period and region under consideration. This inconsistent activity on the part of the Inquisition resulted in the production of but a fragmentary record of the crypto-Jewish communities. And after the inquisitors lost interest in *judaizantes* after the campaigns of the mid-seventeenth century in Mexico and New Mexico, even this meager paper trail disappeared. As a consequence, by the late colonial period, historians no longer had any trial records on which to base their observation of the nature and extent of crypto-Judaism.

Most of the connections cited in this work linking early New Mexico colonists to *converso* family backgrounds are based on solid documentation provided by Inquisition or other church or civil sources. In circumstances where such "hard" evidence of a crypto-Jewish identity is absent, alternative means of formulating logical historical deductions are used—for example, establishing extended-family relationships to those penanced by the Inquisition, connecting a relatively uncommon surname to Jewish populations in a small town in Mexico or on the Iberian Peninsula, associating an individual's occupation with trades characteristically held by Jews and *conversos*, tracing a person's family to the *judería* (Jewish quarter) of a town in Spain or Portugal, documenting a family's possession and reading of the Hebrew Bible or of books cited by the Inquisition as substitutes for the Hebrew Bible, or discovering a family's use of Jewish biblical names for its children.[5] Often the same individual displayed more than one of these traits, thus strengthening the connection.

Some readers who assert a crypto-Jewish heritage may be disappointed not to find in the text specific mention of their individual families. The nature of this kind of study precludes a comprehensive treatment of all such families. Due to considerations of research time and logistics, only nine sample families were selected for extensive genealogical investigation. Those who have already researched their own family histories may well find citations to crypto-Jewish ancestors in the chapters dealing with sixteenth- and seventeenth-century New Mexico. The absence of one's forebears from the discussion and analysis in this work may be due to any number of reasons. The family may have successfully eluded attention from the authorities. Or possibly its surname was so common that it was not possible to differentiate the members of the family from the Old Christians bearing that name in such large communities as Mexico City, Sevilla, and Lisboa. It is hoped that future scholars will take the opportunity to delve deeper into the historical record and discover new and valuable information linking other families to a *converso* past.

The connection of particular surnames with crypto-Jewish origins represents a significant methodological challenge and warrants a detailed discussion. Barely a day passes when Web sites dealing with Sephardic and crypto-Jewish topics do not include conversations assuming the "Jewishness" of a particular last name. To be sure, there did exist certain Spanish names common among *conversos*. But very few could be identified as unique to this community.[6] When Jews converted to Christianity in the fifteenth century, they tended to abandon their Hebrew names in favor of more common Spanish names.

David Gitlitz, in his encyclopedic work on the customs of Iberian and New World crypto-Jews, pointed out that *conversos* tended to take names representing their towns of origin, the name of the saint on whose day they were baptized, or the names of the Old Christians who served as their sponsors during their christening ceremony. The more common the name, the easier it was to gain anonymity within their communities, thus avoiding suspicion on the part of the inquisitors or their Old Christian neighbors.[7] Were there *conversos* by the name of Rodríguez, Martínez, García, Rivera, or Hernández? Of course. Does this indicate that everyone with these names were *conversos*—that these were uniquely crypto-Jewish names? Absolutely not.

Hence the difficulty of tracing the ethnic origins of such early New Mexico colonists as Francisco Rodríguez, Cristóbal Baca, Nicolás Ortiz, and Juan Griego. As will be discussed, there were strong indications that the seventeenth-century settler Juan Griego had been practicing secret Judaism, but it would be impossible to identify his religious background through his surname. One can only imagine the difficulty of researching through the archives of his hometown of Negroponte (today Chalcis, on the Greek island of Euboea), looking for "John the Greek."

Not all surnames present such insurmountable challenges. Some names were less common or had Hebrew origins, and the families with those surnames had emigrated from small towns where people with those family names were identified as having Jewish or crypto-Jewish origins. Such was the case with Alonso Rael de Aguilar, from Lorca, in southeastern Spain; Bartolomé Romero, from Corral de Almaguer, in Castilla, and Simón de Abendaño, from Ciudad Rodrigo, on the Portuguese border, among others.

TERMINOLOGY

Throughout this book, several terms are used to describe the descendants of Jews who converted to Catholicism in Spain and Portugal in the fourteenth and fifteenth centuries. While some of these words are synonyms, others carry subtle differences that require explanation. The most general term utilized here is *converso*, which is Spanish for "convert." Within the set of *conversos*, there were two subsets: (1) those who converted sincerely and truly embraced their new faith, and (2) those who converted in name only and secretly continued to practice their ancestral Jewish religion. Scholars refer to the latter as "crypto-Jews" (*criptojudíos* in Spanish, and *criptojudeos* in Portuguese)[8] or "secret Jews." To confuse the issue, there were another two subsets among *conversos*: (1) *anusim*, which is Hebrew for "forced converts," and (2) *meshumadim*, or "willing converts." "New Christians" (*cristianos nuevos* in Spanish, and *cristãos novos* in Portuguese) was a term often used in the fifteenth and sixteenth centuries by Catholics to refer to converted Jews and their descendants, in contrast to "Old Christians," or those with no Jewish origins. The Inquisition generally referred to those *conversos* and their descendants who engaged in the secret practice of Judaism as *judaizantes* (*judaiçantes* in Portuguese), or "Judaizers." They also often used the word *judíos* (*judeos* in Portuguese), or "Jews." Although *converso* technically referred to only those individuals who actually went through a conversion process, the term is used throughout this book to indicate their descendants as well.

One term that is deliberately not used in this study is *marrano*. Scholars concur that the word is translated as "swine" and was pejoratively applied toward *conversos*. But there exists considerable disagreement about the etymology of the term, as well as whether it was used by Jews against those whom they considered to be apostates or by Old Christians against perceived heretics. Projected origins run the gamut from the Aramaic *maran atha* (Hellenized) to the Hebrew *malah* (to rebel) or the Arabic *mura'in* (hypocrite).[9]

The Spanish linguist Joan Corominas hypothesized that the word *marrano* derived from the Arabic *máhram* (prohibited item) and was used sarcastically by Old Christians toward newly converted Jews and Muslims, due to the repugnance that they displayed toward the consumption of pork.[10] Historian Benzion Netanyahu discerned a Hebrew origin, concluding that *marrano* represented a combination of two Hebrew words: *mumar* (convert) and *anus* (forced convert). The contraction of *mumar-anus* became *marrano*. "The derogatory meaning of 'swine,'" Netanyahu indicated, "may have been attached soon thereafter by the accidental similarity of the words, or may even have been a catalyst in that transformation,"[11] suggesting that such opprobrium was directed toward the Jews who had converted, by those who had not. Linguist Yakov Malkiel put forth the theory that *marrano* represented a variant of the Spanish *barrano* or *albarrano*, meaning "outsider, stranger, person not absorbed into the community," due to the interchangeability of the letters "b" and "m." Once *marrano* became identified with converted Jews, "it was natural for the bigots and fanatics among the speakers of Old Spanish to associate it with its homophone *marrano* [meaning] 'hog, pig' which, at that time, had been in circulation for at least four hundred years."[12]

It is interesting to note that while Netanyahu and Malkiel each found radically different etymological sources for *marrano*, they both concluded that subsequent generations contrived a way to corrupt an otherwise culturally neutral designation and use it to denigrate *conversos* as swine. One scholar contended that the offenders came from the ranks of the Jews, and the other cited Christian origins.

Due to the popularity of Cecil Roth's book *A History of the Marranos* in the early twentieth century,[13] the term assumed a more benign connotation among the English-reading public in recent decades. However, due to its obviously pejorative historical context, the word *marrano* will not be used in this study to refer to the descendants of crypto-Jews.

HISTORIOGRAPHY

While much has been published on the history of crypto-Judaism on the Iberian Peninsula, especially in the past thirty years, the literature dealing with Mexico is considerably more limited. With regard to New Mexico, the field is in its infancy. Early works focused less on the history and more on the contemporary aspects of crypto-Judaism. The first article that appeared on the topic was written by David S. Nidel, who conducted interviews with residents of Albuquerque who asserted a Jewish heritage, reproduced excerpts from the interviews, but offered little in the way of analysis, historical or otherwise.[14] In 1993, Frances Hernández presented a more elaborate discussion of modern vestiges of *converso* culture. She included a brief historical introduction, but disappointingly neglected to include relevant sources to substantiate her allegations of a crypto-Jewish past in New Mexico.[15] Fay Forman Blake was perhaps the first person to investigate the topic, conducting interviews in the mid-1970s with individuals who claimed a *converso* heritage, but not publishing the results of her research until twenty years later. Citing the lack of available documentary evidence, Blake eschewed any elaborate historical analysis, relying instead on contemporary observations to support her hypothesis of a Hispano Jewish presence in New Mexico.[16] In the late 1990s and extending into the early years of the twenty-first century, the field began attracting the attention of prominent scholars from the social sciences, including Tomás Atencio, Seth D. Kunin, Schulamith Halevy, and Janet Liebman Jacobs, whose works will be analyzed later.

With regard to historical works treating the topic of crypto-Jews in New Mexico, very little has been published, save some articles of mine that offer some tentative observations. This book represents the first attempt to provide a comprehensive historical analysis of crypto-Judaism in New Mexico from the earliest European settlement in the late sixteenth century to the mid-twentieth century.

Beginning in the late 1980s and continuing through the next decade, stories appeared in the popular media discussing the phenomenon of crypto-Judaism in New Mexico and the Southwest, focusing on the personal accounts offered by people in the Hispano community.[17] In sharp reaction to these stories, as well as to a brief research note that I placed in the *Jewish Folklore and Ethnology Review*,[18] folklorist Judith S. Neulander published articles highly critical of what she called the "'crypto-Jewish canon,' or a body of demonstrably unfounded beliefs about the cultural past."[19] What others regarded as residual customs of crypto-Judaism, Neulander concluded were either merely manifestations of Adventism or Pentecostal Protestantism or otherwise traceable to non-Jewish origins, theories that I find untenable, as will be demonstrated. Moreover, she insinuated that "the canon's primary academic promoters" (presumably including me) were taking advantage of this misrepresentation for their own commercial gain[20] and had engaged in "prevarication" with regard to the interpretation of history.[21] For their part, Hispanos who asserted a crypto-Jewish past, Neulander claimed, were doing so in order to deny their Indian and African ancestry and to climb the social ladder by identifying themselves as Jews and, thus, white.[22]

Sociologist Michael P. Carroll also questioned the motives of scholars pursuing research into the phenomenon of crypto-Judaism, both historically and ethnographically. Unlike Atencio, Kunin, and Halevy, who expressed strong reservations about Neulander's analyses,[23] Carroll found Neulander's arguments regarding Protestantism credible and thus wondered "why this group embraces that hypothesis so tightly despite the availability of alternative explanations for the evidence that exists and despite the fact that the hypothesis is less plausible than first appears." Carroll ascribed two basic motivations to "this group": (1) the desire to see crypto-Jews as survivors of an inquisitorial "holocaust," and (2) the "orientalization" of New Mexico (that is, a manifestation of earlier Anglo attitudes that romanticized the region as exotic).[24]

The attribution of these sorts of motives to scholars interested in investigating the phenomenon of crypto-Judaism in New Mexico, whether by Neulander (avarice and self-promotion) or by Carroll (ethnographic allegory and orientalism), appears misplaced, at least as they apply to my work. The former represent accusations that are so offensive and unprofessional that they do not warrant serious consideration. The latter, while intellectually intriguing, have never served as an impetus for undertaking the preparation of this study.[25]

To the contrary, I view the question of historical crypto-Judaism in New Mexico from a perspective of intellectual curiosity, based on my observation of a set of intriguing cause-and-effect relationships. It is a logical—indeed, compelling—endeavor to ascertain the existence and nature of a crypto-Jewish presence in New Mexico over the course of the past four centuries, considering that

- Jewish populations existed on the Iberian Peninsula from before the common era until the fifteenth century.
- At the end of the fourteenth century, and culminating with the expulsion and forced conversion of the Jews in Spain and Portugal at the end of the fifteenth century, efforts on the part of the Catholic Church in Spain resulted in a large number of *conversos*.
- A significant number of these Spanish and Portuguese *conversos* continued to practice their ancestral Jewish faith illegally and in secret through the sixteenth and seventeenth centuries.
- Many of these crypto-Jews emigrated to Spanish and Portuguese American colonies where enforcement by inquisitorial authorities was less stringent than on the Iberian Peninsula.
- During and after periods of persecution by the Mexican Inquisition, crypto-Jews and their descendants migrated to frontier areas, including northern New Spain.
- People from these frontier areas migrated to New Mexico from the late sixteenth through the eighteenth century.
- In the late twentieth and early twenty-first centuries, descendants of these early settlers in New Mexico began to publicly assert their crypto-Jewish family histories.

I fully realize that, as is the case in most histories, the data presented in this book will be subject to different interpretations and that some of the observations outlined here will stimulate more questions than they will resolve. It is my hope that this work will encourage other historians to further explore the vast stores of documentation in New Mexico, Mexico, and Europe in order to build on—or reinterpret—the information provided in this book.

NOTES

1. Quoted in Robert Ferry, "The Blancas: Women, Honor, and the Jewish Community in Seventeenth-Century Mexico" (paper presented at the Fourteenth Annual Conference of the New Mexico Jewish Historical Society, Albuquerque, November 10, 2001), pp. 22–23.
2. The term "Old Christian" refers to Iberian Catholics with no *converso* background, as opposed to "New Christians," who either converted from Judaism or descended from those who had.

3. While the records of the Mexican Inquisition have been well preserved in the Archivo General de la Nación (Mexican National Archives, in Mexico City) and in other repositories, those of the Inquisition tribunals of Portugal have suffered severe deterioration over the years, with many trial records rendered totally unreadable. In Spain, the situation is far worse, with the majority of locally generated trial records having been destroyed in the early nineteenth century. See Gustav Henningsen, "El 'Banco de Datos' del Santo Oficio: Las relaciones de causas de la inquisición española (1550–1700)," *Boletín de la Real Academia de la Historia* (Madrid) 174 (1977): 554, and "The Database of the Spanish Inquisition: The 'Relaciones de Causas' Project Revisited," in Heinz Mohnhaupt and Dieter Simon, eds., *Vorträge zur Justizforschung: Geschichte und Theorie* (Frankfurt am Main: Klostermann, 1993), vol. 2, p. 47.
4. *Judaizante* is the Spanish designation for New Christians who persisted in practicing Judaism.
5. These traits will be elaborated on throughout the book.
6. A persistent legend, related to me on many occasions, holds that when the Jews converted to Catholicism and assumed Spanish surnames, they tended to take names from nature: Carrasco and Robledo (oak tree), Espinosa (thorny), Flores (flowers), Jaramillo (willow tree), Luna (moon), Mares (oceans), Naranjo (orange tree), Pino (pine tree), Ríos (rivers), and the like. No scholarly authority could be found to substantiate this theory.
7. David M. Gitlitz, *Secrecy and Deceit: The Religion of the Crypto-Jews* (Philadelphia: Jewish Publication Society of America, 1996), p. 202.
8. "Crypto-Jew" appears to be the term of choice among scholars in the field. This designation was in use as early as the late nineteenth century, when the British historian Lucien Wolf published "Crypto-Jews Under the Commonwealth," *Transactions of the Jewish Historical Society of England* 1 (1893): 55–75, cited in Gitlitz, *Secrecy and Deceit*, p. 651.
9. Yakov Malkiel, "Hispano-Arabic *Marrano* and Its Hispano-Latin Homophone," *Journal of the American Oriental Society* 68 (1948): 176–177.
10. Joan Corominas, *Diccionario crítico etimológico de la lengua castellana* (Madrid: Editorial Gredos, 1954), vol. 3, p. 272.
11. Benzion Netanyahu, *The Marranos of Spain from the Late XIVth to the Early XVIth Century According to Contemporary Hebrew Sources* (New York: American Academy for Jewish Research, 1966), p. 59 n.153.
12. Malkiel, "Hispano-Arabic *Marrano,*" p. 182.
13. Cecil Roth, *A History of the Marranos* (Philadelphia: Jewish Publication Society of America, 1932).
14. David S. Nidel, "Modern Descendants of Conversos in New Mexico," *Western States Jewish History* 16 (1984): 249–262.
15. Frances Hernández, "The Secret Jews of the Southwest," in Martin A. Cohen and Abraham J. Peck, eds., *Sephardim in the Americas: Studies in Culture and History* (Tuscaloosa: University of Alabama Press, 1993), pp. 411–454.
16. Fay Forman Blake, "The Hidden Jews of New Mexico," *Journal of Progressive Judaism* 8 (1997): 5–26.

17. See, for example, Kathleen Teltsch, "Scholars and Descendants Uncover Hidden Legacy of Jews in Southwest," *New York Times*, November 11, 1990, p. 16, and "After 500 Years, Discovering Jewish Ties that Bind," *New York Times*, November 29, 1992, p. 28; Steven Almond, "Hispanics Rediscover Jewish Identity," *New Mexico Magazine*, June 1991, pp. 26, 31; Nancy Plevin, "Secret Jews Step Out of the Shadows," and "'Conversos' Straddle Two Lives," *Albuquerque Journal*, March 31, 1991, pp. B1, B4; Florence Williams, "Keeping the Faith," *New Republic*, October 26, 1998, p. 12; Michael Haederle, "The Hidden Jews of the Southwest," *El Palacio* 98 (1992–1993): 38–43, 56–57; Patricia Giniger Snyder, "America's Secret Jews," *B'nai Brith International Jewish Monthly*, October 1991, pp. 26–30, 38; Howard G. Chua-Eoan, "Plight of the Conversos," *Time* (international edition), March 4, 1991, p. 7; Emma Moya, "New Mexico's Sephardim: Uncovering Jewish Roots," *La Herencia del Norte* 12–32 (1996–2003); and Benjamin Shapiro and Nan Rubin, "The Hidden Jews of New Mexico Radio Project" (National Public Radio): Program One, "Search for the Buried Past" (1988); Program Two, "Rekindling the Spirit" (1992); Program Three, "Return to Iberia" (1995).
18. Stanley M. Hordes, "'The Sephardic Legacy in the Southwest: The Crypto-Jews of New Mexico,' Historical Research Project Sponsored by the Latin American Institute, University of New Mexico," *Jewish Folklore and Ethnology Review* 15 (1993): 137–138.
19. Judith S. Neulander, "The New Mexican Crypto-Jewish Canon: Choosing to Be 'Chosen' in Millennial Tradition," *Jewish Folklore and Ethnology Review* 18 (1996): 19. See also Judith S. Neulander, "Crypto-Jews of the Southwest: An Imagined Community," *Jewish Folklore and Ethnology Review* 16 (1994): 64–68.
20. According to Neulander, "[I]n the Spring of 1994, the canon's primary academic promoters were able to market a commercial crypto-Jewish tourist venture, in cooperation with a number of Hispano subscribers, touting foremost among highlights of the tour, '*Meet descendants of the "Hidden Jews"* at $1,950 per person'" ("New Mexican Crypto-Jewish Canon," p. 33). The reality was far different from that described by Neulander. The ten-day tour focused not on crypto-Jewish sites, but on places of interest associated with nineteenth-century *Ashkenazic* Jews in New Mexico and Arizona. I did, indeed, serve as a resource for the excursion, but my services were limited to offering one lecture on the history of crypto-Judaism in New Mexico and conducting a walking tour of German Jewish sites in Santa Fe and Las Vegas. I had nothing to do with the marketing or promotion of the tour, which was done completely by the sponsor, the American Jewish Historical Society. See also Neulander, "Crypto-Jews of the Southwest," p. 64.
21. Neulander, "Crypto-Jews of the Southwest," p. 64.
22. Ibid.; Neulander, "New Mexican Crypto-Jewish Canon," p. 46. These, as well as many other of Neulander's assertions, were championed by Barbara Ferry and Debbie Nathan in "Mistaken Identity? The Case of New Mexico's 'Hidden Jews,'" *Atlantic Monthly*, December 2000, pp. 85–96. Neulander's arguments will be examined and critiqued in subsequent chapters.
23. Tomás Atencio, "Crypto-Jewish Remnants in Manito Society and Culture," *Jewish Folklore and Ethnology Review* 18 (1996): 59–68; Seth Kunin, "Juggling

Identities Among the Crypto-Jews of the American Southwest," *Religion* 31 (2001): 41–61; Schulamith C. Halevy, "Manifestations of Crypto-Judaism in the American Southwest," *Jewish Folklore and Ethnology Review* 18 (1996): 68–76.

24. Michael P. Carroll, "The Debate over a Crypto-Jewish Presence in New Mexico: The Role of Ethnographic Allegory and Orientalism," *Sociology of Religion* 63 (2002): 1–19.

25. I have long been critical of the "heroes and martyrs" approach to crypto-Jewish history, as well as of the comparison of the persecutions by the Mexican Inquisition and the Holocaust. See Stanley M. Hordes, "Historiographical Problems in the Study of the Inquisition and the Mexican Crypto-Jews in the Seventeenth Century," *American Jewish Archives* 34 (1982): 138–152.

CHAPTER 1

The Origins of Crypto-Judaism on the Iberian Peninsula, 200 B.C.E.–1492

The roots of Jewish settlement penetrate deeply into the history of the Iberian Peninsula. While legend placed Jews in Spain as early as the sixth century B.C.E., after the destruction of the First Temple by Nebuchadnezzar, more solid accounts trace their residence on the peninsula to the Diaspora, which occurred during the time of the Roman Empire, beginning in the second century B.C.E. At this time, Jews, exiled from their ancestral homeland, found themselves scattered across the Mediterranean region, including the southern and eastern coasts of Spain, where they established bases from which they engaged in commerce within Phoenician and Syrian trading networks. Under the administration of the Romans, Spanish Jews enjoyed centuries of relative peace and toleration. After the conversion of the empire to Christianity, however, the situation of the Jews began to erode.[1]

Conflict between Jews and the nascent Christian community began to appear in the early fifth century, when the bishop of Mallorca embarked on a campaign to convert the prosperous Jewish settlement on the island of Menorca.[2] Historian Jane S. Gerber wrote of the "inevitable" confrontation between the two faiths in Spain:

> Christianity defined itself as the successor to its older (and, as is often said, rival) sibling in the divine drama. . . .

> Church thinkers could not simply dismiss Judaism out of hand. Their most troubling challenge was the enigmatic perseverance of the Jewish people after the advent of Jesus had made their religion obsolete. . . .
>
> A fateful rationale was devised from the doctrine of Christian supersession: the Jews would be preserved because their veneration of the Old Testament bore witness to the truth of Christianity. At the same time, they would be tolerated only minimally, so that their debased state itself would provide visible proof of their "rejection" by God.
>
> The paradoxes of a doctrine that simultaneously advocated toleration and discrimination, preservation and persecution, conversion and persuasion, would plague Jews for centuries.[3]

Indeed, from the fifth through the seventeenth century, Jews and, later, crypto-Jews were to suffer greatly from this contradictory policy on the part of the Church, which would eventually come to define Judaism as *la ley muerta de Moisés*, or "the Dead Law of Moses." Over time, Jews would develop strategies for survival, ranging from accommodation to flight to conversion.

EARLY CONFLICTS BETWEEN CHRISTIANS AND JEWS

In the mid-fifth century, the Iberian Peninsula was invaded by successive waves of Germanic bands, the last of which were the Visigoths, who succeeded in driving the others out of the land. The Visigoths practiced Christianity, but maintained significant doctrinal differences from the approximately 8 million Spanish Catholics who fell under their domination. As long as these tensions between Visigoths and Catholics remained in effect, the rulers found the Jews useful as mediators or allies, depending on the exigencies of the day.[4]

Under the Visigoths, patterns of economic life began to emerge among Spanish Jews that would change little for centuries to come. Concentrated for the most part in the towns in the regions of Cataluña and Andalucía, and in the city of Toledo, they held government and military positions; engaged in commerce, both domestic and foreign; and administered the estates of Christian nobles. Some Jews owned land, either farming it themselves or utilizing the services of slave labor. Relations between Jews and the ruling Visigoths were by no means harmonious, especially after their conversion to Catholicism at the end of the sixth century. Codes were enacted that severely restricted the opportunity for Jews to hold office, intermarry, and build synagogues. Increasingly through the sixth and seventh centuries, zealous Visigothic kings sought the conversion of Spanish Jews. Through a combination of positive and negative incentives, they were moderately, although by no means totally, successful in achieving their end. Those who retained their faith, like their descendants who were also forced to pursue their religious beliefs in a hostile environment, tended to observe such basic rituals as sanctification of the Sabbath and festivals, dietary laws, and circumcision.[5]

THE "GOLDEN AGE" OF SPANISH JEWRY UNDER MUSLIM RULE

With the invasion of the Iberian Peninsula by Muslims in 711, Spanish Jews received a reprieve from persecutions and attempts at forced conversions. While the Muslims by no means pursued a policy of total religious freedom, the general atmosphere was one of toleration of non-Muslim practices. Barriers to social and economic mobility, imposed earlier by the Visigoths, were by and large removed. Jewish communities in areas under Arab rule, and eventually in Christian areas as well, were allowed a large degree of autonomy in the administration of their own affairs.[6]

Moreover, Jewish influence manifested itself in the upper echelons of Muslim economy and society, with Jews serving as influential physicians, financial advisers, and ambassadors to the caliphs. Historians have referred to this period as the Golden Age of Spanish Jewry, represented by a fluorescence in almost every aspect of Jewish culture. The era was characterized by such government leaders as Hasdai ibn Shaprut (915–970), literary figures as Yehuda ha-Levi (1075–1141), and philosophers as Bahya ben Joseph ibn Pakuda (ca. 1050–ca. 1100) and, most celebrated of all, the theologian/philosopher Moshe ben Maimon, better known as Maimonides (1135–1204), who still stands as one of the most important spiritual writers in Jewish history.[7]

Geographically, Jewish settlement expanded throughout the Iberian Peninsula, initially to the major cities in Andalucía, Córdoba, Sevilla, and Granada, and eventually, through the twelfth and thirteenth centuries, to the more heavily populated Christian regions of Castilla, León, and Aragón. During the Muslim and early Christian periods, Jews tended to pursue urban trades—as artisans and shopkeepers—in addition to serving as tax farmers for Christian nobles. This latter function earned the enmity of their poorer, more rural Christian neighbors.[8]

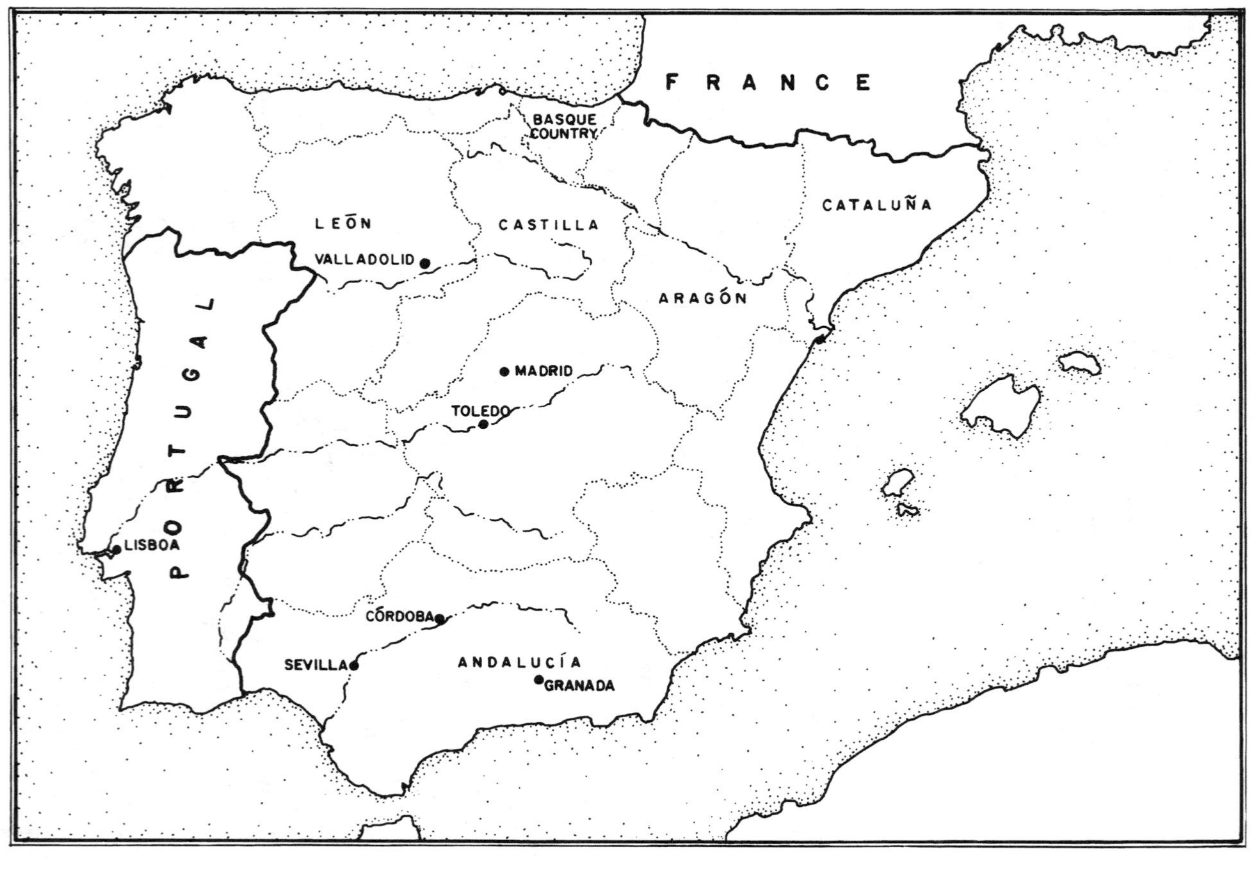

Iberian Peninsula.

CONVIVENCIA AND CONVERSION

The hostility directed against the Jews of Spain by the Christian populace, nurtured by generations of civil war and taxes, in many ways represented a continuation of the anti-Jewish sentiment from the time of Visigothic rule. The new phase began in the eighth century, with the inception of the *reconquista*, the attempt on the part of Christian leaders to reconquer the Iberian Peninsula from the Muslims. Over the course of the eight-hundred-year *reconquista*, this effort became more than just a campaign to defeat the Muslim armies, more than just an attempt to expand the realm of the monarchs of Spain. Rather, it became a veritable crusade against what the Christians regarded as the "infidel," a term that was directed largely against the Muslims, but included the Jews as well.

Despite the hostilities that often plagued the period of the *reconquista*, which pitted Christians against Muslims, with Jews alternatively supporting one side or the other and serving as intermediaries between the two, there occurred long intervals of peaceful accommodation among the three ethnic groups, periods that historians have labeled the *convivencia* (time of coexistence). In the reconquered areas under the control of Christian rulers, Jews played roles similar to those they had under the Muslims, as municipal officials, merchants, financial advisers, tax collectors, and military officers.[9]

In the process of pursuing its conversion efforts through the thirteenth, fourteenth, and fifteenth centuries, the Church utilized peaceful as well as violent means. The more idealistic members of the Church hierarchy sought to win Jewish converts through a prolonged series of debates, or disputations, which pitted theological scholars of both faiths against each other in an attempt to persuade Jews to convert or dissuade them from doing so. The Churchmen aimed their arguments at the Jewish population at large, rather than at the rabbis. They attempted to "instruct," rather than debate, citing Talmudic as well as New Testament sources to prove the absolute truth of their position.[10]

But as the anti-Jewish sentiment that was sweeping through Europe filtered southward into Spain through the mid- and late fourteenth century, conversion efforts on the part of the Church turned increasingly violent. Jews were held responsible for a host of crimes, ranging from poisoning wells to using the blood of Christian children in Passover rites to causing the Black Death. Seizing the opportunity to capitalize on popular antagonism against the Jews, Father Ferrán Martínez in the late 1370s initiated a campaign designed to destroy the Jewish community in Sevilla. Violence broke out in Sevilla in the summer of 1391 and spread northward and eastward to Castilla and Aragón, forcing the residents of the *juderías* throughout Spain to either convert or face death. Approximately 100,000 Jews converted at the point of a sword. Another 100,000 refused to convert and were killed, while another 100,000 escaped.[11]

Whether forced or "gentle," the conversion effort on the part of the Church achieved a high degree of success, especially among those wealthier and better educated members of the Jewish communities. How "Jewish" or "Christian" were the *conversos*? Most historians of the period believe that, generally, the transition from Judaism to Christianity was made without a great deal of inner spiritual conflict, for it represented a change of religion in name only. The bulk of *conversos* and their offspring did not take their new faith seriously. Many *conversos* continued to participate in the social, political, and religious affairs of their synagogues.

Yitzhak Baer articulated the strong ties of the *conversos* to their ancestral faith through the early to mid-fifteenth century:

> Not only did actual converts (*anusim*) try with all their might to live as Jews, but even the children and grandchildren of apostates who had forsaken Judaism of their own free will and choice were now inclined to retrace their steps. The *conversos* secretly visited their Jewish brethren in order to join them in celebrating the Jewish festivals, attended the synagogues, listened to sermons, and discussed points of religion. They did no work on the Sabbath, observed the laws of mourning and the dietary laws, and fasted on Yom Kippur and even women observed the Fast of Esther. They had Jewish prayer books and engaged their own Hebrew teachers and ritual slaughterers. They sent oil to the synagogue for the lamps and were provided by their Jewish brethren with literature that lent them courage to hope for consolation and redemption in days to come.[12]

One of Baer's students, Haim Beinart, who went on to distinguish himself as the dean of Iberian Jewish history, also recognized the strong devotion of a large number of *conversos* to Judaism:

> Their very existence as Jews brought the *conversos* to regret their adherence to Christianity in a moment of weakness and their separation from the Jewish people. The many Inquisition files that have come down to us cover merely a fraction of the people investigated by the Inquisition. They testify to the desire of the *conversos* and their descendants, even after generations of living as

> Christians, to return to their people and their Jewish past. . . . The existence of the Inquisition over hundreds of years and its unrelenting effort to excise the *conversos* who had returned to Judaism are prime proof of the failure of the entire system in its war against Judaism.[13]

Maintaining a view diametrically opposed to the mainstream historiography, Benzion Netanyahu disputed the notion that a significant number of *conversos* continued to practice their ancestral Jewish faith in secret, especially in the generation following the pogroms of 1391. Rather, he asserted, the children of these *conversos* were "born and reared in the Catholic faith and lived according to Catholic law." Moreover, he continued, with regard to those Jews who converted voluntarily through the mid-fifteenth century, "there was no reason to assume that a large number of [these] conversos lived secretly as Jews or lacked devotion to the Catholic faith."[14] Netanyahu rejected the validity of Inquisition records and other Christian sources that documented the alleged secret practices of Judaism on the part of New Christians. He confessed that he was

> baffled by the great credence given by historians to those documents and to the claims made by the Inquisition on their basis. Little value, I thought could be attached to evidence originating in witnesses who remained anonymous and could not be cross-examined by the accused; little weight should be imputed to statements exacted under torture or fear of torture, and little store should be set in documents subjected to the Inquisition's censorship.[15]

Jane S. Gerber took a less dogmatic approach to this issue, recognizing the wide diversity of responses to the conversion process:

> The question of the "Jewishness" of the *conversos* population is complex. Like any group, the New Christians included people with a variety of motives, beliefs, and approaches to life. The convert lived in a kind of "interim" society, his identity perhaps in flux for decades. At any one point, he might well find himself playing more than one role—as a practicing Christian trying to integrate himself into the majority culture socially and economically, as a loving relative still in intimate contact with his Jewish family members. If he met total rejection from the Christian world, he might become more passionately committed to his heritage; conversely, he could counter the difficulties inherent in his new identity by becoming a Jew-baiter.[16]

Perhaps the most cogent response to the revisionist interpretation presented by Netanyahu emanated from historian Michael Alpert. He acknowledged that by the end of the fifteenth century, most of the New Christians probably had assimilated into mainstream Christian society and that the early Inquisition authorities at times exaggerated the behavior of the accused. Nevertheless, Alpert held, "this in itself does not disprove the truth of most of the Inquisition accusations. One cannot simply deny the religious evidence of Judaizing so carefully collected by a scholar of the eminence of Haim Beinart, for instance, in his three volumes reproducing the Inquisition trials of Ciudad Real and his work on other cities."[17] Extending his argument centuries beyond the forced conversions of 1391, Alpert continued:

> Scrutiny of the seventeenth- and eighteenth-century records of the Inquisition's trials suggest that the accused were indeed guilty of Judaizing. Since the records were kept in absolute secrecy, there was no motive for falsifying them. To deny their truth, one would have to suggest that the Inquisition was comparable to the witch-hunts from which Spain, happily, was largely free. However, to accuse a woman of being a witch and flying on a broomstick was irrational. To say that people were cutting a fowl's throat rather than throttling it, or washing all the blood out of a joint of meat, is to describe what Jews did and still do, as moreover the Inquisitors themselves could have seen with their own eyes until the Jews were expelled from Spain in 1492. In any case, no witch in history ever escaped to join a community of witches in another country, while thousands of Spanish and Portuguese Jews fled the Iberian peninsula from the fifteenth until the eighteenth century to do precisely that.[18]

Regardless of how faithful or unfaithful the fifteenth-century *conversos* were to their former religion, the angst of their transition was eased by the new and unprecedented opportunities now available to these New Christians. Barriers that hitherto had prevented them as Jews from rising to economic, social, or political prominence disappeared, and there instantaneously appeared on the scene a new class of nobles, courtiers, municipal officeholders, and literary figures, obviously distinguishable from their Old Christian counterparts by their origin, manner, and appearance.[19]

The presence of a large and prosperous group of apparently insincere converts became increasingly disturbing to the Old Christian community through the fifteenth century. One of the first manifestations of this discontent occurred in Toledo, the scene of an outbreak of extreme violence directed against *conversos* in 1449. Led by Pedro Sarmiento, hostile residents of the city set fire to the house of a *converso* tax farmer following the imposition of a harsh tax against the citizens of Toledo by one of the nobles at the court of Juan II of Castilla. In a manner portending developments later in the century, prominent *conversos* were arrested, tried for Judaizing, and sentenced to be burned at the stake. Hostility toward New Christians quickly spread through the kingdoms, encouraged by the publication of anti-*converso* tracts that were filled with accounts of the desecration of Catholic traditions by a group that the Church regarded as insincere converts from Judaism, many of whom held high positions at court. By the 1470s, the violence had spread to Andalucía, where bloody riots took the lives of *conversos* in Córdoba and other southern towns.[20]

Resentment harbored by Old Christians toward New Christians manifested itself in other ways as well. In the wake of the anti-*converso* riots in Toledo, municipal officials instituted new standards for holding public and private office, barring, for the first time, any Christian of Jewish descent from appointment to such positions. These statutes of *limpieza de sangre* (purity of blood) were to become standard throughout Spain and, ultimately, its overseas empire, in theory at least, over the next four centuries. It was no longer enough just to be a Christian. In order to hold significant posts, one had to be a "pure" Christian, without the stain of Jewish or Muslim blood. What started as a campaign for religious conformity evolved into the establishment of racial and ethnic distinction.

Such discrimination among Christians ran contrary to ecclesiastical law and was opposed by a succession of popes. And while the statutes were taken quite seriously in certain quarters of Spanish society, many institutions enforced them only selectively. Stafford Poole discovered that even within the ranks of the religious orders, the statutes were sometimes ignored. While the Hieronymites incorporated them, the Dominicans did not. The Franciscans enacted a general statute, but were lax in its enforcement. Until 1593, the Jesuits refused to include the statutes among their regulations, owing to the large number of *converso* disciples of Ignacio de Loyola, the founder of the Society of Jesus. Even the Holy Office of the Inquisition was among the last institutions in Spain to adopt statutes of *limpieza*. When it did, the statutes were limited in scope and enforced only when convenient.[21]

The hostilities toward the Jews of the mid-fifteenth century would inevitably be translated into official policy by ruling monarchs. During the civil war that ensued in the 1460s and 1470s in Castilla, *conversos* generally supported Enrique IV's unsuccessful effort to stave off the challenges of his brother Alfonso and, later, of his half-sister, Isabel. The latter two rulers, along with Isabel's consort, Fernando of Aragón, capitalized on the strong anti-*converso* sentiment in the land in order to unite their subjects and thus to solidify control over their dominions.[22]

THE HOLY OFFICE OF THE INQUISITION

The establishment of the Holy Office of the Inquisition in 1481 by Fernando and Isabel, known as the Reyes Católicos (Catholic Monarchs), in concert with Pope Sixtus IV, may be regarded as a logical institutional manifestation of the deeply rooted religious feelings against the *conversos*, as well as a royal desire to implement sovereignty over the newly consolidated realm. Moreover, as recent interpretations suggest, the Catholic Monarchs, operating through the Inquisition, sought to break down the economic power of the increasingly influential middle class, largely composed of Jews and *conversos*.

Scholars of the Spanish Inquisition have expressed sharp differences of opinion about the motivation for the establishment of the Holy Office. Some, such as Haim Beinart, suggested that the Catholic Monarchs set up the tribunal to consolidate their hold over their realm. Others, like Juan Antonio Llorente and Martin A. S. Hume, reflected the Black Legend, anti-Spanish position that Fernando and Isabel organized the Inquisition in order to fill their coffers with the money derived from confiscations. Another theory, put forth by such diverse authors as Henry Charles Lea, Bernardino Llorca, Cecil Roth, and Julio Caro Baroja, held that the institution was truly established in order to ensure orthodoxy within the Catholic Church. In the 1960s, Henry Kamen offered still another theory. The Spanish aristocracy, he maintained, felt that its power was threatened by the increasing activity of the middle class, most of which was composed of Jews and *conversos*. Consequently, it was through the influence of the noble classes that the Catholic Monarchs imposed the Holy Office over the Spanish kingdoms, with the primary purpose of breaking down the economic power of the *converso* community. Thirty years later, Kamen significantly modified his earlier, economic determinist position, recognizing a broader array of causes for the formation of the Inquisition. It was also in the 1990s that Benzion Netanyahu, in his monumental *Origins of the Inquisition in Fifteenth Century Spain*, argued that racial, rather than religious, prejudice motivated its establishment.[23]

As with most historical phenomena, a variety of factors—religious, economic, racial, and political—spurred Fernando and Isabel in 1478 to embark on the three-year process to organize the Holy Office of the Inquisition in Spain. Whatever the deep-seated motivations, accounts of mass backsliding on the part of *conversos*, real or imagined, served as the catalyst for their actions. The institution was to be a royal, not a papal, enterprise, with regional tribunals located throughout the kingdoms, extending as far west as the Canary Islands and, eventually in the next century, across the Atlantic Ocean to Lima, Mexico City, and Cartagena. The Holy Office served the dual purpose of extirpating heresy and enhancing royal power. In 1481, the newly formed tribunal in Sevilla conducted its first auto de fe, implicating scores of *judaizantes*. By the end of the fifteenth century, the Inquisition had penanced tens of thousands of *conversos*, many of whom were burned at the stake.[24]

The establishment of the Inquisition in the 1480s laid the groundwork for the formal expulsion of the Jews from the kingdoms of Spain in the following decade. The trials conducted by the Holy Office focused greater attention on the Judaizing activities of New Christians, thus increasing complaints on the part of Church leaders to Fernando and Isabel of Jews exercising a "pernicious" influence on fragile neophytes. These developments, combined with scandalous fabricated accounts of atrocities perpetrated by Jews on Old Christian populations, resulted in escalating demands by the Church that the Catholic Monarchs take the final step of removing Jews altogether from their kingdoms. Despite the long tradition maintained by Fernando and Isabel of favoring and protecting Jewish interests during their reign, even they could not resist the kind of pressure emanating from such powerful sources.

EXPULSION AND FORCED CONVERSION

The final nail in the coffin of Spanish Jewry came with the fall of the southernmost Muslim kingdom, Granada, at the hands of the Christian armies on January 2, 1492. The eight-hundred-year *reconquista* was finally complete. Fernando and Isabel had effected the military and political unification of Castilla and Aragón. Pressure from the Church now facilitated the religious unification as well. On March 31, 1492, from the Palace of the Alhambra in Granada, they issued an edict that would come to have a profound influence on the history of both the Jews and the Iberian Peninsula. They decreed that within three months (later extended to four), all the Jews living in their kingdoms must convert to Christianity or go into exile.[25]

This watershed event compelled Jews all across Spain to make an extremely difficult choice: either abandon their faith in favor of remaining in their homeland, in which they and their ancestors had lived for more than a millennium, or desert their country in order to remain true to their religion. Estimates vary widely on the number of Jews who opted to leave the Spanish realm, but it seems reasonable to conclude that of the approximately 200,000 to 400,000 Jews living in Castilla and Aragón in 1492, about half chose to leave, most seeking refuge across the frontier in Portugal. Others fled to France, Italy, Morocco, and regions of the eastern Mediterranean controlled by the Ottoman Empire. Those who remained in the Spanish kingdoms submitted to the conversion process and became, at least nominally, Catholic Christians.[26]

To be sure, a large number of the new converts, like many of their predecessors, accepted baptism sincerely; within several generations, their descendants assimilated and acculturated into mainstream Spanish Catholic society, eventually losing all consciousness of their families' Jewish background. But an analysis of contemporary records suggests that a significant number converted *in name only*. Despite outwardly professing Christianity, these individuals continued to practice their ancestral faith, at tremendous personal risk. The observance of Jewish rites, now outlawed, was forced underground, to be practiced only in the secrecy of one's home. No longer Jews, those *conversos* who chose to continue those observances did so as Christians, in violation of ecclesiastical law, and were often prosecuted for these relapses by the Holy Office of the Inquisition, which was charged with the enforcement of Catholic orthodoxy among Spanish Christians, New and Old alike.

The situation was markedly different for those approximately 60,000 to 120,000 Spanish Jews who migrated westward across the Iberian Peninsula to join the smaller native Jewish communities of Portugal.[27] It is estimated that, with the addition of the new immigrants, the number of Jews swelled to make up between 5 and 20 percent of the entire population of Portugal by 1496.[28] But under pressure from his stronger and persuasive neighbors to the east, King Manoel I, in 1496, issued an edict of expulsion of his own, mandating that all the Jews in his realm either convert or leave. Recognizing the importance of his Jewish subjects, however, Manoel effectively eliminated the ability of Portuguese Jews to exercise the latter option by closing all the ports. He then ordered all the Jews to gather in public plazas, where they were baptized en masse. The first two decades were very difficult for these Portuguese *conversos*. Cases were reported of New Christian children being stolen from their homes and taken to the African island of São Tomé, where they perished. Anti-*converso* riots broke out in Lisboa in 1506, resulting in many deaths. And in 1531,

King João III established tribunals of the Holy Office of the Inquisition, designed, theoretically at least, to extirpate the Jewish heresy.[29]

These events served to stimulate a migration of Portuguese crypto-Jews from the more heavily populated cities and towns of the Atlantic coast eastward into the mountains along the border with Spain, where they would be able to live with a greater degree of security. After the disruptions of the first couple of decades, the enforcement of orthodoxy by the authorities relaxed. Conversions on the part of the Portuguese Jews were, for the most part, nominal. Over the next few decades, in sharp contrast with the pressure on Spanish *conversos* to abandon all vestiges of their old faith, the attitude in Portugal was far more tolerant, and Portuguese New Christians tended to continue their observance of Jewish laws and rituals discretely, yet in an atmosphere of relative safety.[30] The ability of these *conversos* to retain their Jewish practices was to have a profound impact on crypto-Jewish life over the next several generations, far beyond the borders of Portugal.

The year 1492 thus represented a significant watershed for Iberian Jews. The ejection of the Muslim armies from the Iberian Peninsula as a result of the conquest of Granada by the Christian forces on January 2 achieved the political unification of Spain under Fernando and Isabel. The edict issued on March 31 by the Catholic Monarchs mandating the expulsion or forced conversion of the Jews marked the end of the open practice of Judaism in Spain for generations to come, forcing all such observances to be conducted in hiding. And the uncovering of the American continent by Christopher Columbus on October 12 foreshadowed vast new opportunities for Spanish and Portuguese crypto-Jews, as it did for thousands of other enterprising individuals from all across Europe.

The timing of the departure of Columbus's expedition, which coincided with the deadline imposed on the Jews to leave the Spanish kingdoms, begs the question of whether Columbus himself was a Jew. Countless authors have weighed in on this issue, professional and amateur alike. Among the most enthusiastic proponents of this thesis was Simon Wiesenthal, whose *Sails of Hope* provided biographical and contextual sources to support the hypothesis of the explorer's Jewishness.[31] Much of the data offered by these advocates is circumstantial, and considerably more in-depth research must be conducted into Columbus's family background before any firm conclusions can be made. What is ascertainable is that at least one *converso* could be found among the crew of his first voyage to the New World. Luis de Torres was recruited specifically because of his knowledge of Hebrew. Because Columbus anticipated landing somewhere in the East Indies, he assumed that there would be found among the local population traders from the Middle East who spoke Hebrew, as well as languages native to the area. Needless to say, when Columbus made landfall in the Bahamas on October 12, 1492, Torres's linguistic skills were rendered somewhat moot.[32]

But far more important than the question of the Jewishness or non-Jewishness of Columbus is the fact that his discoveries, as well as those of subsequent explorers, opened up a "New World" for European expansion. And among the many thousands of Europeans to take advantage of the new commercial opportunities in this New World over the next three centuries were Iberian *conversos* and their descendants.

NOTES

1. Yitzhak Baer, *A History of the Jews in Christian Spain* (Philadelphia: Jewish Publication Society of America, 1971), vol. 1, pp. 15–18; Jane S. Gerber, *The Jews of Spain: A History of the Sephardic Experience* (New York: Free Press, 1992), pp. 2–5.
2. Baer, *History of the Jews in Christian Spain*, vol. 1, pp. 16–17.
3. Gerber, *Jews of Spain*, pp. 5–7.
4. Ibid., pp. 8–9; Haim Beinart, *Los judíos en España* (Madrid: Editorial Mapfre, 1992), p. 39.
5. Baer, *History of the Jews in Christian Spain*, vol. 1, pp. 18–22; Stanley G. Payne, *A History of Spain and Portugal* (Madison: University of Wisconsin Press, 1973), vol. 1, p. 12; Beinart, *Judíos en España*, pp. 39–48; Gerber, *Jews of Spain*, pp. 8–16.
6. For a more elaborate discussion of the nature of religious toleration in Muslim Spain, see Philip K. Hitti, *History of the Arabs* (London: Macmillan, 1937); Gabriel Jackson, *The Making of Medieval Spain* (New York: Harcourt Brace Jovanovich, 1972); Américo Castro, *The Structure of Spanish History* (Princeton, N.J.: Princeton University Press, 1954); and Gerber, *Jews of Spain*, pp. 20–25.
7. Gerber, *Jews of Spain*, pp. 27–89, 311–313. Gerber's extensive bibliographical discussion points the reader to several important sources on the history and literature dealing with the Golden Age.
8. Jackson, *Making of Medieval Spain*, pp. 100–107; Payne, *History of Spain and Portugal*, vol. 1, p. 18; Baer, *History of the Jews in Christian Spain*, vol. 1, pp. 22–24.
9. Gerber, *Jews of Spain*, pp. 92–96. Gerber emphasized that, despite the presence of Jews as financiers, moneylenders, and tax farmers in medieval Spain, they represented only a minority among those who pursued these occupations, most of whom were Christians.
10. Payne, *History of Spain and Portugal*, vol. 1, p. 137; Baer, *History of the Jews*

in Christian Spain, vol. 2, pp. 150–162, 170–243; Gerber, *Jews of Spain*, pp. 101–109.

11. Gerber, *Jews of Spain*, pp. 111–114; Benzion Netanyahu, *The Origins of the Inquisition in Fifteenth Century Spain* (New York: Random House, 1995), pp. 129–167; Antonio Domínguez Ortíz, *La clase social de los conversos en Castilla en la edad moderna* (1955; facsimile, Granada: Universidad de Granada, 1991), pp. 8–10, 26. The numerical estimates were presented by Gerber. Domínguez Ortíz also counted the number of Jews in Spain in 1391 in the range of 300,000, citing the work of Isidro Loeb, "Le Nombre des juifs de Castille et d'Espagne au moyen âge," *Revue d'Études Juives* 14 (1887): 161–183.

12. Baer, *History of the Jews in Christian Spain*, vol. 2, pp. 272–273. See also Julio Caro Baroja, *Los judíos en la España moderna y contemporánea* (Madrid: Ediciones ISTMO, 1978), vol. 1, p. 204. Caro Baroja recognized that while most *conversos* assimilated into mainstream Christian society after 1492, a significant number remained secretly faithful to Judaism. He devoted much of his three-volume work to an analysis of crypto-Judaism in Spain and Portugal.

13. Haim Beinart, *The Expulsion of the Jews from Spain*, trans. Jeffrey M. Green (Oxford: Littman Library of Jewish Civilization, 2002), p. 19.

14. Netanyahu, *Origins of the Inquisition*, pp. 279–280. Netanyahu's views were shared by Francisco Márquez Villanueva, who noted that only a small minority of *conversos* observed their old faith. The *judaizantes*, he felt, were "of no spiritual importance. . . . The importance of the Judaizers is only that they served as a pretext for the establishment of the Holy Office" ("The Converso Problem: An Assessment," in M. P. Hornik, ed., *Collected Studies in Honour of Américo Castro's Eightieth Year* [Oxford: Lincombe Lodge Research Library, 1965], pp. 317–333). See also Norman Roth, *Conversos, Inquisition, and the Expulsion of the Jews from Spain* (Madison: University of Wisconsin Press, 1995).

15. Netanyahu, *Origins of the Inquisition*, p. xvii.

16. Gerber, *Jews of Spain*, p. 123.

17. Michael Alpert, *Crypto-Judaism and the Spanish Inquisition* (Houndsmills, Eng.: Palgrave, 2001), p. 16.

18. Ibid., pp. 16–17.

19. Detailed accounts of upward mobility of Spanish *conversos* may be found in Baer, *History of the Jews in Christian Spain*, vol. 2, pp. 270–277; Manuel Serrano y Sanz, *Origines de la dominación española en América* (Madrid: Veilly-Bailliere, 1918); and Francisco Márquez Villanueva, *Investigaciones sobre Juan Álvarez Gato* (Madrid: Real Academia Española, 1960); "Conversos y cargas consejiles en el siglo XV," *Revista de Archivos, Bibliotecas y Museos* 63 (1957): 503–540; and "Converso Problem."

20. Payne, *History of Spain and Portugal*, vol. 1, p. 209; Netanyahu, *Origins of the Inquisition*, pp. 296–384; Antonio Domínguez Ortíz, *Los conversos de orígen judío despues de la expulsión* (Madrid, 1955), pp. 12–17; Haim Beinart, *Los conversos ante el tribunal de la Inquisición* (Barcelona: Riopiedras Ediciones, 1983), pp. 16–31; Caro Baroja, *Judíos en la España moderna y contemporánea*, vol. 1, pp. 125–148.

21. Stafford Poole, "The Politics of *Limpieza de Sangre*: Juan de Ovando and His Circle in the Reign of Philip II," *Americas* 55 (1999): 359–389, esp. 366–367. Poole acknowledged that initially the statutes of *limpieza de sangre* were designed to serve as a means of racial exclusion, but concluded that by the middle of the sixteenth century they had taken on a less racist and more political tone, used by professional civil servants against the nobility, many of whom were of *converso* origin, to advance the interests of the former. Poole discounted the arguments of Netanyahu and of Roth, in *Conversos, Inquisition*, both of whom he felt exaggerated the racial aspects of the statutes, as well as the "genocidal" character of royal policy. For a general discussion of the concept of *limpieza de sangre*, see Albert Sicroff, *Los estatuos de limpieza de sangre: Controversias entre los siglos XV y XVII* (Madrid: Taurus, 1979); and Antonio Domínguez Ortíz, *Los judeoconversos en la España moderna* (Madrid: Editorial Mapfre, 1992).
22. Fernando and Isabel, despite the anti-*converso* character of their reign, maintained an ambivalent policy toward both Jews and *conversos*, relying on the elite of both groups for political and economic support and, in turn, continuing the long-established tradition of appointing Jews and New Christians to high positions. See Baer, *History of the Jews in Christian Spain*, vol. 2, pp. 304–323.
23. Beinart, *Expulsion of the Jews from Spain*, pp. 19–201; Juan Antonio Llorente, *The History of the Inquisition of Spain* (London: Whittaker, 1826); Martin A. S. Hume, *The Spanish People: Their Origin, Growth and Influence* (London: Heinemann, 1901); Henry Charles Lea, *A History of the Inquisition in Spain*, 4 vols. (New York: Macmillan, 1908); Bernardino Llorca, *La Inquisición en España* (Barcelona: Editorial Labor, 1954); Cecil Roth, *A History of the Marranos* (Philadelphia: Jewish Publication Society of America, 1932); Caro Baroja, *Judíos en la España moderna y contemporánea*, vol. 1, p. 149; Henry Kamen, *The Spanish Inquisition* (London: Weidenfeld and Nicolson, 1965), and *The Spanish Inquisition: A Historical Revision* (New Haven, Conn.: Yale University Press, 1998); Netanyahu, *Origins of the Spanish Inquisition*.
24. Gerber, *Jews of Spain*, pp. 129–130. See also Beinart, *Conversos ante el tribunal de la Inquisición*; and Caro Baroja, *Judíos en la España moderna y contemporánea*, vol. 1, pp. 149–163. An analysis of how the Inquisition functioned as an institution appears in chap. 2.
25. For a comprehensive analysis of the circumstances surrounding the Edict of Expulsion of 1492, see Beinart, *Expulsion of the Jews from Spain*. An informative collection of published primary documents covering the years preceding and following the expulsion is Luis Suárez Fernández, ed., *Documentos acerca de la expulsión de los judíos* (Valladolid: Consejo Superior de Investigaciones Científicas, 1964).
26. Alpert offered a detailed examination of the divergent demographic analyses provided by contemporary and modern historical accounts (*Crypto-Judaism and the Spanish Inquisition*, p. 31). See also Antonio Domínguez Ortíz, "Historical Research on Spanish Conversos in the Last Fifteen Years," in Hornik, ed., *Collected Studies in Honour of Américo Castro's Eightieth Year*, pp. 68–69, citing estimates of Suárez Fernández, "Introduction," in *Documentos acerca de la expulsión de los judíos*, p. 55; Domínguez Ortíz, *Clase social de los*

conversos, pp. 25–32, estimating a population of 180,000 Jews living in the Spanish kingdoms, according to figures of Andrés Bernaldez and Isidro Loeb; and Caro Baroja, *Judíos en la España moderna y contemporánea*, vol. 1, pp. 198–205, counting a total of 400,000 Jews: 160,000 going into exile, and 240,000 choosing to convert and remain in the kingdoms. See also Baer, *History of the Jews in Christian Spain*, vol. 2, p. 438; and Payne, *History of Spain and Portugal*, vol. 1, pp. 211, 229.

27. Payne placed the number at 60,000 (*History of Spain and Portugal*, vol. 1, p. 229); Caro Baroja cited credible sources from the sixteenth and seventeenth centuries that placed the number of Jews crossing into Portugal at 93,000 (*Judíos en la España moderna y contemporánea*, vol. 1, pp. 207–208); Antonio José Sarávia referred to the estimate of 120,000 offered by Abraham Zacuto, a fifteenth-century Spanish Jewish mathematician, who himself found refuge in Portugal (*Inquisição e cristãos-novos*, 6th ed. [Lisbon: Editorial Estampa, 1994], p. 33).

28. Payne offered the 5 percent figure (*History of Spain and Portugal*, vol. 1, p. 229), while Henry Kamen estimated the figure at 20 percent (*Inquisition and Society in Spain in the Sixteenth and Seventeenth Centuries* [Bloomington: Indiana University Press, 1985], p. 221).

29. J. Lúcio de Azevedo, *História dos cristãos-novos portugueses*, 3rd ed. (Lisbon: Clássica Editora, 1989), p. 72.

30. Payne, *History of Spain and Portugal*, vol. 1, p. 230; Kamen, *Inquisition and Society in Spain*, p. 222.

31. Simon Wiesenthal, *Sails of Hope: The Secret Mission of Christopher Columbus*, trans. Richard Winston and Clara Winston (New York: Macmillan, 1973). Jonathan D. Sarna provided a fascinating historiographical essay on the question of Columbus's possible Jewish background ("The Mythical Jewish Columbus and the History of America's Jews," in Bryan F. Le Beau and Menahem Mor, eds., *Religion in the Age of Exploration: The Case of Spain and New Spain* [Omaha, Neb.: Creighton University Press, 1996], pp. 81–95).

32. Meyer Kayserling, "The First Jew in America," in Herbert B. Adams, ed., *Columbus and His Discovery of America* (Baltimore: Johns Hopkins University Press, 1892), pp. 48–49; Sarna, "Mythical Jewish Columbus," p. 85.

CHAPTER 2

The Crypto-Jewish Experience in New Spain, 1521–1649

Crypto-Jews could be found among the members of the early expeditions to the Caribbean islands and, ultimately, to the mainland. By the early sixteenth century, settlements had been established in the major urban centers of Mexico City and Lima. Once tribunals of the Holy Office had been organized in these capitals, inquisitorial persecution stimulated an outmigration of *conversos* from the metropolises to the northern and southern frontiers of North, Central, and South America, extending as far south as Chile and Argentina, and as far north as New Mexico.[1]

THE FIRST CRYPTO-JEWISH SETTLERS IN NEW SPAIN

Hernando Alonso, one of the first individuals to be penanced by the Holy Office of the Inquisition in Mexico for the crime of *judaizante* in 1528, had accompanied the explorer Pánfilo de Narváez from Cuba in 1520, and had joined Fernando Cortés in the conquest of Tenochtitlán (later Mexico City), the legendary *noche triste* flight (when the Aztecs temporarily ousted the invaders), and the recapture of the city in 1521. Alonso, in his brief but enterprising career in New Spain, served the

Viceroyalties of New Spain and Peru, mid-seventeenth century.

nascent Spanish colony in a variety of capacities, as ironsmith, carpenter, miner, and trader of slaves. In addition, he raised livestock on the outskirts of Mexico City, supplying provisions for the capital and thus freeing it from dependence on imported meat from the islands of Hispaniola and Cuba. Based on accounts by several witnesses who testified that Alonso had been practicing Judaic rites, the Inquisition officials in Mexico found him guilty of Judaizing and sentenced him to be burned at the stake. Historian Richard E. Greenleaf theorized that this harsh sentence resulted not so much from the belief on the part of Inquisition officials that Alonso was a confirmed *judaizante*, as from the close political association between him and Cortés.[2]

Indeed, the 1520s witnessed an intense struggle between Cortés and his adversaries, who labored to curb the power of the conquistador. Since the Mexican Inquisition, at this point in its development, was directed by the anti-Cortés Dominicans, *judaizantes* who were allied with the pro-Cortés faction, such as Alonso, suffered a harsher fate than did those who did not have such close ties. Such a New Christian was Diego de Ocaña, who represented the interests of the Spanish Crown, which was seeking to break down the power of Cortés. Ocaña was born in Sevilla to a prominent *converso* family, related to the Xuárez de Benadevas, "Jews of Sevilla," according to the recollection of a Franciscan friar decades later.[3] Ocaña emigrated to Santo Domingo, and ultimately to Mexico City in 1525, where he played a key role in reporting the excesses of Cortés to the royal authorities in Spain. Recognized by government officials as a New Christian, and ordered expelled from the colony, Ocaña was able to avoid deportation by paying a fee, and by justifying the importance of his work on behalf of the king. Three years later, in 1528, Inquisition officials arrested him, accusing him of observing Jewish slaughtering practices and dietary laws. In contrast to the death sentence imposed upon Hernando Alonso, Ocaña suffered only confiscation of his goods and exile to Spain. Within a short time, however, Ocaña was able to return to Mexico, and held the prestigious post of public notary.[4]

The crypto-Jewish community of New Spain in the early sixteenth century was, according to historian Seymour B. Liebman, "undistinguished by learning, morals or skills," from the larger, Old Christian Spanish society.[5] Little has been published revealing any details concerning the social or economic life of Mexican crypto-Jews during this period. An examination of the list of *judaizantes* penanced by the Inquisition from 1528 through 1604 compiled by Liebman, however, reveals that crypto-Jews tended to pursue mercantile trades in greater numbers compared with other endeavors. Occupations connected with the mining sector, such as mine ownership and silversmithing run second, followed by such crafts as tailoring, shoemaking and soapmaking.[6] The large presence of *conversos* among the middle class of Mexican society should not be regarded as a surprising phenomenon, but rather as an extension of the traditional occupational patterns demonstrated by Jews and *conversos* in Spain and Portugal for generations.

The paucity of *judaizante* cases tried by the Mexican Inquisition during the first half-century of Spanish colonization in New Spain suggests that crypto-Jews were able to practice their faith in an atmosphere of relative toleration.[7] This situation began to change in the 1580s, when crypto-Jewish immigration to New Spain increased dramatically. In order to understand the reasons for this demographic phenomenon, it will be necessary to examine contemporary developments on the Iberian Peninsula.

MIGRATION OF PORTUGUESE CRYPTO-JEWS TO NEW SPAIN

It will be recalled that in the wake of the expulsions and forced conversions of the Jews of the 1490s, the policy of the Portuguese authorities was considerably more tolerant than that of the Spanish. But, for a variety of reasons, the last quarter of the sixteenth century witnessed an intensity of royal and ecclesiastical activity against crypto-Jews in Portugal. As in Spain a half-century earlier, middle-class New Christians were beginning to be perceived as a threat by the older, ruling landed aristocracy. Moreover, the Protestant Reformation sparked a new spirit of vigilance in the religious establishment and a consequent strengthening of the powers of the Inquisition.[8] Sealing the fate of the Portuguese crypto-Jews was the union of Spain and Portugal under the rule of Felipe II, who took advantage of a crisis of succession to consolidate his power over the entire Iberian Peninsula in 1581.

The resulting increase in the activity of the Portuguese Inquisition against the crypto-Jews stimulated what Julio Caro Baroja labeled "a veritable invasion" of Portuguese New Christians into the Spanish realm from the 1580s through the early decades of the seventeenth century.[9] According to one account, the mountain town of Castelo Branco, near the Spanish border, was almost completely depopulated in 1625, when the crypto-Jewish residents fled to safer havens in Spain to escape the dreaded Inquisition of Lisboa.[10]

Statistics gleaned from the *procesos* of those crypto-Jews later tried by the Mexican Inquisition concerning the migration and trade patterns of their parents and grandparents substantiate Caro Baroja's contention. Of all the defendants who were able to respond to the inquisitors' queries in this regard, 73 percent descended from Portuguese-born grandfathers and 57 percent from Portuguese-born grandmothers.[11] Data on the mobility of the Mexican crypto-Jews and that of their parents further highlight the migration of New Christians from Portugal to Spain in the late sixteenth and early seventeenth centuries.

The settlement patterns displayed by those crypto-Jews who were caught in the web of the Mexican Inquisition decades later conform closely to those followed by the larger body of New Christians who migrated from Portugal to Spain.[12] Most of these immigrants were attracted to Sevilla and other towns in Andalucía, while others found their way to Madrid and points north. Within a generation or two, many of these Portuguese *conversos* took advantage of their status as subjects of their new sovereign and made their way to Spanish colonies in the New World, including Mexico. Beginning in the 1580s, and continuing through the early decades of the seventeenth century, crypto-Jewish immigration to New Spain increased dramatically. The new arrivals, owing to the atmosphere of relative toleration that they had experienced in Portugal over the previous decades, were considerably more educated and better versed in Jewish doctrine than their coreligionists who had remained under the more repressive environment in Spain. As a consequence, their presence resulted in a new infusion of religiosity in the viceroyalty.[13]

The increase in the number and activity of the crypto-Jews in New Spain did not go unnoticed by the Mexican Inquisition, which had been elevated to the status of a formal tribunal in 1571. Between 1589 and 1604, inquisitors tried almost two hundred individuals for the crime of *judaizante*. This activity of the Mexican Inquisition against crypto-Jews was intense, but short-lived. Following the auto de fe of 1604, the Holy Office lost interest in the prosecution of *judaizante* cases, concentrating instead on more routine, mundane breaches of Catholic orthodoxy, such as blasphemy, bigamy, witchcraft, and the solicitation of sexual favors of women by priests in the confessional. The nucleus of the Mexican crypto-Jewish settlement established in the sixteenth century served to encourage an ever-increasing number of crypto-Jews from Spain and Portugal to flock to New Spain in the early seventeenth century, thus setting the stage for what Seymour Liebman termed "the drama of 1625–1650."[14]

CRYPTO-JEWISH LIFE IN SEVENTEENTH-CENTURY NEW SPAIN

The economic climate in New Spain was extremely favorable for the settlement of crypto-Jewish immigrants from Spain and Portugal in the early seventeenth century. The Mexican economy was experiencing a boom period that had begun at the end of the sixteenth century. The mining sector enjoyed unprecedented expansion from the 1590s through 1620. Agriculture, stock raising, and textile manufacturing kept pace with the demand produced by the mining boom, and the level of trade between New Spain and Europe reached new heights. The succeeding decades witnessed an internalization of the Mexican economy and, despite the falling off of transatlantic trade, a continuation of growth.[15] In this atmosphere of economic expansion, enterprising crypto-Jews found themselves ready and able to participate in all levels of commerce throughout the viceroyalty.[16]

While crypto-Jews were to be found in almost every region of New Spain in the mid-seventeenth century, Mexico City served as the focal point for *converso* society, just as it did for the larger Spanish population. With few exceptions, crypto-Jewish immigrants from Spain and Portugal traveled directly to the capital after landing at the port of Veracruz.[17] The majority of those who settled in Mexico City remained there for many years, establishing themselves in stable occupations and patterns of settlement. Approximately one-third, however, left the capital within a couple of years, searching for greater opportunities in more remote regions of the viceroyalty.[18] As we will see, many left to take advantage of the lucrative trade in the mining regions of Pachuca, Zacatecas, and other parts of northern New Spain. Others set down roots in the ports of Acapulco, Veracruz, and Campeche, where they had direct access to the fleets arriving from Spain and the East Indies. Still others continued westward, in search of greater opportunities in the Philippines.

The crypto-Jews who arrived in Mexico City from their distant homes in Spain and Portugal were quickly absorbed into the mainstream of economic and social life. The established *converso* community in Mexico City was a close-knit group, with a well-developed system of extended-family and patron–client relationships. Several such family networks operated in Mexico City from the 1610s through the 1640s. Each clan generally was headed by a wealthy *patrón*, who not only directed the commercial activities of his family, but also supervised the housing, relocation, marriage, burial, and religious needs of those in his charge. He often financed the passage of a nephew or a cousin from Spain or Portugal, arranged through contacts with relatives in Sevilla or Lisboa.

Simón Váez Sevilla and the Role of Crypto-Jews in Mexican Commerce

To illustrate the effects of the extended-family system on the newly arrived immigrant to New Spain, it would be helpful to examine the inner workings of one such family to see how it absorbed new members into its ranks and assimilated them into the larger community.

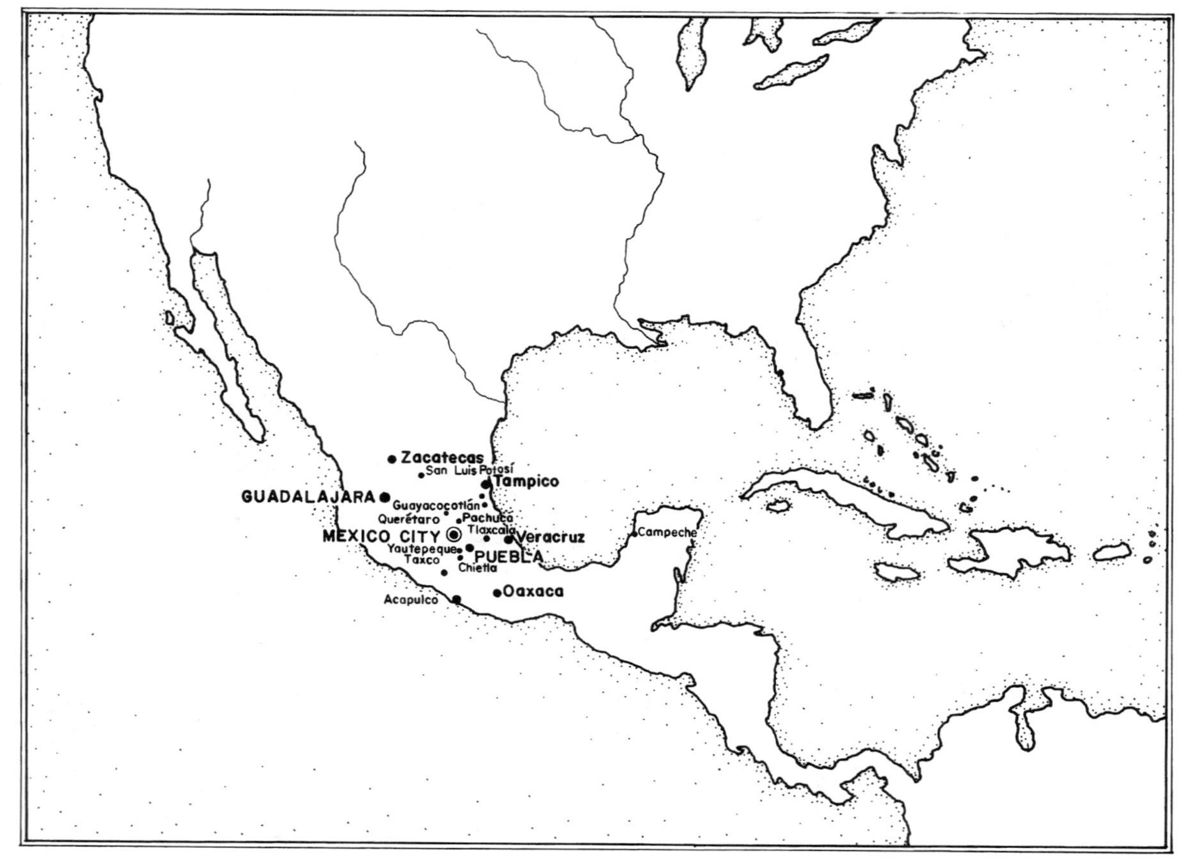

Viceroyalty of New Spain.

The largest family network operating in New Spain was that headed by Simón Váez Sevilla, without question the wealthiest and most powerful crypto-Jewish merchant in the viceroyalty. Váez's commercial scope spanned the Atlantic, Pacific, and Indian Oceans, reaching to such disparate parts of the world as Holland, France, Spain, the Philippines, and Goa, as well as to Peru and Venezuela. He was a member of the *consulado* (merchants' guild) of Mexico City[19] and an influential creditor at the viceregal court.[20] Born in the Galician city of Santiago de Compostela in 1598, Váez spent most of his early life in Castelo Branco, nestled in the mountain range on the Portuguese side of the border with Spain. By age eighteen, he was already active in commerce, both on the Iberian Peninsula and across the Atlantic Ocean. He carried silk for his brother from Sevilla to sell in Lisboa and later sailed to New Spain with a cargo of merchandise, returning to Sevilla shortly thereafter. He made another voyage to New Spain two years later, in 1618, this time not returning to Spain. With the exception of brief excursions to San Luis Potosí, Zacatecas, and Veracruz, made shortly after his arrival, Váez did not leave Mexico City until 1650, when he was exiled by the Inquisition to Sevilla.[21]

Simón Váez's reputation as an influential figure and *patrón* among New Spain's crypto-Jews was well deserved. His large house in Mexico City served as a shelter and stopover for many crypto-Jews recently arrived from Spain and Portugal in the 1620s and 1630s who either were in Mexico temporarily or had not yet found permanent lodging in the city. A substantial number of these new immigrants owed their careers to Váez. The experiences of Manuel de Acosta will illustrate the method by which a newcomer was absorbed into Váez's clan.

The Portuguese-born Acosta worked as an accountant in Sevilla for two crypto-Jewish merchants, Francisco Dias Villaviciosa and his son Antonio. After Antonio married a niece of Váez,[22] Acosta petitioned his employer for permission to travel to New Spain, seeking to capitalize on Antonio's fortuitous marriage. The requisite permission was granted, and Acosta departed for Mexico in 1638, carrying a letter to Váez from his brother asking him to give the young man 300 pesos with which to seek his fortune. Váez indeed fulfilled his obligation as patron to the newly arrived Acosta. After providing him with food and shelter for three months, Váez arranged for him to receive the hand of his niece Isabel Tinoco, along with a generous dowry of 2,000 pesos. In addition, Váez set up Acosta in a lucrative mercantile booth in the *plaza mayor*.[23]

Váez's extended-family system encompassed natural as well as legitimate offspring. From his post in Mexico City, he was able to arrange a marriage between Leonor Váez, his illegitimate daughter living in Valladolid, Spain, and Pedro Fernández de Castro, an itinerant merchant from that city. After only three years of married life, Fernández took the generous dowry supplied by Simón Váez and departed for New Spain, apparently not accompanied by his wife. Fernández moved into Váez's spacious Mexico City house, but before long a quarrel ensued between him and his father-in-law. Váez banished him from Mexico, but still felt compelled to retain him in his commercial network. Fernández spent the next several years as Váez's agent, trading in grain in the Huasteca region.[24]

When necessary, Váez's responsibilities included extricating his clients from difficult legal problems. In 1636, Manuel Dias Santillán, one of Váez's *compañeros* from Castelo Branco, murdered his brother after a family argument over finances erupted into a conflagration that threatened the secret identity of several of Mexico City's crypto-Jews. Váez arranged for a payment of 500 pesos to be made to the jailer in return for the release of Dias. Within twenty-four hours, Dias was freed, all the charges were dropped, and the matter was thus quickly resolved.[25]

There was scarcely a region in the Viceroyalty of New Spain that escaped penetration by crypto-Jews. From Guatemala and Oaxaca in the south, up through Puebla, Tlaxcala, and the Bajío, to the northern mining towns of Tierra Adentro, similar patterns of commercial activity emerged. In each of the principal towns of the outlying areas, *conversos* maintained general stores, supplying the residents of the region with necessary merchandise from Mexico City and abroad, and served their communities as sources of capital. For the replenishment of their stocks, these storekeepers depended on the services of itinerant merchants, many of whom were *conversos* themselves, who traveled back and forth between the sources of supply and the various towns of the periphery. These traders, in turn, received their goods from large-scale operators located either in the ports of Acapulco and Veracruz or in Mexico City. Acting as intermediaries between sources and markets, these wealthy crypto-Jewish merchants usually exerted a high degree of control over the distribution of commodities to the distant regions of the viceroyalty. Dependent family members of the suppliers often served as the traders who carried merchandise to the outlying markets, at the direction of their patrons.

A sizable segment of the crypto-Jewish community, leading relatively stable lives, served the large population centers of Guadalajara and Mexico City, as distributors, storekeepers, and craftspeople. This sector was represented by persons who performed a wide range of functions and lived at various socioeconomic levels. Some barely eked out an existence by working as seamstresses or peddling goods through the streets. Others earned a modest living by operating stalls in the public plazas or maintaining small shops. More successful *conversos* owned large stores and often controlled the distribution of a particular commodity over the entire city.

The trade with the northern mining regions proved to be one of the more significant areas of activity in which New Spain's crypto-Jews participated. These individuals were, for the most part, itinerant merchants, who carried goods to the various towns adjacent to the mining complexes. Other key people lived and owned stores in Zacatecas, Parral, Fresnillo, and other towns of Tierra Adentro, acting as distributors for the merchandise brought to them from the center. In addition, yet other *conversos*, stationed in Mexico City, purchased goods from Europe and Asia for delivery in the north.

The image presented of the mining areas during the first four decades of the seventeenth century by Robert C. West and Peter J. Bakewell is one of a rapidly expanding economy.[26] The increase in production stimulated a demand for foodstuffs and dry goods, a demand that was eagerly met by merchants who flocked to the mining towns to capitalize on these new markets. While much was grown and produced in the areas immediately surrounding the mining centers, a vigorous trade developed between Mexico City and northern New Spain, with sugar, cacao, wine, clothes, and cloth carried northward in exchange for silver.[27] Once these goods reached their destination, they were purchased by the storekeepers in the mining towns and resold to the public.

If the number of stores in a given town was an indication of the degree of mercantile activity, then trade was brisk, indeed, in the north during the first four decades of the seventeenth century. In Zacatecas, the number of shops steadily rose, peaking at ninety-eight in the 1620s, although experiencing a decline through the 1630s. This downturn was due primarily to the rise of the town of Parral, farther north along the Camino Real.[28] In both Parral and Zacatecas, there was a disproportionately large number of shops and shopkeepers in comparison with the Spanish population. Many of the larger shop owners acted as commercial agents for their suppliers in Mexico City and, in turn, maintained their own agents in branch stores in smaller towns.[29]

The experience of crypto-Jews in the northern mining region fit well into this context. Many arrived in New Spain in the late 1610s and the 1620s, and they immediately took advantage of the boom by joining the ranks of those engaged in the lucrative mining trade.

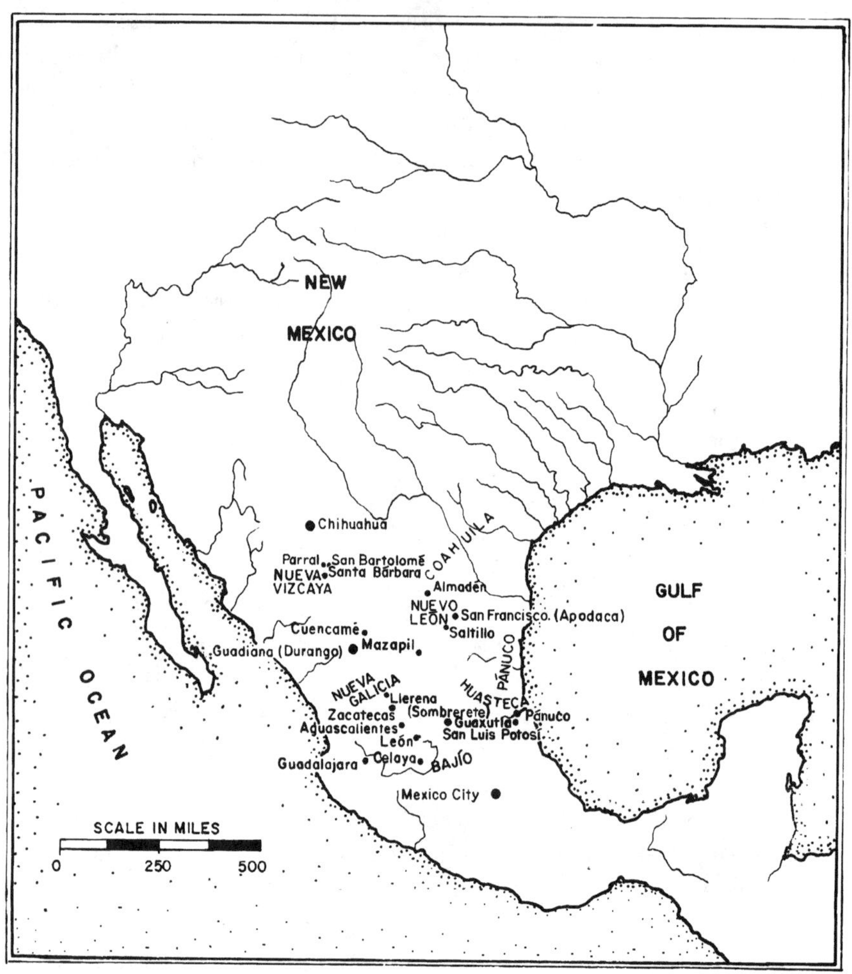

Tierra Adentro: the mining frontier of New Spain.

Those who remained in Mexico City greatly influenced the operation of the trade network that linked the metropolis and the mining areas. The contribution of these individuals was indeed great. They functioned as purchasers of goods from different areas of the viceroyalty and from abroad, as distributors of these commodities throughout the mining districts, as sources of credit, and as guarantors of loans made to their clients. Without having to leave Mexico City, they received on consignment such diverse items as Spanish wine, Philippine silk, Venezuelan cacao, Tlaxcalan cloth, and Campeche wax, and sold this merchandise on credit to traders who made their way to the distant provinces of New Spain. After exchanging these goods for silver in

Zacatecas, Fresnillo, or other towns on the mining frontier, these traveling merchants returned to Mexico City, paid for the merchandise that they had carried, and picked up a new load to begin the cycle again. In turn, the distributors in Mexico City used the silver to repay their debts and purchase new goods. With their profits, they extended credit not only to the traders on their way north, but to various tradespeople and craftspeople in and around the capital.

Among his many commercial activities, Simón Váez Sevilla proved to be instrumental as a supplier of goods for the mining areas. Many of the products that he imported from Europe and Asia, or that he acquired from other parts of the Indies, eventually made their way northward, carried and sold by his agents or associates. While it is difficult to specify the exact nature of all the merchandise traded by Váez, he seems to have dealt heavily in clothes and cloth products, importing raw cloth and sending manufactured clothes to the mining region. Although he obtained most of this fabric from his contacts in Sevilla, he also imported a substantial amount from the Far East and from local textile producers in New Spain, primarily Tlaxcala. To meet the demands of the different markets available to him within the viceroyalty, Váez dealt in merchandise that varied in quality, ranging from fine silks and satins from Asia and Toledo, to coarse wool, flax, and cotton, both imported and domestic.[30] It is unclear whether Váez manufactured clothes from the cloth that he acquired or sold it to others who did so, later purchasing the finished products for resale. In any case, these clothes were carried by members of Váez's trade network to diverse parts of New Spain, including the mining areas. Antonio Váez Casteloblanco, one of Simón Váez's brothers, and Thomás Núñez de Peralta, a brother-in-law, played key roles in transporting these goods to Zacatecas, Guadiana, Cuencamé, and San Luis Potosí, although other traveling merchants also participated in this trade.[31] Simón Váez also imported and distributed saffron, sugar, cinnamon, mules, and a variety of other products throughout the mining region in a similar manner.[32]

Another indication of Váez's influence was his position as creditor, both inside and outside the crypto-Jewish community of New Spain. Among the *conversos* in the viceroyalty, there were few who were not in his debt. At the time of his arrest in 1642 for practicing Judaism, more than 500,000 pesos were owed to his estate. Of this amount, approximately 50,000 pesos were outstanding from Zacatecas and other northern mining towns.[33] Most of the debts owed to Váez by crypto-Jews active in this region derived from advances that he had given to them, either in merchandise or in cash with which to make purchases in other parts of New Spain.[34] In addition, other residents of the mining towns owed him for goods sold on credit by him or his agents. These debtors often included local municipal officials, clerics, and, in some instances, officials of the Inquisition.[35] Váez also extended loans of large sums of money to prominent individuals living in the mining districts, including 28,000 pesos to Isabel Altamirano de Castilla, who had founded a *capellanía* (chaplaincy) in Parral.[36]

Another of the Mexico City crypto-Jews who supplied goods to the northern mining areas was Francisco Franco de Moreira. Although Franco was described by Seymour Liebman as having "lived with great circumspection and apart from any of the Jewish communities in Mexico,"[37] he did maintain commercial relationships with several of his coreligionists in New Spain.[38] Like Váez, Franco acted as both importer and distributor of merchandise. He purchased cacao from Venezuela, cloth from Tlaxcala, and various items from Spain and parts of New Spain, sending these products northward and exchanging them for silver from the mines.[39] While Váez dealt mostly with Zacatecas, Franco concentrated most of his endeavors in Parral. In addition to his trading activities, he acted as commercial agent in Mexico City for several miners and merchants of Parral, exchanging raw silver for specie or merchandise.[40]

Perhaps the most fascinating individuals taking part in this area of trade were those who carried merchandise to the mining towns from the commercial centers of Mexico City, Querétaro, and Guadalajara and from the ports of Acapulco and Veracruz. They made up a mobile, adventuresome group, seldom remaining in one place for more than a few years at a time. For many, their trading experience in the mining areas was but one of many spheres of activity in which they engaged during their lifetimes. With few exceptions, these crypto-Jews were immigrants to New Spain from Portugal and Spain who had come over at a young age to seek their fortunes. Their experiences reflected the needs and the hardships of the environment in which they lived. Some of them participated in the defense of the mining frontier against Indian attacks. Others suffered the loss of their stocks along the highway at the hands of robbers. Regardless of their bases of operation, these traveling merchants found their way to diverse parts of the viceroyalty in their search for sources of supply. In the mining region of the north, they found a lucrative market for their wares.

The danger and risk of their enterprises necessitated the development of interdependence and cooperation among the travelers, both crypto-Jewish and Old Christian alike. Groups of traders often joined in companies for mutual aid and protection. Thomás Treviño de Sobremonte and Diego Rodríguez Árias, both active in trade with the north, had joined with another crypto-Jew, Manuel Rodríguez Núñez, in a trading expedition from Mexico to Acapulco.[41] On several of Thomás Núñez de Peralta's excursions to the northern mining region, he combined his resources with those of Jusepe de Rivera, carrying a large quantity of clothes and other merchandise to San Luis Potosí, Zacatecas, Guadiana, and Cuencamé.[42]

Thomás Treviño de Sobremonte rivaled Simón Váez Sevilla in terms of his wealth and influence within the crypto-Jewish community.[43] In addition to his trade with the northern mining areas, he maintained important operations in Oaxaca. Treviño's business dealings were conducted almost exclusively in Spanish. On at least one occasion, however, he took advantage of his linguistic expertise to handle some sensitive affairs in Nahuatl (the language of the Aztecs). A letter sent to him in Oaxaca by one of his agents operating in the pueblo of San Pablo, written in Nahuatl, warned Treviño of the impending confiscation of his holdings of cochineal (red dye made from the dried bodies of an insect) by the Inquisition:

> Thomás Treviño, may God guard you very much. I received and read your letter. May you continue to be well. We are well here in your Pueblo of San Pablo. We are told that it is not favorable for you to come, because your cochineal is no longer gathered. Many people are looking for and claiming your possessions. . . . We are told that in four weeks you will come. Leave off your business!
>
> Written in the Pueblo of San Pablo on the seventh of September of 1624.
> Your servant [signed] Lásaro Péres.
> Your servant [signed] Pedro Lópes.[44]

Péres and Lópes presumably composed this disturbing letter in the Indian language in order to reach Treviño without arousing the attention of Inquisition officials, who were soon to arrest him for Judaizing.

Demographics of the Mexican Crypto-Jewish Community

Not all Mexican crypto-Jews, of course, earned their living by pursuing mercantile trades. A sizable minority of those *conversos* who were later caught up in the inquisitorial campaign of the mid-seventeenth century, about 17 percent, were engaged in noncommercial occupations. Many of them were tailors, silversmiths, bakers, saddlers, and barbers. The professions were also represented, with four crypto-Jewish doctors, four military officers, one municipal mayor, and one accountant. Other *conversos* could be found as administrators of haciendas, carters, messengers, woodcutters, and farmers. One talented individual even was employed as a singer in the choir in the cathedral of Querétaro. While most women in the crypto-Jewish community claimed to hold no occupation when questioned by inquisitors, it was not uncommon for a *conversa* to earn her living as a seamstress or even as a *curandera* (healer).[45]

In general, the crypto-Jewish community of Mexico was an educated, literate group, compared with the general population. More than 90 percent could read, and 83 percent claimed to be able to write. Only 22 percent had no formal education, and an additional 5 percent had received minimal tutoring from parents or relatives. Most of the community, 73 percent, had some kind of formal education. It was most common for *conversos* to have arranged for their children to study under the direction of a master or tutor. Twenty-two percent had received a higher level of education at some kind of school, university, or monastery. Women demonstrated literary and educational levels far below those of men, but significantly higher than those of the general female population. All the male *conversos* questioned by the inquisitors professed to being able to read and write, whereas the rates for females stood at 68 percent and 50 percent, respectively, far below the 100 percent claimed by their male counterparts. Almost 50 percent of crypto-Jewish women had received no formal education, and only one woman had progressed beyond the tutorial stage.[46]

In regard to an analysis of patterns of personal wealth demonstrated by the crypto-Jewish community of New Spain, any assessment is fraught with methodological challenges. In the first place, the efforts expended by Inquisition officials to ascertain the wealth of those individuals charged with Judaizing met with only limited success. The data in the financial records of the Holy Office thus serve as an accurate measure of the economic status of Mexican *conversos* only to the extent that the authorities succeeded in their investigations. Second, since the Inquisition seized the *conversos'* estates at the time of their arrest, the records reflect their value only at that particular point, obscuring the changes in fortune that these people may have experienced earlier in their careers. Third, there exist few adequate yardsticks against which to measure the wealth of the crypto-Jewish community.[47] Nevertheless, the fiscal records maintained by the Inquisition pertaining to the *judaizantes* are helpful in examining the relative economic success of *conversos* in New Spain at one point in their lives.

Several indicators prove useful in achieving this end. Perhaps the most applicable measure of economic status is the size of the estate seized by the Holy Office at the time of arrest. Inquisition records include such data for sixty-three heads of households arrested in the 1640s on the charge of practicing secret Judaism.[48] Crypto-Jews were represented at all levels of the economic spectrum. Only 22 percent could be found among the extremely poor. Labeled by the treasurer of the Inquisition as "very poor," these people were deep in debt and had no more than a few pesos to their names at the time of their arrest. Another 21 percent held small but modest estates of 200 to 1,000 pesos, a category that economic historian Louisa Schell Hoberman described as "poor." The largest group of crypto-Jews, 43 percent, fell into the category of moderately wealthy, with estates valued at between 1,000 and 15,000 pesos. The top 14 percent, the economic elite of Mexican *conversos*, controlled estates ranging from 15,000 to 70,000 pesos, representing what Hoberman categorized as "well-to-do" to "very wealthy." Falling in the "millionaire" class was Simón Váez Sevilla, whose assets consisted of money, property, and credits amounting to more than 188,000 pesos, according to the financial accounts of the Holy Office.[49]

Other indicators, dowries and incidence of home ownership, help shed light on the economic stratification within the Mexican crypto-Jewish community. Of the twenty-two women for which such data were recorded, more than 81 percent presented their husbands with large dowries of at least 1,000 pesos. While most remained in the 1,000- to 7,000-peso range, some dowries ran as high as 10,000 pesos. The question of the ability of Mexican *conversos* to purchase their own homes may also serve as an indicator of relative affluence. Information on home ownership exists for fifty heads of households and demonstrates that 46 percent were recorded as homeowners. The values of their houses ranged from a modest 1,000 pesos to 14,000 pesos for a more elegant residence.[50]

To this point, crypto-Jews have been considered principally in the context of their role in the commerce of New Spain. In this regard, the *conversos* blended very effectively into the mainstream of Mexican society, not distinguishing themselves as a separate community apart from the general population, except perhaps by the propensity of many to pursue mercantile occupations. In a sense, it is proper to regard the *converso* experience in this light. Crypto-Jews were, first and foremost, Iberians, maintaining the language and customs of their forebears in Spain and Portugal. Many had the opportunity to leave the Spanish dominions in favor of lands where they were free to practice their Judaism openly and in peace, but most opted to remain in familiar cultural surroundings.

Religious and Cultural Life of the Mexican Crypto-Jewish Community

In the seventeenth century, Mexican crypto-Jews were not singled out as a separate group until 1642, when, for a variety of reasons, the Inquisition embarked on a campaign against the community. It must be emphasized that from the 1610s until 1642, neither the Inquisition nor any other religious or political body paid much attention to the crypto-Jews in New Spain. Nevertheless, based on the testimony offered by the *conversos* during the trials of the 1640s, it is evident that in certain respects they did conduct themselves in a manner that reflected a consciousness of their ethnic identity.

The patterns demonstrated by crypto-Jews who resided in Mexico City strongly suggest the presence of a certain degree of ethnocentrism. They tended to live in close proximity to one another, clustered in a three-block area between the cathedral and the church of Santo Domingo. It is not without a touch of irony that the majority of *conversos* maintained their residence within a stone's throw of the Palace of the Inquisition, located directly across from Santo Domingo.

Group consciousness was manifested in other ways as well. *Converso* merchants tended to concentrate their commercial associations within the ethnic community. In almost every area of trade, crypto-Jews relied on one another as sources of supply and credit, as agents in remote regions, as bondsmen, and as partners in business ventures. This is not to say that Old Christians were excluded from *converso* trade channels. Quite to the contrary, *conversos* furnished the Mexican community at large with vital goods and services and, by necessity, dealt with non-*converso* merchants on many levels.

A further demonstration of ethnocentrism may be seen in the propensity of Mexican crypto-Jews to marry within the faith. As a group, they tended to be family oriented. Married *conversos* outnumbered single by a ratio of three to one. The practice of endogamy was almost universal among the *conversos*. More than 95 percent of the marriages were between members of the community. Efforts sometimes were made to "convert" a prospective bridegroom to Judaism in order to gain the approval of the bride's family. In 1638, Isabel Tinoco, niece of Simón Váez Sevilla, found herself being courted by Manuel de Acosta, a young man recently arrived in Mexico City from

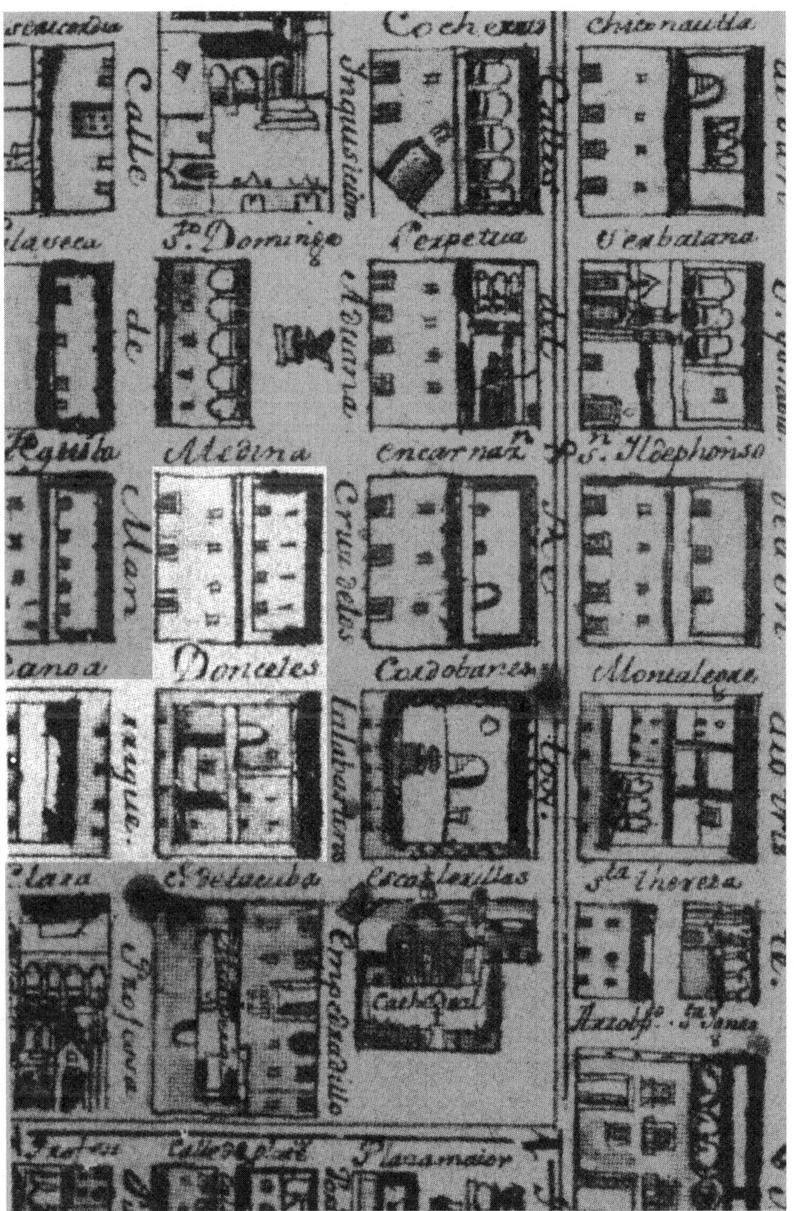

Mexico City in the colonial period, highlighting the area of settlement of crypto-Jews. (From *Planos de ciudades iberoamericanas y filipinas* [Madrid: Instituto de Estudios de Administración Local, 1981], p. 210, pl. 230)

Lisboa. Relations between Acosta and Isabel's family were cordial throughout the courtship, and eventually Acosta asked her grandfather, Antonio Rodríguez Árias, for her hand. On the day that Rodríguez's response was to be delivered, Acosta visited him at his house on Calle Tacuba. During a stroll around the Alameda, Rodríguez offered his consent to the marriage, but only if Acosta abandoned the Law of Jesus Christ in favor of the Law of Moses. Acosta agreed, proceeded to learn the practice of Judaism from Rodríguez's wife, and married Isabel shortly thereafter. Following Rodríguez's death several months later, Acosta was called on by his in-laws to approach the suitor of Isabel's sister and extract from him the same promise that he had made, to forsake Christianity in favor of Judaism.[51]

Perhaps more than any other factor, religious observance served as a vehicle for achieving and maintaining a sense of religious identity within the Mexican crypto-Jewish community.[52] Fast days, especially that of Yom Kippur (referred to as *el día grande*, or "the Great Day"), provided an opportunity for families to interrupt their normal routines and gather in the home of one of the worshipers. Inquisition trial records are filled with detailed accounts of Yom Kippur observances, identifying the location of the services, listing the names of the worshipers, and vividly describing the manner in which the fasts were broken. Not all *conversos* were able to meet the stoic test of the fast. Pedro de Espinosa, a traveling merchant in the mining region of Tierra Adentro, resorted to stealing away from the service at about three o'clock in the afternoon to relieve his hunger.[53]

The Sabbath, regarded by David Gitlitz as "the single most persistent crypto-Jewish custom" in the Iberian world,[54] was also generally observed by Mexican *conversos*. On Friday afternoons, women bathed, donned clean clothes, and put out clean bed and table linen. In the evening, Sabbath lights were kindled, with great care being taken to avoid notice by neighbors and servants. Some *conversos* lit candles, while others used wicks floating in olive oil. Saturday-morning services were generally held at people's homes. The Carvajal family in the 1580s prayed in Latin, with only the Shema recited in Hebrew. Later communities tended to conduct their services in Spanish and Portuguese. No work was performed on the Sabbath. Merchants abstained from selling their wares, and those who prepared meals made certain that all cooking was completed by sundown on Friday evening.[55]

Jewish customs relating to death and dying were also observed by Mexican crypto-Jews. *Conversos* who were about to die would have their heads turned to the wall by family members.[56] Following the death of a member of the community, measures were taken to avoid the administration of the sacrament of last rites. The body was prepared for burial by the family in the traditional Jewish manner, whereby it was bathed, shaved, dressed in a shroud, and then placed in virgin soil. In the 1630s, Mexico City cloth merchant Manuel Álvarez de Arellano took upon himself the obligation of ensuring that shrouds were provided for the cadavers. A common custom among Mexican crypto-Jews was the placing of coins, pearls, or food in the mouths of the deceased to help them on their journey to the next world. As in other parts of the Iberian world, it was important for *conversos* in Mexico to bury their dead within as short a period of time as possible. In contrast to the common Christian practice of burying the body in one place, and later exhuming the decomposed remains and interring them in another, it was essential for crypto-Jews to bury the corpse in virgin soil, ensuring that it would never be disturbed.[57]

Another Jewish rite that was almost universally practiced among Mexican *conversos* was infant male circumcision, which represents the external manifestation of God's covenant with the Jewish people. Although, according to Gitlitz, the ritual was not generally practiced in Spain, it appears to have been observed more diligently among crypto-Jews in Mexico.[58] Inspections by Inquisition surgeons revealed that approximately 80 percent of the male *judaizantes* whom they examined were circumcised. Another 11 percent bore a mark of undetermined origin, raising the suspicion on the part of the inquisitors that some Jewish ritual had resulted in such scarring, either shortly after birth or later in life.[59] When confronted with evidence of their circumcisions, individuals reacted differently. One crypto-Jew made an effort to exonerate himself, explaining to the inquisitors that the scar was due to "an earlier infirmity that I had in those parts." Another dismissed it as the result of "the mischief of women." Still another admitted that he had subjected himself to the ritual, but only to please a Jewish lover in Italy.[60] One of the more curious forms of circumcision was performed by Duarte de León Xaramillo, who cut a small wedge of flesh from the shoulders of his children, both male and female. He reportedly salted and roasted the extracted piece, and then ate it.[61]

These expressions of ethnic identity on the part of the crypto-Jewish community of New Spain were virtually ignored from the 1610s until 1642 by the Holy Office of the Inquisition, the body entrusted with the enforcement of religious orthodoxy in the viceroyalty. With few exceptions, Mexican *conversos* lived their lives, pursued their careers, and discretely practiced their religion in relative obscurity. In the early 1640s, however, a complex series of developments transpired that would dramatically shatter the calm that had prevailed in the *converso* community for the previous four decades.

POLITICAL CHANGE AND INQUISITORIAL PERSECUTION

As spring turned into summer in 1642, the dark clouds that had been gathering for several months broke into a violent storm for the crypto-Jewish community of New Spain. During July, August, and September, scores were arrested by the Holy Office of the Inquisition and charged with the criminal heresy of practicing secret Judaism. By the end of the decade, hundreds of Mexican *conversos* had been convicted of Judaizing, suffering confiscation of their estates and, in a few instances, execution by burning at the stake. The persecution that the crypto-Jews experienced in the 1640s at the hands of the Holy Office represented a departure from the inquisitorial policy pursued over the previous decades. In order to understand why the Mexican Inquisition suddenly embarked on a vigorous campaign against the *conversos*, it is necessary to investigate events that unfolded in both New Spain and Europe during the preceding years.

In 1640, the duque de Bragança, later crowned João IV, led a successful movement for Portuguese independence from Felipe IV of Spain, thus ending a sixty-year period of Spanish domination. The early reports of the Portuguese revolt were received with alarm in Mexico City. Not only had Portugal rebelled, the communiqués read, but the Portuguese had slaughtered three thousand Spanish residents of Brazil, and there were signs that Cartagena would erupt at any moment. A year earlier, the Inquisition of Lima had celebrated its *gran auto de fe*, at which appeared sixty-one Portuguese crypto-Jews, all convicted of having participated in a conspiracy to oust the Spanish authorities in Peru in favor of the Dutch.[62] Officials in Spain and Mexico feared that New Spain was now extremely vulnerable and had to be safeguarded against the Portuguese threat.

By 1641, authorities began to express serious concern about both the external danger of attack on the ports and the threat represented by those in New Spain who might support such an attack by the Portuguese. The bishop of Puebla, Juan de Pálafox y Mendoza, emerged as the most vocal proponent of taking vigilant measures to defend the viceroyalty against this perceived menace. The Portuguese, Pálafox warned the viceroy in November 1641, posed a grave danger due to their wealth and large numbers. They were planning to expend their fortunes to buy up "all the flints and arquebuses, thus secretly controlling all the arms. . . . Veracruz is the principal key to these kingdoms," he continued, "and there are currently in that port more Portuguese than Spanish." Since all the news from Spain and Portugal reached Mexico by way of Veracruz, this situation appeared all the more intolerable.[63]

Pálafox succeeded in convincing Felipe IV to issue a series of *cédulas* (royal decrees) imposing severe restrictions on all Portuguese through 1641 and 1642. The text of these *cédulas* contained ominous references to the danger posed by the concentration of wealthy Portuguese merchants in the vulnerable ports and mining areas. As early as January 1641, Felipe ordered that all Portuguese in New Spain who were in sympathy with the Bragança revolt be expelled and their goods confiscated. In addition, the immigration of all Portuguese to New Spain was to cease immediately.[64] In *cédulas* issued in February 1642, Felipe reflected the growing fear of internal revolt by the Portuguese and concern for the security of New Spain. To defend the port of Veracruz from invasion, he ordered that a platform be constructed overlooking the harbor for the placement of a battery of artillery. He observed that if an insurrection was to break out in New Spain, it would originate among the foreigners residing in the viceroyalty. Specifically, Felipe made reference to a "landed and commercial class" of Portuguese, many of whom were in New Spain without royal license. These individuals, the king continued,

> are great in number and have positioned themselves in the most fortified ports. They are wealthier than the natives [Spanish] and are also more united. In the royal mines they are extremely rich, and I am informed that they plan to seize all the gold and silver and to embezzle my Royal Fifth. They are brazen in their expressions of disloyalty, and are in collusion with the Blacks, who hold them in high regard. Because they had brought such a large number of slaves from Angola and had cared for them, [the Blacks] looked up to them as parents.

Since these Portuguese posed such a grave threat, the king ordered that they were to be removed twenty leagues, or fifty-two miles, from the strategic ports, and the same distance from the northern mining areas of Tierra Adentro.[65]

As if these measures were not severe enough, a special tax was levied against all "vassals of the Portuguese Nation" residing in New Spain. The amount of this *donativo* was calculated on the basis of the value of an individual's estate. Its avowed purpose was to allow the

Portuguese to demonstrate their "fidelity and love" for the king and to help finance the defense effort against the feared invasion of the viceroyalty by enemy forces.[66]

Both inside and outside the ethnic community, Mexican *conversos* were closely identified with their Portuguese origins. As each new report of the Bragança revolt reached New Spain, crypto-Jews increasingly expressed the fear that they would suffer from the repercussions, not because of their religious beliefs, but because of their status as Portuguese.[67]

In late 1641 and early 1642, Simón Váez Sevilla began to take measures to safeguard his possessions, as well as those of his colleagues, from impending confiscation by the Crown. Correspondence between Váez and his commercial agents contains references to his concern about the deteriorating situation. In November 1641, Váez issued instructions to Simón López de Aguarda, his agent in Zacatecas, to sell immediately all his stock for whatever he could salvage and to remit the proceeds to Mexico City: "And if you encounter any problems [from the authorities] on the basis of your status as Portuguese, always say that the cargo is all owned by Simón Váez Sevilla, and since he is a native of His Majesty's kingdoms [Váez was born in Santiago de Compostela], he is entitled to it." Váez further instructed his agent to collect a debt owed to him in Zacatecas, commenting that he would not have done so if the news of the uprising in Portugal had not just arrived in Mexico.[68]

By June 1642, the tone of Váez's letters had become desperate. He warned that officials had been dispatched from Mexico City to Veracruz and to Tierra Adentro in conformity with the royal edicts, with authority to expel the Portuguese from these areas. López was to expend all efforts to liquidate everything immediately and to return to Mexico City, "because the Portuguese will be ousted from all the kingdoms."[69] Testimony offered later before the Inquisition by Váez's son Gaspar confirmed that Váez had taken these precautions "not for fear of the Inquisition, but of . . . Juan de Pálafox . . . , who said for certain that he wanted to divest the Portuguese of their goods. This was the cause for taking the precautions, and no other."[70]

The identification of the Mexican crypto-Jews as Portuguese deeply affected their lives in other ways as well in the early 1640s. Cacao merchant Duarte Castaño related tales of the odyssey undertaken by him and by other *conversos* as a result of the Bragança revolt in Portugal. When news of the rebellion arrived in Caracas in 1640, the governor immediately expelled all Portuguese from the region. Castaño and his colleagues gathered whatever belongings they could manage and sailed for Cartagena, Havana, and, eventually, Veracruz. Before long, however, local authorities began to enforce the royal decree ordering the removal of the Portuguese from the port, so they packed up again and left for Mexico City.[71]

The concern expressed by royal authorities about the loyalties of the Portuguese living in New Spain may well have been justified. The Bragança revolt seems to have found support in certain quarters of the Mexican *converso* community. A letter written in 1641 by Fernando de Mezquita in Veracruz to his brother Luis de Amezquita in Mexico City told of rumors circulating in the port city that a Portuguese ship with 150 soldiers on board had arrived in the Canary Islands and might well continue on to New Spain. "No one here is certain if this news is accurate," Mezquita wrote. "But may God permit that it is, and that our friends may arrive in this land so that all of us may take great satisfaction."[72]

When the inquisitors arrested Luis Núñez Pérez, a Portuguese *converso* cacao merchant, they found among his papers a copy of the treaty negotiated between João IV, the newly proclaimed king of Portugal, and the government of Holland. Núñez had obtained the text of the treaty from an Irish priest who had just arrived in New Spain, and then proceeded to distribute copies to three other Portuguese in Mexico City. Significantly, one of these individuals turned out to be Sebastián Váez de Acevedo, purveyor general of the Spanish *Armada de Barlovento*, strongly suspected of treason by Bishop Pálafox. Whether or not Núñez acted as an enemy agent, this evidence linking him to the Portuguese Crown and to Váez de Acevedo served to confirm in the minds of the inquisitors the danger posed by the Portuguese crypto-Jews to the security of the viceroyalty.[73]

The responsibility of enforcing the anti-Portuguese measures fell initially on the shoulders of the viceroy, Diego López Pacheco y Bobadilla, duque de Escalona. Born in Portugal, and a brother-in-law of the insurgent duque de Bragança, Escalona now found himself in the difficult position of promulgating laws contrary to the well-being of his compatriots and most favored subjects.

During his tenure as viceroy, Escalona had maintained close political and financial ties to Portuguese residents in New Spain, many of whom were members of the crypto-Jewish community. Escalona had appointed several *conversos* to high administrative posts and had borrowed considerable sums from crypto-Jews. In addition to the appointment of Váez de Acevedo as purveyor general, he had named Juan Torres de Rivera as captain of the infantry, to be stationed in the Philippines. At the height of the tension between Spain and Portugal, he commissioned a vessel owned and captained by Portuguese crypto-Jew Diego Rodríguez and dispatched it to Portugal. In addition, Escalona had negotiated loans of substantial amounts from *converso* merchants Simón Váez Sevilla and Antonio Méndez Chillón.[74]

When in April 1641 the decrees issued by Felipe IV reached Escalona in Mexico City, the viceroy chose to ignore them, keeping them secret even from Bishop Pálafox and the *audiencia* of Mexico. Instead, he continued his policy of favoring his Portuguese subjects, thus incurring the jealousy of the Spanish bureaucracy, the suspicion of the king, and the wrath of the bishop, who was keenly sensitive to the threat of both foreign invasion and domestic subversion. In August 1641, Pálafox traveled from Puebla to Mexico City to confront Escalona. The first action that must be taken, he warned, was the removal of Váez de Acevedo and other Portuguese who occupied high positions. Next, all Portuguese should be forced to register their arms, removed from the ports, and prohibited from holding any office that would place them in an advantageous position in case of an insurrection. Escalona turned a deaf ear to the bishop, dismissing his warnings, just as he had Felipe's decrees months earlier. His overtures spurned, Pálafox directed his efforts toward convincing the king of Escalona's unsuitability to continue as the royal representative in such a volatile atmosphere.[75]

Pálafox's entreaties to the king ultimately met with success. On May 23, 1642, news reached Mexico City that he had been appointed to the powerful post of archbishop of Mexico, and on June 9 he received word that he had been named viceroy of New Spain, governor of Mexico, captain-general, and president of the *audiencia*, replacing Escalona as Felipe's representative in Mexico City. Among Pálafox's first acts as viceroy were the arrest of Escalona and the enactment of a broad range of measures to ensure the security of the viceroyalty against external attack and internal subversion.[76]

Within days of Pálafox's assumption of viceregal power, the Holy Office of the Inquisition issued orders for the arrest of almost one hundred persons, most of Portuguese descent, on suspicion of practicing secret Judaism. Correspondence between the tribunal in Mexico City and the Supreme Council of the Inquisition in Madrid clearly placed the mass arrests in the context of the widespread fear that gripped Mexico City in the summer of 1642. In their letters, the Mexican inquisitors made repeated references to the threat posed to New Spain by these *portugueses*, not so much because of their Judaizing activities, but because of their allegiance to the leaders of the Portuguese revolt. One such letter read:

> [In consideration of the inquisitors' obligation to serve God and the king,] in the midst of the great fear generated by this kind of people [the Portuguese], [the inquisitors have been engaged in] preserving the kingdom from the contagion . . . and great dangers that indeed should be regarded seriously. They [the Portuguese] spoke with great desires in anticipation of the arrival of the Portuguese armada, which would be [accompanied by a revolt] of the slaves who live in the sugar mills. In the possession of one of the prisoners [probably Luis Núñez Pérez] was found a copy of the treaty negotiated between the Portuguese crown and the states of Holland after the uprising. We reported all of this to the viceroy, Juan de Pálafox, so that he could vigilantly proceed with the removal of the Portuguese from the ports and mining regions. It is thus clearly evident that this Tribunal has worked actively in the service of Our Lord, the King. We implore of Your Highness that you inform him of this so that he might become better informed of the zeal with which we serve Him. And in order that this Holy Office will always be so vigilant in the defense of this kingdom, may it have the assistance and support of its Catholic and Royal Majesty.[77]

A 1643 manifesto written by Escalona's son, the conde de Santiesteban, corroborates the theory that Pálafox used the Holy Office as a political instrument. After receiving news of the uprisings in Portugal and Cartagena, Santiesteban related, it seemed that "the Indies were now stung, and that it would be prudent to protect the Indies from such dangers. . . . These stringencies were now conferred upon the Tribunal of the Holy Inquisition, upon the royal *audiencia*, upon the royal ministers, and upon powerful individuals."[78]

The anxiety experienced by the crypto-Jews turned to panic by the late spring of 1642. In May, Blanca Méndez de Rivera and her five daughters were arrested by the Holy Office. Since "Las Blancas," as they were known, maintained a reputation both as central figures in the Mexico City *converso* community and as eager gossips, it is probable that the inquisitors singled them out for early attention in order to obtain a comprehensive list of suspected *judaizantes*.[79] The arrest of Las Blancas led to much agitation among the Mexican crypto-Jews. Shortly after the women were taken, sixteen people assembled at the home of Simón Váez Sevilla to vent their frustration, to pray, and to decide on a course of action. In a desperate attempt to keep Las Blancas from implicating them, Váez and his wife sent word by secret messenger to María, Clara, and Margarita de Rivera that they would promise to provide a dowry for their sister Isabel in exchange for their silence. Secret letters written by María de Rivera in her cell to Váez and to Juan Méndez de Villaviciosa reveal that she had been given to understand that Váez offered her a large sum of money if she would not implicate her coreligionists. She expressed the hope "that the alms will be great and very large. You should know that you have enhanced the value of your secret greatly, and if no one besides yourself does not provide such a pledge, do not blame me if the secret is revealed." For her cooperation, María demanded 1,000 pesos. When Váez balked at the amount, she expressed surprise that he would miss the opportunity to take advantage of the "open road to remedy this great danger," but indicated that 500 pesos would be acceptable.[80] Váez made similar attempts to gain the silence of his slaves. If they offered testimony to the Inquisition, he warned, his *compadre*, Garcia de Valdés Osorio, an Old Christian, would purchase them and force them to work in his sugar mill. If they remained loyal, however, they would be rewarded with emancipation.[81]

Anticipating the worst, Mexican *conversos* began to secure their estates against the sequestrations that would take place at the time of their arrest. Váez, his extended family, and other crypto-Jews set out to hide their valuables and to destroy incriminating evidence. He ordered his son to burn commercial papers and account books that not only contained information concerning his assets, but also revealed that he had been carrying on illegal trade with France and Holland over the years. When news of Escalona's ouster reached Váez, he was said to have taken the promissory note for 100,000 pesos in his favor signed by the deposed viceroy and torn it to shreds in order to avoid any further connection with the Portuguese revolt.[82]

On July 12, the day before Váez and dozens of other *conversos* were to be arrested by the Holy Office, one of the inquisitors, Francisco de Estrada y Escobedo, leaked advance news of the arrests to Garcia de Valdés Osorio, who had maintained close commercial relations with Váez. Estrada wanted to warn Valdés to settle his accounts with Váez before Váez's estate was sequestered. Valdés immediately dispatched a messenger to Váez urging his friend to come to his house to discuss some important business matters. Váez complied, carrying with him a large bundle of commercial papers. Upon his arrival, Valdés broke the news of the impending arrests and volunteered to help Váez salvage his estate by accepting temporary custody of a substantial share of his assets. Several cartloads of merchandise had already been hastily sent by Váez to Valdés for safekeeping during the preceding weeks. Váez, fearful of losing all his holdings to the Inquisition, now readily agreed to transfer to Valdés eight notes worth more than 140,000 pesos, with the expectation that they would be returned to him after his release.[83]

That night, agents of the Inquisition arrested seven persons for Judaizing. The next night, thirty more were apprehended. Within a year, over 75 *conversos* had entered the cells of the Holy Office, charged with the criminal offense of observing the Law of Moses. By 1647, more than 130 had been taken. The inquisitors issued warrants for the arrest of many more, but could not follow through on them because the suspects had either died or successfully evaded Inquisition agents.[84]

The process established by the Holy Office for the trial of *judaizantes*, developed over the previous century and a half, was long and tedious, encompassing a multitude of interrogations, admonitions, reports, inspections, and accusations. Officials forced prisoners to bide their time during the long intervals between audiences with inquisitors, resulting in years of incarceration between their arrest and their appearance in the auto de fe.[85] In order to better understand the inquisitorial procedure, it might be helpful to examine in some detail the structure of the trials conducted by the Mexican tribunal against the *judaizantes* in the 1640s.

The first audience that the defendants had with the inquisitors generally did not occur until several weeks after their arrest. Some prisoners languished in jail for over a year before meeting with the authorities. During this first audience, the accused were required to provide information regarding their places of birth and residence and their ages and occupations, and to give an account of their relatives extending back two generations. In addition, they attested to the purity of their lineage; their status as good, baptized Catholics; and their ability to read and write. At this point, the inquisitors asked the defendants to offer a *discurso de la vida* (autobiographical account), a discussion that often continued for many pages, rich with details concerning their experiences in Spain or Portugal, education, travels, family and religious life, and mobility within New Spain. Finally, they were asked if they knew the reason for their arrest and received the first of three formal admonitions to bare their consciences and confess to their crimes. Over the succeeding months (and sometimes years), the inquisitors held periodic audiences with the prisoners, usually according to their own schedules, but sometimes at the request of the defendants who desired to confess.

Of those *conversos* for whom trial records exist in the Archivo General de la Nación in Mexico City, the vast majority, almost 80 percent, confessed to having observed the Law of Moses. Of these, over 50 percent did so immediately at the time of their first interview with the inquisitors. While torture presented itself as a tool available to officials of the Holy Office to gain confessions from recalcitrant suspects, they utilized it sparingly and selectively. Only 31 percent of the *conversos* were forced to submit to the torments of the rack. Efforts to obtain confessions in this manner met with only mixed success. Of those who underwent torture, only 50 percent acquiesced by admitting their guilt. The rest remained steadfast in their denial of any wrongdoing. For some, however, the mere threat of the rack provided sufficient motivation to discharge their consciences. Eighty-three percent of those threatened chose to confess, and it is safe to assume that the implicit fear of the process served as an effective motivation.

Several months after the initial audience with the inquisitors, the defendants were presented with a formal accusation, itemizing in a point-by-point fashion the crimes with which they had been charged. After consultation with their defense lawyer, appointed by the Inquisition, they responded to these charges, acknowledging their accuracy, branding them as complete fabrications, or accepting some combination of both. Following the accusations, male crypto-Jews submitted to the *auto de inspección* (act of inspection), by which they were examined by a team of surgeons seeking evidence of circumcision. Positive determination was interpreted as proof of their guilt. Next, the inquisitors confronted the defendants with a copy of the testimony that had been accumulated over the years since their arrest. Again, they were offered the opportunity to respond to the allegations contained in these anonymous declarations.

All but a few suspects arrested by the Inquisition were found guilty of observing the Law of Moses. Five to seven years after their arrest, they appeared before the inquisitors to receive their formal sentences. Very few *conversos*, less than 7 percent of those sentenced, suffered burning at the stake, and only one of them, Thomás Treviño de Sobremonte, was burned alive. The rest repented at the last moment and were accorded the privilege of being garroted before the pyres were set afire. "Reconciliation" to the Catholic Church was the most common sentence meted out to Mexican crypto-Jews. This penance included confiscation of their estates and exile from the Indies. Over 71 percent of the *judaizantes* emerged as *reconciliados* (persons reconciled to the Church). An additional 12 percent were reconciled, but suffered only confiscation or exile, not both. Another 5 percent were sentenced to serve in the galleys at sea for several years.

Harsher sentences tended to fall on those crypto-Jews who were more religiously observant and better educated, perhaps because they appeared to be more flagrant in their violation of Catholic orthodoxy and, therefore, more dangerous to society. Those who confessed, either immediately or ultimately, to their heresy received more lax sentences than their more recalcitrant cohorts, indicating a policy of rewarding those who cooperated with the inquisitors. No discernable level of association could be ascertained between the size of an individual's confiscated estate and the degree of severity with which he or she was punished.

In the autos de fe of 1646, 1647, 1648, and 1649, 212 *judaizantes* appeared, either in person or in effigy, to be publicly penanced.[86] During these ceremonies, Inquisition officials announced to the assemblage of dignitaries and onlookers the crimes committed by these heretics and the punishments imposed on them. Those to be burned at the stake were "relaxed" to the secular authorities, who without hesitation proceeded to execute the sentences. The remainder, the *reconciliados*, bedecked in their *sanbenitos* (penitential garb), formally recanted their heretical beliefs. The inquisitors placed severe restrictions on the conduct of *reconciliados*. It was forbidden for penanced *judaizantes* and their descendants to wear silk, jewelry, silver, and gold; to bear arms; and to ride on horseback. In addition, they were required to wear their *sanbenitos* for a fixed period of time as a public sign of repentance.

Despite their harsh sentences, it appears that many *reconciliados* managed to avoid compliance with the terms of their exile. In theory, they were supposed to make their way to Veracruz, embark on the first fleet bound for Spain, and report to the tribunal of the Holy Office in Sevilla. The persistent efforts expended by the Mexican inquisitors, the viceroy, and the king to effect the swift departure of these penanced crypto-Jews from New Spain, however, indicates that they had a difficult time in accomplishing this end. From 1647 through 1650, Felipe IV repeatedly issued decrees ordering the generals of the annual fleet to transport the exiled heretics back to Spain. Fearful of the threat that these Portuguese posed to security, the king urged the viceroy and the inquisitors to take all measures to remove the *reconciliados* from the ports and place them immediately on ships bound for Sevilla.[87] As late as November 1651, two and a half years after the *gran auto de fe* of 1649, the viceroy was still reminding Inquisition officials that convicted *judaizantes* yet could be found in New Spain.[88]

The logistical problems faced by the inquisitors in arranging for the deportation of these individuals were compounded by the reluctance of the crypto-Jews to leave the viceroyalty. Not only did the *reconciliados* attempt to avoid or delay leaving the country, but they flagrantly violated other terms of their sentences as well. Inquisitors constantly voiced complaints that the *conversos* used every available pretext to stay in Puebla, rather than complete their journey to Veracruz to board the ships. Nor did they wear their *sanbenitos* in public, attend Mass, or stay within the confines of the city, as mandated by the Holy Office.[89]

When Simón Váez Sevilla and his family emerged from their penitential cells after the auto de fe of 1649, Inquisition officials directed them to leave immediately for Veracruz and board the first ship departing for Spain. They traveled to Veracruz, but instead of sailing across the ocean they disembarked at the nearby port of Campeche, where Váez's old friend Garcia de Valdés Osorio ruled as governor. From this secure position, Váez pleaded to Inquisition officials that he was too ill to travel any farther and too poor to support himself and his family for such a long voyage into exile. During their sojourn in Campeche, Váez and his family were continually harassed by the Inquisition authorities, both for their delaying tactics and for their refusal to wear *sanbenitos*. Although both his state of health and his economic woes were somewhat exaggerated, Váez succeeded in stalling for more than a year before departing for Sevilla. He left in grand style, carrying with him 5,000 pesos (supplied by Valdés), a cargo of chocolate, jewelry, and silver.[90]

Reconciled *judaizantes* Jorge Jacinto Bazán and Miguel Tinoco, staying in Puebla with their families en route to Veracruz, violated the terms of their sentences so flagrantly that they found themselves arrested and tried by the Mexican Holy Office a second time. Both men had been granted permission by Inquisition officials to leave Puebla to trade in the surrounding towns, but only on the condition that they observe the proscriptions regarding their dress and conduct. Once outside the confines of the city, however, Jacinto and Tinoco quickly rid themselves of their *sanbenitos*. Jacinto threw his to the ground and, in an act of defiance, donned his spurs, sword, and dagger (all prohibited items), and then proceeded to stomp on his despised penitential garment. He and his partner then rode on horseback through the countryside in a "scandalous fashion," according to one contemporary account. They were arrested and confined in Mexico City until their exile several months later.[91]

It is known for certain that 26 of the 103 *reconciliados* sentenced to exile actually left New Spain for destinations in Europe. Testimony offered several years later by Simón Váez Sevilla and others reveals that Váez lived in Sevilla and Madrid during the mid-1650s.[92] Simón Fernández de Torres settled in Amsterdam, and Juan Méndez de Villaviciosa opted for life as a merchant in France.[93] Exactly how many convicted *judaizantes* chose not to comply with their exile and remained in New Spain is unknown. The public record includes several trials of those who where apprehended by the Holy Office for violation of their sentences.

If the case of Luis Pérez Roldán was typical of the policy of the Mexican Inquisition in the 1650s, then the Holy Office made little more than a token effort to enforce the sentences of exile. Pérez had been reconciled in the auto de fe of 1649 and banished from the Indies. Three years later, however, he still had not left Mexico City and pleaded with the inquisitors for permission to stay longer. They refused and again ordered him to depart on the next fleet sailing from Veracruz. After another four years passed, word reached the officials that Pérez not only remained in the capital, but conducted business openly in the *plaza mayor*, and without wearing his *sanbenito*. Once more the inquisitors ordered him to leave, and once more he petitioned to remain. At this point, they took action and arrested Pérez on the grounds that such a rebellious attitude would set a dangerous precedent for other *penitenciados* (penanced ones). When he emerged from prison, he was again ordered to leave the viceroyalty without delay. But as late as 1662, more than thirteen years after his initial sentence, Pérez was still to be found in Mexico City, petitioning Inquisition officials to be released from his obligation to wear the *sanbenito*.[94]

Pérez's petition offers a rare opportunity for the modern reader to consider how the stigma of the penitential habit affected those reconciled *judaizantes* who remained in New Spain. In a moving letter, Pérez appealed to the inquisitors' sense of mercy:

> Those who wear the *sanbenito* are detested, not only by Catholics, but also by those of other barbarous nations. I find it impossible to support myself, my family, and my children only because I have retained this disreputable insignia. . . . Please do not allow me or my family to die of hunger. My advanced age [sixty-two] does not permit me to perform manual labor, but I can only find sustenance by the manufacture of arms.[95]

The outcome of Pérez's case is not known, as the Inquisition's record stopped abruptly without indication of resolution. Nor is it clear whether Pérez eventually complied with his sentence of exile or lived out his days in New Spain.

Inquisition records are not the only sources that prove that *penitenciados* remained in the viceroyalty. Civil judicial records reveal that more than a dozen penanced crypto-Jews picked up their business dealings where they had left off before their arrest. A year after his appearance in the auto de fe of 1648, in which he was sentenced to exile, Melchor Rodríguez López was found signing a contract to purchase goods and owning slaves.[96]

The campaigns of the Holy Office of the Inquisition against the crypto-Jews of Mexico in the late sixteenth and mid-seventeenth centuries shattered the calm and relatively tolerant environment that had characterized the decades that preceded them. These periods of persecution demonstrated to the *converso* communities of central Mexico that it was no longer safe to practice their ancestral faith in such close proximity to the inquisitorial authorities. Those who discretely wished to continue to observe the Law of Moses in an atmosphere of security would have to, in the words of María de Rivera, "flee to the ends of the earth," one of which was the far northern frontier of New Mexico.

NOTES

1. The historical literature treating the crypto-Jewish experience in these frontier areas is not well developed, and, as a consequence, the quality is uneven. For an account of crypto-Judaism in Argentina, see Mario Javier Sabán, *Judíos conversos: Los antepasados judíos de las familias tradicionales argentinas* (Buenos Aires: Editorial Distal, 1990). For Colombia, see Daniel Mesa Bernal, *De los judíos en la historia de Colombia* (Santa Fe de Bogotá: Planeta, 1996). For Chile, see Günther Böhm, *Historia de los judíos en Chile*, vol. 1, *Periódo colonial: El bachiller Francisco Maldonado de Silva, 1592–1639* (Santiago: Editorial Andrés Bello, 1984). For Texas, see Richard Santos, *Silent Heritage: The Sephardim and the Colonization of the Spanish North American Frontier* (San Antonio, Tex.: New Sepharad Press, 2000).
2. Richard E. Greenleaf, *The Mexican Inquisition of the Sixteenth Century* (Albuquerque: University of New Mexico Press, 1969), pp. 33–35, 39; Seymour B. Liebman, *The Jews in New Spain: Faith, Flame, and the Inquisition* (Coral Gables, Fla.: University of Miami Press, 1970), pp. 113–115.
3. Autos y diligencias hechas por los sambenitos antiguos y recientes y postura de los que sean de relajados por este Santo Oficio, México, 1574–1632, testimony of Fray Antonio Roldán, México, July 6, 1574, fol. 220v, Ramo de Inquisición, tomo 77, exp. 35, Archivo General de la Nación, Mexico City (hereafter cited as AGN).
4. Greenleaf, *Mexican Inquisition of the Sixteenth Century*, pp. 35–37; Autos y diligencias hechas por los sambenitos antiguos y recientes y postura de los que sean de relajados por este Santo Oficio, fol. 220v, Ramo de Inquisición, tomo 77, exp. 35, AGN.
5. Liebman, *Jews in New Spain*, p. 120.
6. Seymour B. Liebman, *The Inquisitors and the Jews in the New World: Summaries of Procesos, 1500–1810, and Bibliographic Guide* (Coral Gables, Fla.: University of Miami Press, 1974), pp. 37–156.

7. Greenleaf, *Mexican Inquisition of the Sixteenth Century*, p. 81; Liebman, *Jews in New Spain*, pp. 123–130.
8. Stanley Payne, *A History of Spain and Portugal* (Madison: University of Wisconsin Press, 1973), vol. 1, p. 230.
9. Julio Caro Baroja, *La sociedad criptojudía en la corte de Felipe IV* (Madrid: Imprenta y Editorial Maestre, 1963), p. 23.
10. Relación de causa de Sebastián Cardoso, 1642, Ramo de Inquisición, tomo 426, exp. 13, AGN.
11. Data presented here derive from an analysis of trial records from the Mexican Inquisition in the 1640s. See Stanley M. Hordes, "The Crypto-Jewish Community of New Spain, 1620–1649: A Collective Biography" (Ph.D. diss., Tulane University, 1980), p. 41.
12. Caro Baroja, *Sociedad criptojudía*, p. 36.
13. Liebman, *Jews in New Spain*, pp. 135, 151, 184.
14. Ibid., p. 217.
15. Jonathan Israel, *Race, Class and Politics in Colonial Mexico* (Oxford: Oxford University Press, 1975), pp. 20–30.
16. For an excellent contextual examination of mercantile activity among Old Christian traders in seventeenth-century Mexico City, see Louisa Schell Hoberman, *Mexico's Merchant Elite, 1590–1660: Silver, State, and Society* (Durham, N.C.: Duke University Press, 1991). James C. Boyajian offered an outstanding analysis of the interplay among New Christian merchants on the Iberian Peninsula, who supplied the crypto-Jewish merchants with goods for distribution in New Spain (*Portuguese Bankers at the Court of Spain, 1626–1650* [New Brunswick, N.J.: Rutgers University Press, 1983]).
17. Based on the *discursos de la vida* (autobiographical accounts), contained in the Inquisition trials of those arrested in the 1640s, 82 percent of the *converso* immigrants settled initially in Mexico City, 11 percent remained in Veracruz, and the remaining 7 percent scattered throughout the viceroyalty.
18. Approximately 64 percent of the crypto-Jews who settled in Mexico City remained there for five years or longer, while 13 percent left within one year.
19. [Minutes of the *consulado* of Mexico City], August 2, 1635, fols. 4–6, Ramo de Archivo Histórico de Hacienda, tomo 213, exp. 12, AGN. The names of both Simón Váez Sevilla and Sebastián Váez de Acevedo are listed among the members of the *consulado*. Hoberman detailed the structure and function of the *consulado* (*Mexico's Merchant Elite*, pp. 18–21).
20. A large number of debts owed to Váez by various nobles and military officers are revealed in Libro de la razón de la visita de hacienda del Santo Oficio de la Inquisición de la ciudad de México, 1657–1668, Sección de Inquisición, legajo 1737, exp. 20, Archivo Histórico Naciónal, Madrid (hereafter cited as AHN).
21. Proceso y causa criminal contra Simón Váez Sevilla, 1642, fols. 157v–158, 384, Ramo de Inquisición, tomo 398, exp. 1, AGN.
22. Leonor López was the daughter of the prominent Sevilla merchant Francisco Váez Sevilla, brother of Simón Váez Sevilla.

23. Proceso y causa criminal contra Manuel de Acosta, 1643, fols. 55–56, Ramo de Inquisición, tomo 418, exp. 1, AGN. Relations between Acosta and Váez were to sour shortly thereafter, due to a dispute over commercial matters.

24. Proceso y causa criminal contra Pedro Fernández de Castro, 1642, fols. 513–518, Ramo de Inquisición, tomo 409, exp. 4, AGN.

25. Proceso y causa criminal contra Gonzalo Díaz, 1649, fols. 572v–573, Ramo de Inquisición, tomo 431, AGN.

26. Robert C. West, *The Mining Community in Northern New Spain: The Parral Mining District* (Berkeley: University of California Press, 1949); Peter J. Bakewell, *Silver Mining and Society in Colonial Mexico: Zacatecas, 1546–1700* (Cambridge: Cambridge University Press, 1971).

27. Bakewell, *Silver Mining and Society in Colonial Mexico*, pp. 73–76; West, *Mining Community in Northern New Spain*, pp. 77–82.

28. Bakewell, *Silver Mining and Society in Colonial Mexico*, pp. 76–77, citing statistics offered by the seventeenth-century chronicler Alonso de la Mota y Escobar, in *Descripción geográfica de los reinos de Nueva Galicia, Nueva Vizcaya, y Nuevo León* (Guadalajara: Robredo, 1966), p. 67.

29. Bakewell, *Silver Mining and Society in Colonial Mexico*, pp. 77–79; West, *Mining Community in Northern New Spain*, p. 83.

30. Libro primero del juzgado de bienes confiscados, 1661, fols. 266v, 268v, Archivo Histórico, Colección Antigua, tomo 60, Instituto Nacional de Antropología e Historia, Mexico City (hereafter cited as INAH); Libro de la razón de la visita de hacienda del Santo Oficio, fols. 343, 444v, Sección de Inquisición, legajo 1737, exp. 20, AHN; Diferentes autos y papeles tocantes a la visita del tribunal del Santo Oficio de México que sirven para comprovación de los cargos della y de lo demás que se obrado, 1646, fols. 106–107, Sección de Inquisición, legajo 1736, exp. 4, AHN; Escribanía de Juan Oviedo Valdivieso, 1641, fols. 884–889, tomo 469, Archivo General de Notarías, Mexico City (hereafter cited as AGNM).

31. Libro de la razón de la visita de hacienda del Santo Oficio, fols. 417v, 560, 561, 721v, Sección de Inquisición, legajo 1737, exp. 20, AHN; Proceso y causa criminal contra Gonzalo Díaz, fol. 380, Ramo de Inquisición, tomo 431, AGN; Proceso y causa criminal contra Thomás Núñez de Peralta, 1642, Ramo de Inquisición, tomo 395, exp. 5, AGN.

32. Libro primero del juzgado de bienes confiscados, fols. 261v, 265v, tomo 60, INAH; Proceso y causa criminal contra Thomás Núñez de Peralta, Ramo de Inquisición, tomo 395, exp. 5, AGN; Libro de la razón de la visita de hacienda del Santo Oficio, fol. 684v, Sección de Inquisición, legajo 1737, exp. 20, AHN; Escribanía de Juan Oviedo Valdivieso, fols. 687v–689, tomo 469, AGNM.

33. Libro de la razón de la visita de hacienda del Santo Oficio, Sección de Inquisición, legajo 1737, exp. 20, AHN, computed from the *relación de los pleitos* pertaining to Váez. There were possibly more debts outstanding from the mining region, but only debts that specifically cited this origin are included in the figure of 50,000 pesos.

34. Libro de la razón de la visita de hacienda del Santo Oficio, debts owed to Juan

Duarte de Espinosa by Simón Váez Sevilla, fol. 684v, Sección de Inquisición, legajo 1737, exp. 20, AHN; El procurador del Real Fisco contra Jorge Jacinto por quantía de 10 pesos de una arrova de vino perteneciente a Simón Váez, 1644, debts owed to Simón Váez Sevilla by Jorge Jacinto Bazán, fol. 14, Ramo de Inquisición, tomo 392, exp. 13, AGN; Causa criminal contra Antonio Báez, 1623, debts owed to Simón Váez Sevilla by Antonio Váez Casteloblanco, fols. 225v–226, Ramo de Inquisición, tomo 498, exp. 4, AGN.

35. See, for example, Libro de la razón de la visita de hacienda del Santo Oficio, fols. 427v, 430v, 453v, Sección de Inquisición, legajo 1737, exp. 20, AHN.

36. Libro primero del juzgado de bienes confiscados, fols. 270v, 279, tomo 60, INAH; Libro de la razón de la visita de hacienda del Santo Oficio, Sección de Inquisición, legajo 1737, exp. 20, AHN.

37. Liebman, *Inquisitors and the Jews in the New World*, p. 76.

38. Libro primero del juzgado de bienes confiscados, fol. 301, tomo 60, INAH; Libro de la razón de la visita de hacienda del Santo Oficio, fols. 482v–484, Sección de Inquisición, legajo 1737, exp. 20, AHN. For example, Franco purchased cacao for Thomás Méndez and Fernando Gois de Matos, and traded with Pasqual Moreira, Juan Méndez Villaviciosa, and several other crypto-Jews.

39. Libro primero del juzgado de bienes confiscados, fols. 299, 300v–301, 303, 304v, tomo 60, INAH; Libro de la razón de la visita de hacienda del Santo Oficio, fols. 481v, 482v, 486v, Sección de Inquisición, legajo 1737, exp. 20, AHN.

40. Libro de la razón de la visita de hacienda del Santo Oficio, fols. 169–218, 302, Sección de Inquisición, legajo 1737, exp. 20, AHN.

41. Testificaciones de Manuel Rodríguez Núñez contra diversas personas, 1644, fol. 170, Ramo de Inquisición, tomo 414, exp. 2, AGN.

42. Proceso y causa criminal contra Thomás Núñez de Peralta, Ramo de Inquisición, tomo 395, exp. 5, AGN.

43. In *Jews in New Spain*, Liebman devoted a full chapter to Treviño, his personal life, and his role as an important religious leader in the Mexican *converso* community.

44. Cartas misivas y correspondencia comercial, 1624, fol. 338, Ramo de Real Fisco de la Inquisición, tomo 13, exp. 3, AGN. This letter, written in Spanish characters, seems to have been prepared rather hurriedly, as the writer made some obvious mistakes that he might well have easily corrected. Nonetheless, he seems to have known Nahuatl well, as the syntax is native rather than typical of Spanish patterns. In the following transcription, letters in parenthesis were omitted by the writer, while those between the slashes appear unnecessary:

> Tomás Trebiño ma dios mitzpia velsen-
> ca oni(c)ui [error for onicquic] oniuitac moamah quale
> ximoitztica ygu(a)n teg(u)ante quale tion-
> cah nica moaltepeh Sanpablo
> Titolo teguante & [Cipher?] amo guel epa ino
> tigualas ypanpa ayamo tzicoalo

monochistli [error for monochis] ypanpa mieque ipa
te asta tittilancatlatolo moaxca
Ticacisque teguante naguip [contraction for naguipan ypa]
te nochistil [error for monochistla] nica quauhtla
yca ino & titolo teguante
nica nag(u)e semana tigualas
Ticoanas moquenta & Sani-
xqu(i)ch/e/ onitlaquilo nica altepe[tl]
Sanpablo e de setienbre de
1624 años

momasegua momasegual
Lásaro Péres P[o] Lópes

The translation, transcription, and explanation of the letter was provided by Geoffrey Kimball, of Tulane University.

45. This and the succeeding discussions are based on an analysis of trial records from the Mexican Inquisition of the 1640s.

46. Literacy rates among the general population were far lower. France V. Scholes determined that only 15 percent of the men and 10 percent of the women on the far northern frontier could sign their names in the seventeenth century ("Civil Government and Society in New Mexico in the Seventeenth Century," *New Mexico Historical Review* 10 [1935]: 100). For a more extensive discussion of literacy in New Mexico, see Bernardo P. Gallegos, *Literacy, Education, and Society in New Mexico, 1693–1821* (Albuquerque: University of New Mexico Press, 1992).

47. Hoberman's *Mexico's Merchant Elite* represents a notable exception to this paucity of published materials and provides helpful points of comparison relating to the general mercantile community.

48. Figures are derived by adding the value of the person's estate and the debts owed to the estate, minus the debts owed by the estate. To achieve internal consistency, the data have been extracted from one source, the *Memoria* filed by the treasurer (*receptor*) of the Inquisition, Martin Aéta y Aguirre, which reported the amounts confiscated from the *judaizantes*. To this data has been added information relating to Antonio Méndez Chillón, whose estate entered the coffers of the Holy Office after Aéta's report was completed. The *Memoria* is found in Diferentes autos y papeles tocantes a la visita del tribunal del Santo Oficio de México, fols. 343–382, Sección de Inquisición, legajo 1736, exp. 4, AHN.

49. A much larger figure for Váez's estate emerges from an investigation conducted into the financial affairs of the Mexican Inquisition by Pedro de Medina Rico between 1651 and 1669. Hoberman included a table itemizing the assets of seventy-seven merchants active in Mexico City between 1602 and 1660 (*Mexico's Merchant Elite*, pp. 226–228). She categorized the value of their estates as (1) under 1,000 pesos, poor; (2) 1,000 to 9,999 pesos, modest; (3) 10,000 to 24,999 pesos, well-to-do; (4) 25,000 to 49,999 pesos, wealthy; (5) 50,000 to 99,999 pesos, very wealthy; (6) 100,000 to 499,999 pesos, millionaire; and (7) 500,000 to 1 million pesos, billionaire.

50. Hoberman provided useful contextual information regarding the comparative value of houses owned by wealthy Mexico City merchants, describing "[most] *casas principales* [as] ranging from 8,000 pesos to 25,000 pesos in price" (*Mexico's Merchant Elite*, p. 140).

51. Proceso y causa criminal contra Manuel de Acosta, fols. 156–170, Ramo de Inquisición, tomo 418, exp. 1, AGN. Acosta and his newly converted brother-in-law were no strangers to the Law of Moses. Both undoubtedly were descendants of *conversos*. The "conversion" demanded by the families involved adherence to Judaic observances and practices, and thus reflected the strict standards maintained by the Mexican crypto-Jewish community.

52. I make no attempt to undertake a deep analysis of the religious life among Mexican *conversos* in this study. This topic is covered comprehensively in Liebman, *Jews in New Spain*; Martin A. Cohen, *The Martyr: Luis de Carvajal, a Secret Jew in Sixteenth-Century Mexico* (Philadelphia: Jewish Publication Society of America, 1973); and, especially, David M. Gitlitz, *Secrecy and Deceit: The Religion of the Crypto-Jews* (Philadelphia: Jewish Publication Society of America, 1996).

53. Proceso y causa criminal contra Pedro de Espinosa, 1642, fols. 81–85, Ramo de Inquisición, tomo 403, exp. 1, AGN. See also Gitlitz, *Secrecy and Deceit*, pp. 362–366.

54. Gitlitz, *Secrecy and Deceit*, p. 317.

55. Ibid., pp. 317–353.

56. This custom, practiced by crypto-Jews in New Mexico in the seventeenth century, is explained in chap. 5. See also Gitlitz, *Secrecy and Deceit*, pp. 277, 280.

57. Borrador de la relación de las causas que se han despachado desde principio del año del 1634 hasta fin de 1635, Ramo de Inquisición, tomo 381, exp. 5, AGN. The summary of the trial of Simón Montero described the burial of Francisca Núñez. See also Gitlitz, *Secrecy and Deceit*, pp. 277–315.

58. Gitlitz, *Secrecy and Deceit*, p. 204. For a more elaborate discussion of the historical background of the practice of circumcision among Jews and crypto-Jews, see chap. 7.

59. Proceso y causa criminal contra Antonio Caravallo, 1642, fols. 327v–328, Ramo de Inquisición, tomo 409, exp. 2, AGN.

60. Proceso y causa criminal contra Duarte Castaño, 1647, fols. 133–138, Ramo de Inquisición, tomo 497, exp. 8, AGN; Proceso y causa criminal contra Melchor Rodríguez López, 1642, Ramo de Inquisición, tomo 395, exp. 3, AGN; Proceso y causa criminal contra Pedro Fernández de Castro, fol. 521v, Ramo de Inquisición, tomo 409, exp. 4, AGN. See also Gitlitz, *Secrecy and Deceit*, pp. 202–207; and Liebman, *Jews in New Spain*, p. 76.

61. Proceso y causa criminal contra Jorge Duarte, 1648, fol. 116, Ramo de Inquisición, tomo 431, exp. 4, AGN. Gitlitz reported that Xaramillo also performed this ritual on an adult female friend of the family (*Secrecy and Deceit*, p. 206). Liebman indicated his belief that there was no precedent in Judaism for this form of circumcision (*Jews in New Spain*, p. 77).

62. Seymour B. Liebman, "The Great Conspiracy in New Spain," *Americas* 30

(1973): 22, citing José Toribio Medina, *Historia del tribunal de la Inquisición de Lima, 1569–1820* (Santiago: Fondo Histórico y Bibliográfico J. T. Medina, 1956), vol. 2, p. 145. See also Seymour B. Liebman, "The Great Conspiracy in Peru," *Americas* 28 (1971): 176–190; and Harry Cross, "Commerce and Orthodoxy: A Spanish Response to Portuguese Commercial Penetration in the Viceroyalty of Peru, 1580–1640," *Americas* 35 (1978): 151–167.

63. Traslado del papel que remitió a este Santo Oficio el Sr. Obispo Don Juan de Pálafox y Mendoza, visitador general de este Reyno en veinte de noviembre de 1641 que es el original que escribió al ex^mo Sr. Marqués de Villena, Duque de Escalona, Virrey de esta Nueva España segun refiere el dicho Villete, 1641, fols. 84–85, Ramo de Inquisición, tomo 489, AGN.

64. [*Cédula* of Felipe IV], January 7, 1641, fol. 97, Ramo de Inquisición, tomo 489, AGN; Quaderno primero de cédulas reales tocantes a este Santo Oficio, 1555–1776, autos fechos a pedimiento del Sr. Fiscal de Su Magestad de la Real Audiencia sobre que se embarguen partidas pertenecientes a los portugueses del Reyno de Portugal, 1642, Ramo de Inquisición, Lote Riva Palacio, tomo 1, AGN; Ante los oidores de la Contratación . . . en Cádiz y Sevilla para embargar perteneciente a portugueses que venia en los galeones y flotas del aquel año; varios autos y diligencias, 1641–1642, Sección de Contratación, legajo 102B, Archivo General de Indias, Seville. A total of 332,629 pesos' worth of goods sent from New Spain to Portuguese merchants in Sevilla was embargoed in compliance with a royal order of June 17, 1641.

65. Sobre que lo que se debe hacer con los portugueses y demas extranjeros que se encuentran radicados en la Nueva España, February 10, 1642, fols. 528–529, Ramo de Reales Cédulas, tomo 1, exp. 288, AGN; Ordenado al Virrey de la Nueva España, que cumpla las Reales Cédulas expedidas en relación a los portugueses, February 10, 1642, Ramo de Reales Cédulas, tomo 1, exp. 289, AGN.

66. Woodrow Borah, "The Portuguese of Tulancingo and the Special *Donativo* of 1642–1643," *Jahrbuch für Geschichte von Staat, Wirthchaft und Gessellschaft Lateinamerikas* 1 (1964): 386–398; Papeles del Sr. Virrey Conde de Salvatierra acerca del donativo de los portugueses, January 17, 1643, fol. 114, containing a partial accounting of the *donativo* collected from crypto-Jews in New Spain, Ramo de Inquisición, tomo 489, AGN.

67. The synonymity of Jews and Portuguese was to manifest itself again two decades later during the arrests of suspected *judaizantes* in New Mexico, as will be discussed in chap. 5.

68. Francisco Ortuño, en nombre de la Condesa de Peñalva en contra del Real Fisco en juicio sucesorio por los bienes de Simón Váez Sevilla, 1661, containing letter from Simón Váez Sevilla to Simón López de Aguarda, Mexico City, November 21, 1641, Ramo de Real Fisco de la Inquisición, tomo 58, exp. 4, AGN.

69. Ibid., containing letters from Simón Váez Sevilla to Simón López de Aguarda, Mexico City, June 20–21, 1642.

70. Ibid., testimony of Gaspar Váez, 1642. This explanation for Váez's actions apparently was accepted by the inquisitors, who cited the Bragança revolt as a causal factor in the transfer of his goods to another individual.

71. Proceso y causa criminal contra Duarte Castaño, fols. 117, 124v, Ramo de Inquisición, tomo 497, exp. 8, AGN. When Castaño perceived that the situation had calmed down sufficiently, he returned to Caracas. He was later arrested by the Mexican Inquisition in 1647, when he arrived in Veracruz to deliver a cargo of cacao.

72. Proceso y causa criminal contra Luis de Amezquita, 1642, containing letter from Fernando de Mezquita to Luis de Amezquita, Veracruz, August 28, 1641, fols. 5–6, Ramo de Inquisición, tomo 499, exp. 1, AGN.

73. Proceso y causa criminal contra Luis Núñez Pérez, 1642, fols. 465, 467, 479v–480, Ramo de Inquisición, tomo 412, exp. 2, AGN.

74. Relación de las operaciones del Duque de Escalona, Marques de Villena, desde su arribo a Nueva España hasta que fue dispuesto, y copia del manifesto del Conde de Santiesteban, hijo del dicho Sr. Duque, a favor de su padre y la respuesta a este de . . . Don Juan de Pálafox y Mendoza, 1643, MS. 12054, fol. 288, Biblioteca Nacional, Madrid (hereafter cited as BN); Proceso y causa criminal contra Diego Rodríguez, alias Ovandaxo, 1642, fols. 328–338, Ramo de Inquisición, tomo 487, exp. 15, AGN.

75. Relación de las operaciones del Duque de Escalona, MS. 12054, fols. 287v–294, BN.

76. Ibid., fols. 275–284.

77. Cartas originales del Tribunal de México para el Consejo, 1640–1648, containing letter from inquisitors of Mexico to Supreme Council of the Inquisition [1643], fols. 27–28, Sección de Inquisición, legajo 1054, AHN.

78. Relación de las operaciones del Duque de Escalona, MS. 12054, fol. 228v, BN.

79. Francisco de Ortuño, en nombre de la Condesa de Peñalva en contra del Real Fisco, Ramo de Real Fisco de la Inquisición, tomo 58, exp. 4, AGN. In a letter to Simón López de Aguarda written on June 20, 1642, Simón Váez Sevilla referred to the arrest of Las Blancas, "who, it is said, are most indiscrete." Liebman assessed greater responsibility for the mass arrests to the testimony in 1641 of Blanca Méndez de Rivera's relative Gaspar de Robles, who provided the inquisitors with an extensive list of crypto-Jews (*Jews in New Spain*, pp. 225–226). Robert Ferry is preparing a comprehensive historical study of Las Blancas and the role of women in the Mexican crypto-Jewish community in the seventeenth century.

80. Proceso y causa criminal contra Simón Váez Sevilla, testimony of Gaspar Váez and of Isabel Rodríguez, slave of Váez, fols. 74v, 111–113, Ramo de Inquisición, tomo 398, exp. 1, AGN; Proceso y causa criminal contra María de Rivera, 1642, containing letters from María de Rivera to Simón Váez Sevilla and to Juan Méndez de Villaviciosa, n.d., fols. 288–291, Ramo de Inquisición, tomo 403, exp. 3, AGN.

81. Francisco de Ortuño, en nombre de la Condesa de Peñalva en contra del Real Fisco, testimony of Antonia de la Cruz, slave of Thomás Núñez de Peralta and Beatriz Enríquez, brother-in-law and sister-in-law of Váez, Ramo de Real Fisco de la Inquisición, tomo 58, exp. 4, AGN.

82. Proceso y causa criminal contra Simón Váez Sevilla, testimony of Gaspar

Váez, fol. 65, Ramo de Inquisición, tomo 398, exp. 1, AGN; Proceso y causa criminal contra el Bachiller Pedro Tinoco, 1642, fol. 435, Ramo de Inquisición, tomo 396, exp. 2, AGN; Declaraciones hechas ante el comisario del Santo Oficio en la ciudad de Los Angeles, por los bienes secuestrados a Juan Méndez de Villaviciosa, Diego Méndez de Silva, Francisco López, y Simón Baez, 1642, testimony of Padre Fr. Joan de Velasco, fol. 238, Ramo de Real Fisco de la Inquisición, tomo 15, exp. 12, AGN.

83. Resumen de los cargos que resultan asi comunes como particulares de la visita de la Inquisición de México, 1658, Sección de Inquisición, legajo 1737, exp. 11, AHN; Diferentes documentos para prueba de la visita que esta a cargo del Sr. Inquisidor Dr. Don Pedro de Medina Rico, 1656, fols. 382–383, Sección de Inquisición, legajo 1738, exp. 1, AHN; Francisco de Ortuño, en nombre de la Condesa de Peñalva en contra del Real Fisco, Ramo de Real Fisco de la Inquisición, tomo 58, exp. 4, AGN.

84. Libro donde se sientan todos los presos que han entrado en esta cárcel de las casas de Picazo desde trece de julio de 1642 siendo alcaide Pedro Ximénes de Zervera, 1647, Ramo de Inquisición, Lote Riva Palacio, tomo 48, exp. 2, AGN. Data are also extracted from the trial records of *judaizantes* in the Archivo General de la Nación.

85. For a detailed account of the established inquisitorial procedure, see Nicolau Eimeric, *Manual de inquisidores, para uso de las inquisiciones de España y Portugal, o compendio de la obra titulada Directorio de inquisidores* (Mompelier, 1821).

86. Liebman, *Jews in New Spain*, app. A, "Digests and Translations of Official Accounts of Autos-da-fé," pp. 305–333; *Jews and the Inquisition of Mexico: The Great Auto de Fe of 1649 as Related by Mathías de Bocanegra*, ed. and trans. Seymour B. Liebman (Lawrence, Kans.: Coronado Press, 1974). Both works offer elaborate accounts of the ceremonies that surround the autos de fe. No attempt is made in this study to duplicate these accounts.

87. Quaderno primero de cédulas reales tocantes a este Santo Oficio, *cédulas* of October 23, 1647, Ramo de Inquisición, Lote Riva Palacio, tomo 1, AGN; Al Virrey, sobre que remita a España a los reos judaizantes condenados por aquel Tribunal, August 31, 1648, Ramo de Reales Cédulas, tomo 3, exp. 45, AGN; Al Virrey, ordenandole nuevamente que se envien a España los reos condenados por el Tribunal del Santo Oficio, December 11, 1649, Ramo de Reales Cédulas, tomo 3, exp. 88, AGN; Remisión a España de los reos penitenciados por esta Inquisición entregandolos al General de Flota quien dió recivo de ellos, 1650, Ramo de Inquisición, tomo 454, exp. 29, AGN.

88. Sobre remisión de judaizantes a España, 1651, fol. 127, Ramo de Inquisición, tomo 489, AGN.

89. [Report of the *alcalde de las cárceles de penitencia*], 1649, fol. 278, Ramo de Inquisición, tomo 503, exp. 36, AGN; Diligencias fechas contra algunos reconciliados . . . , 1649, fols. 64–77, Ramo de Inquisición, tomo 432, AGN; México—Libro nono de cartas de la Inquisición de la Nueva España, al consejo de Inquisición desde el año de [1649] hasta el de [1653], libro 1055, fol. 31, Sección de Inquisición, AHN.

90. Proceso y causa criminal contra Simón Váez Sevilla, fols. 349–351, 360–386, Ramo de Inquisición, tomo 398, exp. 1, AGN; Francisco de Ortuño,

en nombre de la Condesa de Peñalva en contra del Real Fisco, Ramo de Real Fisco de la Inquisición, tomo 58, exp. 4, AGN.

91. Cabeza de proceso contra Jorge Jacinto Bazán y Miguel Tinoco, penitenciados por el Santo Tribunal, 1649, fols. 522–602, Ramo de Inquisición, tomo 503, exp. 76, AGN.

92. Ynforme del hecho en el [deteriorated] los condes de Peñalba, 1661, testimony of Francisco Martínez de Lugo, Ramo de Real Fisco de la Inquisición, tomo 58, exp. 5, AGN; Diferentes documentos para prueba de la visita que esta a cargo del Sr. Inquisidor Dr. Don Pedro de Medina Rico, declaration of Simón Váez Sevilla, Madrid, January 10, 1655, fol. 382r, Sección de Inquisición, legajo 1738, exp. 1, AHN.

93. Based on a list in Remisión a España de los reos penitenciados por esta Inquisición, Ramo de Inquisición, tomo 454, exp. 29, AGN; and the testimony offered by Váez regarding the whereabouts of other *conversos*, in Francisco de Ortuño en nombre de la Condesa de Peñalva en contra del Real Fisco, Ramo de Real Fisco de la Inquisición, tomo 58, exp. 4, AGN.

94. Proceso y causa criminal contra Luis Pérez Roldán, 1642, fols. 264–326, Ramo de Inquisición, tomo 487, exp. 14, AGN.

95. Ibid., fol. 326. See also Inventario y sequestro de bienes de Luis Pérez Roldán, vecino de esta ciudad de México, 1657, fol. 132, Ramo de Inquisición, tomo 572, exp. 10, AGN. The inventory of Pérez's estate included swords, knives, and shields.

96. Alonso Hernández, maestro de sastre, contra el capitán Melchor Rodríguez López por 127 pesos por que el executó, 1649, legajo 32, Archivo Judicial del Distrito y Territorios Federales, Mexico City.

CHAPTER 3

The Origins of the First Crypto-Jewish Settlement in New Mexico: Luis de Carvajal and the Failed Colony of Gaspar Castaño de Sosa, 1579–1591

Mexican crypto-Jews were able to practice their secret faith in an atmosphere of relative toleration, with the exception of the late sixteenth and mid-seventeenth centuries. During these two periods, due to a series of complex factors, the Holy Office of the Inquisition embarked on vigorous campaigns against the *conversos*. The first of these, which lasted from 1589 to 1601, was initiated in response to the activities of Luis de Carvajal, el Mozo (the Younger), a Portuguese New Christian and nephew of Luis de Carvajal y de la Cueva, the governor of Nuevo León.[1] The persecutions that characterized this era were to have significant ramifications for the settlement of crypto-Jews on the far northern frontier of New Mexico in the succeeding decades.

GOVERNOR LUIS DE CARVAJAL AND THE *CONVERSO* SETTLEMENT OF NUEVO LEÓN

The assumption by Felipe II of Spain of the throne of Portugal in 1581, and the consequent reinvigoration of the Portuguese Inquisition, stimulated a mass migration of Portuguese crypto-Jews to Spain, as well as to Spanish holdings in the New World. The experiences of the Carvajales and their coreligionists in New Spain, in a certain sense, may be seen as a manifestation of this demographic pattern, as many of those arrested for observing the Law of Moses could trace their origins to crypto-Jewish communities in Portugal. But the Mexican career of Luis de Carvajal y de la Cueva long preceded the flood of Portuguese *converso* refugees into the Viceroyalty of New Spain.

Carvajal was born around 1539 in the small northeastern Portuguese town of Mogadouro, nestled in the mountains along the frontier with Spain, the son of Catalina de León and Gaspar de Carvajal. Gaspar had moved to Mogadouro, presumably from the town of Sayago, near Zamora in León, Spain, the home of his parents, Francisca de Carvajal and Gutierre Vasquez de la Cueva. In Mogadouro, Gaspar married Catalina, the daughter of Antonio de León and Francisca Nuñez. Raised in Mogadouro, Luis de Carvajal spent his youth traveling with his father to various places in Spain and Portugal. At age ten, Luis accompanied his uncle to Lisboa, and thence to the Cape Verde Islands, where he stayed for thirteen years, holding the posts of treasurer and royal accountant in the service of the king of Portugal. Around 1562, he returned to Lisboa, and from there traveled to Sevilla, where he married Guiomar de Rivera, the daughter of a Portuguese slave trader.[2] After a failed mercantile venture, Carvajal sailed for New Spain around 1567, carrying a cargo of wine to sell in Veracruz, Mexico City, and Zacatecas.[3]

During the first years of his tenure in the Indies, Carvajal earned a reputation as a bit of a gadfly. Within a year of his arrival, he had secured the post of *alcalde ordinario* (magistrate) of the port town of Tampico, located on the Gulf of Mexico, about three hundred miles north of Veracruz.[4] By 1569, Carvajal owned an *estancia* in the northern frontier province of Pánuco, near the town of Guaxutla. At the same time, he maintained a residence in Mexico City, on Calle Santo Domingo, in the heart of the neighborhood inhabited by crypto-Jews some decades later.[5]

In the mid-1570s, Carvajal was documented as holding various civil and military offices in Pánuco. In addition, he participated in mining enterprises and engaged in selling enslaved Indians to other miners in Mazapíl. It was here in the mid-1570s that he met, and formed a close association with, a cadre of Portuguese military leaders, some of whom were suspected of practicing Judaism. These officers would serve under him in the decade to come, men such as Alberto del Canto, Manuel de Mederos, Diego de Montemayor, and Gaspar Castaño de Sosa. It was also here that he realized the tremendous opportunities even farther out on the northeastern frontier and formulated his strategy for the conquest of Nuevo León.[6]

Southern France, Spain, Portugal, and North Africa.

In 1578, Carvajal sailed back to Spain to seek authorization from the king to undertake his ambitious enterprise, carrying a letter to Felipe II from Fray Pedro de San Luis, *comisario* of the Franciscans in Pánuco, that attested to his status as a good Christian and a loyal servant of royal interests in New Spain.[7] Carvajal took advantage of the opportunity to visit with relatives in Sevilla and Mogadouro, and then headed for Madrid, hoping to secure an audience with Felipe. It took him ten months of lobbying at court before his opportunity finally arrived, but, judging by the results, Carvajal must have felt that the final result was certainly worth the wait. The formal *capitulaciones* agreed to by both Carvajal and the king on May 31, 1579, were very much to Carvajal's advantage. He received authorization to conquer and administer an extensive piece of territory on the northeastern frontier of New Spain, reaching "from the Río Pánuco and port of Tampico, to the mines of Mazapíl and surrounding area, to the limits of the pacified lands, and to Nueva Galicia and the jurisdiction of Nueva Vizcaya."[8] Under the terms of the agreement, Carvajal was required "to bring to that province up to one hundred men, sixty of whom shall be married farmers, together with their wives and children. The remainder shall consist of soldiers and artisans for the aforesaid population."[9] Carvajal was appointed governor and captain-general "of the New Kingdom of León for all the days of [his] life and, afterward, for those of [his] son or heir."[10]

Two weeks after the proclamation of these *capitulaciones*, Felipe issued a decree in Toledo, presumably at Carvajal's request, that was to have a profound impact on the ethnic composition of the new colony and, ultimately, on the religious fabric of the Viceroyalty of New Spain:

> The King. [To] Our Officials residing in the city of Sevilla in the House of Trade of the Indies. I order you to allow Captain Luis de Carvajal de la Cueba to return to New Spain, and that you allow him to bring with him one hundred men, sixty of whom shall be married farmers, together with their wives and children, and the remainder soldiers and artisans for the discovery and pacification of the provinces that shall be called the New Kingdom of León, the same lands that I have ordered taken by means of the contract and agreement, *without asking any of them for any information whatsoever. And for the present, we entrust the aforesaid Captain Luis de Carvajal to exercise much care that they be persons clean, and not of the [category of people] prohibited from crossing to those parts*, and principally not to take any married man who leaves his wife in these kingdoms [emphasis added].[11]

Thus it is clear that Felipe ordered his officials not to conduct any investigations into the ethnic background of the colonists to be recruited by Carvajal to populate the new settlement of Nuevo León.[12] Almost a century earlier, King Fernando and his successor, Carlos V, had imposed restrictions on the immigration of New Christians to the Indies.[13] To be sure, many *conversos* and their offspring settled there legally, but did so under assumed names or doctored *limpiezas de sangre.* By waiving the requirement to produce proof of Old Christian background, the king now provided the opportunity for dozens of crypto-Jewish refugees to emigrate to New Spain.

With his mandate from Felipe II clearly articulated, Carvajal immediately began to recruit more than one hundred people from Spain and Portugal, the majority of them New Christians.[14] In January 1580, Carvajal's party departed from Sevilla on the ship *Santa Catarina.*[15] While the other vessels in the fleet sailed directly to Veracruz, the *Santa Catarina* broke away from the convoy and landed instead at the port of Tampico, possibly to avoid inspection by royal immigration officials, at the end of September. Upon their arrival, some of the passengers remained in the service of Governor Carvajal, while others dispersed to more distant parts of the viceroyalty.[16]

The new arrivals were joined by other Spanish and Portuguese from Pánuco, Saltillo, and the Huasteca, eager to take advantage of the opportunities presented by the opening of Nuevo León for European settlement. Some had served with Carvajal in the 1560s and 1570s, while others were new to the frontier. One historian speculated that of the 259 colonists who comprised the original Nuevo León settlement, at least 177, or over 68 percent, were New Christians.[17]

Carvajal's enterprise was plagued with problems from the outset. In the first place, much of the territory that he had been assigned overlapped with lands in Nueva Vizcaya and Nueva Galicia, already occupied and administered by other officials. The consequent jurisdictional disputes that arose among these officials resulted in the creation of powerful enemies for Carvajal in the capital. More important, despite the modest success of some mining endeavors, the new colony was overly dependent for its economic base on the raiding of Indian villages and the enslaving of their people.

Beginning in 1586, the royal authorities in Mexico City began cracking down on the governor's slaving activities. Since the early years of Spanish conquest and colonization of the Indies at the end of the fifteenth century, the question of enslavement of Native Americans had divided the Spanish authorities, religious and civil alike. One school of thought held that, as subject people, Indians could and should provide forced labor for their European masters. But others believed that the indigenous peoples of the Americas, in contrast to the enslaved black people imported from Africa, were human beings, with souls to save, and thus deserved protection from such obligations. Theologians such as Fray Bartolomé de las Casas led a campaign in the early years of the sixteenth century to mitigate the abuses of the colonial system and successfully lobbied royal officials to pass a series of laws designed to protect Indians from arbitrary enslavement. Institutional means were developed to exact labor and tribute from subjugated peoples, with elaborate theoretical safeguards to limit the nature and extent of the servitude. Outright slavery of the indigenous peoples was eventually prohibited, except in cases of military resistance to Spanish authority. In practice, of course, such legalistic distinctions were often blurred. Military and civil officials interpreted these laws to fit their own exigencies, resulting in contentious differences among bureaucrats with regard to what constituted violation of the protective laws.[18]

Concomitant with this struggle was the effort to break down the power of ambitious and independent-minded conquistadores, who, in the minds of royal authorities in Spain and Mexico City, were intent on establishing their own fiefdoms on the frontier. In what may, perhaps, appear to represent a cynical policy, the Crown empowered these enterprising individuals to conquer and settle a given area, often at their own expense, and then, once the area was pacified, attempted to reign them in by selectively accusing them of violations of humanitarian laws that the royal officials had conveniently ignored during the initial phase of the conquest.[19]

It is within this context that the relationship between Governor Luis de Carvajal and his superiors in Mexico City must be examined. Carvajal's tenure happened to coincide with the administration of Viceroy Álvaro Manrique de Zúniga, marqués de Villamanrique, a strong advocate of centralization. As Richard E. Greenleaf described:

> The Marqués de Villamanrique was a stern viceroy of New Spain, a man determined to enforce the spirit as well as the letter of the law. Earlier viceroys had compromised in narrowing the gap between theory and practice in colonial administration, but Villamanrique delved into political and financial matters with a tenacity that often antagonized vested interests. Perhaps, with his penchant to reorganize administrative processes and to consolidate royal power, Villamanrique was stubborn and inflexible. His enemies in Guadalajara called him intemperate. But he always seemed to uphold the king's prerogatives and the public

interest with an impartial mind when he enunciated policies and saw to their enforcement.[20]

Once Carvajal had completed the subjugation of the Indians of Nuevo León, Villamanrique began to question the activities of the governor as they pertained to his treatment of the native peoples. The first accusation arose in 1587, when he was charged with having enslaved some five hundred Indians who had rebelled against his authority, but had subsequently surrendered and asked to be baptized.[21] By January 1589, Carvajal found himself under arrest by order of Villamanrique, accused of flagrantly violating the viceroy's express orders.[22]

But for all the legal difficulties suffered by Governor Carvajal in the late 1580s, it was the Judaizing activities of his relatives, especially his nephew Luis de Carvajal, el Mozo, that resulted in his ultimate demise. The policy of the Spanish colonial authorities in New Spain tended to be one more of toleration than persecution, relative to the more harsh practices pursued by the Holy Office of the Inquisition in Spain. For the first few years of the Inquisition's existence, it appears that the crypto-Jewish settlers of Nuevo León and Mexico City were left alone to worship as they pleased, as long as they did so quietly. This atmosphere of calm was soon to be shattered, however, when the governor's nephew betrayed the standard of discretion.

LUIS DE CARVAJAL, EL MOZO, AND THE INQUISITORIAL PERSECUTIONS OF THE 1580S AND 1590S

Born in Benavente, Spain, just across the Portuguese border from Mogadouro, young Luis de Carvajal sailed to Nuevo León on the *Santa Catarina* as a boy of fifteen, in the company of his parents, Francisco Rodríguez de Matos and Francisca Nuñez de Carvajal, sister of the governor.[23] As a young man, he participated fully in the establishment of the new colony and was considered as the heir to the governorship. Between 1584 and his arrest for Judaizing in 1589, Luis, el Mozo, traveled extensively around the viceroyalty, making several trips between Nuevo León and Mexico City, engaging in trade in the mining towns of Taxco and Zacatecas, and eventually settling in the capital.

Shortly after his arrival in New Spain, Luis, el Mozo, had been told of his Jewish roots by older relatives. In contrast to the response of his contemporaries, young Luis decided that if he was a Jew, he was going to live openly as a Jew. Not only did he begin to practice his religion in full view, but he initiated efforts to reconnect other New Christians with Judaism. Even in the atmosphere of relative toleration demonstrated by New Spanish society, this behavior could not be endured. The Holy Office of the Inquisition in Mexico City, recently elevated to the status of tribunal, had been watching the growth of the Portuguese *converso* community in New Spain over the previous few years and had expressed concern about the potential for the spread of the practice of *la ley muerta de Moisés*, or "the Dead Law of Moses." In 1587, the Mexican inquisitors complained to their superiors in Madrid: "In this land there are large numbers of Portuguese, growing day by day, almost all merchants, a frugal people, and very industrious, most of whom are confessed Judaizers. And as we understand that the inquisitors in Spain have arrested and punished some of those [Portuguese] who have traveled to Castilla as a result of the joining of the kingdoms, it is possible that they have also crossed to the Indies."[24]

The reaction of the inquisitors in Mexico was strong and swift. Between 1589 and 1596, almost two hundred persons were arrested for the crime of *judaizante*, focusing on the Carvajal family and extending to crypto-Jews all over the viceroyalty. Luis, el Mozo, was arrested in 1589 and reconciled in the auto de fe of 1590. Undeterred by this castigation, and encouraged by a temporary amnesty issued by the Supreme Council of the Inquisition in Madrid, young Carvajal resumed his proselytizing efforts immediately after his release from jail. The pardon notwithstanding, the Holy Office in Mexico City rearrested Luis, convicting him for relapsing into Judaism. He was burned at the stake in the auto de fe of 1596, along with several members of his family.[25]

Among the extended family of the Carvajales to be caught in the web of *judaizantes* in the 1590s was Simón de Paiba, a relative of Melchor de Paiba, who was among the early explorers in New Mexico. Born in Portugal around 1545, Simón emigrated to Mexico, eventually settling in the mining town of Pachuca. He married Beatríz Enríquez, who was known as "La Paiba," also Portuguese, and they had three children: Pedro, Diego, and Catalina. Catalina married Manuel de Lucena, whose home, according to Martin A. Cohen, "had become a mecca for Judaizers" and was frequented by Luis, el Mozo, and his brother Baltasar Rodríguez. Lucena's devotion to Judaism was shared by Paiba's children and was "surpassed by his mother-in-law, Beatríz Enríquez de Payba."[26] Diego, born in Sevilla around 1564, had served as a soldier in Guatemala and, at the time of his arrest by the Holy Office in 1589, was engaged in trading in Mexico

City. At his trial, he testified that his priest had told him, "All of his race and generation were Jews, and descendants of the Tribe of Benjamin."[27]

Paiba's wife, Beatríz, and his children Catalina and Pedro appeared as *reconciliados* in the auto de fe of 1596. Diego was reconciled in the auto of 1589, rearrested in 1595, convicted of relapsing, and relaxed and burned at the stake, along with Luis, el Mozo, and other members of the family. Simón died shortly thereafter. He was convicted posthumously of having practiced Judaism, and his remains were disinterred and burned in the auto de fe of 1601.[28]

Diego Díaz Nieto (Neto in Portuguese) and his clan was another *converso* family caught up in the persecutions of the Carvajales who had probable links to an early New Mexican explorer, Juan Rodríguez Nieto. Díaz Nieto's paternal grandparents—Manuel Díaz, alias Ruy Gómez Nieto, and Francisca Rodríguez, alias Cecilia Rodríguez Cardoso—fled from Oporto when the situation for crypto-Jews deteriorated in Portugal after 1535. They first sought refuge in the Low Countries and then relocated to Italy, eventually settling in Ferrara, which was considered to be a safe haven for Spanish and Portuguese crypto-Jews. The family, for a time, abandoned the veneer of Catholicism, lived openly in Ferrara as Jews, and took Jewish first names. Manuel Díaz and Francisca Rodríguez became Yitzhak and Rivkah (Isaac and Rebecca) Nieto. Ruy Díaz (father of Diego Díaz Nieto) took the name Yaacov (Jacob), and his sister, Beatríz, became Esther.

When the New Christians were expelled from Ferrara in 1551, Ruy/Yaacov Díaz returned to Portugal and was forced to live underground again. But four years later, he returned to Ferrara and married a cousin, Ines Nuñez, alias Esther Nieto, the daughter of Marcos Díaz, alias Salomon Israel. In 1573, their union produced Diego, who, while living as a Jew in Ferrara, was known as Yitzhak. Diego/Yitzhak Díaz Nieto received a formal Jewish education in Italy and married a cousin, Rivkah, who was brought over from Portugal. An economic downturn forced the family to seek their fortune in Venice, but they ultimately returned to the Iberian Peninsula, where they again had to profess Catholicism, living secretly as Jews. In Madrid, Díaz Nieto and his family were welcomed into the crypto-Jewish community and met Jorge de Almeyda, the brother-in-law of Luis, el Mozo. It was Almeyda who was instrumental in convincing the Díaz Nietos to emigrate to New Spain, enlisting them to carry the reprieve (short-lived, as it turned out) issued by the Supreme Council of the Inquisition in favor of his brother-in-law and two other family members.

The family arrived in Veracruz in the spring of 1594, having exhausted their savings on the cost of the necessary immigration papers and passage. They observed Passover in Puebla before continuing their journey to Mexico City. In the capital, they met with Luis, el Mozo, who was pleased not only with the valuable papers that they had brought, but also with the sophisticated level of knowledge of Judaism that they had acquired in Italy. Not only was Diego Díaz Nieto fluent in Hebrew, but he could recite almost the entire Torah by heart, and the Psalms and Prophets as well. But the fertile religious life enjoyed by the Díaz Nietos and their cohorts in Mexico City was not to last long. Diego and his family were arrested by the Holy Office and emerged reconciled in the autos de fe of 1596 and 1601.[29]

The campaign of the Holy Office in Mexico City against the crypto-Jews of Nuevo León in the late 1580s and 1590s was to have a direct impact on the exploration and settlement of New Mexico at the end of the sixteenth century. During the previous decade, Governor Luis de Carvajal had surrounded himself with a coterie of talented military leaders who played a prominent role in advancing the northern limits of the Viceroyalty of New Spain. In certain of these endeavors, it appears that crypto-Jews from Spain and Portugal served as full participants. The arrest of the governor by Mexican inquisitors in 1590 stimulated one of these captains, Carvajal's second-in-command, Gaspar Castaño de Sosa, to embark on a hastily organized, illegal, and ill-fated expedition northward to establish a colony in the far northern frontier of New Mexico.

THE FAR NORTHERN FRONTIER OF NEW SPAIN AS REFUGE

The frontier had long served as a destination for crypto-Jews fleeing from the Holy Office. In the late fifteenth century, *conversos* seeking to avoid persecution in Spain and Portugal initially had fled to the rugged mountainous regions separating the two countries. When the opportunity arose, others sought shelter in the remote Canary Islands and, still later, in the distant colonies of the Americas. With the establishment of the Inquisition in Mexico in 1571, crypto-Jews were compelled to look for a safe haven elsewhere.

Before, during, and after the two aberrant periods of inquisitorial persecution against the crypto-Jews in New Spain, it appears that the far northern frontier served as a refuge for *conversos* attempting to avoid arrest by the Holy Office. In her groundbreaking book, Solange Alberro emphasized the role of the frontier as sanctuary in her analysis of seventeenth-century Zacatecas.[30] The second most important

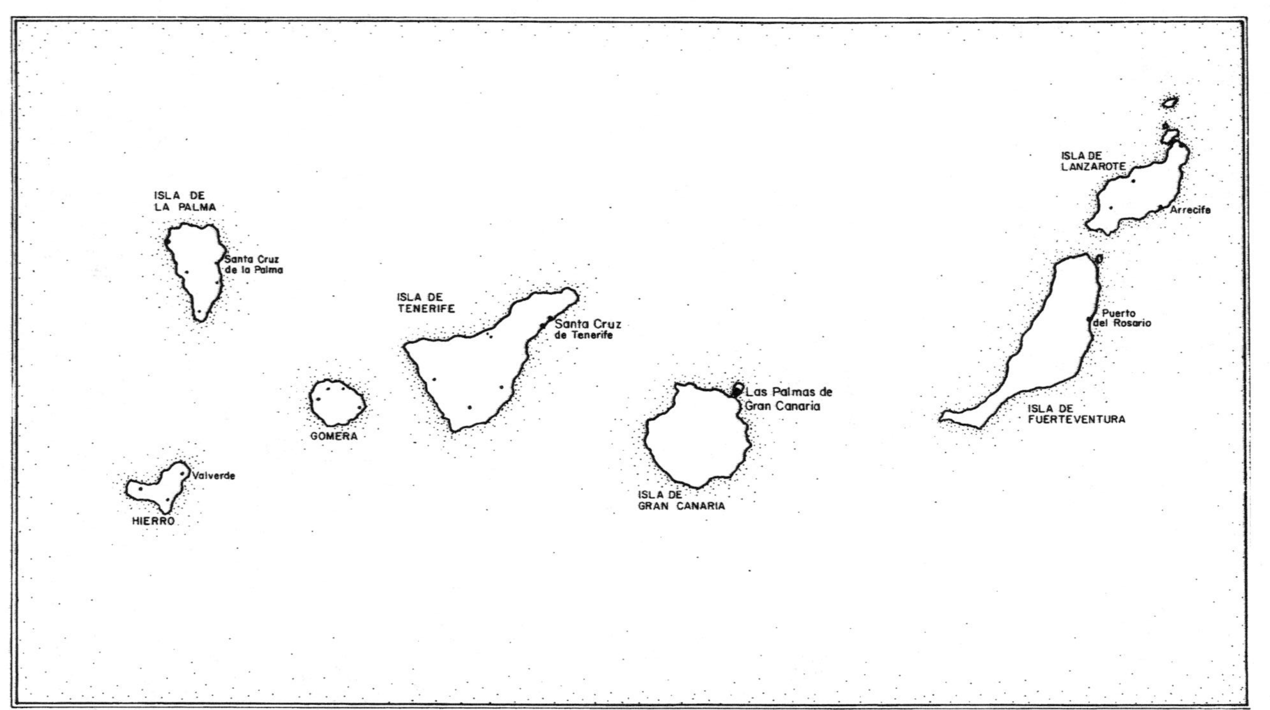

Canary Islands.

city in the Viceroyalty of New Spain, Zacatecas served as an important mining center and mercantile distribution point for the region.[31]

Alberro argued that the great distance of Zacatecas from the center of authority in Mexico City, and its geographic isolation from other major communities, "facilitated laxity and backsliding, practically ensuring exemption from punishment" by the Holy Office.[32] The permissive atmosphere of this northern mining community fostered an environment where heretical acts lost their character as social transgressions, and, as a consequence, behavior that would not have been tolerated in the capital passed virtually unnoticed in Tierra Adentro. The frontier offered two major advantages for crypto-Jews seeking anonymity: remoteness from Inquisition officials and an ample market for the goods and services provided by *converso* merchants. Alberro observed that although several members of this community were denounced before the Mexican tribunal, only a minority of these cases were ever prosecuted.[33] Despite the formal prohibition of Judaizing activity in New Spain, the practice of the Law of Moses in Zacatecas was, according to Alberro, "conscious, coherent, and deliberate," thus indicating that the northern mining region functioned effectively as an area of safety.[34]

"If Zacatecas constitutes a zone of refuge in comparison with the central region of the viceroyalty," according to Alberro, "New Mexico is, as [France V.] Scholes states, 'a heaven for social outcasts from the mining camps of Zacatecas, Santa Bárbara and Parral.' . . . That is to say, the zone of refuge from the zone of refuge."[35] Indeed, it appears that New Mexico, like Zacatecas and Nuevo León before the persecutions of members of the Carvajal family, also served as a focus of settlement for a number of crypto-Jews seeking to escape arrest by the Mexican tribunal of the Holy Office of the Inquisition.

The origins of European exploration of New Mexico date back to 1540, when Francisco Vázquez de Coronado led an expedition of more than one thousand men and women north and west from Mexico City into what is today the American Southwest.[36] The Spanish explorers, in search of the mythical, wealthy "Seven Cities of Cíbola," found little in the way of precious metals. But, perhaps more important, they encountered groups of sedentary Indians, whom they labeled "Pueblos" because the populations were concentrated in towns. A combination of severe winters, the failure to discover the treasures of "Cíbola," and a debilitating injury to Vázquez compelled the Spanish to return home to Mexico, thus leaving the colonization of New Mexico for another, more permanent enterprise five decades later.[37]

The intervening years witnessed a succession of small-scale forays into New Mexico, most of which involved the participation of subordinates of Governor Luis de Carvajal of Nuevo León. The first of these endeavors was initiated by a Franciscan friar, Agustín Rodríguez, who had heard of groups of settled Indians in the far north who had not yet been exposed to Christian missionary efforts. Accompanied by two other friars and a military escort of eight soldiers, commanded by Captain Francisco Sánchez Chamuscado, the party departed from Santa Bárbara in June 1581, reaching the first of the pueblos of New Mexico within two months. Finding a fertile field for his conversion efforts, Fray Agustín, together with one of his colleagues, remained at the pueblo of Puaray, in the Middle Río Grande Valley, just north of present-day Albuquerque, while Sánchez Chamuscado and his troops headed home.[38]

Reflecting a mixture of euphoria over the encounter with "civilized" Indians, ripe for proselytizing in what the explorers named "San Felipe del Nuevo México," and concern about the safety of the two friars, Spanish colonial authorities realized the efficacy of mounting another expedition to the north. The man chosen to lead this rescue operation was Antonio de Espejo, *familiar* (agent) of the Holy Office of the Inquisition, a successful cattle rancher, convicted murder conspirator, and comrade-in-arms of Governor Carvajal. Historians differ over who appointed Espejo to lead the new expedition northward. According to biographers George P. Hammond and Agapito Rey, Espejo owed his authority to Captain Juan Ontiveros, *alcalde mayor* (mayor) of the small frontier community of Cuatro Cienegas. Diego Pérez de Lujan, the chronicler of the expedition, wrote that the orders had come not from Ontiveros, but from Juan de Ibarra, the lieutenant governor of Nueva Vizcaya.[39] However, documents in the Archivo General de Indias tell another story. During the course of an investigation, undertaken in 1587, into the conduct of Carvajal, the governor himself claimed to have commissioned Espejo to embark on his mission northward, an allegation supported by seven witnesses.[40]

Espejo departed from the mining town of San Bartolomé in November 1582, with eighteen soldiers and two Franciscan priests. When he arrived at Puaray the following February, he discovered that both friars had been killed. Undeterred, Espejo and his party visited the territory occupied by the Río Grande pueblos and then headed west, reaching as far as Zuni and the Hopi country in present-day Arizona. Although Espejo had experienced some violent encounters with the Pueblo people, which resulted in the death of dozens of Indians, the report that he brought back to Mexico was essentially a positive one, promoting the mineral wealth of the newly discovered lands, the potential for renewed missionary efforts, and the opportunities for Spanish settlers to establish a farming and ranching colony on the far northern frontier.[41]

News of the uncovering of "another new world," in the words of the archbishop of Mexico, spread quickly. By April 1583, Felipe II had issued a decree ordering the viceroy of New Spain to engage the most competent person he could find to organize and lead an enterprise to establish a permanent colony in New Mexico. The next decade witnessed a fierce competition among prominent military men in New Spain for the privilege of heading the new expedition. But this struggle was to be interrupted by the illegal exploits of one of the aspirants, Gaspar Castaño de Sosa, whose destiny it was to link the history of the crypto-Jews of New Spain with that of the European settlement of New Mexico.

GASPAR CASTAÑO DE SOSA AND THE FIRST *CONVERSO* FORAY INTO NEW MEXICO

Little is known about the background of Gaspar Castaño de Sosa. Details about his age and place of birth are, unfortunately, lost to history. Seventeenth-century chronicler Alonso de León, writing about a half-century after Castaño's death, characterized him as "a man of great heart and spirit . . . courageous, accommodating and liberal with all, which explains why the men under his command were so loyal."[42] Castaño first appeared in the records in the late 1570s, accompanying Alberto del Canto in the founding of Saltillo and then serving as its first *alcalde mayor*. By 1583, he found himself in the service of Governor Luis de Carvajal, who named him as *alcalde mayor* of San Luis Potosí, and granted him lands for a ranch, which he named San Francisco (today, Apodaca, Nuevo León). Castaño participated in the conquest and settlement of the mines of Almadén (today, Monclova, Coahuila), León, Coahuila, and San Luis Potosí, rising in the ranks to assume the position of lieutenant governor of Nuevo León.[43]

León identified Castaño as "Portuguese,"[44] a term that contemporaneously was synonymous with "Jew."[45] Indeed, many Castaños and Sosas could be found among *judaizantes* penanced by the tribunals of the Inquisition in Spain, Portugal, and Mexico in the sixteenth and seventeenth centuries.[46] In his book on the history of the persecutions of the Carvajales, Martin Cohen determined that Castaño was related to one of the Judaizers of Nuevo León, Manuel de Herrera. Similarly, Richard Santos, writing about the *conversos* in South Texas, referred to Castaño as a "suspected Crypto-Jew."[47] Eugenio del Hoyo pointed to Castaño's Portuguese origins and his possible identity as a *judaizante*. He quoted from the testimony of Luis de Carvajal, el Mozo, in his trial for heresy: "Item: I know that Manuel de Herrera, Portuguese, and relative of Captain Castaño, is a Jew and observes and believes in the said Law [of Moses]." Hoyo also established a familial relationship between Castaño and the crypto-Jew Simón de Paiba of Pachuca.[48] Considering the large percentage of New Christians in Nuevo León in the late 1580s (over 68 percent, according to Hoyo),[49] the high level of *judaizante* activity uncovered by the Mexican Inquisition in the province during this period, and the close relationship between Castaño and Carvajal, there is a substantial likelihood that Castaño was of *converso* background or even a practicing crypto-Jew. Castaño's behavior during the years from 1590 to 1592 lends credence to this hypothesis.

Carvajal's difficulties with both the civil and inquisitorial authorities had finally come to a head, with his arrest by the viceroy in January 1589;[50] his transfer to the Inquisition jail three months later, on April 14, 1589;[51] and his appearance in the auto de fe of February 24, 1590.[52] Upon his initial capture by the civil authorities, Carvajal appointed his lieutenant governor, Gaspar Castaño de Sosa, to govern Nuevo León in his stead.[53] Shortly after receiving news of his superior's public disgrace, Castaño began plans to abandon the colony. By July 27, 1590, just five months after Carvajal was penanced by the Holy Office, Castaño had abandoned the town of Almadén, depopulating the colony of its European population, and headed northward into uncharted territory, toward the ultimate destination of New Mexico.

In view of the challenges facing Castaño in the summer of 1590, why did he opt to embark on his dangerous trek northward? To be sure, the material difficulties in the settlement may have served as a motivator for the inhabitants of Nuevo León to leave in search of greener pastures elsewhere. The mines of Almadén, which had shown so much promise just a decade earlier, had begun to play out, and the settlers were starting to drift away. Castaño provided a detailed description of the plight of the colony in the spring of 1590:

> The reason for abandoning my former settlement [Almadén] was sufficient in my opinion, in that the mines were unprofitable and lacking in ores. Where there were any, they did not contain enough silver to pay even for the charcoal used in smelting. Surely this explanation will be believed, since we had constructed water mills, and others run by mulepower, for smelting, grinding and refining, which we would not have abandoned without cause

> after everything had been done so laboriously and at, God knows, what expense. This work cost me more than fifteen thousand pesos, for most of which I am in debt. . . . Moreover, I had in operation a farm from which I obtained many supplies. All of these things were lost because there was [no] silver, and the land was such that we could not support ourselves there without resorting to acts which would have been in a sense wrongful. That was the principal reason for abandoning the site. In addition, the settlers and other people were leaving that region.[54]

But it is also likely that, given the demographics of the colony and the acceleration in the campaign by the Holy Office of the Inquisition against crypto-Jews all across the viceroyalty, many residents became apprehensive about lingering any longer than necessary. León, writing in the seventeenth century, linked Castaño's departure to the death of Carvajal, which he believed had taken place just months before. Hoyo found this hypothesis intriguing: "In reality, the *entrada* to New Mexico of Castaño de Sosa represented nothing other than a flight, the intent to put space between him and the authorities, in view of the unique and weak legal status of his lieutenant governorship." The problem with this conjecture, Hoyo continued, was that Carvajal appears to have been still living in October 1590, three months *after* Castaño left Nuevo León. Hoyo based his doubts on the fact that Viceroy Luis de Velasco, in a letter dated October 6, wrote as though the governor was alive.[55] Indeed, notarial records from Mexico City indicate that Carvajal was very much among the living on October 13, when he executed a power of attorney relating to legal proceedings initiated against the marqués de Villamanrique, the former viceroy.[56] Formal notice of Carvajal's death on February 13, 1591, was issued by the viceroy in a letter to the king ten days later.[57] León and Hoyo were on the right track with regard to their assessment of the motivation for Castaño's hasty departure. But it was not Carvajal's death, but his conviction by the Mexican Inquisition and his presence as a *reo penitenciado* in the auto de fe of February 1590, that appears to have served as the motivation for the flight.

Castaño's desperate decision in the summer of 1590 was a risky one. The expedition that he was undertaking ran counter to royal policy. Under the terms of Spanish law, settlers could not just pick up and leave, abandoning an established colony. To undertake an enterprise of this sort required permission from the proper authorities in Mexico and Spain. Evidence had to be presented that the expedition was sufficiently staffed and supplied. Until the 1570s, ambitious and enterprising individuals had, indeed, been able to venture forth into the hinterland to advance the frontier of New Spain, as well as their own fortunes. From time to time, the viceroy in Mexico City would act to curb these activities, once he perceived that the interests of the Crown had been satisfied.

The Colonization Laws of 1573 sought to formalize and centralize the process by which expeditions into the frontier were initiated.[58] The laws made it very clear that anyone seeking to undertake a venture to discover new lands needed the permission of royal authorities:

> No person, regardless of status or condition shall by his own authority undertake any new discovery, neither by sea or land, or embark on any expedition to a new population or settlement in lands that have been discovered, or about to be discovered, without Our license and provision, or that of an official whom we authorize to give such permission, under penalty of death and confiscation of all goods by Our chamber. And we order that none of Our viceroys, *audiencias*, governors, and other justices of the Indies issue any license to undertake new discoveries without first sending it to us for consultation and approval.[59]

With regard to efforts to colonize territory already discovered, the viceroy in Mexico City was empowered to sanction such an enterprise, provided that notice of the settlement be forwarded to the king: "But, in the cases of [lands] already discovered, [royal officials] may give permission to establish whatever settlements as they see fit, providing that, in so doing, all the laws contained in this book are observed, and that notice of the settlement in these discovered lands be sent to us afterward."[60] In both cases, the express authorization of Crown officials was essential. Whether Castaño considered his mission one of discovery or of colonization, he had to secure such license from Mexico City before he left. It was never granted.[61]

Not that Castaño hadn't tried in vain to obtain proper authorization from royal authorities. On May 27, 1590, he sent trusted captains Francisco Salgado and Manuel de Mederos to Mexico City to communicate with Viceroy Velasco. According to Castaño's account, he waited almost a month for the return of his emissaries, anticipating the viceroy's consent. But, much to his dismay, not only did he fail to secure such approval, but he received a most unwelcome visit from his rival, Juan Morlete,[62] who brought word from Velasco that his request had been denied and that he was specifically forbidden to undertake the expedition without permission. It was strongly represented to him that he return to the capital to answer directly to the viceroy. But out of fear that the community would disintegrate in his absence, he chose to send another representative, Alonso Ruíz, to again try to make his case at court.[63] But this time, instead of waiting for a reply, Castaño chose to violate Viceroy Velasco's express order and departed into the wilderness with approximately 170 men, women, and children, bound for New Mexico.[64]

The sudden and illegal departure of Castaño's expedition, the coincidence of timing with the conviction of Governor Carvajal, Castaño's own ethnic background and familial ties to known Judaizers, and the absence of a priest or a member of a religious order from his company (the only expedition into the northern frontier of its day to fail to include such representatives)[65] all suggest strongly that the lieutenant governor initiated the dangerous *entrada* into New Mexico at least partially for the purpose of leading other crypto-Jews to a secure haven on the far northern frontier.

This hypothesis is strengthened by an examination of the ethnic origins of certain of the participants in the enterprise. Unfortunately, no muster roll has ever been uncovered for the expedition, thus limiting the number of clues that would offer insights into the Iberian roots of the colonists. As a matter of fact, only thirty-three of the individuals are even named in the contemporary documentation,[66] leaving approximately 80 percent of the settlers unidentified. Nevertheless, not all the participants in Castaño's colonization effort remain lost to history. A comparison of names found in the official journal of the expedition with trial records of the Holy Office of the Inquisition in Mexico, Spain, and Portugal establishes with varying degrees of certainty that crypto-Jews could be found among the European settlers heading north.

One of the members of Castaño's expedition who can be linked to *converso* origins was Alonso Jaimes. Born in the Canary Islands, Jaimes tried to pass himself off as an Old Christian before immigration officials in an attempt to emigrate to Mexico in 1574. He had convinced Francisco Rodríguez to perjure himself by alleging that Jaimes was "free from all Muslim or Jewish blood." Recognizing the attempt to circumvent the prohibition of descendants of Jews from emigrating to the New World, Inquisition officials in the Canaries arrested Jaimes and accused him of being "a descendant of a line of *conversos*, reconciled by the Inquisition." Unbeknownst to either Jaimes or Rodríguez, the inquisitors had maintained a dossier on Jaimes's family, tracing it back five generations to Jews from Spain who, after converting to Catholicism in 1492, had sought refuge in the Canaries. Jaimes's grandfather Pedro de Almonte and great-grandparents Marcos Alonso de

Almonte and Beatris Alonso were born in the southwestern Spanish town of Lepe, near the Portuguese border. They were all identified as *conversos* and penanced by the Inquisition in the nearby town of Gibraleón. Rodríguez was fined 8 *ducados* for his perjury. And, despite all the attention from the Las Palmas tribunal of the Holy Office, Jaimes apparently was able to emigrate to New Spain within a few years after this unpleasant encounter with the Inquisition officials.[67]

Melchor de Paiba, according to Hoyo, was "undoubtedly" related to Simón de Paiba, a devout crypto-Jew in Pachuca, and was the uncle of *judaizante* Manuel de Herrera, which also linked him by blood to Gaspar Castaño de Sosa. Melchor had been in the company of Governor Carvajal since 1583.[68]

Juan de Victoria Carvajal, also known as Juan de Carvajal,[69] was thirty years old when he joined Castaño's expedition to New Mexico. He was born in 1560 in Yautepeque, in the Marquesado del Valle, south of Mexico City, the son of Juan de Carvajal.[70] That young Juan de Victoria Carvajal was counted among Governor Luis de Carvajal's retinue in the late 1580s, and that he had known Carvajal since age eleven, suggest strongly that he maintained some kind of family connection with the governor and thus was tied by blood to the *judaizantes* of Nuevo León penanced by the Mexican Inquisition in the 1590s.[71] It is possible that Victoria Carvajal may even have been the governor's first cousin, as Inquisition records identify Carvajal's paternal uncle as the "man of arms" Juan de Carvajal, the name of Victoria Carvajal's father.[72]

Juan Rodríguez Nieto, a thirty-five-year-old soldier in the company of Castaño, was likely a cousin of the prominent crypto-Jew Diego Díaz Nieto of Mexico City. Both were born in the vicinity of Oporto, Juan around 1557,[73] and Diego in 1573. Inquisition records from the 1590s identify Díaz Nieto's paternal grandparents as Manuel Díaz, alias Ruy Gómez Nieto, also from Oporto, and Francisca Rodríguez, alias Cecilia Rodríguez Cardoso.[74] The coincidence in family names and birthplaces points to a probable family relationship between the two men. Moreover, when offering testimony the year after his return to Mexico in a legal action relating to Castaño's expedition, Rodríguez Nieto referred to himself as a "bad Christian," the only witness in the proceeding to make such a self-incriminating reference.[75]

Other participants on the expedition may well have had ties to crypto-Judaism in Mexico and Spain as well. Was Pedro de Íñigo, for example, the same man as Pedro de Íñiguez, of Pazarón, Spain, who accompanied Governor Carvajal to Nuevo León in 1580?[76] Without more corroborating documentation, one is left only to speculate.

The itinerary followed by Castaño and his followers in 1590 is well known to students of New Mexican history.[77] The party left the mining community of Almadén on July 27 and headed north, reaching the Río Grande on September 9. The precise location of Castaño's crossing of the Río Grande is a subject of scholarly debate. Albert H. Schroeder and Don S. Matson, as well as George Hammond and Agapito Rey, placed the site near Del Rio, Texas. But Richard Santos claimed that the expedition had made the crossing farther downriver, near Piedras Negras. He identified the name of the crossing as *el paso grande de los judíos* (the great crossing of the Jews), but offered no primary citation for this, beyond his reference to its use by the United States–Mexico Border Commission in 1850.[78] From there, they proceeded upriver to the confluence with the Río Pecos and continued up the Pecos, arriving at the pueblo of Pecos just before New Year's Day 1591. After a violent exchange between the Spanish and the inhabitants of the pueblo, which resulted in the killing of several Indians, Castaño then crossed Glorieta Pass, explored the pueblos of northern New Mexico, returned southward to visit those of the Galisteo Basin, and, by early March, continued southward, establishing his headquarters in the Middle Río Grande Valley, near the pueblo of Santo Domingo.

By this time, the royal officials in Mexico City had long received word of Castaño's unauthorized departure from Nuevo León. The earliest confirmation of Viceroy Luis de Velasco's acknowledgment of this news derives from a letter written on September 24, 1590, to Juan Morlete, *alcalde mayor* of Saltillo, advising him to prepare for an expedition northward to apprehend Castaño and his followers and bring them back to Mexico City.[79] Several days later, on October 1, Velasco followed up with formal instructions for the arresting party. He outlined the principal objectives of the mission:

> to put a stop to the expedition planned and undertaken by Gaspar Castaño and his men in contravention of my specific order as well as the general orders of His Majesty; to check the injuries and excesses against the poor natives which have done such great disservice to our God our Lord and his Majesty; and to insure the punishment of those who perpetrated the offenses, as well as giving satisfaction to the Indians for the abuses already suffered and assurance that they will not be so abused in the future but will receive only wholehearted friendship and good treatment.[80]

Apparently, the reputation that Castaño had earned a decade earlier for having organized slaving parties had come back to haunt him. A

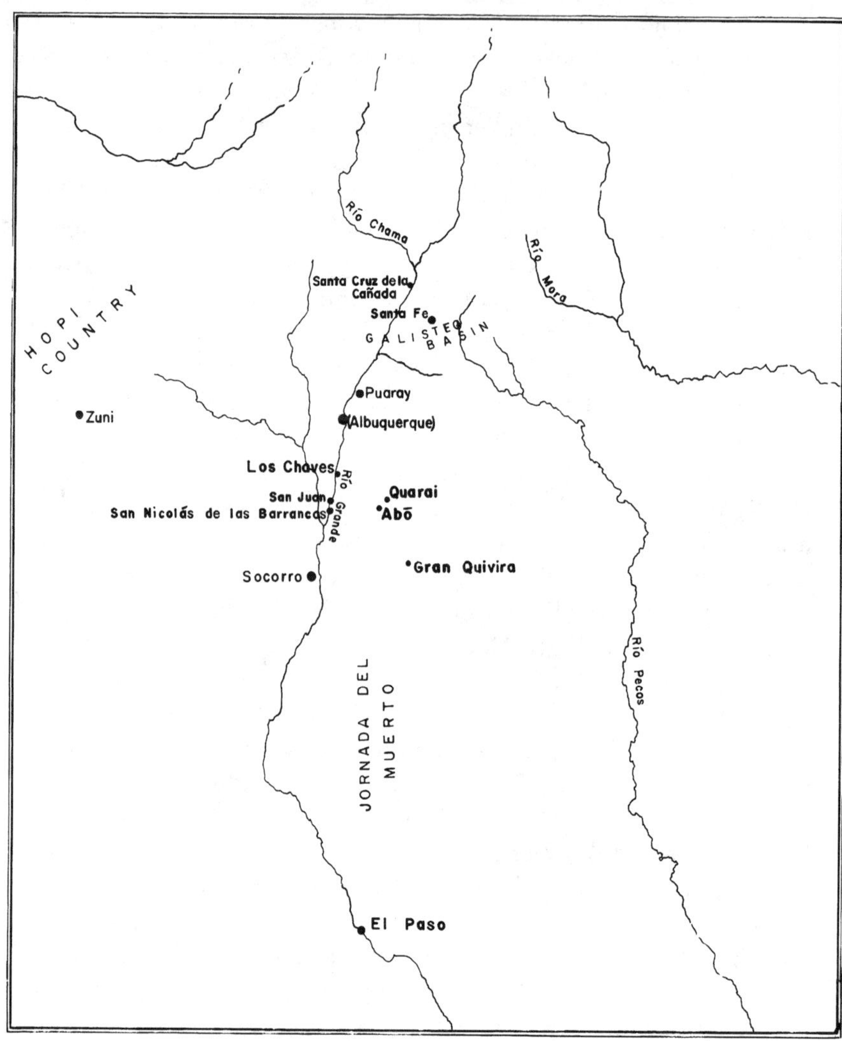

New Mexico, sixteenth and seventeenth centuries.

week later, as if to put another nail in Castaño's coffin, the viceroy appended to another order a copy of a royal *cédula* issued by Felipe II. "No person appointed by this Luis de Carvajal shall go there [New Mexico]," the king ordered, clearly referring to Castaño. "To the contrary, the viceroy shall nominate and indicate who shall have this authority, as he sees fit."[81]

Morlete departed from Saltillo with forty men; followed the more traditional route directly up the Río Grande, rather than retracing Castaño's trail up the Pecos; and arrived at Castaño's camp near Santo

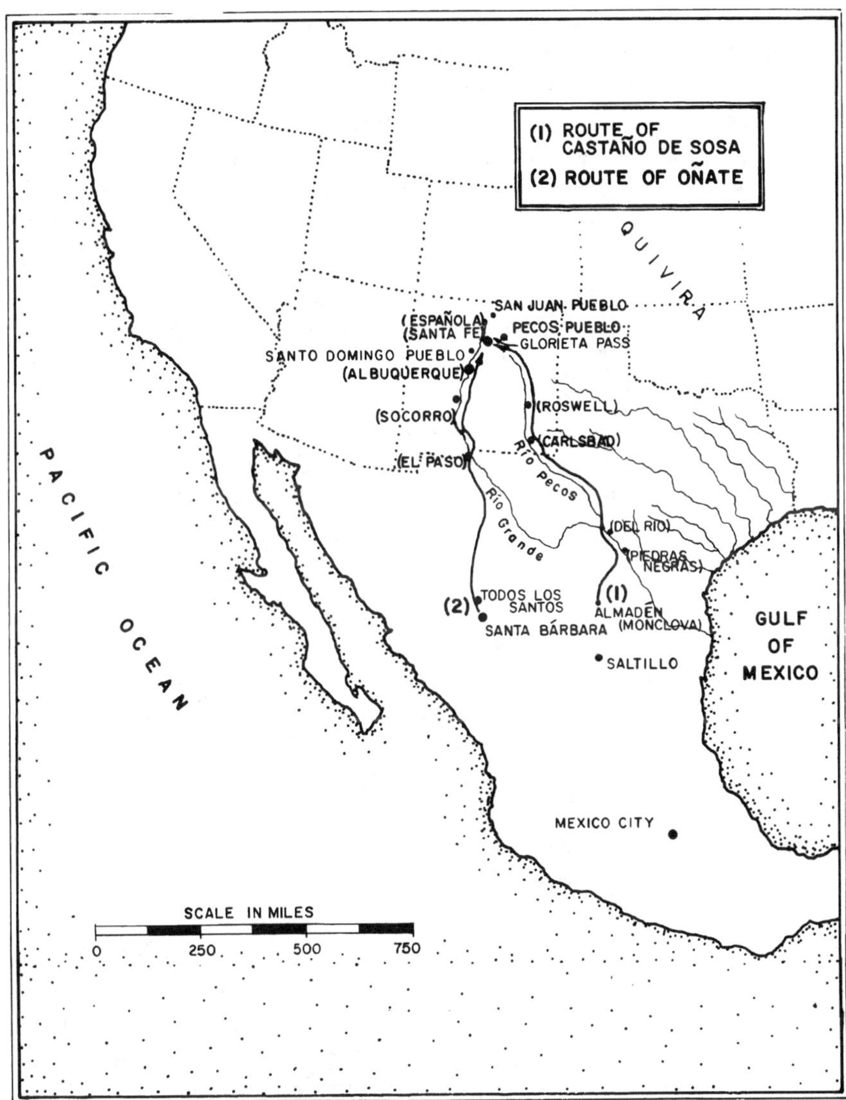

Routes of the expeditions of Gaspar Castaño de Sosa (1590) and Juan de Oñate (1598).

Domingo on March 29, 1591. When presented with the viceregal order for his arrest, Castaño submitted to his captor without resistance. Morlete placed him in shackles, and the combined parties began their long trek southward to Mexico City.[82]

Although the order for Castaño's arrest included no accusation of religious heresy, one wonders if fear of religious persecution was in the back of the minds of the lieutenant governor and his party. Nineteenth-century Mexican historian Vicente Riva Palacio put forth this idea in his analysis of Castaño's arrest: "[Castaño de] Sosa knew not the cause of his arrest, nor was he so informed, leaving him to wonder if he had been taken because he had embarked on the expedition without permission of the viceroy, or for having been considered as a suspect in the proceedings that the Inquisition initiated against Luis de Carvajal and his family for secretly practicing Judaism."[83]

On the return trip to Mexico City, on July 27, 1591, Castaño wrote an impassioned letter to Viceroy Velasco, defending his actions and explaining his motivation for having undertaken the expedition northward. He had no intention of deceiving the viceroy, Castaño wrote, but he was relying in good faith on the authority that he presumed he had been granted by Governor Carvajal. Besides, in sending messengers to Mexico City, he had made a sincere effort to inform the authorities of his plans, anticipating that the viceroy would give his consent. He left before word of such approval arrived, he explained, "because circumstances forced me to depart in order to hold my people, who were beginning to leave me, and some of the Indians, too, were running away. I went on, but with the firm intention of delaying action (as I did) during the time required for the round trip to bring your Grace's order." Moreover, the mission to New Mexico was successful, in that he discovered lead and silver mines and was able to secure the allegiance of the Pueblo Indians to the king. Castaño also outlined the reasons why he felt it necessary to abandon the Nuevo León settlement the previous year and defended himself against the charges that he had engaged in illegal slaving operations.[84]

This letter is important because it not only details Castaño's actions, but also contains rhetorical allusions that may indicate a Jewish identity. The message includes no reference to such Catholic images as Christ and the Trinity (save one appeal to the "Christian charity" of the viceroy), but invokes only the name of God. The text is punctuated with phrases such as "as God is my witness," "God was pleased to lead me," "if God brings us safely to your city," "Almighty God knows my innocence," "God knows," "once I have found my way to your presence by God's will," and "if God wills my release from my present captivity." More important, Castaño's prose, on several occasions, cites the monotheistic concept of the oneness of God, with such phrases as "I invoke the Lord God as the sole and true judge," "I humbly beseech that you will pardon that failure, for the love of the One Single God," and "I beg and implore, in the name of the One Single God."[85]

In his encyclopedic work analyzing crypto-Jewish customs in Spain and Mexico, David Gitlitz stressed the importance of monotheism among the *anusim*: "The central and most common precept for the Iberian crypto-Jews was the belief in a unitary God in contrast to what they considered to be the tripartite or plural God of the Christians. Jews are uncompromising monotheists for whom belief in a single God is the most important article of faith."[86] To reinforce this point, Gitlitz cited several examples where the crypto-Jews, including members of the Carvajal community, invoked the phrase *un solo Dios*—which he translated alternatively as "one single God" or "one God alone, "as opposed either to the Trinity (collectively) or to God, Christ, or the Holy Spirit (individually).[87]

The message of Castaño to the viceroy reflects this singular emphasis on God, in contrast with more typical letters written by other Spanish residents of the New World in the sixteenth century. Among the correspondence included in James Lockhart and Enrique Otte's compilation of letters can be found some that, while citing the name of God, also include references to having mercy on the enemy, "in order not to hinder any whom the Holy Spirit should illumine in our holy Catholic faith," or refer to a priest who is "serv[ing] God and his majesty, and [dying] for the faith of Jesus Christ."[88] Similarly, a letter written in 1542 by the governor of Peru to his wife begs her to give thanks "to God our Lord and the glorious virgin our Lady, his mother."[89] And Bernal Díaz del Castillo, the famous chronicler who accompanied Fernando Cortés in the conquest of Mexico in 1519, wrote decades later to the king, "I . . . pray to our Lord Jesus Christ that he guard your majesty and our lords the illustrious princes."[90]

The import of his invocation of the deity notwithstanding, Castaño's appeal to the viceroy had little effect. On February 13, 1593, the *audiencia* of Mexico convicted him of treason for having disobeyed royal authorities "by having invaded the territory of peaceful Indians, having raised the banners and having left for the provinces of New Mexico." Castaño was sentenced to exile in the Philippine Islands for six years. His conviction was appealed to the Council of the Indies in Sevilla, and was overturned, but Castaño was not to survive long enough to savor the victory. He died in the Philippines soon after his arrival, killed during a revolt of Chinese galley slaves in October 1593.[91]

What became of the survivors of Castaño's ill-fated expedition? Most of them, according to Hoyo, either settled in Saltillo or returned to Nuevo León, joining Diego de Montemayor, another former captain of Governor Carvajal, in the founding of the town of Monterrey in 1596.[92] But while most returned to familiar territory on the northeastern frontier, others sojourned in Mexico City, which by the mid-1590s was immersed in the campaign by the Holy Office of the Inquisition against the Carvajal family and, indeed, the entire crypto-Jewish community of Mexico.

The participation of crypto-Jews in the early conquest and colonization efforts of Luis de Carvajal in Nuevo León and Gaspar Castaño de Sosa in New Mexico set the stage for the next phase of Spanish settlement on the far northern frontier of New Spain. Some of the participants in these enterprises, who to this point had evaded persecution by the Inquisition, were to find themselves actively involved in this endeavor.

NOTES

1. To avoid confusion between these two individuals, Governor Luis de Carvajal will be referred to as Carvajal and his nephew, as Luis, el Mozo. The Spanish form of names is used here. In Portugal, Carvajal would have been Carvalho; Nieto, Neto; Nuñez, Nunes; Castaño, Castanho; González, Gonçalves; and so on.
2. Eugenio del Hoyo pointed out that several other members of Carvajal's extended family had engaged in the slave trade and that Carvajal himself, during his late teens and early twenties, had participated in these endeavors during his tenure in the Cape Verde Islands. This, according to Hoyo, occurred "precisely during those decisive years when his character was forged and his life was oriented," presaging Carvajal's slaving activities among the Indians of Nuevo León years later (*Historia del Nuevo Reino de León [1577–1723]* [Monterrey: Instituto Tecnológico y de Estudios Superiores de Monterrey, 1972], pp. 103–104).
3. Proceso contra Luis de Carvajal, Governador del Nuevo Reino de León, natural de la Villa de Mogadorio, 1589, fol. 50, Ramo de Inquisición, Lote Riva Palacio, tomo 11, exp. 3, Archivo General de la Nación, Mexico City (hereafter cited as AGN).
4. Hoyo, *Historia del Nuevo Reino de León*, pp. 104–106.
5. Pleito de hexecución de Gonzalo de las Casas contra Luis de Carabajal, 1571, Ramo de Civil, tomo 921, exp. 43, AGN. The suit was executed against Carvajal for nonpayment relating to the purchase of a burro. Carvajal's house was initially seized, and then returned after the authorities ruled in Carvajal's favor. With regard to the location of the crypto-Jewish neighborhood in Mexico City, see chap. 2.
6. Hoyo, *Historia del Nuevo Reino de León*, pp. 92, 107–110, 147–148, 229.
7. Antonio F. García-Abásalo, *Martín Enríquez y la reforma de 1568 en Nueva España* (Seville: Diputación Provincial de Sevilla, 1983), p. 368, citing Fray Pedro de San Luis a Felipe II, San Luis de Tampico, March 12, 1578, Sección

de Audiencia de México, legajo 103, R. 2, Archivo General de Indias, Seville (hereafter cited as AGI).

8. Asiento y capitulación con el Capitán Luys de Carvajal sobre el descubrimiento y población del Nuevo Reyno de León, Aranjuéz, May 31, 1579, fol. 1v, Sección de Indiferente, legajo 416, L. 7, AGI.

9. Ibid., fol. 3r.

10. Ibid., fol. 4v.

11. Orden del rey a la Casa de Contratación, Toledo, June 14, 1579, fol. 7v, Sección de Indiferente, legajo 416, L. 7, AGI. See also Richard E. Greenleaf, *The Mexican Inquisition of the Sixteenth Century* (Albuquerque: University of New Mexico Press, 1969), p. 170; Martin A. Cohen, *The Martyr: Luis de Carvajal, a Secret Jew in Sixteenth-Century Mexico* (Philadelphia: Jewish Publication Society of America, 1973), p. 56; and Alfonso Toro, *La familia Carvajal* (Mexico City: Editorial Patria, 1944), p. 41.

12. This interpretation is consistent with that of Vicente Riva Palacio, *México a traves de los siglos* (Barcelona: Establecimiento Tipo, 1888–1889), vol. 2, pp. 446–447. Hoyo, apparently unaware of the existence of the royal order of June 14, 1579, took issue with Riva Palacio's observation regarding the waiving of the investigation into the colonists' *limpieza de sangre*. Noting that article 9 of the *capitulación* included no such waiver, he dismissed the idea. Hoyo did, however, acknowledge that Carvajal succeeded in avoiding investigation of his colonists, but he claimed that the governor had done so by circumventing the law. As will be demonstrated later, Hoyo believed that "almost all of them [the colonists] were Jews of Portuguese origin" (*Historia del Nuevo Reino de León*, pp. 112–113).

13. Richard E. Greenleaf, *Zumárraga and the Mexican Inquisition, 1536–1543* (Washington, D.C.: Academy of American Franciscan History, 1961), p. 89.

14. Hoyo calculated that 75 percent of the passengers on the *Santa Catarina*, which sailed from Sevilla in January 1580, were confirmed *conversos* and presumed that the rest were as well (*Historia del Nuevo Reino de León*, pp. 221–231). See also Greenleaf, *Mexican Inquisition of the Sixteenth Century*, p. 170; Eugenio del Hoyo, "Notas y comentarios a la 'Relación' de las personas nombradas por Luis de Carvajal y de la Cueva para llevar al descubrimiento, pacificación y población del Nuevo Reino de León, 1580," *Humánitas* 19 (1978): 251–281; George Alexander Kohut, "The Martyrdom of the Carabajal Family in Mexico, 1590–1601," *Jewish Tribune* (Portland, Ore.), March 25, 1904, p. 5; Toro, *Familia Carvajal*, p. 43; and Seymour B. Liebman, *The Jews in New Spain: Faith, Flame, and the Inquisition* (Coral Gables, Fla.: University of Miami Press, 1970), pp. 144–145.

15. According to Hoyo, the name of the ship carrying the passengers bound for Nuevo León was *Santa Catarina* (*Historia del Nuevo Reino de León*, p. 221). Cohen contends that the name of the vessel was *Nuestra Señora de la Luz* (*Martyr*, p. 63).

16. Hoyo, *Historia del Nuevo Reino de León*, pp. 114–116, 221–234, and "Notas y comentarios."

17. Hoyo, *Historia del Nuevo Reino de León*, pp. 268–272. Hoyo observed that

Nuevo León was not unique in this sense, but that other parts of New Spain had significant *converso* populations at this time as well. Nor did Hoyo contend that all descendants of Spanish and Portuguese Jews were practicing Judaizers.

18. Clarence H. Haring, *The Spanish Empire in America* (New York: Harcourt, Brace & World, 1947), pp. 38–68.
19. Ibid., pp. 20–22.
20. Richard E. Greenleaf, "The Little War of Guadalajara—1587–1590," *New Mexico Historical Review* 43 (1968): 122.
21. Cohen, *Martyr*, pp. 110–111.
22. Greenleaf, "Little War of Guadalajara," p. 124; Peter Gerhard, *The Northern Frontier of New Spain* (Princeton, N.J.: Princeton University Press, 1982), p. 348. See also George P. Hammond and Agapito Rey, *The Rediscovery of New Mexico: The Expeditions of Chamuscado, Espejo, Castaño de Sosa, Morlete, and Leyva de Bonilla and Humaña* (Albuquerque: University of New Mexico Press, 1966), pp. 296–298, citing Viceroy Villamanrique to Luis de Velasco, February 14, 1590 [issuing instructions regarding the arrest of Carvajal], Sección de Audiencia de México, legajo 22, AGI.
23. For further details on the life and Judaizing activities of Carvajal, el Mozo, and other members of the Carvajal family, see Toro, *Familia Carvajal*; Cohen, *Martyr*; *The Enlightened: The Writings of Luis de Carvajal, el Mozo*, trans. and ed. Seymour B. Liebman (Coral Gables, Fla.: University of Miami Press, 1967); Liebman, *Jews in New Spain*, chaps. 7 and 8; and Greenleaf, *Mexican Inquisition of the Sixteenth Century*, pp. 169–171.
24. [Mexican Tribunal to Supreme Council of the Inquisition], Mexico, November 6, 1587, libro 1048, fols. 243r–244r, Sección de Inquisición, Archivo Histórico Nacional, Madrid (hereafter cited as AHN).
25. [Mexican Tribunal to Supreme Council of the Inquisition], October 21, 1594, libro 1048, fols. 363r–364r, Sección de Inquisición, AHN; [Mexican Tribunal to Supreme Council of the Inquisition], March 31, 1595, libro 1049, fol. 4v, Sección de Inquisición, AHN; Cohen, *Martyr*; Eva A. Uchmany, *La vida entre el judaísmo y el cristianismo en la Nueva España, 1580–1606* (Mexico City: Archivo General de la Nación and Fondo de Cultura Económica, 1992), p. 55; Toro, *Familia Carvajal.*
26. Cohen, *Martyr*, p. 128. Simón de Paiba had died before the occurrence of the activities outlined in the Inquisition trials, described by Cohen.
27. Uchmany, *Vida entre el judaísmo y el cristianismo*, pp. 88–89.
28. Ibid., p. 88.
29. Ibid., pp. 41–63; Liebman, *Jews in New Spain*, pp. 194, 306, 310.
30. Solange Alberro, *Inquisición y sociedad en México, 1571–1700* (Mexico City: Fondo de Cultura Económica, 1988).
31. Peter J. Bakewell, *Silver Mining and Society in Colonial Mexico: Zacatecas, 1546–1700* (Cambridge: Cambridge University Press, 1971).
32. Alberro, *Inquisición y sociedad en México*, p. 390.
33. Ibid., pp. 390–402.

34. Ibid., p. 408.

35. Ibid., pp. 391–392; France V. Scholes, "The First Decade of the Inquisition in New Mexico," *New Mexico Historical Review* 10 (1935): 216.

36. No studies have yet been undertaken to ascertain the participation of crypto-Jews in the Vázquez de Coronado expedition, but recent genealogical research has established that Vázquez's wife, Beatríz de Estrada, was the granddaughter of Men Gutiérrez, relaxed in effigy by the Inquisition of Toledo, for having practiced Judaism. See José Antonio Esquibel, "The Jewish-Converso Ancestry of Doña Beatriz de Estrada, Wife of Don Francisco Vásquez de Coronado," *Nuestras Raíces* 9 (1997): 134–143.

37. Herbert Eugene Bolton, *Coronado: Knight of Pueblos and Plains* (New York: Whittlesey House, 1949); Richard Flint and Shirley Cushing Flint, eds., *The Coronado Expedition to Tierra Nueva: The 1540–1542 Route Across the Southwest* (Boulder: University of Colorado Press, 1997).

38. For a detailed account of the Rodríguez–Sánchez Chamuscado expedition, see Hammond and Rey, *Rediscovery of New Mexico*, pp. 6–15, 67–150.

39. Hammond and Rey, *Rediscovery of New Mexico*, pp. 18–19; George P. Hammond and Agapito Rey, *Expedition into New Mexico Made by Antonio de Espejo, 1582–1583* (Los Angeles: Quivira Society, 1929), p. 28.

40. Ynformación resibida de officio en la audiencia real del nuevo reyno de galicia contra lo que hiso de parte Luis de Caravajal de la Cueva, governador y capitán general del nuevo reyno de León va al real consejo de las yndias, 1587, fols. 4v, 14v, 24r, 44r, 50v, 56r, 60v, 65v, Sección de Audiencia de Guadalajara, legajo 47, N. 47, AGI.

41. Hammond and Rey, *Rediscovery of New Mexico*, pp. 15–28, 153–231.

42. Alonso de León, *Relación y discursos del descubrimiento, población y pacificación de este Nuevo Reino de León . . .* (1649), in Genaro García, ed., *Documentos inéditos o muy raros para la historia de México* (Mexico City: Editorial Porrúa, 1975), pp. 50, 52.

43. Hoyo, *Historia del Nuevo Reino de León*, p. 148; Hammond and Rey, *Rediscovery of New Mexico*, p. 29; Ynformación resibida de officio en la audiencia real del nuevo reyno de galicia contra lo que hiso de parte Luis de Caravajal de la Cueva, fol. 17v, Sección de Audiencia de Guadalajara, legajo 47, N. 47, AGI; Traslado de las ynformaciones, autos y otras diligencias que se hizieron contra el Capitán Gaspar Castaño de Sosa y sus soldados sobre aver ydo al nuevo méxico, 1592, fol. 5r, Sección de Audiencia de México, legajo 220, AGI.

44. Alonso de León, *Historia de Nuevo León, con noticias sobre Coahuila, Tamaulipas, Texas y Nuevo México, escrita en el siglo XVII* (Monterrey: Universidad de Nuevo León, 1961), pp. 55–57.

45. See, for example, Cohen, *Martyr*, pp. 27–28, 295; Edward Glaser, "Referencias antisemitas en la literatura peninsular de la Edad de Oro," *Nueva Revista de Filología Hispánica* 8 (1954): 41; Miriam Bodian, *Hebrews of the Portuguese Nation: Conversos and Community in Early Modern Amsterdam* (Bloomington: Indiana University Press, 1997), p. 13; António Vieira, *Obras escolhidas* (Lisbon: Livraria Sá de Costa, 1951–1954), vol. 4, p. 182; Liebman, *Jews in New Spain*, p. 183; Charles Boxer, *The Dutch in Brazil, 1624–1654* (Oxford:

Clarendon Press, 1957); James Howell, *Epistolae Ho-Eliane, Familiar Letters, Domestic and Foreign* (London, 1645); and Hoyo, *Historia del Nuevo Reino de León*, p. 202.

46. See, for example, Processo de Gaspar Afonso Castanho, 1592, Lisboa, no. 12839; Processo de Nicalou Castanho, 1554, Lisboa, no. 5944; Processo de Jorge Castanho, 1629, Coimbra, no. 1939; Processo de Manoel Castanho, 1626, Coimbra, no. 5040; Processo de Isabel Castanho, 1591, Evora, no. 1641; Processo de Diogo Castanho, 1589, Evora, no. 3649; Processo de Alvaro Fernandes Castanho, 1635, Evora, no. 10531; Processo de Gaspar de Sousa, 1621, Lisboa, no. 8485; Processo de Briolana de Sousa, 1599, Coimbra, no. 7994; and Processo de Joana de Sousa, 1618, Lisboa, no. 2743, all in Secção de Inquisição, Arquivo Nacional da Torre do Tombo, Lisbon.

47. Cohen, *Martyr*, pp. 103–104; Richard Santos, *Silent Heritage: The Sephardim and the Colonization of the Spanish North American Frontier* (San Antonio, Tex.: New Sepharad Press, 2000), pp. 297–298. Neither Cohen nor Santos provided any references to document these assertions.

48. Hoyo, *Historia del Nuevo Reino de León*, pp. 147–148, 229; in *Rediscovery of New Mexico*, Hammond and Rey consistently misidentified Paiba as Pavía.

49. Eugenio de Hoyo, "¿Sefarditas en el Nuevo Reino de León?" *Humánitas* 12 (1971): 247–254, and *Historia del Nuevo Reino de León*, p. 268.

50. Hoyo, *Historia del Nuevo Reino de León*, p. 134; Cohen, *Martyr*, p. 143.

51. Expediente de las raciones diarias que recibian los presos de la [*sic*] carceles secretas del Santo Oficio, 1589, fol. 149, Ramo de Inquisición, tomo 213, exp. 12, AGN. On February 26, 1590, Governor Carvajal was removed from the Inquisition jail and returned to the royal prison.

52. Proceso contra Luis de Carvajal, Governador del Nuevo Reino de León, fol. 69, Ramo de Inquisición, Lote Riva Palacio, tomo 11, exp. 3, AGN; José Toribio Medina, *Historia de la Inquisición en México* (Mexico City: Ediciones Fuente Cultural, 1905), p. 128; Uchmany, *Vida entre el judaísmo y el cristianismo*, p. 55.

53. Hoyo, *Historia del Nuevo Reino de León*, p. 133.

54. Hammond and Rey, *Rediscovery of New Mexico*, pp. 308–309, citing Captain Gaspar Castaño de Sosa to the viceroy, July 27, 1591, Sección de Audiencia de México, legajo 22, AGI. See also *A Colony on the Move: Gaspar Castaño de Sosa's Journal, 1590–1591*, ann. Albert H. Schroeder and trans. Don S. Matson (Santa Fe: School of American Research, 1965), p. 6.

55. Hoyo, *Historia del Nuevo Reino de León*, pp. 140–141.

56. Escribanía de Antonio de Villalobos, 1580–1603, October 13, 1590, Archivo General de Notarías, Mexico City.

57. Hammond and Rey, *Rediscovery of New Mexico*, p. 302, citing Don Luis de Velasco to the king, February 23, 1591, Sección de Audiencia de México, legajo 22, AGI.

58. Joaquín Francisco Pacheco and Francisco de Cárdenas y Espejo, eds., *Colección de documentos inéditos relativos al descubrimiento, conquista y organización de las antiguas posesiones españoles* (Madrid: Imprenta de Hospicio, 1871), vol. 16, pp. 142–187.

59. Ibid., p. 143.

60. Ibid.

61. Dorothy Hull argued that Castaño did, indeed, fulfill these requirements ("Castaño de Sosa's Expedition to New Mexico," *Old Santa Fe* 3 [1916]: 332). Schroeder and Matson claimed that the law regarding "discoveries" did not apply, since New Mexico had been discovered years earlier (Castaño de Sosa, *Colony on the Move*, pp. 4–5). Schroeder and Matson held that Castaño fulfilled his obligation by "ma[king] an effort" to comply with the law regarding colonization by seeking, although not receiving, permission. This interpretation ignores the clause specifically requiring prior permission to have been granted by the viceroy. Hull, too, misread the provision, incorrectly believing that formal notice of the settlement could be given by the head of the expedition to the viceroy, whereas, according to the law, such notice was required to be forwarded by the viceroy to the king.

62. Some historians have speculated that Morlete was also a crypto-Jew. See, for example, David T. Raphael, *The Conquistadores and Crypto-Jews of Monterrey* (Valley Village, Calif.: Carmi House, 2001), pp. 149–151.

63. Hammond and Rey, *Rediscovery of New Mexico,* pp. 30, 306–307, citing Captain Gaspar Castaño de Sosa to the viceroy, July 27, 1591, Sección de Audiencia de México, legajo 22, AGI.

64. Castaño de Sosa, *Colony on the Move*, p. 11; Hammond and Rey, *Rediscovery of New Mexico*, p. 51.

65. Castaño de Sosa, *Colony on the Move*, p. 9.

66. Based on an analysis of names found in "Report on the Exploratory Expedition to New Mexico Undertaken on July 27, 1590, by Gaspar Castaño de Sosa while he was Lieutenant Governor and Captain General of New León," in Hammond and Rey, *Rediscovery of New Mexico*, pp. 245–295.

67. Proceso seguido en el S.O. contra Francisco Rodríguez, vecino de Garachico, porque en cierta información de limpieza de sangre que para pasar Indias con cierta cantidad de vino hizo Juan Núñez Jaimez, declaro ser este cristiano viejo, siendo notorio descendiente de los Almonte, naturales de Lepe, reconciliados por el Tribunal, 1584, fols. 941r–943v, Fondo Antiguo, CXXXIII–20; Libro segundo de genealogías, 1628, fols. 1r, 36v, Fondo Antiguo, CLII–2, both in Museo Canario, Las Palmas.

68. Hoyo, *Historia del Nuevo Reino de León*, p. 229.

69. Castaño de Sosa, *Colony on the Move*, p. 179. Schroeder and Matson deduce that Juan de Carvajal and Juan de Victoria Carvajal, who formed part of the expedition to New Mexico to reinforce the colony of Juan de Oñate some ten years later, were the same person. Contemporary records appear to corroborate this conclusion, with documentation from 1587 and 1600 offering the same date of birth for Juan de Carvajal and Juan de Victoria Carvajal. See Ynformación resibida de officio en la audiencia real del nuevo reyno de galicia contra lo que hiso de parte Luis de Caravajal de la Cueva, testimony of Juan de Caravajal, Guadalajara, September 1, 1587, fol. 43r, Sección de Audiencia de Guadalajara, legajo 47, N. 47, AGI.

70. George P. Hammond and Agapito Rey, *Don Juan de Oñate, Colonizer of New*

Mexico, 1595–1628 (Albuquerque: University of New Mexico Press, 1953), p. 153.

71. Ynformación resibida de officio en la audiencia real del nuevo reyno de galicia contra lo que hiso de parte Luis de Caravajal de la Cueva, testimony of Juan de Caravajal, fol. 43r, Sección de Audiencia de Guadalajara, legajo 47, N. 47, AGI.

72. Proceso contra Luis de Carvajal, Governador del Nuevo Reino de León, fol. 50, Ramo de Inquisición, Lote Riva Palacio, tomo 11, exp. 3, AGN.

73. Informaciones de oficio y parte, Domingo Martínez de Zearrata y Pedro de Zearrata, participación en la jornada a Nuevo México en busca de Capitán Gaspar Castaño, 1592, fol. 6v, Sección de Audiencia de México, legajo 220, N. 24, AGI.

74. Uchmany, *Vida entre el judaísimo y el cristianismo*, pp. 41, 200, 314.

75. Informaciones de oficio y parte, Domingo Martínez de Zearrata y Pedro de Zearrata, fol. 6v, Sección de Audiencia de México, legajo 220, N. 24, AGI.

76. "Pedro Íñiguez, natural de Pazarón, soltero, hijo de Alonso Íñiguez y de Juana Íñiguez, al Nuevo Reino de León, con Luis de Carvajal—1580" (no. 3.615), in María del Carmen Galbis Díaz, ed., *Archivo General de Indias: Catálogo de pasajeros a Indias, siglos XVI, XVII y XVIII*, vol. 6, *1578–1585* (Seville: Ministerio de Cultura, 1986), p. 455.

77. For a detailed account of the expedition, see Hammond and Rey, *Rediscovery of New Mexico*, pp. 31–39, 245–295; Hull, "Castaño de Sosa's Expedition to New Mexico" and Castaño de Sosa, *Colony on the Move*.

78. Castaño de Sosa, *Colony on the Move*, pp. 32–33; Hammond and Rey, *Rediscovery of New Mexico*, p. 249; Santos, *Silent Heritage*, pp. 286–287.

79. Hammond and Rey, *Rediscovery of New Mexico*, pp. 42–43.

80. Ibid., p. 299, citing [Instructions to Captain Juan Morlete for an expedition to New Mexico in pursuit of Gaspar Castaño de Sosa and his companions], Mexico City, October 1, 1590, Sección de Audiencia de México, legajo 220, exp. 30-A, AGI.

81. Hoyo, *Historia del Nuevo Reino de León*, p. 139, citing Carta de don Luis de Velasco II al Rev. Mexico, October 8, 1590, Sección de Audiencia de México, 58–3-11 [old citation], AGI. Hoyo indicated that the king was enjoining Castaño from traveling to Nuevo León, but the context of the document clearly made reference to New Mexico.

82. Hammond and Rey, *Rediscovery of New Mexico*, pp. 43–47.

83. Riva Palacio, *México a traves de los siglos*, p. 443.

84. Hammond and Rey, *Rediscovery of New Mexico*, pp. 305–311, citing Captain Gaspar Castaño de Sosa to the viceroy, July 27, 1591, Sección de Audiencia de México, legajo 22, AGI.

85. Ibid. Hammond and Rey translated the original, "un solo Diós," as "the One God," but I have taken the liberty of amending the translation of that phrase to "the One Single God." See El Virrey a S.M., descubrimiento de Nuevo México. Capitulaciones con Juan Bautusta. Franciscanos, Mexico, 1592, Anexo, Gaspar Castaño al Virrey, sobre su entrada en Nuevo México.

Desde el camino del norte, July 27, 1591, 5ff., Sección de Audiencia de México, legajo 22, N. 88, AGI.

86. David M. Gitlitz, *Secrecy and Deceit: The Religion of the Crypto-Jews* (Philadelphia: Jewish Publication Society of America, 1996), p. 101.

87. Ibid., pp. 101–102, 125, 224, 238–239, 367, 408.

88. Don Alonso Enríquez de Guzmán to Fray Francisco de Bobadilla, Guaytará, Peru, January 1, 1538, in James Lockhart and Enrique Otte, trans. and ed., *Letters and People of the Spanish Indies: The Sixteenth Century* (Cambridge: Cambridge University Press, 1976), pp. 148–154.

89. Lic. Cristobal Vaca de Castro, governor of Peru, to his wife, Doña María de Quiñones, Cuzco, November 28, 1542, in Lockhart and Otte, trans. and ed., *Letters and People of the Spanish Indies*, p. 175.

90. Bernal Díaz del Castillo to Emperor Charles V, Santiago, Guatemala, February 22, 1552, in Lockhart and Otte, trans. and ed., *Letters and People of the Spanish Indies*, p. 73.

91. Hoyo, *Historia del Nuevo Reino de León*, pp. 145–146; Hammond and Rey, *Rediscovery of New Mexico*, p. 48.

92. Hoyo, *Historia del Nuevo Reino de León*, pp. 146–147. Some historians have postulated that the early settlers of Monterrey included a substantial number of crypto-Jews. See, for example, Hoyo, *Historia del Nuevo Reino de León*, pp. 268–272, and "¿Sefarditas en el Nuevo Reino de León?" David Albert Cossío, *Historia de Nuevo León* (Monterrey: Cantú Leal, 1925–1933), vol. 2, p. 275; and Raphael, *Conquistadores and Crypto-Jews of Monterrey*. Anthropologist Marie Theresa Hernández offered a fascinating discussion linking the Carvajal settlement, the reestablishment of the Nuevo León colony in the late 1590s, and the emergence of a consciousness of a Jewish past among *nuevoleneses* at the turn of the twenty-first century (*Delirio: The Fantastic, the Demonic, and the Réel* [Austin: University of Texas Press, 2002]).

CHAPTER 4

Juan de Oñate and the Participation of Crypto-Jews in the First Permanent Colony in New Mexico, 1595–1607

COMPETITION FOR THE GOVERNORSHIP OF NEW MEXICO

After the aborted expedition of Gaspar Castaño de Sosa into New Mexico, and an even more ephemeral incursion in 1593, led by Francisco de Leyva de Bonilla and Antonio Gutiérrez de Humaña,[1] former associates of Luis de Carvajal y de la Cueva, Viceroy Luis de Velasco realized the pressing need to establish a defensive outpost on the far northern frontier of New Mexico. He refocused his attention on the task of selecting the most appropriate candidate for the job. Felipe II had expressed interest in such an enterprise since 1583, and several seasoned candidates applied for the position, including Hernán Gallegos and Antonio de Espejo, both of whom had made forays into New Mexico and knew well the territory in question.[2] Serious consideration had been given to the proposals submitted by Cristóbal Martín in 1583 and by Juan Bautista de Lomas y Colmenares in 1589. The *audiencia* of Mexico had gone so far as to draft a formal contract with Martín, by which he promised to support the expedition with 50,000 pesos and three hundred men,[3] but the expedition never materialized. Viceroy Álvaro Manrique de Zúniga, marqués de Villamanrique, acted favorably on Lomas's bid, and forwarded it to the Council of the Indies with his strong recommendation. The paperwork languished in Sevilla, however, and there the proposal died, due, most likely, to the Crown's reluctance to accept the grandiose terms submitted by Lomas.[4]

Among the frontier officials least disappointed with the news of Lomas's fate was Francisco de Urdiñola. A soldier of fortune with considerable military and administrative experience in Nueva Vizcaya, Urdiñola felt that he was the most logical individual to lead the official expedition northward to New Mexico. Lomas and Urdiñola had come to be bitter rivals over the previous few years, and Urdiñola hoped to take advantage of Lomas's bad fortune. Preliminary consultations with Viceroy Velasco in 1594 resulted in the drafting of a contract by which Urdiñola would head the expedition to the north. But before the year was out, his candidacy came under a cloud, as authorities in Nueva Galicia accused him of having murdered his young wife and two of his servants the previous year. Urdiñola's biographer, Vito Alessio Robles, believed the charges to have been bogus and suspected that Lomas was behind the accusations, pointing out that two of Lomas's sons-in-law sat on the *audiencia* of Guadalajara, the body that formulated the indictments.[5]

Urdiñola demanded that he be tried not in civil court, but by the Inquisition. Two years earlier, he had successfully applied for the position of *familiar* of the Holy Office, which accorded him the privilege of being exempt from civil authority in a matter such as this. After a bitter jurisdictional dispute between inquisitorial and *audiencia* officials, the former prevailed, and Urdiñola was allowed to defend himself in a more sympathetic venue. He was ultimately exonerated of the murder charges, but, in the process, he lost the confidence of the viceroy to conduct the New Mexico enterprise.[6]

Writing to the king in early 1595, Viceroy Velasco outlined the accusations brought against Urdiñola and his efforts to defend himself against these charges. Velasco accurately anticipated that Urdiñola's trial was likely to be long. For this reason, he announced to the king that "the expedition to New Mexico is suspended, because, as I have communicated to you [in October 1594], there does not exist in this kingdom any man to whom I could entrust the task."[7] Four months later, Velasco still considered the mission to be on hold, having ruled out both Urdiñola and a last-ditch effort by Lomas, and again expressed the view that "up to now no other [qualified] candidate has presented himself to apply for the expedition."[8]

Urdiñola's problems with the murder charges clearly served as the principal reason for Velasco to have put the New Mexico project on hold. One may, perhaps, also speculate whether Urdiñola's position as *familar* of the Holy Office of the Inquisition gave the viceroy some pause as well. During the spring of 1595, when Velasco was contemplating what to do with Urdiñola, the inquisitors of the Mexican tribunal were strongly promoting the virtues of their agent. Urdiñola, they believed, was a "very rich and honorable man" who deserved and was destined to secure the contract for the expedition to New Mexico, but for the twisted machinations of his rival, Lomas y Colmenares.[9] In view of the zeal with which the royal officials protected their prerogatives, especially in regard to missions to the frontier, it is conceivable that Velasco considered the potential for Urdiñola to have harbored dual and competing loyalties—to both the royal authorities and, perhaps more intense, the powerful Mexican inquisitors.

THE FAMILY ORIGINS OF JUAN DE OÑATE

If by the spring of 1595, Velasco still had not found a viable and trustworthy candidate to lead the expedition to establish a defensive outpost on the far northern frontier of New Mexico, his efforts were soon to be rewarded, in the form of the son of a wealthy and prominent miner from Zacatecas, Juan de Oñate. Oñate, in many ways, presented himself as the perfect person for the job. Raised in both Mexico City and the northern mining region, he was equally urbane and rustic, gentleman and adventurer. Born in Zacatecas in 1552, Oñate participated in the expansion of Spanish territory beyond Zacatecas and Pánuco—as soldier, explorer, and miner—gaining experience that he would draw on later in his career. In this sense, he followed in the footsteps of his father, Cristóbal de Oñate, who had arrived in Mexico in the wake of the conquest of Tenochtitlán by Fernando Cortés. The elder Oñate had served in a variety of administrative posts in the capital and achieved recognition for his military exploits during the Mixtón Wars against the Chichimeca Indians (1540–1542). He was counted among the founders of the city of Zacatecas and rose to great prominence as one of the pioneer miners in the region. Both father and son married into even more distinguished families, Juan entering into a union with Isabel de Tolosa Cortés Moctezuma, the granddaughter of the famous conquistador and the great-granddaughter of the vanquished Aztec emperor.[10]

Until recent years, historians portrayed Juan de Oñate's family background as not dissimilar from those of other prominent and successful adventure-seekers in sixteenth-century New Spain. Biographer Marc Simmons traced his paternal line to the Pérez and González families of the town of Oñate, in the Basque country of northern Spain, presumably of pure Old Christian origin. On the maternal side, nothing was discussed beyond the fact that the family descended from the Salazares of Granada.[11] Nor did Donald Chipman shed any further light on the family of Oñate's mother in his otherwise thorough treatment of the Oñate genealogy.[12] It was not until the late 1990s that historical scholarship began to question the long-held assumption that the first governor of New Mexico was, as the contemporary documents attempting to prove one's *limpieza de sangre* alluded, "free from all stain of Jewish or Moorish blood."

In 1998, two scholars argued that, to the contrary, Oñate did, indeed, descend from converted Jews on his maternal side. Donald T. Garate pointed to the office of treasurer of the mint and other high administrative positions held in Spain by one of Oñate's maternal great-grandfathers and great-great grandfathers, and concluded that "despite the fact that the intent of a *prueba* [proof of nobility] was to prove that the candidate had no Jewish or Moorish heritage, a close examination of the original document lends support to the premise that Oñate did have Jewish ancestry through his maternal grandmother."[13]

The other historian, José Antonio Esquibel, presented a far more comprehensive analysis of the question of the Jewish ancestry of Oñate. After conducting exhaustive genealogical research, Esquibel determined that Oñate's fourth great-grandmother had been a member of a very prominent Jewish family of Burgos: his maternal grandmother, Catalina de la Cadena y Maluenda, was the daughter of Pedro de Maluenda, whose paternal great-grandmother was María Núñez Ha-Leví, the sister of the chief rabbi of Burgos, Salomón Ha-Leví. Their father, Isaac Ha-Leví, and grandfather Abraham Ha-Leví, according to Esquibel,

> came from the kingdom of Aragón to the city of Burgos in the mid-fourteenth century. At this time the Jewish community of Burgos was regarded as the most prosperous in terms of wealth and social influence in the Christian society of Castile, a status that progressively deteriorated into one of impoverishment by the beginning of the fifteenth century. Isaac Ha-Leví and his wife Doña María had eight children born between 1352 and 1380, all raised in the Jewish faith. Several of the Ha-Leví progeny proved to be exceptional individuals in the Jewish community of Burgos, and their conversion to Christianity precipitated their establishment as a socially, politically, economically, and religiously influential extended family.[14]

Rabbi Salomón was no exception. Like many fourteenth-century rabbis, he was also proficient in the fields of law and medicine. Well respected both in Spain and abroad, he was called on to represent the interests of the Castilian Jewish community in the Vatican. But on the eve of the anti-Jewish persecutions that swept many parts of Spain in the early 1390s, Salomón Ha-Leví decided to convert from Judaism to Catholicism, along with his mother, his children, and two of his siblings, including María Núñez, the ancestor of Juan de Oñate.

Adopting a new name, Pablo de Santa María, he joined the priesthood, rose in the ranks to bishop and, finally, archbishop, and distinguished himself by his writings and diplomatic services to the Church. Two of his sons also became priests and, ultimately, bishops. Conversion to Catholicism by the Ha-Leví family opened up new opportunities for social and economic advancement, of which the succeeding generations took full advantage. María Núñez's son Alvar Rodríguez de Maluenda, the third great-grandfather of Juan de Oñate, served as *regidor* (councillor) of Burgos. His son Hernando de Maluenda held the post of treasurer of the mint of Burgos; in turn, his son, Pedro de Maluenda, Oñate's great-grandfather, was a judge.[15]

In addition to these ancestors of Oñate, the family of Pedro de Maluenda's wife, Catalina de la Cadena y Martínez de Lerma, Oñate's great-grandmother, could be traced to a Jewish background. Esquibel cited the research of Yolanda Guerrero Navarrete in his observation that the Martínez de Lermas "were originally a Jewish mercantile family" who converted to Catholicism in the late fourteenth century and prospered as a *converso* commercial family in fifteenth-century Burgos. Moreover, the Maluenda family was also of Jewish origin, Juan Garcés de Maluenda having married María Núñez Ha-Leví around the time of her conversion.[16]

To add even more to the equation, recent scholarship has determined that Viceroy Luis de Velasco, who chose Oñate to lead the expedition to New Mexico, traced his ancestry back five generations through the Álvarez de Toledo family to Jewish roots. His great-grandfather Don Alonso Álvarez de Toledo was known as one of the wealthiest and most influential of the *converso* figures at the court of the infante Enrique II in the mid-fifteenth century, serving as *contador mayor* (chief accountant) of Castilla and *regidor* of Toledo. Some sources even establish a genealogical link with the same Ha-Leví/Santa María line as that maintained by Oñate.[17]

Could Juan de Oñate have known about his family's illustrious Jewish origins? Absent any documentation that would so indicate, one is only left to guess. Garate suspected that Oñate could have had no such knowledge, pointing out that during the course of the family's efforts to prove its noble ancestry in the seventeenth century, all the witnesses "emphatically den[ied]" that the family had any Jewish background. What Garate seems to have ignored is that those offering testimony in support of their friends, families, and neighbors tended not to raise any questions that might adversely affect the outcome of the investigation. Besides, they were seldom asked about the family history beyond two or three generations, thus eliminating the need to lie about any of the Oñates of earlier generations having been Jews or first-generation *conversos*.

Nor did Garate believe that Oñate could have known anything about the history of his family beyond two or three generations, based on the premise that people today possess no such awareness, and "it would not have been any different in Oñate's day."[18] This reasoning appears flawed. In the first place, many noble families commissioned and promoted formal family histories to prove their "noble" lineages. It certainly would not have been inconceivable for members of the Oñate–Salazar family to have done so and, thus, to have known the religion of their progenitors. Moreover, Esquibel discussed the degree to which descendants of the Ha-Leví family of Burgos maintained a memory of their ancestry for more than two hundred years after the conversion of Rabbi Salomón Ha-Leví in 1390:

> The descendants of the Ha-Leví family of Burgos became so widespread and so interrelated with Castilian nobility that a royal decree was issued by King Felipe III (r. 1598–1621) in recognition of a papal brief written by Pope Clement VIII (1592–1605) accepting their *limpieza de sangre*, or purity of bloodline, and officially recognizing the Ha-Leví family as an honorable and noble family of Christian blood and faith. The papal dispensation was given because of services provided by their descendants to the Church and because the Ha-Leví were believed to be descended of the same Hebrew tribe as the Virgin Mary.[19]

On the question of whether Oñate knew about his Jewish origins, Esquibel concluded, "One can only speculate that members of the Oñate-Salazar-Mendoza-Zaldívar families of New Spain and New Galicia may have been aware of their Jewish ancestry through oral family history passed on by Oñate's mother, Doña Catalina de Salazar."[20] And if he was aware of his *converso* roots, was he a practicing crypto-Jew? Again, the contemporary documentation is silent on this question. Esquibel asserted that he was not and, indeed, that the original conversion in 1390 by Rabbi Salomón Ha-Leví and his family put to rest any such suspicions:

> Their sincere and complete acceptance of the Christian faith was solidly confirmed by the decision of Don Pablo de Santa María (formerly Salomón Ha-Leví) and two of his sons to join the clergy as ordained Catholic priests. . . .
>
> Further evidence of the Ha-Leví's sincere conversion and their rapid integration into the Christian society of Castile can be found in the public work and life of Don Alvar García de Santa María (b. 1380, Burgos), the youngest brother of Don Pablo, who enjoyed a highly distinguished career beginning in the court of Enrique III.[21]

But as the experience of the Carvajal family of Mexico City and Nuevo León demonstrates, neither the presence of priests in the family nor the participation of relatives in matters of state is inconsistent with the practice of crypto-Judaism. The placement of family members in strategic civil and religious positions not only offered an effective cover for heretical activities, but also afforded a certain degree of protection from inquisitorial prosecution.

Whether or not Juan de Oñate knew about his Jewish heritage, when he sought and accepted the royal commission to lead the expedition to New Mexico in 1595, he apparently, knowingly or unknowingly, included among the ranks of his colonists a number of New Christians seeking to avoid persecution by the Holy Office of the Inquisition, which was in the midst of its vigorous campaign against the Carvajales and the rest of the crypto-Jewish community of New Spain.

RECRUITMENT FOR THE EXPEDITION TO THE NORTH

Immediately following the formal signing of his contract with Viceroy Luis de Velasco on September 21, 1595, Juan de Oñate and his close circle of advisers—his nephews Cristóbal, Juan, and Vicente de Zaldívar—began their efforts to enlist soldiers and colonists from various parts of central Mexico and the northern mining areas for the great mission to New Mexico. Oñate's contract called for him to supply two hundred fully armed men for the enterprise, along with an extensive array of livestock and supplies. He hoped to far exceed this number of soldiers during his recruitment campaign in 1595 and 1596. But unanticipated administrative difficulties resulted in the postponement of the final authorization of the expedition until January 1598, which hampered Oñate's ability to attract and hold potential participants. Three major factors were responsible for these problems:

the replacement of Viceroy Velasco by Gaspar Zúñiga y Acevedo, conde de Monterrey, in late 1596; challenges to Oñate's candidacy by rivals, old and new, in the persons of the indefatigable Juan Bautista de Lomas y Colmenares and Spanish aristocrat Pedro Ponce de León; and, finally, the efforts of viceregal bureaucrats who seemed intent on postponing Oñate's departure.[22]

During this delay of more than two years, Oñate's recruits spent most of their time languishing in camps in Zacatecas and other parts of the northern mining region, playing the familiar military game of hurry-up-and-wait. Records from the two major inspections of the expedition—undertaken by Lope de Ulloa y Lemos at the mining town of Casco in February 1597 and by Juan de Frías Salazar at Santa Bárbara the following December—include a detailed list of colonists and thus provide abundant demographic information about those individuals who were to form the first permanent European settlement in what is today the American Southwest. Among those names can be counted *converso* survivors of Gaspar Castaño de Sosa's expedition who found themselves in central Mexico, quite possibly at no small risk during the most intense phase of the inquisitorial persecutions of the mid-1590s, and, as a consequence, were eager to join an enterprise that would take them to a remote corner of the empire. For his part, Oñate would certainly have profited greatly from the experience of those soldiers who knew well not only the territory, but also the Pueblo Indians who inhabited the lands that he was about to enter. The inclusion of these individuals would have allowed him to establish his colony on a much more stable footing.

One of these veterans of Castaño's expedition to return to New Mexico with Oñate, Juan de Victoria Carvajal, son of Juan de Carvajal, is listed as a military officer in both Ulloa's and Salazar's muster rolls. He is described as being "of medium stature [with] chestnut-colored beard." Although the record indicates that he was accompanied by his "children and family," the only members specifically named in the inspections are his sons, Gerónimo and Estevan. Other sources suggest that his wife, Isabel Holguín, daughter of Juan López Holguín and Catalina de Villanueva, was included among the party. Among the items furnished by Victoria Carvajal were a set of armor, a harquebus, four saddles, fifteen horses, and a leather shield. He also brought along a male servant.[23]

Juan Rodríguez Nieto, another survivor of Castaño's mission, joined the Oñate camp late, missing Ulloa's inspection, but arriving in time to be counted among the troops for Salazar's muster roll of December 1597. Described as being of "medium stature and somewhat gray," the forty-year-old Rodríguez brought with him a sword, a harquebus, armor for himself and his horse, nine horses, ironware, and a tent.[24] This appears to be the same Juan Rodríguez who was identified by the Mexican Inquisition as a fugitive the previous year and who was burned in effigy in the auto de fe of 1601 for practicing Judaism.[25]

Although he could not be found on either of the official muster rolls, Alonso Jaimes, whose *converso* roots were discussed earlier, served as one of Oñate's captains when his troops were stationed in Casco during Ulloa's inspection in the winter of 1597.[26] No further documentation could be found linking Jaimes with Oñate's expedition, and it is assumed that he did not make the journey to New Mexico, but remained in the Zacatecas area.[27]

In addition to those New Christian participants in Castaño's enterprise who journeyed to New Mexico with Oñate, several others among his ranks could be traced to Jewish origins or activities in Mexico and on the Iberian Peninsula. Cristóbal de Herrera, for example, signed up as a young man of nineteen. Born in Jeréz de la Frontera to Juan de Herrera, he is described in the muster roll as "tall, swarthy [and] beardless."[28] He participated in the campaign against the pueblo of Ácoma in 1598,[29] and his presence was noted in New Mexico as late as February 1601, in connection with the alleged murder of Pedro de Aguilar by Juan de Oñate.[30] Herrera did not remain long in the colony, however. At some point in the next decade, he returned to Zacatecas and lived there as a merchant. In 1614, he was denounced before the Inquisition on suspicion of practicing Judaism. During the proceedings, one of the witnesses related a conversation between him and Herrera pertaining to the arrest of eight Portuguese for teaching the Law of Moses to the Indians in Oaxaca. "The Portuguese are intelligent," Herrera was reputed to have said, "and, since the Law of Moses was attractive, that is why they are drawn to it. And that anyone who would like to could read it, and that he [Herrera] had read it."[31] He apparently survived the denunciation unscathed and three years later contracted marriage with a local woman.[32] In 1626, however, Herrera was again denounced, this time by a woman who had been told by her parents "that Cristóbal de Herrera, *vecino* of this city [Zacatecas], and married there, is the son of a woman who was sentenced by the Inquisition of Sevilla to wear the *sanbenito* for eight or ten years, and was required to work in a convent."[33] In her book about the history of the Inquisition in Zacatecas, Solange Alberro referred to Herrera as "a true Judaizer."[34]

Bartolomé Romero was another colonist who may be traced to

probable Jewish origins in Spain. Born in the eastern La Mancha town of Corral de Almaguer in 1557,[35] Romero was one of the first officers to enlist with Oñate and can be found in the muster rolls of both Ulloa and Salazar, accompanied by his wife, Lucía Robledo, daughter of Pedro Robledo and Catalina López. He is described as the son of Bartolomé Romero and as being "of good stature, swarthy [and] black bearded." He brought with him an impressive array of supplies for the expedition, including a cart with oxen, a plowshare, three coats of mail, two swords and a javelin, a lance, a harquebus, a pistol, twenty horses, some with armor, and six mules.[36] Romero served as one of Oñate's most trusted captains, representing the governor in his relations with the Pueblo Indians and testifying on his behalf before hostile royal officials. When some disgruntled soldiers conspired to desert the colony, Romero actively opposed them.[37]

Documents pertaining to Romero's hometown strongly suggest Jewish roots for the family. Before the expulsion of the Jews in 1492, the small town of Corral de Almaguer (population 1,200 in 1575)[38] included a Jewish population worthy of note.[39] A royal order issued in 1483 mandated that the village's Jews restrict themselves to living in their own quarter, indicating that they had began to spill out of their neighborhood and mingle with the Christian population.[40] The Inquisition of Cuenca was particularly active in its pursuit of crypto-Jews in Corral de Almaguer, especially in the early decades of the sixteenth century. A trial against Diego Hernández, conducted in 1518, included testimony by Juana Gómez, "wife of Romero" and fifty years old, who indicated that she was a *conversa*.[41] Assuming that the marriage between Gómez and Romero had taken place approximately thirty years earlier—that is, around 1488—both wife and husband were likely to have still been Jews.

About three generations later, in the mid- to late sixteenth century, the community's concern about the issue of *limpieza de sangre* started to manifest itself in the sacramental records, to the point that a newborn's status as a New Christian began to be referenced as part of the official baptismal record. Such documentation from Corral de Almaguer reveals the presence of several Romeros, listed either as New Christians or as godparents for New Christians.[42] Yet another Romero, Isabel, from Quintanar de la Orden, located about fourteen miles from Corral de Almaguer, was tried and convicted for practicing Judaism by the Inquisition of Cuenca in 1589.[43] Her marriage to Alonso del Campo may well have reflected the same Romero–Campo *compadrazgo* relationship demonstrated by Bartolomé Romero's family in Corral de Almaguer.

Bartolomé Romero's baptismal record, from April 1557, cites his parents as Bartolomé Romero and María de [Ad]eva. His godparents included Blas Ramírez and Juan Martínez del Campo.[44] Unfortunately, neither the baptismal records before 1539 nor any of the contemporary marriage records for Corral de Almaguer are extant, and thus it is not possible to specifically track Bartolomé's ancestors any farther back than his parents' generation. Nevertheless, the unusual nature of his mother's last name allows us to surmise that the maternal line likely derived from a prominent Jewish family, the Benadevas.[45]

Testimony from the Mexican Inquisition in 1574, originally recorded at the trial of Diego de Ocaña for *judaizante* four decades earlier, reveals valuable information about the family of Ocaña's mother, the Benadevas: "[T]his witness knows that in this city [Mexico], the Xuárez de Benadeva family, Jews of Sevilla, is widely recognized as being of the generation of Jews."[46] Records from Sevilla from around the turn of the fifteenth century are replete with references to *converso* Benadevas, some of whom fled that city, and others of whom were penanced by the Inquisition. Pedro Fernández Benadeva, for example, was cited as having been burned at the stake in 1481, while his son escaped to Rome. Other of his children remained in Sevilla, at least temporarily, living in the parish of San Bartolomé in what, in pre-expulsion times, had been within the Jewish quarter. In 1515, seven *converso* priests, including Alonso and Juan Benadeva, were reconciled by the Inquisition of Sevilla for practicing Judaism. As late as 1569, the stigma of descent from the "caste of Benadeva" was still strong enough to destroy the opportunity of Gaspar Sánchez de Villafranca, great-great-grandson of Pedro Fernández Benadeva, for promotion within the Church.[47] Life in Sevilla for the Benadevas was certainly fraught with danger in the early sixteenth century, and it would not have been surprising for members of the family to have sought more secure opportunities elsewhere, including, perhaps, the small farming community of Corral de Almaguer and, later, the far northern frontier of New Mexico.

Other participants in Oñate's expedition display more tenuous, but still very possible, links to *converso* families in Mexico, Spain, and Portugal. Diego Landín, for example, appears on Salazar's muster roll as a forty-year-old native of Coimbra, Portugal, the son of Diego González. Other documentation from the same inspection shows him as "Blandín."[48] He is likely the same person as Captain Diego González, who served under Governor Luis de Carvajal in Nuevo León in the early to mid-1580s.[49] Rather than volunteering for service in Oñate's mission to the north, Landín appears to have participated as the result of a penalty imposed on him by the *audiencia* of México. But whatever stigma may have been attached to Landín's presence on the expedition, it apparently had no effect on the level of confidence that Oñate accorded him, as he was entrusted with a packet of letters sent back to Mexico City in March 1598.[50] The governor later was prosecuted by the viceroy for allowing Landín to leave New Mexico before the completion of his sentence.[51]

Landín found himself in trouble with the inquisitorial authorities in Celaya in 1606, when he was denounced for asserting that "God, because He is God, had spoken more truth than he had, and that he had spoken as much truth as had the saints."[52] Fray Angelico Chávez suggested that Landín was the father of New Mexican colonists Domingo and Sebastián González, progenitors of the González Lobón–González Bernal–González Bas family.[53] Inquisition records from Portugal lend credence to this link, indicating that several members of the Brandón and Brandão families of Coimbra and Lisboa were penanced for practicing Judaism in the sixteenth and seventeenth centuries, including Francisco Lobó, son of Jorge Brandão; Francisca Fernandes, daughter of Duarte Brandão and María Gonçalves; and Alvaro Gomes, son of Gomes Brandão and María Gonçalves.[54] It is possible that Diego Landín also was connected with the family of Francisco López Blandón, penanced by the Mexican Inquisition in 1635 and again in 1649.[55]

Other participants in Oñate's enterprise may have had *converso* ties as well, but, due to crucial gaps in the contemporary documentation, such links will have to remain speculative at best. Baltasar Rodríguez, for example, served as Oñate's representative during the process of appraising the equipment and supplies as part of Ulloa's inspection in Casco in 1597.[56] Could he have been the same Baltasar Rodríguez who was the brother of Luis de Carvajal, el Mozo, and who had avoided arrest by the Mexican Inquisition in 1589 and been burned in effigy as a fugitive in the auto de fe of 1590? Martin A. Cohen documented Rodríguez's escape from Mexico to Madrid, where he lobbied at court to secure his brother's release, and ultimately to the Vatican to pursue the same end. The last documented communication from Italy by Rodríguez, who by this time had adopted the name David Lumbroso, is dated March 2, 1595.[57] It is conceivable that Rodríguez could have made his way back to New Spain in 1596 and, as a merchant with family ties to some of the colonists heading north, could have sought refuge on the fringes of the northern frontier.

Pedro Robledo, the father-in-law of Bartolomé Romero, also fits into this category. Born around 1537 in the small town of La Carmena, on the outskirts of Maqueda,[58] Robledo had spent much of his life in the city of Toledo, located about twenty-five miles from his hometown, before emigrating with his family in 1574 to New Spain.[59] He had served as *familiar* of the Inquisition in Toledo and had successfully applied for the same position shortly after his arrival in Mexico.[60] What motivated Robledo to gather his wife, Catalina López, four sons, and two daughters and to leave the relative security of Mexico City for the distant frontier is unknown. Robledo's family background remains a mystery, as the sacramental records of La Carmena were destroyed in the Spanish Civil War of 1936 to 1939.[61] What is known is that several families of Robledos were living in the old Jewish quarter of Toledo in the early to mid-sixteenth century[62] and were pursuing professions associated with *converso* families.[63] Unfortunately, due to the absence of specific records pertaining to Pedro's family, the common nature of the name Robledo, and the large population of Toledo, any definitive connection to the *converso* community of Toledo would be most tentative. Robledo died during the trek northward to New Mexico in 1598, but his granddaughter, Ana, the daughter of Lucía Robledo and Bartolomé Romero, carried on the Robledo name in the colony, passing it down through her children, Francisco, Juan, and Andrés Gómez Robledo.[64]

It is important to remember that, in contrast to the earlier *entradas* to New Mexico, which were designed to be temporary, the Oñate expedition signaled a firm commitment on the part of the Crown to establish a permanent colony on the far northern frontier of New Spain. While the last large foray into the region by Francisco Vázquez de Coronado almost six decades earlier had been dependent for its sustenance on supplies provided by Native Americans along the way, Oñate made certain that his enterprise was well provisioned and self-sufficient. The extensive preparations for the first major colonizing effort in the mid-1590s by Oñate mark a significant watershed in the history of New Mexico. No longer would New Mexico be considered purely as *terra incognita*, fit for only small exploratory bands of soldiers and missionaries. The commitment made by Oñate and his backers, as well as by the Crown, began a new stage in the history of the northern frontier, an obligation to establish a settlement in New Mexico, to convert the Indians, and to serve as a bulwark against potential threats from other European powers. As such, no longer would expeditions be sent northward with the expectation of living off the land. Rather, the Oñate colonizing expedition was the first to depart from north-central New Spain well provisioned with enough supplies not only to last the journey northward, but to equip the new colony with the basics of European civilization.

THE FIRST PERMANENT EUROPEAN SETTLEMENT IN NEW MEXICO

After interminable delays, the expedition finally departed from the mining town of Todos los Santos on January 21, 1598, with an estimated 460 people: 129 soldiers, an almost equal number of women and children, and about 200 others, including a mix of free and servant Indians, blacks, mestizos, and mulattos.[65] By April 20, the party had reached the Río Grande and, ten days later, just downriver from El Paso, celebrated what many regard as the first formal European Thanksgiving in what later was to become the United States.[66] It was there that Juan de Oñate, holding the dual offices of governor and *adelantado* (person who advances the frontier), issued his famous proclamation, taking possession of "all the kingdoms and provinces of New Mexico" in the name of the king.[67] The party continued up the Río Grande, crossing the dreaded *jornada del muerto* (journey of the dead man), reconnecting with the river just south of Socorro, and continuing upstream until they reached the confluence of the Río Grande and Río Chama. Oñate established his capital in this location, called San Gabriel del Yunque, just across the Río Grande from the pueblo of San Juan. Along the route, the governor solicited and accepted oaths of allegiance to the king by the various groups of Pueblo Indians who inhabited the Río Abajo and Río Arriba—the lower and upper reaches of the Río Grande.[68]

Once the headquarters was established, Oñate then set out to expand his mission. The pueblos were parceled out among the Franciscans who accompanied the expedition for teaching of Christian doctrine. To get a better understanding of the resources in the area, he assigned his officers the task of exploring the region, southeast to the Salinas province and west to Ácoma, Zuni, and the Hopi country, in search of the "South Sea"—the Pacific Ocean. All did not go smoothly in the first years of the colony's existence. At the pueblo of Ácoma, thirteen soldiers, including one of the governor's nephews, were killed after a dispute over the pueblo's supplying of provisions. To avenge their deaths and, more important, to set an example for other Pueblo Indians who might harbor any thoughts of rebellion, Oñate ordered the pueblo attacked, resulting in hundreds of Ácomas killed and many more captured. The male prisoners were sentenced to have one foot amputated, followed by twenty years of servitude. The younger men, as well as the women, endured the sentence of servitude, while the children were removed from their parents and turned over to the Franciscans for a Christian upbringing.[69]

The potential for military resistance on the part of the pueblos now very much evident, Oñate realized that in order to establish the colony on a more secure footing he would have to obtain additional support from the capital. In early 1600, he sent his most trusted soldiers, among them Juan de Victoria Carvajal, to Mexico both to convince the viceroy that New Mexico possessed sufficient material resources to justify the supplemental investment and to recruit soldiers and settlers to reinforce the fledgling settlement.

While some of Oñate's officers abandoned their commander and opted to stay in Mexico City, Victoria Carvajal, by now a seasoned veteran and a member of Oñate's council of war, remained loyal and helped direct the effort to engage fresh troops to reinforce the struggling colony in New Mexico. In the late summer of 1600, he embarked on his third, but by no means last, trip north, accompanied by seventy-two men, women, and children.[70] At some point during the campaigns in New Mexico, Victoria Carvajal must have been wounded in action, as the muster roll compiled in 1600 describes him as having a scar above his right eye.[71]

REINFORCEMENTS

Among the fresh troops of *converso* origins to head north in 1600 was a young man from the Canary Islands, Cristóbal de Brito. Born on the island of La Palma around 1575 to Tomé Yañes de la Calle and Leonor Luys, the tall and black-bearded Brito left the Canaries at an early age to seek his fortune in the New World.[72] Tomé Yañes de la Calle, the third generation to have that name, married Luys sometime before 1569.[73] The Brito name derived from his great-great-grandparents: Ines de Brito and Tomé Yañes de la Calle (I), alias Tomé Yañes de Brito. Some of their children took the surname Yañes; others, Brito; and still others, Yañes de Brito. In Cristóbal's line, the Brito surname took three generations to resurface.[74] The Brito and Yañes families were prominent merchants in the Canary Islands throughout the sixteenth century[75] and were well represented in the crypto-Jewish population, not only in the Canaries, but in Spain and Portugal as well.[76] Moreover, the Britos could be found among those families who had escaped from the Iberian Peninsula and found refuge in England in the seventeenth century.[77] In his pioneering study of Jews in the Canary Islands, Lucien Wolf cited Pedro Yañes, *portugues*, as one of "the names of Jews or persons denounced as such."[78] In consideration of the unusual surname and the timing of the denunciation, it is likely that he was the same Pedro Yañes as Cristóbal's great uncle Pedro Yañes de Brito, a merchant from La Palma who died sometime before 1554. Pedro had been in business with his brother Manuel, who carried cargos of wine, fish, and cheese from La Palma to destinations in the Caribbean.[79]

Another immigrant from La Palma with *converso* roots who enlisted with the reinforcements in 1600 was Juan Ruíz de Cáceres. Tall, eagle-faced, and heavy-bearded, Ruíz is listed in the muster roll as a native of that island, born around 1570.[80] He can be identified as the son of Pedro Ruíz and Margarida Martín, and the grandson of Luisa de Carmona and Juan Ruíz, a prominent La Palma merchant who, like the family of Cristóbal de Brito, was engaged in importing and exporting merchandise.[81] Luisa was the sister of Catalina de Carmona and Diego de Carmona, all of La Palma. These siblings were undoubtedly descendants of the *converso* silversmith Diego Carmona, born around 1465 and married to Isabel de Carmona. Diego, Isabel, and their entire family were convicted and reconciled by the Holy Office of the Inquisition of Sevilla for practicing Judaism. They fled to the Canary Islands, where they had ten children, five of whom survived, including a Catalina de Carmona. A son, Gonzalo, married María de Casañas, the daughter of a *converso* from Orihuela, Spain, and lived on the island of La Palma. They very likely were the parents of Luisa and thus the great-grandparents of colonist Juan Ruíz de Caceres.[82]

The reinforcements who arrived in New Mexico in December 1600 helped stabilize the fragile colony. But by the summer of 1601, Oñate had left on an unsuccessful mission eastward in search of the mythical kingdom of Quivira and had reached as far as Kansas before realizing the chimerical nature of the quest. During his absence, a rebellion broke out among the ranks, resulting in a significant number of his settlers abandoning the province.[83] Many of his troops remained loyal, however, and offered testimony in support of the governor.[84] Bartolomé Romero was one of seven colonists who penned the following letter to the king backing up Oñate and advocating support for a transition from a military encampment to a permanent civilian settlement in New Mexico:

> We come to these kingdoms of New Mexico by order of your majesty and have served here with our goods and persons in the company of Governor Don Juan de Oñate among the barbarous [*sic*] natives in order to pacify the land and to get them to acknowledge your majesty as their true master and king. The benefits thus

far derived have been so small and our losses so great that we have decided, as befitting the royal service of your majesty, to build a villa here in order that the foundations of this colony might be more stable. So, as faithful vassals of your majesty, we sought means of settling the land when others were abandoning it, but because of our large expenditures we were unable to transform our military organization to a civilian one until now. If this change had not been made, we would have been compelled to turn back, forced by our poverty and our great privations. If your majesty does not deign to give us some aid, as the governor asks, it will not be possible, even if were are ready to die a thousand times in your service, to endure this situation beyond the period of five years, the time agreed upon in the original contract for earning the right to enjoy our privileges.

The governor is unable to help us because, as a loyal subject, he has spent his wealth and that of his relatives serving your majesty in these first settlements and in discovering new ones toward the South sea [Pacific Ocean], from which he has just returned with his men. These services exacted many hardships and expenditures, and unless your majesty favors us all, this land cannot be settled nor can we obtain the increase of the royal crown that we so greatly hoped for. We humbly ask for instructions, as our lives, honor, and wealth will always be at your service. May the Lord preserve your majesty, as your kingdoms and subjects need. New Mexico, January 1, 1602.

[signed] Alonso Gómez, Bartolomé Romero, Juan de Ynojosa, Antonio Gutiérrez Bocanegra, Gonzalo Hernández. Before me, Alonso Varela, chief notary of the *cabilido* [All with rubrics][85]

Oñate, for his part, also turned to the Crown for help. Taking a two-pronged approach, he sent his nephew Vicente de Zaldívar to Mexico, while his brother Alonso de Oñate appealed to royal authorities in Spain. Although his efforts were neither as successful nor as timely as he had hoped, Alonso de Oñate, with the assistance of Zaldívar, who had sailed to Spain to help with the lobbying effort, received permission in the summer of 1603 to recruit some forty ship pilots, musketeers, and shipwrights to reinforce the colony in New Mexico.[86] By March 20, 1604, Alonso had gathered in the port of Sevilla thirty-one men (one with his wife and children) from various parts of Spain and Portugal, ready to embark on the transatlantic voyage.[87]

One of these recruits, the Portuguese Francisco Gómez, was to be accused of practicing Judaism in New Mexico some decades later. The ethnic origins and religious persuasions of the others are unknown. Alonso de Oñate's strenuous efforts to protect these colonists from the prying eyes of the Inquisition officials at the port of Veracruz on the arrival of the ship in June 1604, however, suggests that he may well have been aware of the suspicious backgrounds of some members of the group.

When the ship carrying the reinforcements docked at Veracruz on June 30, it was met by an agent of the Holy Office of the Inquisition, a thirty-six-year-old native of Oviedo, Andrés Menéndez de Bovela y Solis, who boarded the vessel and proceeded to conduct what he expected to be a routine investigation of the passengers and cargo. Both Menéndez and the ship's captain, Juan Núñez, knew the procedure. Núñez gathered the requisite papers that he had brought from Inquisition officials in Sevilla, and placed them on a table for Menéndez's inspection. The captain then informed Menéndez that among the cargo were several boxes of books that belonged to some of Oñate's soldiers. The agent responded that none of these boxes was to be released until he had had the opportunity to inspect them, under penalty of excommunication and a substantial fine of 100 *ducados*.

But at that point, a royal treasury official, Pedro Coco Calderón, intervened, demanding that Menéndez specify what he was looking for. The representative of the Inquisition simply responded that he was under instructions to examine the boxes that belonged to the soldiers and other passengers. Coco then inquired sharply why the agent was meddling into matters that were under his jurisdiction. As the argument between the two bureaucrats escalated, Alonso de Oñate entered the scene and, according to testimony offered by Menéndez, shoved him, demanding that he "get out of here! For what reason are you hanging around my boxes?" Oñate, upset with the agent's answer, angrily repeated his demand that Menéndez vacate the premises.[88]

Correspondence from Menéndez's superior to the inquisitors in Mexico City places Alonso de Oñate's actions in a broader perspective. Fray Francisco Carranco, *comisario* of the Holy Office in Veracruz, in complaining about the rude manner in which Menéndez had been treated, cited the precise instructions that he had been given the previous year. In order to counter the spread of heretical books published in countries other than Spain that were finding their way into New Spain through the port of Veracruz, Carranco and his staff had been ordered to inspect each arriving ship, confiscate the offending books, and arrest those who carried them. He emphasized the need to inspect the books carried by *gente sospechosa* (suspicious people), particularly applying this appellation to the Portuguese and other foreigners on board:

> This order of yours I obey, especially as it applies to the ships arriving from Spain, and with regard to the inspection of the ship chartered by Alonso de Oñate, with soldiers and other persons destined for New Mexico, whose passengers brought many chests, and because they are people not known [to us], nor are they people who provide us with any sense of security, due to their communication with the English in Sevilla, I am moved to order that they should not be unloaded on shore without requesting my permission, so that I may inspect them and ascertain if any of them contained any of the aforesaid [heretical] books, *given that among the aforesaid passengers were included Portuguese* and those from kingdoms other than Castilla [emphasis added].[89]

Examined in the context of the list of colonists, the actions taken by Alonso de Oñate and the concerns expressed by the Inquisition officials in Veracruz are quite telling. Of the thirty-five colonists on board, all but one, the Portuguese Francisco Gómez, were born in Spain. Yet Carranco noted the suspicious character of the Portuguese and other foreign passengers, indicating that a number of those brought over by Oñate, despite their Spanish birth, were regarded as outsiders and potential heretics. And, in view of the Inquisition's linking of Portuguese and Jews, the preoccupation of the *comisario* with the questionable religious beliefs of some of these passengers leads to the strong suggestion that not only Francisco Gómez, but others as well, may have been New Christians. The attempt by Oñate to bully his way past the Inquisition officials in Veracruz lends credence to this idea. It is curious to note that of the thirty-five people recruited by Oñate to reinforce his brother's colony, only Gómez appears to have arrived in New Mexico.

The lack of support from Spain and Mexico, the failure to find significant lodes of precious metals, the allegations of abuse of the Pueblo Indians, and the dissension among the ranks of the colonists all combined to seal the fate of Juan de Oñate as governor of New Mexico. By 1607, both Oñate and the royal authorities had come to the same conclusion. Before the viceroy got around to enforcing the king's order to remove Oñate from office, the governor had submitted his resignation.[90]

As one chapter of New Mexico's history closed, another opened. Many of the Spanish and Portuguese men, women, and children who had emigrated to the far northern outpost in the various waves of settlement between 1598 and 1604 stayed on and formed the nucleus of the farming and ranching colony that was to cope with struggles—material, political, and spiritual—through the seventeenth century. Among those who persevered were the descendants of crypto-Jews who had successfully evaded arrest by the Inquisitions of Spain, Portugal, and Mexico by finding refuge in this remote community. Over the succeeding decades, they would be joined by more coreligionists, some of whom would find relative peace and security, while others would find their ethnicity and observances tangled up in the nasty web of frontier politics.

NOTES

1. For a more extensive discussion of the Leyva de Bonilla–Gutiérrez de Humaña expedition, see George P. Hammond and Agapito Rey, *The Rediscovery of New Mexico: The Expeditions of Chamuscado, Espejo, Castaño de Sosa, Morlete, and Leyva de Bonilla and Humaña* (Albuquerque: University of New Mexico Press, 1966), pp. 48–50.
2. George P. Hammond and Agapito Rey, *Don Juan de Oñate, Colonizer of New Mexico, 1595–1628* (Albuquerque: University of New Mexico Press, 1953), p. 4.
3. Asiento y capitulación que hizo la Audiencia de México con Cristóbal Martín, sobre ir, en persona, al descubrimiento, pacificación y población de Nuevo México, bajo las condiciónes que expone, Mexico City, October 26, 1583, Sección de Patrononato, legajo 22, R. 6, Archivo General de Indias, Seville (hereafter cited as AGI).
4. Asiento y capitulación que el virrey de Nueva España, Marqués de Villamanrique, hizo con Juan Bautista de Lomas Colmenares, sobre el descubrimiento y población de las provincias del Nuevo México, Mexico, March 11, 1589, Sección de Patrononato, legajo 22, R. 8, AGI; Capitulaciones hechas por Juan Baptista de Lomas Colmenares con el virrey de Nueva España, Marques de Villamanrique, sobre el descubrimiento de Nuevo México, Mexico, February 15, 1589, Sección de Patrononato, legajo 22, R. 9, AGI. Marc Simmons concluded that Lomas "aimed at nothing less than creation of a semiautonomous principality on the Río Grande," demanding huge territorial and administrative authority (*The Last Conquistador: Juan de Oñate and the Settling of the Far Southwest* [Norman: University of Oklahoma Press, 1991], pp. 55–56). See also Vito Alessio Robles, *Francisco de Urdiñola y el norte de la Nueva España* (Mexico City: Imprenta Mundial, 1931), pp. 195–196.
5. Alessio Robles, *Francisco de Urdiñola*, pp. 217–224; Simmons, *Last Conquistador*, pp. 56–58; Richard E. Greenleaf, "The Little War of Guadalajara—1587–1590," *New Mexico Historical Review* 43 (1968): 131.
6. Alessio Robles, *Francisco de Urdiñola*, pp. 231–232; Simmons, *Last Conquistador*, p. 58. See also Ynformación de la limpieza del linaje del Capitán Francisco de Urdiñola, natural de la provincia de Guipúzcoa, y Leonor de Lois,

su muger, vecinos del Río Grande y Mazapíl. Familiar del Santo Oficio, Mexico, September 1592, Ramo de Inquisición, tomo 197, exp. 6, Archivo General de la Nación, Mexico City (hereafter cited as AGN); Documentos relativos al proceso contra el Capitán Francisco de Urdiñola, familiar, por homicidio de Domingo Landaverde, Las Nieves, Zacatecas, October 1593, Ramo de Inquisición, tomo 214, exp. 20, AGN; and Proceso criminal sobre competición de jurisdición con la Real Audiencia de Guadalaxara contra el Capitán Francisco de Urdiñola, familiar del Santo Oficio de la Inquisición de México, 1595, Sección de Inquisición, legajo 1734, no. 5, Archivo Histórico Nacional, Madrid (hereafter cited as AHN).

7. Viceroy Luis de Velasco to the king, Mexico, January 30, 1595, fol. 1v, Sección de Audiencia de México, legajo 23, N. 4, AGI.

8. Viceroy Luis de Velasco to the king, Mexico, April 6, 1595, item 27, Sección de Audiencia de México, legajo 23, N. 13, AGI.

9. [Correspondence between Supreme Council of the Inquisition and Mexican Tribunal], 1595–1603, libro 1049, fol. 7r, Sección de Inquisición, AHN.

10. For details on the life of Cristóbal de Oñate and the early years of Juan de Oñate, see Simmons, *Last Conquistador*, pp. 17–47; George P. Hammond, *Don Juan de Oñate and the Founding of New Mexico* (Santa Fe: El Palacio Press, 1927), pp. 15–18; and Hammond and Rey, *Don Juan de Oñate, Colonizer*, p. 6.

11. Simmons, *Last Conquistador*, pp. 13–32.

12. Donald Chipman, "The Oñate-Moctezuma-Zaldivar Families of Northern New Spain," *New Mexico Historical Review* 52 (1977): 297–310.

13. Donald T. Garate, "Juan de Oñate's *Prueba de Caballero*, 1625: A Look at His Ancestral Heritage," *Colonial Latin American Historical Review* 7 (1998):132–133, 144.

14. José Antonio Esquibel, "New Light on the Jewish-Converso Ancestry of Don Juan de Oñate: A Research Note," *Colonial Latin American Historical Review* 7 (1998):182–183.

15. Ibid., pp. 183–186; Judith Gale Krieger, "Pablo de Santa María: His Epoch, Life, and Hebrew and Spanish Literary Production" (Ph.D. diss., University of California, Los Angeles, 1988), p. 71. Krieger's dissertation offers an excellent detailed account of the life, times, and writings of Salomón Ha-Leví/Pablo de Santa María.

16. Esquibel, "New Light," pp. 182–183, citing Yolanda Guerrero Navarette, *Organización y gobierno en Burgos durante el reinado de Enrique IV de Castilla, 1453–1476* (Madrid: Universidad Autónoma, 1986), pp. 164–166.

17. José Antonio Esquibel, "The Álvarez de Toledo Family" (manuscript, Hispanic Genealogical Research Center of New Mexico, Albuquerque), pp. 1–6.

18. Garate, "Juan de Oñate's *Prueba de Caballero*," pp. 141–142.

19. Esquibel, "New Light," p. 187, citing Ángel Montenegro Duque, José Luis Moreno Peña, and Sabino Nebreda Pérez, *Historia de Burgos: Edad media* (Burgos: Caja de Ahorros Municipal de Burgos, 1987), p. 422; and Antonio Domínguez Ortíz, *Los conversos de orígen judio despues de la expulsión* (Madrid, 1955), p. 79.

20. Esquibel, "New Light," p. 187.

21. Ibid., p. 185.

22. For details on these developments, see Simmons, *Last Conquistador*, pp. 58–89; Hammond, *Don Juan de Oñate*, pp. 18–89; and Hammond and Rey, *Don Juan de Oñate, Colonizer*, pp. 7–16, 42–93, 169–198.

23. Hammond and Rey, *Don Juan de Oñate, Colonizer*, pp. 153, 280, 294; David H. Snow, *New Mexico's First Colonists: The 1597–1600 Enlistments for New Mexico Under Juan de Oñate, Adelante [Adelantado] and Gobernador* (Albuquerque: Hispanic Genealogical Research Center of New Mexico, 1996), pp. 25, 30; *History of New Mexico by Gaspar Pérez de Villagrá, Alcalá, 1610*, trans. Gilberto Espinosa (Los Angeles: Quivira Society, 1933), p. 225; Fray Angelico Chávez, *Origins of New Mexico Families in the Spanish Colonial Period* (Santa Fe: Gannon, 1975), pp. 14–15.

24. Hammond and Rey, *Don Juan de Oñate, Colonizer*, pp. 272–273, 290.

25. Seymour B. Liebman, *The Inquisitors and the Jews in the New World: Summaries of Processos, 1500–1810, and Bibliographic Guide* (Coral Gables, Fla.: University of Miami Press, 1974), p. 130; Alfonso Toro, ed., *Los judíos en la Nueva España: Documentos del siglo XVI correspondientes al ramo de Inquisición* (Mexico City: Archivo General de la Nación y Fondo de Cultura Económica, 1932, 1993), pp. 12, 62, which lists the trials of Ruy Díaz Nieto and Juan Rodríguez in succession as *expedientes* 1 and 2 of Ramo de Inquisición, tomo 157, AGN.

26. Hammond and Rey, *Don Juan de Oñate, Colonizer*, pp. 130, 148; Snow, *New Mexico's First Colonists*, pp. 20, 38.

27. Captain Alonso Xaime[s] is cited as *padrino* for the marriage of Francisco Álvaro and Juana Quintero, October 4, 1624, Libro de matrimonios, 1605–1626, fol. 88v, Archivo Parroquial de Zacatecas, Mexico.

28. Hammond and Rey, *Don Juan de Oñate, Colonizer*, p. 297.

29. Villagrá, *History of New Mexico*, p. 224.

30. Hammond and Rey, *Don Juan de Oñate, Colonizer*, p. 1130.

31. Causa contra Cristóbal de Herrera, mercader, vecino de la ciudad de Zacatecas, 1614, testimony of Julian Rozo, May 9, 1614, fols. 171–200, Ramo de Inquisición, tomo 309, AGN, typescript in Liebman Papers, box 2, vol. 5, pp. 194–197, Latin American Library, Tulane University, New Orleans. Both documents indicate that Herrera was from Jeréz de la Frontera, the son of Juan de Herrera. Seymour B. Liebman incorrectly attributed the quote to Rozo (*The Jews in New Spain: Faith, Flame, and the Inquisition* [Coral Gables, Fla.: University of Miami Press, 1970], p. 208) and incorrectly cited that Herrera was accused of teaching the Law of Moses to the Indians (*Inquisitors and the Jews in the New World*, p. 86).

32. Marriage of Cristóbal de Herrera and Bernardina de Porras, August 15, 1617, Libro de matrimonios, Archivo Parroquial de Zacatecas.

33. Testificaciónes procedentes de diversas comisaros denuncias declaraciónes, y otros asuntos todos concernientes al Sto. Oficio con su índice alfabético y foliado particularmente del 1 a 370, deposición de Juana Bautista Conte, biuda, contra Xptóbal de Herrera, mercader, Zacatecas, May 4, 1626, fols. 154 (287) r–v, Ramo de Inquisición, tomo 356, exp. 6, AGN.

34. Solange Alberro, *Inquisición y sociedad en México, 1571–1700* (Mexico City: Fondo de Cultura Económica, 1988), pp. 405–406.

35. Baptism of Bartolomé Romero, April 5–7, 1557, Libro primero de bautismos, 1539–1574, fol. 359v, Corral de Almaguer, AHN. The part of the page indicating the date is torn, but the previous entry is April 5, and the subsequent entry is April 7.

36. Expediente de concesión de licencia para pasar a Nueva España a favor de Pedro Robledo, vecino de Carmena, con su muger, Catalina López, y a sus hijos, Ana, Diego, Luis y Lucía, y a su sobrino Luis, a vivir con sus primos, Miguel de Sandoval y Catalina Sánchez, vecinos de México, 1574, Sección de Contratación, legajo 2055, no. 77, AGI; Hammond and Rey, *Don Juan de Oñate, Colonizer*, pp. 153, 264–265, 293; Snow, *New Mexico's First Colonists*, pp. 29, 42; Chávez, *Origins of New Mexico Families*, p. 95. Lucía was also known as Luisa.

37. Hammond and Rey, *Don Juan de Oñate, Colonizer*, pp. 708–711, citing [Report of the people who remained in New Mexico], 1601, testimony of Bartolomé Romero, San Gabriel, October 3, 1601, Sección de Audiencia de México, legajo 26, AGI.

38. *Relaciones de pueblos del obispado de Cuenca* (Cuenca: Diputación Provincial de Cuenca, 1983), p. 443.

39. José Luis Lacave, *Juderías y sinagogas españolas* (Madrid: Editorial Mapfre, 1992), p. 317.

40. "Carta a las justicias de Corral de Almaguer para que se obligue a los judíos a vivir en el recinto señalado, November 24, 1483" (no. 1351), in Pilar León Tello, ed., *Los judíos de Toledo* (Madrid: Consejo Superior de Investigaciones Científicas, 1979), vol. 2, p. 485, citing Luis Suárez Fernández, ed., *Documentos acerca de la expulsión de los judíos* (Valladolid: Consejo Superior de Investigaciones Científicas, 1964), pp. 212–213; and Registro General de Sello, fol. 69, Archivo General de Simancas.

41. Proceso de Diego Hernández, cristiano nuevo del Corral de Almaguer, judaismo, relajado, 1518, fol. 47r, Archivo de la Inquisición, legajo 71, exp. 1044, Archivo Diocesano de Cuenca (hereafter cited as ADC). Gómez's testimony is the source of some confusion, as three folios later, at fol. 50r, she is described as a *xpiana vieja* (Old Christian).

42. See, for example, baptism of Alonso, hijo de Alonso Romero y Ana Fernández [in margin: *cristiano nuevo*], March 26, 1581, fol. 19r; baptism of Lucía, hija de Andrés González y María Fernández, cristianos nuevos, compadres: Andrés Romero y Marí Romero, hijos de Sebastián Romero, July 8, 1589, fol. 19r; and baptism of Luis, hijo de Luisa, cristiana nueva (no tiene padre), compadres: Bernardino Díaz y su mujer, Polonia Romero, May 27, 1590, fol. 263r, all in Libro tercero de bautismos, 1580–1599, Corral de Almaguer, AHN. The Libro segundo de bautismos (1574–1578) was too deteriorated to examine, and thus any relevant information that may be in it is lost to history.

43. Proceso de Isabel Romero, muger de Alonso del Campo, Quintinar de la Orden, judaísmo, reconciliada, 1589, legajo 323, exp. 4642, ADC.

44. Baptism of Bartolomé Romero, April 5–7, 1557, Libro primero de bautismos,

fol. 359v, Libros de bautismos, Corral de Almaguer, AHN. Romero's mother is cited as María de Eva, but other baptismal documents indicate that María's last name was Adeva. See, for example, baptism of María, hija de Alonso Crespo and María de Adeva, January 12, 1558, where the *padrina* is listed as "María de Adeva, mujer de Bartolomé Romero" (fol. 62v). Juan Martínez del Campo and Catalina Martínez, the wife of Pedro Martínez del Campo, served as *padrinos* for the baptism of Bartolomé's younger brother, Juan, September 12, 1559 (fol. 16v).

45. The name Adeva/Benadeva may have several different etymological explanations. The prefix *ben* is the Hebrew word for "son of." Gutierre Tibón cites the name Benadiba as a Sephardic Jewish name from Morocco, deriving from (son of) Adiba, which, in turn, derives from the Arabic word for either jackal (*adib*) or wolf (*adz-dzib*) (*Diccionario etimológico comparado de los apellidos españoles, hispanoamericanos y filipinos* [Mexico City: Fondo de Cultura Económica, 1992], p. 4). Other possible Hebrew derivations might include Ben Adiv, from *adiv*, meaning "cultured or literate," and Ben Nadiv, from *nadiv*, translated as "prince, noble, or generous." Another potential origin might be the Moorish Spanish *bena diba* (good pearl), a vernacular allusion to the Hebrew name of some fifteenth-century Jewish families in the Iberian Peninsula (Francine Landau and Amir Shomroni, e-mail messages to author, April and October 2003).

46. Autos y diligencias hechas por los sanbenitos antiguos y recientes y postura de los que sean de relajados por este Santo Oficio, México, 1574–1632, testimony of Fray Antonio Roldán, México, July 6, 1574, fols. 220v–221r, Ramo de Inquisición, tomo 77, exp. 35, AGN. For details of the trial of Diego de Ocaña, see Richard E. Greenleaf, *The Mexican Inquisition of the Sixteenth Century* (Albuquerque: University of New Mexico Press, 1969), pp. 35–37; and Arnold Wiznitzer, "Crypto-Jews in Mexico During the Sixteenth Century," *American Jewish Historical Quarterly* 41 (1962): 168–214.

47. Juan Gil, *Los conversos y la inquisición sevillana* (Seville: Universidad de Sevilla, 2000), vol. 2, pp. 37, 104–105, 116, 135–137, 330–331.

48. Hammond and Rey, *Don Juan de Oñate, Colonizer*, pp. 227–228, 300.

49. Ynformación resibida de officio en la audiencia real del nuevo reyno de galicia contra lo que hiso de parte Luis de Caravajal de la Cueva, governador y capitán general del nuevo reyno de León va al real consejo de las yndias, 1587, testimony of Capitán Diego González, Guadalajara, September 1, 1587, fol. 48r, Sección de Audiencia de Guadalajara, legajo 47, N. 47, AGI. González testified that he was approximately thirty years old in 1587, placing his date of birth around 1557, which correlates with the information offered by Diego Landín in Salazar's muster roll of 1597. Since the roster cites his paternal family name as González, it is likely that Diego Landín and Diego González were the same person.

50. Hammond, *Don Juan de Oñate*, p. 93; Hammond and Rey, *Don Juan de Oñate, Colonizer*, p. 312.

51. Hammond and Rey, *Don Juan de Oñate, Colonizer*, p. 1110.

52. Contra Diego Landín, por aver dicho que Diós por ser Diós avía dicho mas verdad que el y que dezía tanta verdad como avían dicho los santos, Celaya,

September 24–November 8, 1606, fols. 372–373, Ramo de Inquisición, tomo 171, exp. 111, AGN.

53. Chávez, *Origins of New Mexico Families*, p. 39.

54. Processo de Francisco Lobo, 1604, Coimbra, no. 2838; Processo de Francisca Fernandes, 1535, Coimbra, no. 4345; Processo de Alvaro Gomes, 1547, Lisboa, no. 191, all in Secção de Inquisição, Arquivo Nacional da Torre do Tombo, Lisbon (hereafter cited as ANTT). Blandín and Brandón (and, presumably, Brandão) are variations of the same name. See Tibón, *Dicciónario etimológico*, p. 43.

55. Liebman, *Inquisitors and the Jews in the New World*, p. 48. Blandín and Blandón are variations of the same name. See Tibón, *Dicciónario etimológico*, p. 43.

56. Hammond and Rey, *Don Juan de Oñate, Colonizer*, pp. 102, 108, 130, 132.

57. Martin A. Cohen, *The Martyr: Luis de Carvajal, a Secret Jew in Sixteenth-Century Mexico* (Philadelphia: Jewish Publication Society of America, 1973), pp. 182–186, 233, 265, 332 n.43. Liebman indicated that Rodríguez had taken the name Jacob Lumbroso (*Jews in New Spain*, p. 193; see also Liebman, *Inquisitors and the Jews in the New World*, pp. 55, 134). At times, the inquisitors expected crypto-Jews to return to Mexico after attempting to secure the freedom of their relatives in Spain. See Cohen, *Martyr*, p. 264.

58. Hammond and Rey, *Don Juan de Oñate, Colonizer*, p. 290.

59. Chávez, *Origins of New Mexico Families*, p. 93; Expediente de concession de licencia para pasar a Nueva España a favor de Pedro Robledo, vecino de Carmena, Sección de Indiferente, legajo 2055, no. 77, AGI.

60. Pedro Robledo, familiar de la Inquisición de Toledo, pide que se le admita información de su título y que se le nobre familiar en México, 1591, fol. 5, Ramo de Inquisición, tomo 213, exp. 19, AGN.

61. Parish priest, Asunción de Nuestra Señora, personal communication, September 1999.

62. Baptism of Luisa, hija de Gaspar Rodríguez y María Sedeno, . . . comadre mayor: Magdalena de Robledo, March 28, 1566, Libro de bautismos, 1563–1572, fol. 97r; marriage of Benito Ramos con Ysabel de Bargas, compadres: Francisco López y Ysabel de Robledo, August 11, 1574, Libro de matrimonios, 1574–1641; marriage of Juan Sánchez de Robledo con María de Vargas, testigos: Diego Álbarez y Sayabedra y Melchor Díaz, October 27, 1577, Libro de matrimonios, 1574–1641, all in Parroquia de Santo Tomé, Toledo; Linda Martz and Julio Porres, *Toledo y los toledanos en 1561* (Toledo: Patronato "José María Cuadrado," del Consejo Superior de Investigaciones Científicas, 1974), app., doc. 1, "Relación de los vecinos que parece que ay en la Ciudad de Toledo en este presente año de Mil y Quinientos y Sesenta y Uno (Archivo General de Simancas, . . . Hacienda, serie 2, legajo 183)," listing four Robledo families in the parishes of Santo Tomé, San Martín, and San Román, which composed a large portion of the Jewish and, later, *converso* quarter of Toledo. Lacave pointed out that, in contrast to other communities in Spain, the old Jewish quarter of Toledo was not exclusively inhabited by Jews (*Juderías y sinagogas españolas*, pp. 294–309). Nevertheless, he continued, Jews composed a majority of the population in neighborhoods like Santo Tomé and San Román. See also Linda Martz, "Relaciónes entre

conversos y cristianos viejos en Toledo en la edad moderna: Unas perspectivas distintas," *Toletum* 37 (1997): 49–51.

63. [Juan Robledo, apothecary of Toledo, rents shops in the Plaza de San Salvador from Domingo Pérez], June 11, 1567, fol. 586v, Notarías, Bernardino de Navarra, legajo 1973, Archivo Provincial de Toledo. The parish of San Salvador was also one with a large concentration of *conversos* in the sixteenth century. See Martz, "Relaciónes entre conversos y cristianos viejos en Toledo," pp. 49–51.

64. For more on their lives and their experiences with the Holy Office of the Inquisition, see chap. 5.

65. The number and ethnic composition of the recruits are based on calculations derived from Snow, *New Mexico's First Colonists.*

66. Hammond, *Don Juan de Oñate*, pp. 94–95; Hammond and Rey, *Don Juan de Oñate, Colonizer*, pp. 16, 314–315; Simmons, *Last Conquistador*, pp. 100–101; Leon Metz, "El Paso Can Take Pride in First Thanksgiving," *El Paso Times*, March 29, 1998, p. 15. Although the ceremony took place on the right bank of the Río Grande, the river has changed course over the past four centuries, placing the site today on the United States side of the present border with Mexico.

67. Hammond and Rey, *Don Juan de Oñate, Colonizer*, pp. 329–336.

68. Hammond, *Don Juan de Oñate*, pp. 95–105; Hammond and Rey, *Don Juan de Oñate, Colonizer*, pp. 16–17, 315–323, 337–353; Simmons, *Last Conquistador*, pp. 101–11.

69. Hammond, *Don Juan de Oñate*, pp. 106–123; Hammond and Rey, *Don Juan de Oñate, Colonizer*, pp. 17–22, 428–479; Simmons, *Last Conquistador*, pp. 133–146.

70. Hammond, *Don Juan de Oñate*, pp. 124–130; Hammond and Rey, *Don Juan de Oñate, Colonizer*, pp. 23–24, 512–579; Simmons, *Last Conquistador*, pp. 146–148, 152.

71. Hammond and Rey, *Don Juan de Oñate, Colonizer*, pp. 542, 553, citing Inspection made by Don Juan de Gordejuela and Juan Sotelo, San Bartolomé, August 26–28, 1600.

72. Hammond and Rey, *Don Juan de Oñate, Colonizer*, p. 551, citing Inspection by Gordejuela and Sotelo, August 28, 1600. Hammond and Rey mistranscribed the name of Brito's father in the original record as Tremiñez de la Calle. Based on research in the Archivo Histórico Diocesano de La Laguna de Tenerife; Iglesia del Salvador, Santa Cruz de la Palma; and Archivo-Biblioteca José Pérez Vidal, Santa Cruz de la Palma, his name should read Tomé Yañes or Tomiañes.

73. Baptism of Juana, hija de Pedro Luys y Leónor Francisca, vecinos de la Breña, padrinos: Tomé Yañes de la Calle y su muger, Leonor Luys, April 7, 1569, Libro primero de bautismos, fol. 55v, Iglesia del Salvador, Santa Cruz de la Palma.

74. This genealogy is based on research conducted in various civil and church records in the Canary Islands.

75. Luis Agustín Hernández Martín, *Protocolos de Domingo Pérez, escribano público*

de La Palma (1546–1533) (Santa Cruz de la Palma: Caja General de Ahorros de Canarias, 1999), nos. 7, 19, 27, 38, 57, 84–85, 89–91, 626–627, 631, 720, 822.

76. Relación de las personas que salieron a el auto público de la fe que se zelebró por el Santo Oficio de la inquisición de Sevilla en la Plaza de San Francisco della día de el Glorioso Apostol San Andrés de este Presente año de 1624, judaizantes: no. 9, Gaspar Fernández de Brito, vecino de Sevilla, portugues, descendiente de cristianos nuevos de judíos, 1624, Sección de Inquisición, legajo 2075, pt. 2, exp. 31, AHN; Processo contra Diego López de Perea, vecino de la ciudad de Guadalajara, judaizante, Toledo, 1543, testimony of Francisco Díaz de Olmedilla, implicating Juan de Brito, Guadalajara, July 31, 1518, Sección de Inquisición, legajo 160, exp. 9, AHN; Culpas de Judaismo: Culpas vindas das inquisições espanholas contra judaiçantes de Portugal; correspondencia das referidas inquisições; listas dos acusados por culpas diversas, 1587–1635; relación de personas que estan presas en el Santo Oficio de la Inquisición de Sevilla por ser observantes de la ley de Moysen . . . [no date, but placed between documents dated 1604 and 1623]; Diego de Brito, natural de la ciudad de Bejar de officio de sedero que de presente residia en Sevilla, de hedad de 60 años, Secção de Inquisição, Coimbra, livro 70, ANTT.

77. Cecil Roth, *A Life of Menasseh Ben Israel: Rabbi, Printer, and Diplomat* (Philadelphia: Jewish Publication Society of America, 1934), p. 257, citing Domingo Váez de Brito/Abraham Israel de Brito as a member of the "Marrano colony" of London in the seventeenth century.

78. Lucien Wolf, ed., *Judíos en las Islas Canarias: Calendario de los casos extraídos de los Archivos de la Inquisición canaria de la colección del Marqués de Bute* (Tenerife: Editorial J.A.D.L., 1988), p. 121, referring to vol. 6, 1st ser. (1527–1560).

79. Wolf cited the denunciation of Pedro Yañes as occurring between 1527 and 1560 (*Judíos en las Islas Canarias*, p. 121). Cristóbal de Brito's great-uncle Pedro Yañes de Brito was born before 1526 and was deceased as of December 20, 1554. See Hernández Martín, *Protocolos de Domingo Pérez*, nos. 84, 85, 89, 90, 627.

80. Hammond and Rey, *Don Juan de Oñate, Colonizer*, p. 551, citing Inspection by Gordejuela and Sotelo, August 28, 1600.

81. Baptism of Ana, hija de Pedro Ruíz y Margarida Martín, September 30, 1571, Libro primero de bautismos, 1546–1605, fol. 84v, Iglesia del Salvador, Santa Cruz de La Palma. No baptismal records could be found for Juan Ruíz de Cáceres, but—given the date, the name of the father, and the information in the muster roll of 1600 identifying Pedro Ruíz as his father—Ana was likely the sister of Juan. Hernández Martín, *Protocólos de Domingo Pérez*, nos. 338, 339, November 4, 1553, citing Juan Ruíz married to Luisa de Carmona, deceased, with children: Pedro, Melchora, and Catalina. The Cáceres name appears to have derived from some tangled branches of the family tree, where Lucas de Riberol, both the brother-in-law and the nephew-in-law of the elder Juan Ruíz, was married to María de Cáceres, daughter of Alonso de Cáceres and Violanta Infante (no. 108, August 26, 1546).

82. Luis Alberto Anaya Hernández, *Judeoconversos e Inquisición en las Islas Canarias,*

1402–1605 (Las Palmas: Cabildo Insular de Gran Canaria, 1996), pp. 153–154, 231.

83. Hammond, *Don Juan de Oñate*, pp. 136–153; Hammond and Rey, *Don Juan de Oñate, Colonizer*, pp. 24–29; Simmons, *Last Conquistador*, pp. 160–169.

84. Hammond and Rey, *Don Juan de Oñate, Colonizer*, pp. 701–739, citing [Report of the people who remained in New Mexico], Sección de Audiencia de México, legajo 26, AGI.

85. Hammond and Rey, *Don Juan de Oñate, Colonizer*, pp. 761–762, citing Sección de Audiencia de México, legajo 121, AGI.

86. It must be remembered that Oñate had still hoped to discover a route to the sea and thus would be in need of shipbuilders and pilots. See Hammond, *Don Juan de Oñate*, pp. 161–163; and Simmons, *Last Conquistador*, pp. 170–171.

87. Relación de pasajeros a Nueva España encabezada por Alonso de Oñate, encargado de llevar refuerzos para la jornada de Nuevo México, dirigida por su hermano Juan de Oñate y el maestre de campo Vicente de Saldívar; le acompañan los siguientes pilotos, mosqueteros y carpinteros de ribera, Sevilla, March 20, 1604, Sección de Contratación, legajo 5281, no. 45, AGI. Although the topic of the recruits is discussed in various secondary works, the list itself has never been published. Consequently, to mitigate this gap in the record, following are the names, occupations, and origins of the reinforcements as listed in this document:

Juan Bernardo de Quiros	alferez, natural de Oviedo, hijo de Juan Bernardo de Quiros
Francisco de Guevara	mosquetero, natural de Granada, hijo de Gonzalo Fernández de Córdoba
Jorge de Portales	mosquetero, natural de Granada
Juan López de Cardenas	mosquetero, natural de Córdoba, hijo de Juan de Arriola
Domingo Lázaro	mosquetero, natural de Velilla de Ebro, hijo de Juan de Arreguí
Cristóbal Rodríguez Lobato	mosquetero, natural de Ayamonte, hijo de Pedro de Castro
Rodrigo de Castro	mosquetero, natural de Ayamonte, hijo de Pedro de Castro
Hernando Martín	mosquetero, natural de Écija
Francisco Gómez	mosquetero, natural de Lisboa
Melchor de Tornamira	mosquetero, natural de Tudela
Hernan García	mosquetero, natural de Martos, hijo de Alonso García de Cuenca
Juan de Alarcón	mosquetero, natural de Argamasilla de Alba, hijo de Bartolomé de Chillerón
Pedro García Cabeza	mosquetero, natural de Santaella, hijo de Juan García
Miguel Fernández	mosquetero, natural de Santaella, hijo de Juan Bermejo
Felipe de Liaño	mosquetero, natural de Madrid
Hernando Laviano	mosquetero, natural de Azpeita

Juan de Tolosa	mosquetero, natural de Madrid, hijo de Juan de Tolosa
Martín de Velasco	mosquetero, natural de Orihuela
Francisco Vallejo	mosquetero, natural de Toledo
Francisco Martínez	mosquetero, natural de Madrid
Miguel de Bengoechea	mosquetero, natural de Tolosa
Antonio Gutiérrez	mosquetero, natural de Toro
Andres Juárez	mosquetero, natural de Fuente Obejuna, hijo de Sebastian Rodríguez
Juan Gómez	mosquetero, vecino de Puebla de Guzman, hijo de Hernando Álvarez
Felipe de Ávila	mosquetero, natural de Málaga
Diego Ruíz de Aldana	mosquetero, natural de Cabra, hijo de Diego Ruíz de Aldana
Juan González	mosquetero, natural de Islas Canarias, hijo de Domingo González
Diego Rodríguez	mosquetero, natural de las Islas Canarias, hijo de Baltasar Medrano
Alonso Diez	mosquetero, natural de Oviedo, hijo de Alonso Diez
Cristóbal de Melgarejo	maestro mayor de carpintería, natural de Málaga, hijo de Juan Martínez de Santaella y Bernardina de Melgarejo, con su mujer Andrea de Lara, natural de Antequera, hija de Juan de Lara y María de Lara, y con sus hijos María, Cristóbal y Catalina
Juan Bautista de Avila	piloto, natural de Sevilla, hijo de Cristóbal Rodríguez y Ana de Ávila

88. Don Alonso de Oñate, impedió la visita de un navío en la Veracruz, Veracruz, July 2–7, 1604, fols. 201, 222–226, testimony of Andres Menéndez de Bovela y Solis, July 2, 1604, fols. 223r–224r, Ramo de Inquisición, tomo 368, AGN.

89. Ibid., containing letter from Fray Francisco Carranco to Tribunal de México, July 3, 1604, fols. 222r–v; and letter from Fray Francisco Carranco to Sr. Inquisidor Lic. General Bernardo de Quiros, July 7, 1604, fols. 201r–v.

90. Simmons, *Last Conquisitador*, pp. 178–182; Hammond, *Don Juan de Oñate*, pp. 171–174.

CHAPTER 5

Franciscans, the Inquisition, and Secret Judaism in New Mexico, 1610–1680

The independent-minded Juan de Oñate was replaced by Governor Pedro de Peralta in 1610, but the centralization of power by royal authorities did little to achieve the goal of political or economic stability in New Mexico. The decades that followed were characterized by material challenges, conflicts between Spanish colonists and Pueblo Indians, and intense political infighting between civil and religious officials. These developments contributed to the outbreak of the Pueblo Revolt of 1680, which succeeded in driving the European settlers into a thirteen-year exile.

The revolt resulted in the destruction of virtually all the documents that had been produced and kept in New Mexico, leaving historians with few records on which to rely in analyzing this most fascinating period. Fortunately, pioneer scholars such as France V. Scholes scoured the repositories in Spain and Mexico in the 1930s and 1940s, and brought to light correspondence, reports, investigations, trials, pronouncements, and other archival material that pertains to this remote frontier outpost. Thus thanks to these efforts, it has been possible to reconstruct, at least in part, how the various conflicts played out in the young colony.[1]

Despite the methodological challenges posed by the paucity of documents, it is clear that descendants of crypto-Jews from Spain and Portugal continued to find their way to New Mexico during the seventeenth century. These colonists, together with those who had arrived earlier, were to play a significant role in the economic, social, and political development of the struggling settlement, and find themselves participants, either willingly or unwillingly, in the fierce struggle for power between representatives of the church and of the state that characterized the period.

CHALLENGES FOR THE NEW COLONY

The physical environment that formed the context for the new colony was considerably less than hospitable. While it was the intention of Juan de Oñate and the royal officials to establish a self-sufficient colony in New Mexico, the European settlers quickly came to depend on the goods and services grudgingly provided by the Pueblo Indians, who had been living in the region for several centuries. The institutional means whereby the Spanish exacted food and supplies from the Indians, which had evolved over the previous hundred years or so, was known as the *encomienda*. Under this system, individual communities of Indians would be *encomendados*, literally "entrusted" to a Spanish settler to provide labor and tribute, in return for religious training and protection. Borrowed from the Iberian Peninsula, where, during the *reconquista*, this process served the Christians well against the Muslims, it devolved into little more than slavery in the early years of the conquest and settlement of the New World. But by the seventeenth century, the Crown had attempted to ensure that proper legal safeguards were put into effect to limit the extent of abuse by Spanish settlers.[2]

Initiated in New Mexico by Governor Juan de Oñate during his administration, the practice continued throughout the seventeenth century, whereby governors, in order to reward soldiers and other settlers for their services, would grant certain pueblos (or portions thereof) to them in *encomienda*. Part of the recipients' obligations involved being on call in case the governor needed military assistance, thus serving, in the absence of a standing army, as a sort of militia and providing horses and weapons in times of defense. The *encomenderos*, those Spanish colonists who held the *encomiendas*, were not expected to reside in the area of their charges; most maintained their principal residence in the capital, established in Santa Fe in the first decade of the century, while making periodic trips to the pueblos whenever necessary.[3]

While the distribution of Native labor constituted the major share of the governor's obligations, he was also responsible for the administration of justice and, in coordination with the town council, the construction and maintenance of public works in Santa Fe. Moreover, he oversaw the defense of the colony from attacks by Plains Indians on Pueblo and Spanish residents of the Río Grande Valley, the upper reaches of the Río Pecos, and the Galisteo Basin. The Navajos to the west and the Apaches to the east and south had long posed a threat to the Pueblo Indians, alternately engaging in trading and raiding activities. The introduction of the Europeans into the area did little to mitigate their sense of insecurity.[4]

Superimposed on the civil structure, and in direct competition for authority and the fruits of Pueblo labor, were the Franciscan friars. After the royal officials realized that the far northern region had failed to live up to its potential as *un otro México* (another Mexico) in terms of its material resources, the salvation of the souls of the Pueblo Indians became the principal focus—indeed, the raison d'être—of the colony. Thus the Franciscans, imbued with a sense of missionary zeal, saw themselves as the true representatives of Spanish civilization, the true guardians and protectors of the faith. Members of the Franciscan order had played a leading role in the spiritual conquest of Mexico during the very early years of settlement, and the friars were later assigned the most challenging task of conducting proselytizing work among the Pueblo Indians in New Mexico.[5]

The missionary zeal spawned during the sixteenth century carried over into the seventeenth, when the friars took their charge very seriously. They compelled the Pueblo people to serve as laborers in the construction of mission churches and exacted food and supplies for their sustenance. Regarding the Native practices as heathen and idolatrous, the friars imposed severe punishment on the Pueblo Indians, who, despite their status as newly baptized Catholics, continued to observe their traditional dances and other customs. In certain instances, their sacred kivas were desecrated and their religious leaders executed.[6] From a twenty-first-century perspective, these actions appear cruel and certainly counter to modern standards of tolerance and cultural relativism. But examined in the context of the seventeenth century, the behavior of the Franciscans was consistent with European Christocentric attitudes.

THE STRUGGLE FOR POWER BETWEEN CHURCH AND STATE

In theory, the Spanish civil and religious leaders had similar goals—the security and well-being, both material and spiritual, of the colony.

But in practice, overlapping areas of authority, combined with limited resources, resulted in abuses of power on the part of both governors and friars, ranging from the trivial to the capital, in seventeenth-century New Mexico. Both factions maintained their own set of weapons in their respective arsenals. The governor controlled the military forces, while the Franciscans held the power of excommunication and served as agents of the Holy Office of the Inquisition, authorized to initiate charges of heresy. The struggle between the two forces began almost immediately after the arrival of Governor Pedro de Peralta in 1610 and accelerated exponentially through the succeeding decades. It culminated in the 1660s, with the campaign of the Franciscans, acting with the authority of the Inquisition, against Governor Bernardo López de Mendizábal; his wife, Teresa de Aguilera y Roche; and his supporters—all accused of secret Judaism and other heresies.

The feud began innocuously enough, with a tiff between Governor Pedro de Peralta and Fray Isidro Ordóñez in 1613 regarding the question of who had authority over a military expedition to collect tribute from the Indians of the pueblo of Taos. On the way north from Santa Fe, the soldiers sent by Governor Peralta encountered Fray Isidro, who ordered them back to the capital so that they could observe the Feast of Pentecost. They dutifully obeyed, and, on their arrival, the governor immediately sent them back to Taos because of the high priority of a prompt collection of corn. For Peralta's part, the men could just as well honor their observance of the feast day by attending Mass at one of the mission churches along the route. Ordóñez responded to this challenge of his authority by invoking his power as agent of the Inquisition and threatening excommunication if the governor did not revoke his order within two hours.

Predictably, the order of excommunication was executed, but later withdrawn. In the wake of this dispute, though, more recriminations, arrests, insults, and threats were exchanged. Indignities endured by Peralta ranged from having his chair removed from the church and thrown into the street just before Mass; through being labeled as a Lutheran, a heretic, and even a Jew and suffering incarceration under Ordóñez's order; to receiving another order of excommunication. By the time Peralta was replaced as governor in 1614, the small Spanish community was hopelessly polarized between pro-governor and pro-Franciscan factions. This legacy of division was to transcend generations, characterizing life in New Mexico for decades to come.[7]

The names and faces changed, but the issues remained the same, and the consequences escalated, both for the individuals involved and for the colony as a whole. Fray Isidro left New Mexico in 1617 and was replaced by Fray Estevan de Perea, whose battles with Governor Juan de Eulate from 1618 to 1626 mirrored those waged between Fray Isidro and Governor Peralta.[8] A decade or so later, Governor Luis de Rosas incurred the wrath of the Franciscans who were operating in the colony during his tenure in office, which culminated in a revolt by his detractors, his arrest and murder, and the subsequent retribution and decapitation of the rebels.[9] This violent episode set the stage for the even more dramatic conflict of the 1660s, when pro-clerical forces, acting with the authority of the Holy Office of the Inquisition, successfully conspired to bring down the governor, his wife, and his supporters.

THE PARTICIPATION OF *CONVERSOS* IN THE COLONY

Despite the turmoil and division that characterized the first several decades of European settlement in New Mexico, the colony experienced a period of growth, with immigrants from Spain, Portugal, and Mexico accompanying the Franciscan merchant caravans and royal military expeditions on the long and perilous trek up the Camino Real from Mexico City to the far northern outpost. Among these new settlers were descendants of *conversos*, some of whom were later found to be exhibiting indications of crypto-Jewish practices, joining those who had journeyed to New Mexico with Juan de Oñate around the turn of the seventeenth century.

The Mexican Inquisition, represented in the colony by the Franciscan friars, initially appeared unconcerned about the possibility of Jewish heresy in its midst. This inattention stemmed from a variety of factors, including the general disinterest of the Mexican Holy Office in *judaizante* cases in the early seventeenth century, the remoteness of New Mexico from the capital, and, perhaps most significantly, the preoccupation of the Franciscans with their struggle for power with the civil authorities.

One of the *converso* descendants to take advantage of the relatively tolerant environment in New Mexico was Simón de Abendaño. Born in the town of Ciudad Rodrigo, located on the border between Spain and Portugal, Abendaño emigrated to the New World and up to New Mexico at some point during the 1600s or 1610s.[10] The surname Abendaño or Abendaña is long associated with Jewish families in Spain and the Sephardic diaspora.[11] Abendaños could be found among the Jewish and crypto-Jewish communities of Murcia and Lorca from the fifteenth to the seventeenth century. The municipal archives of Murcia cite Mayr Abendanno as selling sheep and goats to the city's slaughterhouse in 1469. That same year, Mose Abendanno was apprehended along with "many other armed Jews," attempting to enter the Moorish quarter of the city in search of one of his servants.[12] The municipal census of the town of nearby Lorca for 1660 includes Don Herónimo Abendaño and his wife, Doña Beatríz Riquelme.[13] The Riquelme family of Murcia was suspected of practicing secret Judaism a century earlier.[14] It is interesting to note that Abendaño and Riquelme lived next door to Juan de Osca Alzamora and Juliana Rael de Aguilar, the parents of future New Mexico resident Alonso Rael de Aguilar, whose Jewish roots will be discussed.

The Jewish population of Ciudad Rodrigo can be traced back at least to the twelfth century.[15] By 1486, on the eve of the expulsion of the Jews from Spain, Jews constituted about 9 percent of the town's population, quite a remarkable representation, compared with 2 percent for the country as a whole. The same year, Mose Habendyño was counted as one of the more affluent residents of the *judería*,[16] and Perucho de Abendaño served as *mayordomo del consejo*, charged with supervision of municipal finances. The Jews of Ciudad Rodrigo suffered along with those in the rest of the kingdom as a result of the Edict of Expulsion issued by Fernando and Isabel in 1492. Because of the town's proximity to Portugal, many of them chose to escape across the border, rather than convert to Christianity. So many of Ciudad Rodrigo's Jews chose to leave, and so devastating was their departure to the economy of the town, that within months the Catholic Monarchs proclaimed that all the Jews from Ciudad Rodrigo who wished to return could do so, with full restitution of the goods that they had abandoned when they left. The only condition was that they convert to Catholicism.[17] The appeal seems to have had no small success, as a substantial *converso* community could be found living in the old Jewish quarter a century and a half later.[18]

Unfortunately, the baptismal and marriage records of the parish of San Juan Bautista (which formed part of the old Jewish quarter of Ciudad Rodrigo) for the period when Simón de Abendaño was born either did not survive or are so badly deteriorated as to prevent examination, and thus the genealogical information concerning his parents and other relatives are forever lost. Documents from the 1590s through the mid-seventeenth century, however, show several members of the Abendaño family living in the old *judería*, including a wool merchant, Joan de Abendaño, married to Leonor Hernández and residing on Calle de Santiago, in close proximity to the former synagogue, which had been converted into a hospital.[19]

Just decades after Simón de Abendaño left for the New World, the

Holy Office of the Inquisition in Valladolid discovered "a conspiracy and congregation of *judaizantes* in Ciudad Rodrigo." The documentation that emerged from the crackdown on this group by the inquisitors provides a unique glimpse of the inner workings of the secret Jewish community in this town. According to testimony presented in 1647 and 1651, the men among the crypto-Jews of Ciudad Rodrigo would gather at a designated home each Friday night at 10:00 P.M. The house had to be large enough to accommodate the worshipers and had to have a secret door, separate from the principal entrance, in order for the participants to avoid detection. At one point, the meetings were held at the home of Paulo de Herrera, on the plaza, but were shifted to that of Antonio Espinosa, which did have a separate entrance. Espinosa, curiously enough, had served as auditor of the local military post. For purposes of security, an elaborate series of passwords and countersigns were required, whereby the person desiring entrance said, "La nación." The man guarding the door answered, "Quién?" (Who is it?), to which the first one replied, "Ismael." Details about prayers are absent from the testimony, but practices allegedly involved the abuse and burning of Catholic images. The participants in the services included shoemakers, apothecaries, and notaries who lived in Ciudad Rodrigo (some on the same streets as the Abendaños mentioned earlier) and elsewhere. None of the witnesses indicated that women attended the services.[20]

Whether or not the family of Simón de Abendaño participated in such ceremonies is unknown. But given the Jewish origin of this uncommon surname, the inclusion of Abendaños among the pre-expulsion Jews of Ciudad Rodrigo, and the presence of Abendaños in the town's *judería*, it is likely that Simón's family formed an integral part of the *converso* community. Little is known about his life in New Mexico in the early seventeenth century, beyond the fact that he had married María Ortiz, daughter of Juan López Holguín and Catalina de Villanueva, and that their daughter María de Abendaño married Diego de Vera,[21] whose family connections to *converso*s in the Canary Islands appear to be clear.

Born in La Laguna, on the island of Tenerife, in 1590,[22] Diego de Vera emigrated to Mexico in the late 1610s and lived with a cousin, Juana Perdomo. After a year or so, he traveled north to New Mexico, and in 1622, he wed María de Abendaño. Within three years of Vera's marriage, Fray Alonso de Benavides arrived in Santa Fe as custodian of the Franciscans. Perhaps because Fray Alonso had inside information or because he wanted to salve his guilty conscience, Vera confessed to the prelate that, despite his marriage to María, he already had a wife, whom he had left behind in the Canaries.[23] His trial for bigamy before the inquisitors in Mexico City in 1626 reveals considerable demographic information that, when linked with data from Inquisition, notarial, and sacramental records in the Canary Islands, suggests a connection with a family of crypto-Jews who had fled to the islands from various parts of Spain after the expulsion.

During his trial, Diego mentioned a relative, Juana de Vera.[24] A review of sacramental records for Las Palmas, Gran Canaria, suggests strongly that all the Veras living on that island belonged to the same family and that, through Juana de Vera, Diego de Vera was related to Francisco de Vera Moxica.[25]

In July 1609, Vera Moxica had applied for a license to travel to the Indies. Hoping that no one would delve into his family's past, he presented testimony that he and his ancestors were "people clean of all [bad] race, and without stain or descent of Moors or Jews, nor anyone penanced by the Holy Office of the Inquisition."[26] Unfortunately for him, for the previous hundred years or so, the Inquisition of Las Palmas had maintained a comprehensive file on the crypto-Jews of the island, including the Vera family. Within a few weeks, he and the witnesses from whom he had suborned false testimony found themselves on trial, during which the inquisitors presented Vera Moxica with the damaging information that they had accumulated:

> The aforesaid Francisco de Vera Mújica, [is the] notorious descendant of Jews, confessants and *reconciliados*, . . . as the son of Pedro de Vera Mojica, resident at present of this aforesaid city, and the aforesaid Pedro de Vera Mojica, his father, the son of Martín de Vera, also a resident of [Las Palmas], and town councillor, and the aforesaid Martín de Vera, paternal grandfather of the aforesaid Francisco de Vera Mojica, son of Alonso de la Barrera, and the aforesaid Alonso de la Barrera, paternal great-grandfather, son of Gonzalo de la Barrera, resident of Villalva, and reconciled by this Holy Office of the Inquisition, and Gonzalo de Barrera, the paternal great-great-grandfather, the son of Pedro Alonso de la Barrera and Isabel González, his wife, both condemned by the Holy Office of the Inquisition.[27]

This indictment was accompanied by a complete genealogy of the Vera family going back five generations and detailing their migration from Valladolid, Jerez, Villalba, Gibraleón, Lepe, and Trigueros to the Canaries. It appears from this document that it was Francisco's paternal great-grandfather, Alonso de la Barrera, who left his native Valladolid in 1498, at age twelve, presumably with his parents, and his paternal great-grandmother, Ana de Vera, who left Jerez around the same time, just a few years after the Edict of Expulsion. Escape from inquisitorial persecution is strongly suggested as a motivating factor, as the genealogy refers to Alonso's grandfather, also named Alonso, as having been condemned by the Inquisition.[28]

Vera Moxica was fined 20 *ducados* for his infraction and was warned never to use this kind of false information for such purposes in the future.[29] Whether he ever actually made it to the Indies is unknown. For his part, New Mexican bigamist Diego de Vera allegedly sailed back to Tenerife to renew his relationship with his first wife, never to see María de Abendaño again.[30] One of the two daughters he left behind in Santa Fe, Petronila, married Pedro Romero, the grandson of Bartolomé Romero.[31]

Another Vera descendant, whose connection to the family members just discussed is unclear, was to reveal even more about the extent of Jewish practices in seventeenth-century New Mexico. Manuel Jorge, likely a relative of a Tangier-born Portuguese merchant,[32] also named Manuel Jorge, and his wife, Ana de Vera, was born about 1635.[33] The elder Manuel Jorge was born around 1592 and emigrated to the mining frontier of northern New Spain between 1615 and 1620. He first established himself as a merchant in Cuencamé and later moved to Parral, to take advantage of the mining boom of the early 1630s. Jorge maintained close commercial relationships with the wealthy and powerful Portuguese crypto-Jewish merchants of Mexico City, including Francisco Franco de Moreira and Simón Váez Sevilla, both of whom capitalized local merchants in the northern mining areas. Rick Hendricks and Gerald J. Mandell observed that all those chosen by Manuel Jorge and Ana de Vera to be godparents of their children were Portuguese as well. These authors hypothesized that the Jorge family, as well as their inner circle of friends and associates, were of New Christian ancestry and "may or may not have been crypto-Jews." They suggest that the campaign of the Holy Office against the *judaizantes* of New Spain in the 1640s motivated one of Jorge's sons, Antonio Jorge de Vera, to flee from Parral to New Mexico in 1649.[34]

The likelihood that the members of the Jorge family were practicing crypto-Jews is demonstrated by an incident involving a daughter of the younger Manuel Jorge, who appears to have migrated to New Mexico in 1655, joining his cousin Antonio, and worked as a blacksmith and an armorer in Santa Fe. He was described as *de nación portugués*,[35] which was often used as a euphemism for a *judaizante*. The older of his two daughters, during her confession in 1656 to Fray Miguel Sacristán, guardian of the Convento de la Imaculada Concepción in Santa Fe, disclosed that "she observed the Law of Moses with exquisite rites and ceremonies." Because of her very young age (which was not specified in his account), Fray Miguel could not offer her absolution. Nor did he report her family's heresy to any of the authorities, "because [the Inquisition] was five hundred leagues [1,300 miles] distant, and there was no minister of the Holy Tribunal here."[36] This story was related in the testimony of a colleague of Fray Miguel, Fray Nicolas de Villar, before local agents of the Mexican Inquisition in 1661, five years after the girl had confessed. It has importance not only because it indicates that Judaism was being practiced in seventeenth-century New Mexico, but, more significantly, because it shows that such observances appear to have been common knowledge. Moreover, despite his awareness of this heresy, neither the Franciscan clergyman nor his superiors took any action to suppress it. What became of the unnamed daughter is not known. Manuel Jorge appears to have returned to Parral by the early 1660s, but his cousin Antonio remained in New Mexico, served as a military officer, and married Gertrudis Baca. Their descendants were to play significant roles in the history of Santa Fe and Río Abajo over the next four centuries.

Awareness of a Jewish family background appears not to have presented a barrier even to advancement within the Franciscan order. Fray Estevan de Perea, who participated in the church–state struggle in the early decades of the seventeenth century, served as the first custodian of the Franciscans in New Mexico, holding that position from 1616 to 1621 and, again, from 1629 to 1631. If there was any investigation into Fray Estevan's genealogy in advance of his first term, its records appear not to have been preserved in the Archivo General de la Nación in Mexico City. The second time around, however, the Mexican Inquisition conducted a comprehensive inquiry into the *limpieza de sangre* of the prelate. According to the documents gathered from agents of the Holy Office in Spain and Portugal, Perea was born in the town of Villanueva del Fresno, located just on the Spanish side of the border with Portugal, about halfway between Badajóz and the southern Mediterranean coast. Both of his parents, however, were Portuguese, his paternal side from Beja and maternal side from the small town of Motrinos, just across the border from Villanueva del Fresno, in the vicinity of Monsaráz.[37] So many Jews had settled in this area—not only the normal mix of merchants and bankers, but also farmers and distributors of land—that the region was known by the thirteenth century as the Vale de Judeo (Valley of the Jew).[38]

One of the investigations, conducted by the inquisitors of Llerena,

Spain, found that while several witnesses attested to the purity of blood of Perea's family,

> two of the witnesses, one being fifty years old, says that he heard it said that Estevan Núñez, maternal grandfather of the applicant, was a resident and native of Monçaráz and of a village called Mohinos [Motrinos], and that the common people of Villanueva questioned the purity of his blood and said that he had an admixture of new Christian blood. The other witness, seventy-six years old, says that he had heard it said among other witnesses of Villanueva that Inéz Núñez, mother of the applicant, was tainted with new Christian blood, he does not know whether through Estevan Núñez, her father, or Juana Hernández, her mother; this witness has the same suspicion concerning the religious, and intimates that the defect is through the father, Estevan Núñez, rather than through the mother.[39]

Despite these indications that Fray Estevan de Perea may well have had Jewish roots on his mother's side, the Franciscans chose to ignore this damaging evidence, confirming him to his post as custodian, and he remained among the Franciscans in New Mexico until his death in 1638 or 1639.[40]

The endogamous marriage patterns exhibited by Mexican crypto-Jews in the seventeenth century appear to have been consistent with those of their coreligionists in New Mexico, many of whom also married within a tight group of New Christians. Simón de Abendaño married María Ortiz, daughter of Juan López Holguín and Catalina de Villanueva. María Ortiz's sister Isabel became the wife of Juan de Victoria Carvajal, who had served with Gaspar Castaño de Sosa and Juan de Oñate.[41] And Felis de Carvajal, one of their sons, wed Juana de Arvízu, granddaughter of Francisco Gómez.[42] María de Abendaño, daughter of Simón de Abendaño and María Ortiz, married Diego de Vera. One of their daughters, Petronila, married Pedro Romero, grandson of Bartolomé. Lucía Robledo married Bartolomé Romero, and their daughter Ana became the wife of Francisco Gómez. One of their sons, Andrés Gómez Robledo, married Juana Ortiz, daughter of María de Vera, the other daughter of María de Abendaño and Diego de Vera.[43] Portuguese colonist Domingo González married Magdalena de Carvajal, likely daughter of Juan de Victoria Carvajal, and became the progenitors of the González Lobón family.[44]

In terms of occupational patterns, it appears that these families distinguished themselves in significant military and civil positions—

military officers, town councillors, mayors, and lieutenant governor and even governor of the province. Portuguese immigrant Francisco Gómez, who had been recruited by Alonso de Oñate to reinforce the colony in 1604, "became the most outstanding military official in New Mexico, . . . occupying every office of importance, including that of High Sheriff [*alguacil mayor*] of the Holy Office," according to historian Fray Angelico Chávez.[45] France Scholes referred to Gómez as New Mexico's "most important military figure during the first half of the seventeenth century."[46] Gómez also owned significant *estancias*, one at the old Spanish capital at San Gabriel de Yunque, across the river from the Tewa pueblo of San Juan, at the confluence of the Río Grande and the Río Chama, and two others in the Río Abajo region, near Socorro, one named San Juan and other San Nicolás de las Barrancas.[47]

Gómez's children inherited both the wealth and the call of public service. The oldest, Francisco Gómez Robledo, served in the military, holding the ranks of sergeant, *maese del campo* (field commander) and sergeant major, before his arrest by the Inquisition in 1662 for practicing Judaism.[48] In addition to the *estancias* that had belonged to his father, Gómez Robledo owned a house on the corner of the plaza in Santa Fe, consisting of a living room, three other rooms, a patio, and a garden. His enhanced social and economic status was reflected by the large number of *encomiendas* that he held, including those at the pueblos of Ácoma, Tesuque, Taos, and Pecos, and half of the *encomiendas* at Sandía and Abó.[49] Following his release from the Inquisition jail, he also served as member of the town council of Santa Fe.[50] Among the most curious entries in the inventory of his personal papers that was conducted after Gómez Robledo's arrest was "an account of services, including a royal order [conferring upon him the title] of *cavallero hijodalgo*," indicating that, despite his somewhat questionable ethnic background, his services to the king warranted a recognition of knighthood.[51]

Francisco's younger brothers Andrés and Bartolomé Gómez Robledo also served as members of the Santa Fe town council.[52] Andrés held the high military rank of *maese del campo* and formed part of the General Council of the Kingdom, along with his older brothers.[53] Bartolomé was commissioned as ensign and sergeant major[54] and occupied the important post of secretary to the governor and war under Governor Bernardo López de Mendizábal.[55]

The children and grandchildren of Bartolomé Romero, a captain in the expedition of Juan de Oñate, followed in their elder's footsteps. Sons Bartolomé II and Mathías and grandson Diego all held high military rank, with Diego and Mathías serving also as protectors of the Indians. Bartolomé and Mathías participated in municipal affairs as members of the town council, and Bartolomé served as *alcalde ordinario*. Diego appears to have been the most affluent of the offspring, holding *encomiendas* at the pueblos of Cochití and Cuyamungué, and half of the *encomienda* at Zía, and possessing a "fine and spacious house" in the capital, as well as ample tracts of cultivated land in Santa Fe, Pecos, and Los Chávez.[56] Other *converso* settlers in New Mexico, including members of the González Lobón, González Bernal, Ruíz Cáceres, and Victoria Carvajal families, demonstrated similar career patterns.[57]

THE PARTICIPATION OF *CONVERSOS* IN THE CHURCH–STATE CONFLICT

As major participants in the political and military affairs of the colony, several of these families allied themselves with various factions during the vicious struggle between the civil authorities and the Franciscan friars during the seventeenth century. Although there were exceptions, most sided with the governors and their supporters. Captain Francisco Gómez and his sons, for example, demonstrated remarkable consistency in their allegiance to the king's representatives throughout the period. In the struggles between Governor Juan de Eulate and Fray Estevan de Perea in the 1610s and 1620s, Gómez strongly defended the interests of the governor. In 1622, in the midst of the difficulties, he was placed in command of the caravan to carry goods south to Mexico City. Fray Agustín de Burgos wished to use the caravan as an opportunity to smuggle reports back to the viceroy, informing him of the abuses suffered by the Franciscans at the hands of the anticlerical secular authorities. But Gómez refused to carry what he considered to be seditious material that would be counter to his superiors' interests. As a result of Gómez's action, the friars came within a hair's breadth of abandoning New Mexico entirely, and it was only through the desperate intervention of Fray Estevan that the mission was saved.[58]

Gómez also testified on behalf of Eulate when the governor was accused of having made the heretical claim that the state of marriage was preferable to that of celibacy—that is, that of priests—and that married men contributed more to society than did priests.[59] In his declaration before Fray Alonso de Benavides on May 19, 1626, Gómez attested that "about six years ago, more or less, upon his arrival in Santa Fe from New Spain, it was heard around town that Don Juan de Eulate, who was governor of these provinces at the time, had said that the state of married persons was as good as that of members of the religious orders. He [Gómez] does not remember very well if [Eulate] said this, or if he even said that the state maintained by the religious is bad."[60] Not only did Gómez question whether the governor had actually expressed these thoughts, but, in describing the offending expression, he softened the language to render the status of married persons only equal to, not better than, that of the priests.

Gómez's role in defending the interest of the secular officials solidified during the more intense rivalry between Governor Luis de Rosas and the Franciscans, from 1637 to 1641. In this cause, he was joined by other descendants of New Christians. On at least two occasions, Gómez wrote strong letters in defense of Rosas's actions to counter the accusations of the clerics. One of the issues surrounded the governor's alleged mishandling of the policy toward the Apaches, whose recurring raids on the pueblos antedated the arrival of the Spanish. The establishment of the colony in New Mexico by the members of Juan de Oñate's expedition merely exacerbated the problem, creating more tensions and, at the same time, offering a more attractive target for the attacks. By the time Rosas assumed his duties, the threat had reached a crisis stage. His approach to the problem was not met with universal praise. Some accused him of needlessly provoking nonhostile bands, while failing to prepare adequate defenses for the predictable counterattack. Captain Francisco Gómez, however, perceived the situation in a different light and expressed his views freely to the viceroy in a letter dated October 26, 1638:

> For forty years I have served His Majesty in these provinces, since the time of the *adelantado* Don Juan de Oñate, for which services I have been granted the post of sergeant major of these provinces by Viceroy Marqués de Cerralvo. By virtue of my office and status as an old soldier, I present to Your Excellency an account of this land. And it is [true], Sir, that the enemy Apaches are restless, as they have always been, but they are well-castigated, as it seems that they are, at the present time, intimidated to the point where they have retreated, and the land has been opened up for the discoveries made by our *capitán general* [Governor Rosas], and that the discovery of the kingdom of Quivira [located on the eastern plains of New Mexico, and extending eastward], has been incredible, in view of the fact that it has always been understood that such an enterprise required greater forces and expenditures. And although all the generals that we have had longed for this discovery, none had acted as boldly as our *capitán general*, who had tried and succeeded in this endeavor. But it is no wonder that in his

> military exploits and their execution, he demonstrated that he is a real soldier, and his work has so demonstrated.[61]

In the same letter to the viceroy defending Rosas's actions, Gómez expressed criticism of the friars and voiced his concern about their unchecked power and influence in the civil sphere:

> And if these friars impede his efforts through lawsuits (a regular occurrence for them, from which they have not held back with any governor), this should demonstrate how just they are. There is no commandment for these [friars] that this practice should continue. And in this fashion they have caused the land to be so needy and afflicted, that the soldiers have become desperate, a fact that is clearly understood, as the friars are the owners of the riches of the land, and are not subject to any secular judge. And the clergy who the people have here act to cloak their own defects: the clergy of this kingdom are not mindful of this land and do not punish anyone [in need of it], except with a reprimand, [and only] if this is required, and so nothing comes of this. And in this way they are the owners of the land, as well as the wealth that is attached to it. And with these lawsuits they claim to use both jurisdictions [secular and religious]. And it is unfortunate that a governor who should be rewarded is instead so vexed, to say the very least. Moreover, the incumbent, who has governed and who continues to govern, performs considerable services to His Majesty, and provides many honors to those poor soldiers, with such grace, and gives help so freely, with the result that all feel comforted and consoled. And thus, in the name of all, and with the order of all, I humbly entreat Your Excellency to grant us the favor of keeping him in this office, so that in so doing we will receive your favor. . . .
>
> Santa Fe, October 26, [1]638
> [signed] Francisco Gómez.[62]

So closely identified with the pro-Rosas faction was Gómez that after the death of Rosas's successor, Governor Juan Flores de Sierra y Valdes, in 1641, he, as Flores's designated lieutenant governor, was prohibited by the anti-Rosas town council from assuming his responsibilities as acting governor. His son-in-law Pedro Lucero de Godoy, also a supporter of Rosas, served as one of the town's *alcaldes* and would have been in a position to back Gómez in his claim to office, but for reasons unknown chose not to act.[63] The family tradition of supporting the civil over the religious authorities was to continue with the next generation. Gómez's son Francisco Gómez Robledo was to pay dearly for his allegiance to Governor Bernardo López de Mendizábal two decades later.

Other colonists with crypto-Jewish family connections served the cause of royal authorities as well. Before the anti-Rosas faction took over the town council of Santa Fe in 1639, the governor's allies had held sway. Among the pro-Rosas council members was Mathías Romero, a son of Bartolomé Romero.[64] So, too, did the Portuguese Sebastián González participate in the sack of the mission church of Socorro in 1640. To add the proverbial insult to injury, it was reported that González donned the habit of one of the Franciscan friars and ordered the Indians of the mission to kiss his hand.[65]

GOVERNOR BERNARDO LÓPEZ DE MENDIZÁBAL, DOÑA TERESA DE AGUILERA Y ROCHE, AND THE INQUISITORIAL PERSECUTIONS OF THE 1660S

Following the violence and strife during the tenure of Governor Luis de Rosas in the early 1640s, relations between civil and religious leaders in New Mexico seemed to improve, at least temporarily, and the colony enjoyed a decade or so of relative peace. The arrival of a new and contentious governor in 1659 opened old wounds, however, and the next several years were to witness accusations and counteraccusations, resulting in midnight arrests by the Inquisition, long and protracted trials for heresy, disrupted families, ruined careers, and untimely deaths. For the first time in the colony, the question of crypto-Judaism being practiced, by both pioneer families and recent immigrants, was discussed openly. As with the persecutions of the *judaizantes* farther south in New Spain, issues extraneous to that of heresy served as the catalyst for agents of the Inquisition to embark on a campaign against their political adversaries who were suspected of practicing the Law of Moses. And, as in the earlier periods of persecution, the documents resulting from the Inquisition testimony and trials demonstrate clearly that, despite the prohibition of the practice of Judaism in the colony, certain families did engage in Jewish observances. Moreover, these records show that the celebration of such rituals was common knowledge, but that no one seems to have expressed concern until the Holy Office embarked on its aberrant mission in the early 1660s.

The new round of conflict between church and state began with the arrival in New Mexico of Governor Bernardo López de Mendizábal and his wife, Teresa de Aguilera y Roche, in June 1659. López was about thirty-six years old when he was appointed governor of New Mexico, the latest in a series of military and civilian posts that he had held over the previous decade and a half in Cartagena de Indias and New Spain.[66] He was born and raised in the village of Chietla, near Puebla, in central Mexico, where his parents operated a sugar-growing and -producing operation. Despite the pretense of nobility and affluence projected by López, his actual situation was far from comfortable. The failure of the family hacienda had resulted in financial near ruin. His maternal uncle Roque de Pastrana had to scrape together enough money to pay the debts accumulated by López's father, Cristóbal López de Mendizábal, and thus keep him from being thrown in jail. After Cristóbal's death, his widow, Leonor de Pastrana, continued to struggle to keep the creditors at bay.[67] López clearly regarded the appointment to high office as an opportunity for financial gain, a means to recover from the setbacks suffered by his family's enterprises. López's preferred method of operation appears to have been the exercising of a monopoly over the distribution of playing cards in whatever region happened to fall under his administration. His experience in 1654, when he borrowed money to purchase two hundred decks for resale in Guayacocotlán, seems to have worked well. On the eve of his departure for New Mexico in December 1658, he tapped the same source to purchase one thousand decks for what he expected to be willing customers on the far northern frontier.[68]

The family background of Doña Teresa de Aguilera y Roche was more distinguished than that of her husband. She was born in the Italian town of Alexandria Ultra el Po, located about halfway between Milan and Genoa, into a family that included an interesting mix of Spanish diplomats and Irish refugees. Her maternal grandfather, Juan de Roche, probably known in Ireland as John Roach, was forced to flee that island during the war with England. Aguilera's mother, María de Roche, met Melchor de Aguilera in Madrid, where they married, and she followed him to various diplomatic and administrative posts in Italy, France, and, eventually, Cartagena de Indias, where a union was arranged between Teresa and the young aspiring officer López de Mendizábal.[69]

The stormy tenure of López as governor of New Mexico reflected a continuation of the contentiousness between civil and religious officials that had characterized the earlier decades of the seventeenth century. López's predecessor, Juan Manso de Contreras, who held the position since 1656, enjoyed friendly relations with the Franciscans, no doubt because he was the younger brother of Fray Tomás Manso and had accompanied him on the mission supply caravans from Mexico City to Santa Fe. Little is known about the details of the Manso administration, other than that the governor pursued a harsh policy toward the Pueblo Indians in regard to the practice of their ancestral religion.[70] Manso also managed to create enemies among prominent Spanish colonists as well. For reasons that remain unclear, he arrested Francisco de Anaya Almazán, who had served in several important military and administrative positions. Anaya managed to break out of jail, with the help of Pedro Lucero de Godoy and Francisco Gómez Robledo. Anaya fled to Mexico City, along with his wife, Juana López; their two sons, Cristóbal and Francisco; their daughter Ynéz; and her husband, Alonso Rodríguez. In the viceregal capital, they met and developed a close relationship with López de Mendizábal and Doña Teresa. Partisans of Manso later alleged that the Anayas used their access in order to poison López's mind against the governor. According to one account, Anaya even exerted his influence to gain López's appointment as governor.[71] The close association between the Anaya family and Governor López would soon come back to haunt them.

With the papers certifying his appointment in hand, López and his wife left Mexico City for New Mexico around Christmas of 1658. The behavior exhibited by the new governor—and the reaction of the community—during one of his first stops set the tone for the next couple of years. On June 30, 1659, the entourage arrived at the Convento de Nuestra Señora de Socorro. Historian Joseph P. Sánchez described the scene, based on documents from the Mexican Inquisition:

> With church bells ringing and trumpets blaring, the father-guardian, Fray Benito de la Natividad, sprinkled holy water on the governor and the caravan and directed them to the church. Appreciative of the gesture, but unimpressed, Governor López mumbled that the friars could do a little better in receiving him. Someone later swore they had heard him say, "They should receive me like the most Holy Sacrament on the Feast of Corpus Christi." Before long, everyone in the province was either aghast at the comment or secretly in admiration of his bold sense of humor.[72]

Over the next several months, López succeeded in agitating and alienating virtually every friar in the province with his irreverent words and hostile policies, which included the encouragement of the Pueblo Indians to perform their traditional kachina dances, the elimination of the requirement for the Pueblos to provide forced labor for the Franciscans, the interference with other prerogatives of the Franciscans, a nasty investigation into the policies of his predecessor, the removal of Manso's appointees from civil and military positions, and the gross profiteering at the expense of both the Pueblo Indians and the Spanish colonists.[73] As had Governor Rosas's policies earlier in the century, López's actions brought about his own downfall as well as that of his loyal followers.

Word of the strife between the governor and the friars traveled fast, and by late 1660, the viceroy in Mexico City had decided to replace López with Diego Dionísio de Peñalosa Briceño y Berdugo. Although Peñalosa complied with his obligation to conduct a *residencia*, or investigation of his predecessor's conduct in office,[74] the Franciscans were out for blood. The next year, invoking their status as representatives of the Holy Office of the Inquisition, they began their own investigation into the suspicious heretical practices of López, his wife, and a number of their supporters. Fray Alonso de Posada, acting in his capacity as *comisario* of the Inquisition, conducted interviews with dozens of witnesses, including friars, soldiers, and, most important, servants and other intimates of the governor and his wife, who were in a position to offer incriminating testimony about details of their daily life.

The materials that Fray Alonso gathered were sent to the tribunal of the Holy Office in Mexico City. On the basis of this evidence, the inquisitors returned formal indictments and orders for the arrest of, first, four of López's closest officers and, later, the governor and his wife. The cases against Captain Nicolas de Aguilar, Sergeant Major Diego Romero, and Captain Cristóbal de Anaya Almazán were based on general issues of heresy related to their hostility to the friars and their laxity in enforcing orthodoxy among the Pueblo Indians. The charges against Sergeant Major Francisco Gómez Robledo were far more serious, involving family practices of Judaism. The indictments against Governor López and Teresa de Aguilera y Roche, while including a broad array of accusations of general heresy, also included important provisions relating to their own Jewish origins and practices.[75]

In May 1662, the first shoe fell, with Fray Alonso conducting almost simultaneous arrests of the four officers. He began with Captain Nicolas de Aguilar, whom he found at the Convento de San Antonio at the pueblo of Isleta on May 2, at 7:00 A.M., in the company of Captain Andrés López Sambrano, Captain Bartolomé Romero II, his nephew Sergeant Major Diego Romero, and Captain Juan Luján. The officers were on their way back to Santa Fe, after having conducted an inspection of the Hopi country, and had just arrived at the pueblo. Posada and his associates arrested Aguilar and placed him in one of the cells of the convent. Six hours later, they apprehended Diego Romero and put him in an adjoining cell. They were taken together to the convent at the pueblo of Santo Domingo, headquarters of the Franciscans in New Mexico.[76] Fray Alonso rushed back to Santa Fe, and, two days later, he and two other friars arrived at the residence of Sergeant Major Francisco Gómez Robledo at 5:00 A.M., finding, to no one's surprise, that he was asleep. They ordered him to get up and dressed, and they escorted to him to his cell in a nearby convent.[77] Two weeks after the arrest of Gómez Robledo, on May 14, former governor Juan Manso, acting in his capacity as high sheriff of the Holy Office and under the orders of Fray Alonso, interrupted Captain Cristóbal de Anaya Almazán during a midday conversation that he was conducting with two friars and two brother officers, at the pueblo of Sandía, and placed him under arrest at one of the cells of the convent.[78] Within a short period of time, both Gómez Robledo and Anaya Almazán were taken to join Aguilar and Romero at the convent at Santo Domingo.[79]

The other shoe fell on August 26. At 10:00 P.M., after a nasty exchange between Fray Alonso and Governor Peñalosa over the disposition of López's belongings, Posada, in the name of the Holy Office of the Inquisition, took the former governor into custody.[80] And at 4:00 A.M. on August 27, without warning, the inquisition agents burst into the home of Teresa de Aguilera y Roche. In his formal account of the arrest, Fray Alonso's secretary spared no effort to record every prurient detail:

> And having opened the door . . . they found the aforesaid Doña Teresa de Aguilera y Roche seated on her bed, half-dressed, and there next to her were two beds, one in which were sleeping Doña Ana Robledo [mother of Francisco Gómez Robledo] and Catalina de Zamora, and in the other Antonia Gonzales, all citizens of this town of Santa Fe who had come there to keep Doña Teresa company, as her husband had been arrested earlier by the governor of these provinces, Don Diego de Peñalosa, imprisoned in the house of Maese del Campo Pedro Lucero de Godoy, and guarded by four guards. The high sheriff entered the room first, and said to Doña Teresa de Aguilera that she was under arrest by the Holy Office by virtue of a special order, at which point Doña Teresa broke into tears, and with great emotion asked how such an important lady as her could be treated in such a fashion. She insisted that she was a Catholic Christian, and had no idea why she was being treated so maliciously. And turning her face twice to the image of Our Lady, she pleaded for justice (with exclamations) against those who were the cause of such an affront. And that the inquisitors should know *who she is*. And if she had

> wanted to martyr herself, than she would have already done so. And later, Doña Ana Robledo, Doña Catalina [de Zamora], and Antonia Gonzales were told to get dressed and to go home, taking their beds with them, which they did. And the aforesaid Doña Teresa de Aguilera was kindly ordered to finish getting dressed, and she put on a blue doublet. And below, an under waistcoat of crimson damask, a blouse of Rouen worked with silk, and adorned with scarlet petticoats, with five lace garnitures of silver, some *nagrillas o tapapiés* [long, silk skirt] of baize, a locally made blanket, and some coral bracelets. . . . She was arrested and placed in a small windowless cell in the convent, illuminated by only a skylight, with a bed with two coarse mattresses, two linen sheets, a cotton bedspread and a striped tablecloth.[81]

Within five weeks of the arrest of the former governor and his wife, all six prisoners were removed from their cells and sent, under armed guard, on the long trek southward to stand trial before the Mexican Holy Office.[82] On April 11, 1663, they were placed in the *carceles secretas* of the Palace of the Inquisition, on the northeastern corner of the Plaza de Santo Domingo in Mexico City, where they were to spend several very unpleasant years waiting for the interminably slow grinding of the wheels of inquisitorial justice to complete their turn. Three of them faced charges involving, among other heresies, the observance of the Law of Moses. One of the others, although not explicitly accused of practicing Judaism, expressed the fear that he would be regarded by the community as having done so. The record of their trials reveals much about the background of these individuals, the Jewish rites that were practiced in seventeenth-century New Mexico, and, more important, the awareness of the Spanish colonists that Judaism was being practiced secretly in their midst.

A little over two weeks after his incarceration in Mexico City, Bernardo López de Mendizábal was summoned by the inquisitors for his first audience. As were all the others accused of heresy, he was asked to give his name, place of birth and residence, age, occupation, and genealogy back two generations; a description of other family relationships; and a brief biography. He also offered an assessment of his status as an Old Christian, free from any stain of Jewish or Moorish blood; a proof of his ability to read, write, and recite Catholic prayers; and an account of his last confession and communion. He was then presented with a list of charges brought against him, which proceeded for one hundred pages.

Among the many charges amassed against López in the 260-count indictment brought by the inquisitors was that he was "an observer of Jewish rites and ceremonies, believing in them . . . as a descendant on the maternal line, of a person noted and vehemently suspected of the observance of the dead and expired Law of Moses, as he was penanced by this Holy Office of that which he had been accused."[83] Article 253 named the ancestor as Juan Núñez de León, "*balancario* [person who weighs and adjusts the coins in the mint], formerly employed in the royal treasury of this city [Mexico], penanced by this Holy Office in the public auto de fe celebrated in the *convento* of San Francisco of this city in the Chapel of San José Domingo, April 20, 1603, [reconciled for practicing Judaism]."[84]

Indeed, despite pious protests that López's ancestors were all "Basques, Old Christians, nobility and knights," it is clear from an examination of Inquisition trial records that his mother's maternal grandfather, Juan Núñez de León, had been arrested, tried, and convicted of practicing Judaism in Mexico City around the turn of the seventeenth century. Núñez's *proceso* indicated that he was born into a mercantile family in the town of Cea, in the Spanish province of León, around 1545. His parents and grandparents were from the area around Cea, Grajal, and Sahagún, the site of a significant Jewish population in the fifteenth century.[85] Núñez emigrated to New Spain in 1564 and served in several midlevel bureaucratic positions for the archbishop for about six years. He then worked as a merchant, selling his wares under the *portales* of Mexico City, until he was selected by the viceroy to serve as the *balancario* of the royal treasury. Shortly after his arrival in Mexico, he had married Leonor Váez, and they had three children, among whom was Mariana de León, born around 1568, who married the prominent merchant Pablo de Pastrana. This union produced four children, including Leonor de Pastrana, born in 1590, the mother of Governor López.[86]

A native of the "kingdom of Toledo," Pablo de Pastrana sailed to New Spain and settled in Puebla. He quickly developed a reputation as a wealthy man, maintaining a warehouse worthy of note.[87] He quite possibly descended from the Pastrana family of Guadalajara, cited by the Inquisition of Toledo as *judaizantes* in the 1530s.[88] Leonor, daughter of Pablo de Pastrana and Mariana de León, married Captain Cristóbal López de Mendizábal, native of the Basque town of Oñate. Together they operated a sugar plantation in Chietla. After the death of her husband and the demise of the sugar operation, Mariana moved to Mexico City, living "in her own houses across from the baptismal font of the Church of Santo Domingo," in the neighborhood occupied by so many of the Mexican *judaizantes* caught up in the campaign by the Inquisition in the 1640s.[89]

In response to the charge relating to his Jewish ancestor, López began to weave a tangled web of denials and rationalizations. He first dismissed the allegation, claiming that he had no idea that such a person existed in his genealogy, and certainly he had never met him. Nor should the sins of this "bad man," whoever he was, be transferred to him. He never tried to hide anything like this, he claimed. Besides, it would have been impossible to hide such a relative from the Inquisition. In any case, he continued, even if he had forgotten to mention this, as well as some other things, the issue was not terribly significant. Besides, he had been preoccupied with other, more important issues, and he should just be considered as having exercised poor judgment.[90]

Many of the allegations relating to the Jewish practices observed by López were also levied against his wife, Doña Teresa de Aguilera y Roche, whose audience followed that of López by four days. Like her husband, Doña Teresa protested that she was a good and faithful Christian and that "her parents, grandparents and relatives have all been considered as Catholic Christians, clean of all bad race; that she has never been arrested, penanced, reconciled or castigated by the Holy Office of the Inquisition." She indicated that she could read well, but conceded that "she did not know how to write fluently" (somewhat of an understatement, considering the paleographical challenge presented by her correspondence with the inquisitors), and that she had been instructed by teachers hired by her parents in a convent in Milan. She reported that she attended confession and took communion only once a year, as required by the Church, and last had done so during Holy Week in Santa Fe, the previous year.[91]

Most of the charges levied against her and her husband revolved around Sabbath observances, such as bathing and changing linens and clothes on Friday, in preparation for the Jewish day of rest, and reciting prayers on Friday evening. The inquisitors considered the testimony of some twenty-six witnesses. Some statements were little more than hearsay, but others were eyewitness accounts, not only by servants, but also by close friends and associates who maintained a degree of intimacy with the family. One of these couples, Pedro de Arteaga and Doña Josepha de Sandoval, had accompanied the governor and his wife in the wagon-train escort to New Mexico in 1658/1659[92] and continued a close relationship during their tenure in Santa Fe. Their observations, along with those of the servants, in regard to Doña Teresa's Sabbath eve hygienic practices were duly noted by the inquisitors. According to his testimony, Arteaga "knows that Doña Teresa de Aguilera every Friday put on clean clothes with particular care, on her bed, as well as her person and on the table, and she washed her face; even in very bad weather, when it was snowing, she never failed to wash herself and change her clothes, as it was Friday."[93] Sandoval testified:

> Every Friday, without fail, by order of Bernardo López de Mendizábal and Teresa de Aguilera, clean clothes would be put on the bed and the table, and although this could have been left until the next day, it wasn't permitted; and that the aforesaid [people] put on clean clothes on Saturday.
>
> As a person who always visited Doña Teresa, she observed that every Friday that she was in her company, she washed her head, and sometimes her feet, as well, every Friday. With regard to the washing of her head, she never failed to do so. And that later, after she washed her head, she would close herself off . . . in a separate room alone, putting in water, and saying that she was closing herself off in order to wash her [private] parts; and that she would stay there for three hours. And in this space of time, no one would be permitted in. And it seemed to this witness scrupulous and suspicious, that if she had had the opportunity to spy on her, she would have done so.[94]

Arteaga supplemented his wife's testimony by explaining that modesty did not appear to account for Doña Teresa's actions, "and that this witness suspected that she [Doña Teresa] closed herself off with such fear when she left to clean her parts in the aforesaid room, when in other occasions she did not exhibit such fear when Doña Josepha would see her entire body in her bed."[95] Moreover, Sandoval commented on the infrequency of both López's and Doña Teresa's compliance with the sacraments of confession and communion. She testified that she almost never saw either of them attend Mass or take communion. Nor did either of them invoke "the name of God, the Holiest Mother or any of the saints."[96]

Not surprisingly, both Doña Teresa and her husband denied these charges, arguing that although they did wash themselves on Friday, they did so on other days as well, and that they changed their clothes three times a week, not only on Friday. And if she took the occasion to wash her head, she swore that she did not wash anything else, including her feet, or cut her nails or close herself off for any purpose. Regarding the accusation that she used Saturday as an occasion to groom herself, Doña Teresa's testimony indicated, "It is true that on Saturdays she fixed her hair, as generally did all the other women, and for this reason she was always accustomed to doing so, because later on Sunday, there was no time to fix herself up before going to Mass, except to tend somewhat to one's hair. But in no manner did she, or does she, do so in observance of the Law of Moses, or any other."[97]

Francisco Gómez Robledo languished in his cell for three months before his first audience with the inquisitors in Mexico City on July 4, 1663. In his initial encounter, he tried to impress them with the military credentials of his father and his ties to the Oñate family, stretching the truth just a bit in his assertion that the elder Francisco Gómez "was the first to conquer New Mexico." As far as his own career was concerned, he touted his contributions as "soldier and conquistador, undertaking many risks and enterprises, bearing the costs himself, without receiving any salary, serving as royal ensign of the aforesaid town of Santa Fe, captain of the infantry, sergeant major, and commander of the companies of New Mexico, and *maestre del campo* of the company, and member of the town council and *alcalde ordinario* of the aforesaid town."[98]

After offering an account of his genealogy and collateral relationships, he indicated that he had been taught to read and write by his father, "since up there [New Mexico], there are no teachers to give such instruction, and he has not studied any field, whatever, because there is no one there to so teach." All his ancestors, he alleged, were honorable Old Christians and defenders of the Holy Faith. Nor were any of them ever arrested, penanced, reconciled, or condemned by the Holy Office.[99]

Unfortunately for Gómez Robledo, several witnesses had presented testimony in New Mexico that called into question his family's ethnicity. Thomás Pérez Granillo attested, "Many years ago a man—he [Pérez] could not recall his name—had told Francisco Gómez, the elder, that he [Gómez] was Jew, and that he would prove it, and that the aforesaid man who had so said, left New Mexico."[100] Subsequent testimony by Fray Antonio de Ybargaray added more specifics to this allegation:

> [A]bout twenty-nine years ago [ca. 1634] there arrived in this kingdom a Portuguese soldier, Manuel Gómez, who stayed with Francisco Gómez, Portuguese by nationality, resident of this town (now deceased [as of 1662]). It was common knowledge that the aforesaid Manuel Gómez said to him [Francisco Gómez] that he was a Jew, and he had known him as such, that the two of them were born on the same street in Lisboa. For that reason, the aforesaid Francisco Gómez, along with his [family] wanted

to kill the aforesaid Manuel Gómez, who then fled to New Spain. Ever since this transpired, until his death, about three or four years ago [ca. 1658 or 1659], Francisco Gómez never took any action to prove his character.[101]

Former governor Juan Manso corroborated this incident, adding that "the aforesaid Francisco Gómez did not defend himself, nor did he prove who he was."[102]

So, too, did Fray Nicolas de Chaves link Gómez Robledo to a Jewish background, on the basis of his father's ethnicity: "Francisco Gómez [Robledo] is suspicious, as he is the son of a Portuguese, and his father, also named Francisco Gómez, is well known throughout that kingdom as a Portuguese, now for years has been referred to as a Jewish dog."[103] The testimony of these witnesses—as well as that of the New Mexicans Juan Griego, Antonio López Zambrano, Domingo López de Ocanto, Fray García de San Francisco, and (even his cousin) Diego Romero—makes it clear that the Jewish identity of the Gómez family was suspected throughout the province, not only at the time of Gómez Robledo's arrest in 1662, but for decades earlier.[104]

Further information about the Jewish observances maintained by the Gómez household was provided by Diego de Melgarejo in an account of a conversation between Bernardo López de Mendizábal and Francisco Gómez Robledo. According to Melgarejo's testimony, López, in a loud voice and in the presence of a group of Santa Feans, had confronted Gómez Robledo, asking him for his reaction to the statement made by a former governor that "your father, Francisco Gómez, was a Jew, and that he died with his face turned to the wall."[105]

The practice of turning a person's face to the wall just before the moment of death was described by David Gitlitz as "one of the most common and most persistent [crypto-Jewish] death-related customs" and one of several examples of Jewish practices mentioned by the Mexican Inquisition in its Edict of Faith, issued in 1639.[106] Another New Mexican family that observed this Jewish custom was that of Juan Griego, one of the old soldiers of Oñate. Doña Teresa de Aguilera y Roche, in a statement made in her own defense against charges of Judaizing, declared that the nonagenarian Griego "died with a *çapote*[107] in his mouth, and with his face against the wall, without desiring to reconcile himself, or to be a Christian, even in this hour [of his death], and as a consequence, they say that he was buried in the hills of Santa Ana."[108]

The most compelling evidence presented against Gómez Robledo, however, was that he was found to have been circumcised, a practice that was considered by the inquisitors as a certain indication of Judaizing.[109] Several witnesses presented testimony that not only Francisco but also his younger brothers Juan and Andrés were circumcised. In his testimony, Domingo López de Ocanto conveyed the impression that knowledge of the circumcisions was widespread among the entire community: "He replied that he only knows that Juan Gómez and Andrés Gómez, sons of Francisco Gómez, deceased, citizens of the town of Santa Fe, who are of the age of this witness, when they were young boys used to bathe together, and that it appeared to him that they had their parts circumcised, *and that all of the young men of that age know this* [emphasis added]."[110] The circumcision of the Gómez Robledo brothers had been the topic of conversation among others as well. Antonio López Zambrano testified that "when he was stationed in the province of Zuni, he heard from the mouth of padre fray Fernando de Monroy, that Domingo López de Ocanto had told him that the aforesaid sons of Francisco Gómez were circumcised, and later, the same young man, Domingo López, in the presence of the aforesaid friar and of this witness, affirmed and confirmed this."[111] As a result of this revelation, the Inquisition prosecutor, Rodrigo Ruíz, suggested that "Juan and Andrés Gómez, brothers, sons of Francisco Gómez and Doña Ana Romero [Robledo], with regard to the aforesaid sign of circumcision or cutting, which demonstrates that they are observers of Judaism, as a consequence should be severely castigated by the Holy Office with the penalties established by law."[112] Neither Juan nor Andrés Gómez Robledo, the stern admonition of Ruíz notwithstanding, was ever arrested by the Inquisition.

The testimony concerning the Gómez Robledo brothers was confirmed by the surgeons and physicians engaged by the Holy Office of the Inquisition during the trial of Francisco Gómez Robledo. The inquisitors included as an integral part of their investigation a process called the *auto de inspección*, whereby a male defendant was examined by a group of surgeons to determine if he had been circumcised. On September 5, 1663, Gómez Robledo submitted to this procedure, which was conducted by Sebastian del Castillo and Andrés Alberto, surgeons of Mexico City, and Diego de Rocas, barber of the Mexican Inquisition (barbers and surgeons during this period often performed the same functions), accompanied by a secretary and a jailer. Their report was conclusive: "They said that they saw and recognized that the defendant, in his genital parts, had on the ligament [that joins the prepuce and the penis] a scar of the size of a grain of barley, more or less, and two other signs, one on the left side of the ligament, and the other one on the right side, smaller than that on the left side, with scars that appear to have been made with a sharp instrument, and this is the truth by the oath that they swore."[113]

Gómez Robledo's response to this finding, issued two weeks after the inspection, was indignant. Reflecting arguments typical of those utilized by *judaizantes* caught up in the celebrated campaign two decades earlier, he contended that "[the information] contained in this chapter is false, because neither he nor his brothers are circumcised, and it is true that in the part of his genitals he had some small ulcers, and they left the marks that are referred to in the chapter, but they do not represent a circumcision, nor anything of the like."[114] But five months later, he backtracked on his assertions regarding the circumcision of his brothers:

> He said that when the doctors and surgeons examined him, it was a cloudy day, and one of them wore eyeglasses, because he was old, and the others were distracted and did not see, and thus they were mistaken, and he asks that this be recognized as a mortification by God, our Lord. And it is true that on the ligament he had some small ulcers, and there, where he had them, the doctors say nothing, and that on the side of the ligament he has a small vein which in dehooding in the genital, makes a scar, and appears to be a mark, but that in looking at it, it is clearly not a mark, and this is the truth by the oath that I make. . . .
>
> [A]nd although it could have been by indication, that which the other witness says, that the brothers of the confessant, when they were young boys, were seen to have had a certain mark in the manner indicated by the witness, that cannot serve as evidence against *this* confessant; moreover, when, by the inspection that took place, the marks that the surgeons found could not be considered as circumcision, as this, in the Old Law was in a different place from where the incision or marks that he had declared to be from the ulcers that he had in that part [emphasis added].[115]

Gómez Robledo requested, and was granted, a second inspection. This time, to ensure a closer degree of scrutiny, the three original surgeons were joined by Don Pedro de los Arcos y Monroy, the official physician of the Mexican Holy Office. The defendant could not have been pleased with the results:

> They said that the aforesaid Sergeant Major, Francisco Gómez, not only had on his prepuce marks that they have declared, according to and as they have said, but more recently they found that on the interior part of the prepuce a medium-size transver-

> sal mark and scar, the size of half a fingernail, and it is evident by the composition and evenness of the part, that they appear to be made by a sharp instrument; although this is not infallible, that they could *not* originate from another cause, and that which they have said is true, by virtue of the oath that they took [emphasis added].[116]

Captain Cristóbal de Anaya Almazán was arrested on an unspecified charge of heresy. The accusations against him had nothing to do with Judaism, but involved his views, contrary to Church doctrine, about the role of priests in administering the sacrament of baptism. He confessed his guilt, was found guilty, and, rather than having to appear in an auto de fe, was required to return to New Mexico and admit his sins before the friars and the general community, which he did at the pueblo of Sandía in July 1665.[117] The next year, he expressed anxiety about the perception that he, like Gómez Robledo, López de Mendizábal, and Teresa de Aguilera y Roche, had been associated with the practice of Judaism:

> Item—he also says and declares that in August of the previous year [1665], in the pueblo of Sandía, having complied with the order that he had brought from the Holy Tribunal, Don Fernando de Durán y Chaves said to the witness that he had taken back that which the Holy Tribunal had ordered, to which the witness responded to him, I, too, take back what I said so that the people should not be saying what is being said, *that perhaps they arrested me for practicing Judaism*, which was said before Don Agustín de Chaves, Padre Fray Raphael, and Doña Catalina Vasques, from which I also ask for mercy as a Catholic Christian [emphasis added].[118]

What was the outcome of the trials of these prominent New Mexicans before the Holy Office of the Inquisition in Mexico City? Cristóbal de Anaya Almazán was given a slap on the wrist and allowed to return to his home. Diego Romero and Nicolas de Aguilar were convicted on several relatively minor counts of heresy, unrelated to any Jewish practices, and eventually were sentenced to a ten-year exile from New Mexico.[119] Bernardo López de Mendizábal died in the Inquisition jail in September 1664, before any determination could be made of his guilt or innocence. He ultimately was absolved, and his remains were exhumed from the unconsecrated grave in which he had been buried and transferred to the Church of Santo Domingo in Mexico City.[120] In December 1664, the inquisitors suspended the trial of Doña Teresa de Aguilera y Roche, after extracting the sum of 4,000 pesos from her to cover the expenses that she had incurred during the four years and two months that she had been incarcerated.[121] And Francisco Gómez Robledo, despite the strength of the testimony against him, combined with the confirmation of his circumcision, was absolved of all charges of Judaism.[122]

How are these absolutions of López, Aguilera, and Gómez Robledo to be explained? Why, after collecting so much damaging evidence over three years, did the Mexican inquisitors simply drop these cases? France Scholes, writing in the 1940s, decades before the development of any elaborate literature offering a context for the history of crypto-Judaism in Mexico, believed that the argument presented by the prosecution was essentially weak and politically motivated. He dismissed the value of the testimony presented against the governor and his wife, as well as that against Gómez Robledo, arguing that "actual eyewitness accounts . . . were given by only four or five persons who were members of the López household" and that such testimony represented nothing more than "petty gossip and spiteful rumor-mongering. Much of the testimony against Teresa was based on stories told by ignorant, prying servants who had incurred her displeasure."[123]

To be certain, much of the evidence offered by the Inquisition officials was hearsay. But a considerable number of those bearing witness in the trials of López and Aguilera did present firsthand accounts of their behavior. That some were servants in their household should not categorically negate the veracity of their reports. And not all the deponents were servants, but intimates who had direct knowledge of the couple's weekly personal routines. Moreover, that López's maternal great-grandfather had been convicted of practicing Judaism in Mexico six decades earlier, a detail that the governor had conveniently neglected to mention in his discussion of his family history, gives the Inquisition's charges more plausibility. With regard to the case against Gómez Robledo, the testimony pertaining to the widespread reputation in the New Mexican community of his father, Francisco Gómez, as a Portuguese Jew was enhanced by the accounts of the family turning Gómez's head to the wall at the point of death, the eyewitness reports of the circumcision of two of the Gómez Robledo brothers, and, perhaps most important, the judgment of the Inquisition physicians and surgeons that Francisco himself had been circumcised.

Were the arrests politically motivated? All indications point to the conclusion that they were. The Franciscans were extremely upset about the policies and behavior of Governor López and clearly used their authority as agents of the Holy Office of the Inquisition to break down his power by incarcerating him, his wife, and his closest political and military associates, thus removing them from the scene. But it is fallacious to conclude that simply because there was a political motivation for the actions against López, Aguilera, and Gómez Robledo, there was no valid basis for the charges of the practice of Judaism. It must be remembered that political concerns extraneous to the issue of heresy had served as the catalyst for the major campaign by the Inquisition against the *judaizantes* of New Spain two decades earlier. That the inquisitors had capitalized on the anti-Portuguese sentiment that gripped the viceroyalty in the 1640s in no way diminishes the validity of their accusations of observance of the Law of Moses.

The more interesting issue raised by the aberrant crackdowns by the Inquisition against the crypto-Jews of Mexico and, particularly, New Mexico in the sixteenth and seventeenth centuries relates to the ability of these people to practice their Jewish observances in such a manner that the general community was aware of their activities, yet seems not to have cared, except to the extent that some may have benefited politically from the arrest and consequent removal of their rivals. All things being equal, the "heretical" activities of the crypto-Jews likely would have been barely noticed and would have passed without official comment. Had it not been for the political conflicts between Governor López and the Franciscans, and the consequent Inquisition trials, the observations of Pedro de Arteaga and Doña Josepha de Sandoval with regard to the Sabbath eve rituals of Doña Teresa de Aguilera would have remained a topic of conversation between the two of them. The distinguished political and military career of Francisco Gómez Robledo would have continued to flourish, as had his father's, despite the common knowledge that the elder Gómez had lived and died as a Jew and that Francisco and his brothers bore the distinguishing mark of circumcision.

But in 1660, all things were not equal. The Franciscan friars were sorely upset with the policies practiced by López and regarded the governor and his cronies as a distinct threat to the social, moral, and economic order of the colony. Thus what would have been regarded as "tolerable" behavior on the part of the governor and his wife under ordinary circumstances was cited as grounds for removal from office and expulsion from New Mexico. That Doña Teresa, her husband, and others, like Francisco Gómez Robledo, were not convicted of the crimes of which they were accused had less to do with the strength of the evidence against them than with the disinclination of the Holy Office of the Inquisition or anyone else in authority in Mexico City to prosecute cases against crypto-Jews. The energy generated during the intense campaign of the Inquisition against *judaizantes* in the 1640s had long since expired. By the time Governor López and his New Mexican cohorts arrived in Mexico City for trial, the Mexican Inquisition was in the throes of a decades-long investigation into the fiscal and procedural abuses perpetrated by a group of corrupt inquisitors. The new corps of inquisitors, it appears, went through the motions of investigating cases of crypto-Judaism, but were far more interested in pursuing other, less spectacular heresies.

As in Mexico during the 1640s, in New Mexico two decades later, the authorities tended not to persecute all those who might have been practicing Judaism secretly, but pursued only the high-profile cases. It is also interesting to note that while the Inquisition authorities disrupted the life of Francisco Gómez Robledo, neither of his circumcised brothers, Juan and Andrés, was touched. Siblings José, Ana María, and Francisca escaped notice completely, and brother Bartolomé fled New Mexico with Francisco's horses and mules, as well as the income from the *encomienda* of the pueblo of Ácoma, presumably to come to the aid of his brother who was incarcerated in Mexico City.[124] Nor was Manuel Jorge or his family ever prosecuted, despite the allegation that they "observed the Law of Moses with exquisite rites and ceremonies," which emanated from his daughter's confession. With regard to the others whose New Christian origins have been mentioned, the documentary record that has survived the ages is silent. Perhaps by the late seventeenth century, they had abandoned or forgotten their ancestral Jewish faith. Or possibly they continued to maintain their beliefs and practices in secret, successfully managing to avoid detection by authorities. In the absence of documentation, the facts will never be known for certain.

What became of these Spanish and Portuguese colonists who were caught up in the nightmare of the 1660s? Bernardo López de Mendizábal, as noted, died in his Inquisition cell in 1664. After her release from jail in 1664, Doña Teresa de Aguilera y Roche did not return to New Mexico, but remained in Mexico City. Her problems with the Inquisition officials were far from over, however. For years afterward, she was engaged in litigation with the Holy Office over the disposition of her husband's estate, which had been embargoed on his arrest. The dispute lasted for fourteen years after Doña Teresa's death in 1680 and was finally resolved on July 16, 1694, when the inquisitors released some 6,500 pesos from López's estate to Doña Teresa's heirs.[125] Cristóbal de Anaya Almazán remained in New Mexico through the 1660s and 1670s. Members of his family were to suffer violent deaths during the Pueblo Revolt of 1680, when his neighbors from the pueblo of Santo Domingo sacked his *estancia* at Angostura. One of his nephews, Francisco, returned to New Mexico with Diego de Vargas in the 1690s and served as the progenitor of the Anaya family, which was to distinguish itself over the succeeding centuries.[126] Francisco Gómez Robledo returned to New Mexico after his release from the Inquisition jail and managed to escape from Santa Fe during the Pueblo Revolt. He was counted among the Spanish refugees in El Paso and was cited as deceased by 1693. Apparently, the only legitimate descendant of the elder Francisco Gómez documented to have returned to New Mexico after its reconquest by Vargas was Francisca Gómez Robledo, daughter of Andrés and married to Ignacio Roybal.[127]

After the brief, but intense activity by the agents of the Holy Office of the Inquisition in the 1660s, the policy soon returned to one of toleration. In 1680, accumulated grievances against the Spanish authorities, both civil and religious, exacerbated by several years of drought and food shortages, finally pushed the beleaguered Pueblo Indians over the edge. In August, Spanish settlements fell victim to attacks all across the province. Men, women, and children; priests, soldiers, and civilians; Old Christians and New Christians—all could be found among those killed as revenge for eight decades of abuse. Governor Antonio de Otermín, seeing his capital laid waste, hastily organized a retreat of the surviving colonists southward to begin a thirteen-year exile in the area around El Paso. Among the refugees were the nieces and nephews, the grand-nieces and grand-nephews, the grandchildren and great-grandchildren of the *converso* settlers: Carvajales, Romeros, Gómez Robledos, Jorges, Veras. Many of these individuals and their offspring returned to New Mexico in the 1690s, accompanied by others of crypto-Jewish descent from Mexico, Spain, Portugal, and even France. This new generation of New Christians, and their descendants, would participate fully in the reestablishment of Spanish New Mexico and become instrumental figures in the economic and political development of the colony in the eighteenth century.

NOTES

1. Richard E. Greenleaf, "France V. Scholes: Historian's Historian, 1897–1979," *New Mexico Historical Review* 75 (2000): 324.
2. The historical literature treating the institution of the *encomienda* has evolved greatly over the past several decades, from excessively theoretical evaluations to more in-depth, site-specific studies. See, for example, Leslie Byrd Simpson, *The Encomienda in New Spain: The Beginning of Spanish Mexico*, rev. ed. (Berkeley: University of California Press, 1982); Charles Gibson, *Spain in*

America (New York: Harper & Row, 1967); Clarence H. Haring, *The Spanish Empire in America* (New York: Harcourt, Brace & World, 1947); Silvio Zavala, *La encomienda indiana* (Mexico City: Editorial Porrúa, 1992); Robert Himmerich y Valencia, *The Encomenderos of New Spain, 1521–1555* (Austin: University of Texas Press, 1991); James Lockhart, "Encomienda and Hacienda: The Evolution of the Great Estate in the Spanish Indies," *Hispanic American Historical Review* 49 (1969): 411–429; Wendy Kramer, *Encomienda Politics in Early Colonial Guatemala, 1524–1554: Dividing the Spoils* (Boulder, Colo.: Westview Press, 1994); and Luis F. Calero, *Chiefdoms Under Siege: Spain's Rule and Native Adaption in the Southern Colombian Andes, 1535–1700* (Albuquerque: University of New Mexico Press, 1997).

3. John L. Kessell, *Kiva, Cross, and Crown: The Pecos Indians and New Mexico, 1540–1840* (Washington, D.C.: National Park Service, 1979), pp. 98–99.

4. Testimonio del ynforme que su ssa. el Dr. Don Bernardo López de Mendizábal, governador y capitán general de este Reyno, hace al Exmo. Señor Virrey de la Nueva España, Santa Fe, September 8, 1660, fols. 313r–339r, Ramo de Concurso de Peñalosa, tomo 1, Archivo General de la Nación, Mexico City (hereafter cited as AGN); [*cédulas* pertaining to the conditions in New Mexico, hostility with Apaches, resupply, etc.], September 11, 1678–October 5, 1678, fols. 297r–302v, Ramo de Reales Cédulas Duplicadas, tomo 31, exp. 296, AGN; Kessell, *Kiva, Cross, and Crown*, p. 94.

5. Robert Ricard, *The Spiritual Conquest of Mexico: An Essay on the Apostolate and the Evangelizing Methods of the Mendicant Orders in New Spain, 1523–1572*, trans. Lesley Byrd Simpson (Berkeley: University of California Press, 1966); France V. Scholes, *Church and State in New Mexico* (Albuquerque: University of New Mexico Press, 1937).

6. Ramón Gutiérrez, *When Jesus Came, the Corn Mothers Went Away: Marriage, Sexuality, and Power in New Mexico, 1500–1846* (Stanford, Calif.: Stanford University Press, 1991), pp. 71–72, 104–105, 114, 120–130; Kessell, *Kiva, Cross, and Crown*, pp. 120–121, 164, 224–226; Joseph P. Sánchez, *The Río Abajo Frontier, 1540–1692: A History of Early Colonial New Mexico* (Albuquerque: Albuquerque Museum, 1987), pp. 89–94.

7. Scholes, *Church and State in New Mexico*, pp. 19–37.

8. Ibid., pp. 43–102.

9. Ibid., pp. 115–191.

10. Fray Angelico Chávez, *Origins of New Mexico Families in the Spanish Colonial Period* (Santa Fe: Gannon, 1975), p. 1, citing Ramo de Inquisición, tomo 495, fols. 89–103, AGN.

11. Gutierre Tibón cited the name as "one of an illustrious Sephardic family; its principal branches are those of London and Amsterdam. Jacob A. translated into Spanish the *Cuzary* (Amsterdam, 1666), which Yehuda Halevi had written in Arabic" (*Diccionario etimológico comparado de los apellidos españoles, hispanoamericanos y filipinos* [Mexico City: Fondo de Cultura Económica, 1992], p. 2). The *Encyclopedia Judaica* refers to Abendaña as a "Sephardi family, with members widely dispersed among the ex-Marrano communities of Northern Europe. The name, Abendaña is Arabic in origin, commonly written in Hebrew, אבן-דנא, דנא" (Cecil Roth and Geoffrey Wigoder, eds., *Encyclope-*

dia Judaica [Jerusalem: Keter, 1972], vol. 1, pp. 65–67). The encyclopedia listed eight prominent individuals by that name who distinguished themselves in seventeenth-century England, Germany, Holland, India, and New York.

12. "Obligación de carnecerías, February 14, 1469" (no. 751) and "Prohibición de entrar en la morería a la búsqueda de moros cautivos fugados, December 11, 1469" (no. 746), in Luis Rubio García, ed., *Los judíos de Murcia en la baja edad media (1350–1500): Colección documental* (Murcia: Universidad de Murcia, 1994), vol. 2, pp. 9 (citing Libro de actas, 1468–1469, fol. 104r, Archivo Municipal de Murcia), 14–15.

13. Padrones [ecclesiastical censuses] de Santiago, San Mateo, San Juan, y Santa María, 1660, Archivo Histórico Municipal de Lorca.

14. Jaime Contreras Contreras, *Sotos contra Riquelmes: Regidores, inquisidores y criptojudíos* (Madrid: Muchnik, 1992), p. 314.

15. Feliciano Sierro Malmierca, *Judíos, moriscos e Inquisición en Ciudad Rodrigo* (Salamanca: Diputación de Salamanca, 1990), p. 23.

16. María Fuencisla García César, *El pasado judío de Ciudad Rodrigo*, Fontes Iudaeorum Regni Castellae, vol. 6 (Salamanca: Universidad Pontificia de Salamanca, 1992), p. 93, citing Lybro de las colaçiones desta çibdat e sus arrabales del repartimiento de la puente, año de mil e quatrocientos e ochenta e seys años.

17. Carlos Carrete Parrondo, *Provincia de Salamanca*, Fontes Iudaeorum Regni Castellae, vol. 1 (Salamanca: Universidad Pontificia de Salamanca, 1981), p. 73, Edict of November 10, 1492, citing Registro General de Sello, fol. 40, Archivo General de Simancas.

18. Ángel Bernal Estévez, *El consejo de Ciudad Rodrigo y su tierra durante el siglo XV* (Salamanca: Diputación de Salamanca, 1989), pp. 199–207, 301–304. See also Relaciones de causas y autos de fe, 1559–1715, Sección de Inquisición, legajo 2075, pt. 2, exps. 38, 40, Archivo Histórico Nacional, Madrid (hereafter cited as AHN); and Relaciones de las causas de fe, 1622–1699, Sección de Inquisición, legajo 2135, exps. 23, 24, AHN.

19. Marriage of Joan de Abendaño, natural de Peñaranda, con Leonor Hernández, hija de Diego Hernández, August 30, 1596, Parroquia de San Juan Bautista, libro 219, matrimonios, fol. 1v; marriage of Juan de Pedraça, hijo de Pedro de Pedraça y Francisca de Cisneros, vecinos de Villa Vieja, con María de Avendaño, hija de Xptóbal de Avendaño, difunto, y Francisca Hernández, vecinos de Ciudad Rodrigo, August 2, 1623, libro 219, matrimonios, fol. 34r; baptism of María, hija de Christóbal de Avendaño y Francisca Hernández, August 17, 1605, libro 219, bautismos, fol. 16r; baptism of Francisco, hijo de Pero Hernández, curador, y de Ana Hernández, padrinos: Joan de Avendaño y Leonor Hernández, October 29, 1606, libro 219, bautismos, fol. 18r; Padrones, 1598, 1612–1615, 1617–1623, 1625, 1629, showing Juan de Avendaño, wool merchant, living on Calle de Santiago, all in Archivo Diocesano de Ciudad Rodrigo.

20. Relaciones de las causas de fe del año pasado de 1648 (Valladolid), testimony of Antonio Rodríguez del Cano, Antonio de Espinosa, Antonio Rodrigues, Acacio Bustillo, Antonio López Coletero, Christóbal Ramos, Domingo Hernández, Diego Malo, Francisco de Herrera, Gaspar de Herrera, Gaspar Ro-

dríguez del Cano, Juan de Ysla, Miguel Bázquez, and Paulo de Herrera, fols. 15v–23r, Sección de Inquisición, legajo 2135, exp. 23, AHN; Relaciones de las causas de fe que se han fencido en la Inquisición de Valladolid en el año pasado de 1651, testimony of Juan del Cerro, fols. 1r–v, Sección de Inquisición, legajo 2135, exp. 24, AHN.

21. Chávez, *Origins of New Mexico Families*, p. 1.

22. Baptism of Diego de Vera, April 29, 1590, Nuestra Señora de la Concepción, Libro segundo de bautismos, fol. 44r, Archivo Histórico Diocesano de La Laguna de Tenerife.

23. John B. Colligan, "More About Diego de Vera Perdomo," *Herencia: Quarterly Journal of the Hispanic Genealogical Research Center of New Mexico* 7 (1999): 2.

24. Ibid., p. 7.

25. Libros 2–5 de bautismos, 1529–1587, Archivo Histórico Diocesano de Canarias, Las Palmas.

26. Relación de las causas despachadas este anno, en la inquisición de Canaria desde primero de enero de 1609 asta fin del dicho anno, Francisco de Vera Mojíca, 1609, Sección de Inquisición, legajo 1829, exps. 2–20, AHN.

27. Proceso seguido en el S.O. contra Estévan de Jerez, por declarar en cierta información que Francisco de Vera Muxíca era cristiano viejo siendo como era, descendiente de judíos, conversos, etc., 1609, fol. 818v, Fondo Antiguo, XCIV-10, Museo Canario, Las Palmas.

28. Alonso de la Barrera and Doña Ana de Vera, Canaria, 1528, Libro primero de genealogías, fols. 130r–131r, Fondo Antiguo, CLII-1, Museo Canario.

29. Relación de las causas despachadas este anno, en la inquisición de Canaria desde primero de enero de 1609, Sección de Inquisición, legajo 1829, exps. 2–20, AHN.

30. Chávez, *Origins of New Mexico Families*, p. 112.

31. José Antonio Esquibel, "The Romero Family of Seventeenth-Century New Mexico," part 1, *Herencia: Quarterly Journal of the Hispanic Genealogical Research Center of New Mexico* 11, no. 1 (2003): 1–30, and "Romero Family," part 2, *Herencia* 11, no. 3 (2003): 2–20; Causa contra el Capitán Diego Romero, natural de la Villa de Santa Fe en Nuevo México, por hereje, 1663, fol. 71v, Ramo de Inquisición, tomo 586, exp. 1, AGN. Bartolomé Romero's *converso* roots are discussed in chap. 4.

32. Rick Hendricks and Gerald J. Mandell postulated that the Manuel Jorge of New Mexico was a close relation of the Manuel Jorge family of Parral ("Francisco de Lima, Portuguese Merchants of Parral, and the New Mexico Trade, 1638–1675," *New Mexico Historical Review* 77 [2002]: 261–293). The likelihood of a blood relationship is strengthened by the narrative offered by Doña Teresa de Aguilera y Roche, in the statement that she offered in her defense before the Mexican Inquisition, which declared that the Manuel Jorge of New Mexico "is my mortal enemy, along with all of the Veras always, and his wife through him" (El Señor fiscal del Santo Oficio contra Doña Teresa de Aguilera y Roche, mujer de Don Bernardo López de Mendizábal, por sospechosa de delitos de judaismo, 1663, statement in her defense, fol. 156, Ramo de Inquisición, tomo 596, exp. 1, AGN).

33. Testamento de Manuel Jorge, Parral, June 7, 1655, fols. 72r–74r, microfilm, reel 1654B, Archivo Histórico de Parral. Manuel Jorge, the elder, was cited as a resident of Parral, a native of Portuguese Tangiers, and the son of Antonio Jorge and María Álvares, both deceased. In his will, he listed his wife as Ana de Vera, daughter of Captain Gaspar de Vera and María Delgado, both deceased. He indicated that the union had produced nine children: Antonio (who at the time lived in New Mexico), Manuel, María, Ana, Diego, Pedro, Juana, Lucía, and Ysabel. See also Hendricks and Mandell, "Francisco de Lima." John Kessell and Rick Hendricks appear to have confused the two Manuel Jorges, considering them to have been one person (*By Force of Arms: The Journals of Don Diego de Vargas, 1691–1693* [Albuquerque: University of New Mexico Press, 1992], pp. 211–212 n.46). See also Chávez, *Origins of New Mexico Families*, p. 51.

34. For an elaborate discussion of the Portuguese New Christian connections of the elder Manuel Jorge in Cuencamé, Parral, and Mexico City, see Hendricks and Mandell, "Francisco de Lima." While they held out the possibility that Jorge and his associates may have been crypto-Jews, they conclude that "in all probability, they were not," on the basis that they "bent over backward in efforts to demonstrate their loyal Christianity." As discussed elsewhere in this book, I believe that outward expressions of Catholic piety and the secret practice of Judaism are not mutually exclusive.

35. Proceso contra Bernardo López de Mendizábal, gobernador de Nuevo México, por proposiciones heréticas y sospechoso de judaizante, 1662, testimony of Fray Nicolas de Villar Santa Fe, September 27, 1661, fol. 162r, Ramo de Inquisición, tomo 593, exp. 1, AGN.

36. Ibid.

37. Genealogía del Pe. Fr. Estévan de Perea, predicador y custodio de las Provincias de México, 1628, fol. 1r, Ramo de Inquisición, tomo 365, exp. 11, AGN; "Carta de los señores del convento con el testimonio de la Ynquisición de Llerena de las ynformaciones de Fray Estéban de Perea . . . para que se junte con las que se hizieron en la Ynquisición de Ebora. . . . (1628–1633)," in Charles Wilson Hackett, ed., *Historical Documents Relating to New Mexico, Nueva Vizcaya, and Approaches Thereto, to 1773, Collected by Adolph F. A. Bandelier and Fanny R. Bandelier* (Washington, D.C.: Carnegie Institution, 1937), vol. 3, pp. 128–129, citing Ramo de Inquisición, tomo 268, exp. 5, fol. 3r, AGN.

38. José Pires Gonçalves, *Monsaráz: Vida, morte e ressurreição de uma vila alentejana* (Lisbon: Edição de Casa do Alentejo, 1966), pp. 13–14.

39. "Carta de los señores del convento con el testimonio de la Ynquisición de Llerena de las ynformaciones de Fray Estéban de Perea," in Hackett, ed., *Historical Documents*, vol. 3, pp. 128–129. Scholes dismissed this testimony as "some rumor that [Perea's] maternal grandfather came from a line of new [*sic*] Christians" ("Problems in the Early Ecclesiastical History of New Mexico," *New Mexico Historical Review* 7 [1932]: 62).

40. Scholes, *Church and State in New Mexico*, p. 116.

41. Chávez, *Origins of New Mexico Families*, p. 14.

42. Ibid., p. 15.

43. See chap. 4 and Chávez, *Origins of New Mexico Families*, pp. 35–37, 77.

44. Chávez, *Origins of New Mexico Families*, pp. 38–39.

45. Ibid., p. 35.

46. Scholes, *Church and State in New Mexico*, p. 120.

47. Autos de prisión, embargo y remate de bienes del Sargento Mayor Francisco Gómez Robledo, fecho el año de 1662, inventory of estate of Francisco Gómez Robledo, Santa Fe, May 4, 1662, fols. 246r–247r [second set of folios bearing these numbers], and inventory of estate of Francisco Gómez Robledo, Estancia de San Nicolás de las Barrancas, May 18, 1662, fol. 250r, Ramo de Concurso de Peñalosa, tomo 2, legajo 1, no. 6, AGN. For a discussion of the location of the southern two *estancias*, see Stanley M. Hordes, "Irrigation at the Confluence of the Río Grande and Río Chama: The *Acequias* de Chamita, Salazar and Hernández, 1600–1680" (report, state of New Mexico, on the relation of *S. E. Reynolds, State Engineer, Plaintiff* v. *Roman Aragon, et al., Defendants*, no. 7941—Civil, Río Chama Mainstream Section, Río Chama Ditches, June 24, 1996), pp. 5–9.

48. Testimonio de Francisco Xavier, Santa Fe, August 9, 1662, fols. 86v–87r, Ramo de Concurso de Peñalosa, tomo 1, AGN; Testimonio a la letra que el Señor Capitán y Sargento Mayor D. Diego Dionísio de Peñalosa Briceño y Verdugo, Governador y Capitán General del Nuevo México mandó trasuntar de la Residencia que remitió al Exmo. Señor Virrey de la Nueva España de la que dió el Capitán D. Bernardo López de Mendizábal. Año de 1661, testimony of Diego Romero, Santa Fe, October 13, 1661, fol. 218v, Ramo de Concurso de Peñalosa, tomo 1, legajo 1, no. 2, AGN.

49. Autos de prisión, embargo y remate de bienes del Sargento Mayor Francisco Gómez Robledo, inventory of estate of Francisco Gómez Robledo, Santa Fe, fol. 246r [second set of folios bearing this number], Ramo de Concurso de Peñalosa, tomo 2, legajo 1, no. 6, AGN.

50. [*Cédulas* pertaining to the conditions in New Mexico, hostility with Apaches, resupply, etc.], fol. 302r, Ramo de Reales Cédulas Duplicadas, tomo 31, exp. 296, AGN.

51. Autos de prisión, embargo y remate de bienes del Sargento Mayor Francisco Gómez Robledo, inventory of estate of Francisco Gómez Robledo, Santa Fe, fols. 246v–247r [second set of folios bearing these numbers], Ramo de Concurso de Peñalosa, tomo 2, legajo 1, no. 6, AGN.

52. [*Cédulas* pertaining to the conditions in New Mexico, hostility with Apaches, resupply, etc.], fol. 302r, Ramo de Reales Cédulas Duplicadas, tomo 31, exp. 296, AGN.

53. Chávez, *Origins of New Mexico Families*, p. 37.

54. Ibid., p. 36.

55. Testimonio a la letra que el Señor Capitán y Sargento Mayor D. Diego Dionísio de Peñalosa Briceño y Verdugo, declaración de Governador Bernardo López de Mendizábal, fol. 153, Ramo de Concurso de Peñalosa, tomo 1, legajo 1, no. 2, AGN.

56. Causa contra el Capitán Diego Romero, fols. 71r–v, Ramo de Inquisición, tomo 586, exp. 1, AGN; Testimonio a la letra que el Señor Capitán y Sar-

gento Mayor D. Diego Dionísio de Peñalosa Briceño y Verdugo: declaration of Governador Bernardo López de Mendizábal, fol. 153; testimony of Bartolomé Romero, Santa Fe, October 8, 1661, fol. 195; and testimony of Diego Romero, Santa Fe, October 13, 1661, fol. 218r, Ramo de Concurso de Peñalosa, tomo 1, legajo 1, no. 2, AGN; [*cédulas* pertaining to the conditions in New Mexico, hostility with Apaches, resupply, etc.], fol. 302r, Ramo de Reales Cédulas Duplicadas, tomo 31, exp. 296, AGN; Testimonio de Sargento Mayor Diego Romero, Santa Fe, July 8, 1661, fol. 139, Ramo de Concurso de Peñalosa, tomo 1, AGN; Autos de prisión, embargo y remate de bienes del Sargento Mayor Diego Romero—Año de 1662, inventory of estate of Diego Romero, Santa Fe, May 4, 1662, fols. 297r–v, Ramo de Concurso de Peñalosa, tomo 2, legajo 1, no. 7, AGN; Chávez, *Origins of New Mexico Families*, pp. 95–97.

57. Chávez, *Origins of New Mexico Families*, pp. 14–15, 38–40, 99.

58. Scholes, *Church and State in New Mexico*, p. 120.

59. Ibid., pp. 90–91 n.3.

60. Testificaciónes procedentes de diversas comisarios denuncias, declaraciónes, y otros asuntos todos concernientes al Santo Oficio con su índice alfabético y foliado particularmente del 1 a 370, denunciation of Francisco Gómez, Santa Fe, May 19, 1626, fols. 269v–270r [405v–406r], Ramo de Inquisición, tomo 356, exp. 6, AGN.

61. Scholes, *Church and State in New Mexico* pp. 120, 145 n.14, citing Gaspar Pérez de Villagrá, *Historia de la Nueva México* (Mexico City: Museo Nacional, 1900), vol. 2, app. 3, pp. 9, 10 [7–8], translated by Stanley M. Hordes.

62. Villagrá, *Historia de la Nueva México*, vol. 2, app. 3, pp. 7–8. This segment of the letter was not included in Scholes, *Church and State in New Mexico*. Rather, Scholes mistakenly indicated that the information contained therein comprised a separate letter, dated two days later.

63. Scholes, *Church and State in New Mexico*, pp. 154–155.

64. Ibid., p. 126.

65. Ibid., pp. 141, 151 n.58, citing Testimony before Fray Tomás Manso, 1644, Sección de Patronato, legajo 247, sec. 7, Archivo General de Indias, Seville.

66. Among other offices, López de Mendizábal held the post of *alcalde mayor* de San Juan de los Llanos and *corregidor* de Guayacocotlán. See Protestación, México, April 15, 1652, fol. 118v, Notaría 110, Toribio Cobian, tomo 726 bis, 1650–1652, Archivo General de Notarías, Mexico City (hereafter cited as AGNM); Poder (Pueblo de Epecontepeque [?], provincia de Guayacocotlán), February 24, 1656, fols. 11r–12r, Notaría 110, Toribio Cobian, tomo 728, 1656, AGNM; and Primera audiencia de Don Bernardo López de Mendizábal, por proposiciones irreligiosas y escandalosas, México, April 28, 1663, fol. 2r, Ramo de Inquisición, tomo 594, exp. 1, AGN.

67. Cartas referentes al ingenio de Cristóbal de Mendizábal, Puebla, 1650, fols. 164–173, Ramo de Inquisición, tomo 436, exp. 31, AGN; Protestación, fol. 118v, Notaría 110, Toribio Cobian, tomo 726 bis, 1650–1652, AGNM.

68. Obligación, Bernardo López de Mendizábal to Antonio Urrutia de Vergara, México, May 23, 1654, fol. 187r, Notaría 110, Toribio Cobian, tomo 727 bis,

1654, AGNM; Obligación, Bernardo López de Mendizábal to Antonio Urrutia de Vergara, December 20, 1658, fol. 465r, Notaría 110, Toribio Cobian, tomo 729, 1658, AGNM.

69. El Señor fiscal del Santo Oficio contra Doña Teresa de Aguilera y Roche, Primera audiencia, México, May 2, 1663, fols. 56r–59r, Ramo de Inquisición, tomo 596, exp. 1, AGN.

70. France V. Scholes, *Troublous Times in New Mexico, 1659–1670* (Albuquerque: University of New Mexico Press, 1942), pp. 1–18. For an account of Manso's career before and after his term as governor, see Rick Hendricks and Gerald J. Mandell, "Juan Manso, Frontier Entrepreneur," *New Mexico Historical Review* 75 (2000): 339–367.

71. [Interrogatory presented by former governor Juan Manso pertaining to the suit against General Don Bernardo López de Mendizábal], Santa Fe, August 9, 1662, fols. 82r–v: testimony of Francisco Xavier, Santa Fe, August 9, 1662, fols. 86v–87r; and capitán Juan Barela de Losada, Santa Fe, August 14, 1662, fol. 96v, Ramo de Concurso de Peñalosa, tomo 1, AGN. See also Scholes, *Troublous Times in New Mexico*, p. 35.

72. Sánchez, *Río Abajo Frontier*, p. 90, citing Proceso contra Bernardo López de Mendizábal, testimony of Fray García de San Francisco, Convento de San Antonio de Senecú, May 9, 1661, Ramo de Inquisición, tomo 593, AGN.

73. Scholes, *Troublous Times in New Mexico*, pp. 34–87; Sánchez, *Río Abajo Frontier*, pp. 90–95.

74. Testimonio a la letra que el Señor Capitán y Sargento Mayor Don Diego Dionísio de Peñalosa Briceño y Verdugo, December 13, 1660–October 29, 1661, fols. 148–364, Ramo de Concurso de Peñalosa, tomo 1, legajo 1, no. 2, AGN.

75. Scholes, *Troublous Times in New Mexico*, pp. 99–105.

76. Auto de prisión, embargo y remate de bienes del Capitán Nicolas de Aguilar, Isleta, May 2, 1662, fols. 569r–v, Ramo de Concurso de Peñalosa, tomo 1, legajo 1, no. 5, AGN; Autos de prisión, embargo y remate de bienes del Sargento Mayor Diego Romero, Isleta, May 2, 1662, fols. 296r–v, Ramo de Concurso de Peñalosa, tomo 2, legajo 1, no. 7, AGN. See also Scholes, *Troublous Times in New Mexico*, p. 129.

77. Autos de prisión, embargo y remate de bienes del Sargento Mayor Francisco Gómez Robledo, May 4, 1662, fol. 247r, Ramo de Concurso de Peñalosa, tomo 2, legajo 1, no. 6, AGN.

78. Auto de prisión y embargo de bienes con su remate del Capitán Christóval de Anaia Almasan, May 14, 1662, fol. 381r, Ramo de Concurso de Peñalosa, tomo 3, legajo 1, no. 22, AGN.

79. Scholes, *Troublous Times in New Mexico*, pp. 129–130.

80. Ibid., pp. 134–137.

81. Prisión y embargo de bienes de Doña Teresa de Aguilera y Roche, Santa Fe, August 27, 1662, fols. 396r–397r, Ramo de Concurso de Peñalosa, tomo 1, AGN.

82. Autos de prisión, embargo y remate de bienes del Sargento Mayor Francisco

Gómez Robledo, October 5, 1662, fols. 263r–v, Ramo de Concurso de Peñalosa, tomo 2, legajo 1, no. 6, AGN.

83. Acusación del fiscal del Santo Oficio contra Bernardo López de Mendizábal, por judaizante y otros delitos, México, 1663 [incorrectly written on the document as 1648], fol. 201r, Ramo de Inquisición, tomo 421, exp. 6, AGN.

84. Ibid., fol. 248r.

85. Evelio Martínez Liébana, *Los judíos de Sahagún en la transición del siglo XIV y XV* (Valladolid: Junta de Castilla y León, Consejería de Cultura y Turismo, 1993).

86. Proceso contra Juan Núñez, balanzario de la real caja, por alumbrado y sospechoso de judaizante, México, 1598, fols. 160r–161v, Ramo de Inquisición, tomo 210, exp. 2, AGN; Luis Romera Iruela and María del Carmen Galbis Díez, *Catálogo de pasajeros a Indias durante los siglos XVI, XVII y XVIII* (Seville: Archivo General de Indias, 1981), vol. 4, p. 387, March 2, 1564, entry 3.177, III-23v.

87. Primera audiencia de Don Bernardo López de Mendizábal, fols. 2v–3r, Ramo de Inquisición, tomo 594, exp. 1, AGN.

88. Proceso contra Diego López de Perea, vecino de la ciudad de Guadalajara, judaizante, Toledo, 1543, testimony of Francisco Díaz de Olmedilla, Guadalajara, July 31, 1518, Sección de Inquisición, legajo 160, exp. 9, AHN; Proceso contra Juan de Pastrana, mercader, vecino de Guadalajara, Toledo, 1538, Sección de Inquisición, legajo 173, exp. 13, AHN. Juan de Pastrana was the son of Leonor de Pastrana, the same name as Pablo's daughter.

89. Primera audiencia de Don Bernardo López de Mendizábal, fols. 2v–3r, Ramo de Inquisición, tomo 594, exp. 1, AGN.

90. Ibid., response of Don Bernardo López de Mendizábal, México, December 1, 1663–March 14, 1664, fol. 280r.

91. El Señor fiscal del Santo Oficio contra Doña Teresa de Aguilera y Roche, Primera audiencia, fols. 59r–61r, Ramo de Inquisición, tomo 596, exp. 1, AGN.

92. Chávez, *Origins of New Mexico Families*, p. 7.

93. El Señor fiscal del Santo Oficio contra Doña Teresa de Aguilera y Roche, testimony of Pedro de Arteaga, Santa Fe, October 24, 1661, fol. 18, Ramo de Inquisición, tomo 596, exp. 1, AGN.

94. Ibid., testimony of Josepha Sandoval, Santa Fe, October 31, 1661, fol. 26v.

95. Ibid., testimony of Pedro de Arteaga, fol. 18.

96. Ibid., testimony of Josepha Sandoval, fol. 26v.

97. Ibid., response of Doña Teresa de Aguilera y Roche, México, October 26, 1663, fols. 100r–v. See also Scholes, *Troublous Times in New Mexico*, pp. 162–165.

98. Proceso y causa criminal contra el sargento mayor Francisco Gómez Robledo, por sospechoso de delitos del judaismo, y haver dicho proposiciones heréticas, Primera audiencia, México, July 4, 1663, fols. 341v–342r, Ramo de Inquisición, tomo 583, exp. 3, AGN.

99. Ibid., fols. 344r–v.

100. Ibid., testimony of Thomás Pérez Granillo, Santa Fe, July 23, 1661, fols. 278r–v.

101. Ibid., testimony of Fray Antonio de Ybargaray, Santa Fe, March 6, 1662, fols. 295r–v.

102. Ibid., testimony of Juan Manso, México, May 21, 1660, fol. 275r.

103. Ibid., testimony of Fray Nicolas de Chaves, México, September 18, 1660, fol. 270v.

104. Ibid., testimony of Juan Griego, fols. 297r–298r; Antonio López Zambrano, fols. 299r–v; Domingo López de Ocanto, fols. 301r–v; Fray García de San Francisco, fols. 305r–v; and Diego Romero, fols. 307r–309r, Santa Fe and México, May 9, 1661–October 26, 1663.

105. Ibid., testimony of Diego de Melgarejo, Santa Fe, October 26, 1661, fol. 293r.

106. David M. Gitlitz, *Secrecy and Deceit: The Religion of the Crypto-Jews* (Philadelphia: Jewish Publication Society of America, 1996), pp. 277, 280, 305 n.12, 627. According to Gitlitz, "One of the most common and persistent death-related customs is for family and friends to turn the dying person's face towards the wall. The custom appears to derive from 2 Kings 20:2, which recounts how when Hezekiah was dying he 'turned his face to the wall, and prayed to the Lord,' who then healed him. A 1639 Mexican Edict of Grace considers as a sign of Judaizing that 'when some person is at the point of death, he turns to the wall to await death,' and many Judaizers, such as Clara Rodríguez . . . were accused of turning their sick spouse's face toward the wall before death. In some places this custom persisted even after its original intent had been transformed. Bernardino de San Juan's mother . . . taught her that 'when someone was about to die you should turn their face toward the East so that they suffer less'" (p. 280).

107. Fruit of the *zapote* tree, according to the Royal Spanish Academy, *Diccionario de autoridades* (1726–1737; reprint, Madrid: Editorial Gredos, 1976), vol. 3, p. 560. On the placement of food in the mouth of the deceased by Mexican crypto-Jews, see chap. 2.

108. El Señor fiscal del Santo Oficio contra Doña Teresa de Aguilera y Roche, statement in her defense, fol. 148, Ramo de Inquisición, tomo 596, exp. 1, AGN.

109. See chap. 2 and Gitlitz, *Secrecy and Deceit*, pp. 202–207.

110. Testificaciones que se an sacado a pedimiento del dr. fiscal de uno de los quadernos que se remitieron por el comisario del Nuevo México contra Juan Gómez, vezino de dicho Nuevo México, 1662–1663, testimony of Domingo López de Ocanto, Convento del Sr. San Francisco del Pueblo de Sandía, April 4, 1662, fol. 119v, Ramo de Inquisición, tomo 598, exp. 7, AGN; Proceso y causa criminal contra el sargento mayor Francisco Gómez Robledo, testimony of Domingo López de Ocanto, Sandía, April 4, 1662, fol. 301r, Ramo de Inquisición, tomo 583, exp. 3, AGN. López added that Juan Gómez Robledo also had a *colita*, or little tail, protruding from the area just above his buttocks, an observation shared by other witnesses about Juan

as well as Francisco. Chávez described this phenomenon as "an abnormal coccyx" (*Origins of New Mexico Families*, p. 36).

111. Proceso y causa criminal contra el sargento mayor Francisco Gómez Robledo, testimony of Antonio López Zambrano, Santa Fe, May 3, 1662, fol. 299r, Ramo de Inquisición, tomo 583, exp. 3, AGN.

112. Testificaciones que se an sacado a pedimiento del dr. fiscal de uno de los quadernos que se remitieron por el comisario del Nuevo México contra Juan Gómez, petition by Dr. Rodrigo Ruíz, México, July 23, 1663, fol. 116r, Ramo de Inquisición, tomo 598, exp. 7, AGN.

113. Proceso y causa criminal contra el sargento mayor Francisco Gómez Robledo, Auto de inspección, México, September 5, 1663, fols. 353r–v, Ramo de Inquisición, tomo 583, exp. 3, AGN. The anatomical term *frenillo*, translated here as "ligament," refers to the "ligament that holds the prepuce to the penis" (*Gran diccionario de la lengua castellana [de autoridades]* [Barcelona: Fomento Comercial del Libro, 1932], vol. 3, p. 109).

114. Proceso y causa criminal contra el sargento mayor Francisco Gómez Robledo, response of Francisco Gómez Robledo, México, September 28, 1663, fol. 383r, Ramo de Inquisición, tomo 583, exp. 3, AGN.

115. Ibid., February 13, 1664, fols. 373v–375v.

116. Ibid., Segundo auto de inspección, México, June 23, 1664, fols. 380r–v. Scholes appears to have misread the original document when he indicated that the inspection revealed that "it *was* possible that they had resulted from another cause [emphasis added]" (*Troublous Times in New Mexico*, p. 193). Kessell depended on Scholes's mistranslation in arriving at his conclusion that Gómez Robledo may not have been circumcised and that allegations of his Judaism were just an "ugly lie" (*Kiva, Cross, and Crown*, pp. 191, 185). Unfortunately, in her effort to discredit the historical basis for crypto-Judaism in New Mexico, folklorist Judith S. Neulander failed to consult the original record, relying instead on Scholes ("The New Mexican Crypto-Jewish Canon: Choosing to be 'Chosen' in Millennial Tradition," *Jewish Folklore and Ethnology Review* 18 [1996]: 49). The procedure whereby the foreskin was not entirely removed as part of the ritual circumcision is consistent with the conclusion reached by Gitlitz: "By the seventeenth century in Mexico, some Judaizing *conversos* did not remove the foreskin at all, but rather scarred it with a longitudinal cut in an attempt to comply with the requirement of the law and deceive the Inquisitors. When Inquisition doctors examined Gabriel de Granada in Mexico in 1645 they 'found a mark . . . running longitudinally and with a scar, made apparently with a cutting instrument'" (*Secrecy and Deceit*, p. 206).

117. Proceso y causa criminal contra Cristóbal de Anaya por proposiciones heréticas, 1661, Ramo de Inquisición, tomo 582, exp. 1, AGN. See also Scholes, *Troublous Times in New Mexico*, pp. 187–190.

118. Denunciaciones contra Juan Domínguez de Mendoza. Nuevo México, 1667, denunciation of Christóbal de Anaia Almazán, Santo Domingo, May 3, 1666, fols. 66v–67r, Ramo de Inquisición, tomo 610, exp. 7, AGN.

119. Causa contra el capitán Diego Romero, Ramo de Inquisición, tomo 586, exp. 1, AGN; El Señor fiscal del Santo Oficio contra el Capitán Nicolas de

Aguilar por proposiciones, 1661, Ramo de Inquisición, tomo 512, exp. 2, AGN. See also Scholes, *Troublous Times in New Mexico*, pp. 172–183.

120. Primera audiencia de Don Bernardo López de Mendizábal, fols. 293r–294r, Ramo de Inquisición, tomo 594, exp. 1, AGN. See also Scholes, *Troublous Times in New Mexico*, pp. 157–158.

121. El Señor fiscal del Santo Oficio contra Doña Teresa de Aguilera y Roche, fol. 250, Ramo de Inquisición, tomo 596, exp. 1, AGN.

122. Proceso y causa criminal contra el sargento mayor Francisco Gómez Robledo, Sentencia, México, October 24, 1664, fols. 382r–383r, Ramo de Inquisición, Tomo 583, exp. 3, AGN.

123. Scholes, *Troublous Times in New Mexico*, pp. 160, 196–197.

124. Chávez, *Origins of New Mexico Families*, p. 36, citing "Case against Nicolás de Aguilar, testimony of Fray Salvador de Guerra, June 13, 1662," in Hackett, ed., *Historical Documents*, vol. 3, p. 138.

125. El maestre del campo Thomé Domínguez de Mendoza, vecino de las provincias del Nuevo México, en nombre del capitán Don Diego de Peñalosa y Briseño, goberndor de dichas provincias sobre los bienes que se le embargaron por el Pe. Fray Alonso de Posada . . . se depositaron. Pide se le entreguen, 1663–1694, fols. 41r–44r, 65r–66r, 125r–126r, Ramo de Concurso de Peñalosa, vol. 3, AGN.

126. Chávez, *Origins of New Mexico Families*, pp. 4–5, 125.

127. Ibid., pp. 36–37. Ignacio Roybal's possible *converso* roots are discussed in chap. 6.

CHAPTER 6

The Role of Crypto-Jews in the Life of the New Mexico Colony, 1680–1846

With the reconquest of New Mexico by Diego de Vargas in 1692/1693, Spanish royal sovereignty was reestablished over New Spain's far northern frontier province. The new generation of administrators, both civil and religious, brought with them new attitudes and new approaches to governing. The Franciscan leaders modified significantly their hard-line approach toward Pueblo religious practices and followed a more effective strategy of missionization. Royal officials and friars cooperated more often than feuded, recognizing the need to present a united front in the face of enemies, both real and potential. Concerns for collective security also served as a motivation for Pueblo and Spanish settlers to pursue a policy of rapprochement following the bloodletting of the revolt and reconquest. The two groups realized that they had a mutuality of interest in effecting the common defense of their respective communities against the growing threat from attacks by nomadic tribes—Apaches, Comanches, Navajos, and Utes.

The new era of cooperation between governors and friars in the eighteenth century, combined with the general lack of interest on the part of the Mexican Inquisition in the prosecution of *judaizante* cases throughout the Viceroyalty of New Spain, resulted in the elimination of the factors that had contributed to the persecution of crypto-Jews in Mexico and New Mexico in the late sixteenth and mid-seventeenth centuries. Gone were the massive campaigns against the Mexican *conversos*, which had motivated crypto-Jews to escape to the extreme frontier regions of the north. Gone were the fierce struggles between civil and religious leaders in New Mexico, which had provoked the Franciscans to capitalize on the New Christian background of their political enemies by fomenting charges of heresy. But, as a result of these important historical developments, gone, too, were the rich trial records of the Holy Office of the Inquisition, which had provided such a treasure trove of demographic information on the background and practices of *conversos* in New Mexico.

As a consequence, it is relatively difficult to determine the extent to which those who resettled New Mexico in the eighteenth century demonstrated a crypto-Jewish heritage. In attempting to resolve this question, it will be necessary to identify the ethnic background of some of the new colonists who migrated northward with Diego de Vargas and to examine the patterns of marriage within this group, as well as between them and those seventeenth-century *converso* families who returned to New Mexico after the reconquest, in order to discover possible indications of endogamy. The types of careers that these colonists pursued might also serve as clues of ethnicity. Did they occupy positions typical of those held by New Christians in other parts of the Hispanic world?

In order to begin the process of identifying which of the post-reconquest families had the highest potential to demonstrate these traits, it is necessary to take a two-pronged approach, examining the lives of both the descendants of the pre–Pueblo Revolt New Christians who returned to New Mexico and the ancestors of the nine sample individuals mentioned in the introduction, who, in the late twentieth century, either asserted a crypto-Jewish past or demonstrated ethnographic traits or a medical/genetic profile suggestive of such a heritage. There certainly was overlap between these two groups, as evidenced by their family histories; that is, among the ancestors of the twentieth-century informants were some who could be traced to New Mexican *converso* families from the sixteenth and seventeenth centuries. It also appears that marriages and other close associations took place between the pre-revolt New Christians and the post-revolt ancestors, from the 1680s until the end of the Mexican period.

THE SPANISH RECONQUEST OF NEW MEXICO

During their thirteen-year exile, from the Pueblo Revolt of 1680 until the final reconquest of New Mexico in 1693, the refugees in El Paso—who included not only Spanish colonists, but also displaced Indians from the pueblos of Isleta and Socorro—lived a bleak existence. They were able to eke out a living by scratching the ground for a few crops, while enduring shortages of food and livestock and suffering constant attacks by Sumas, Mansos, and Apaches. The desperation of this situation moved Governor Antonio de Otermín to embark immediately on a series of military campaigns to reconquer the province from the rebellious Pueblos, but victory eluded him and his troops. The temporary campsites that had been established along the lower Río Grande began to take on an air of permanence, and the colonists resigned themselves to a long wait before a more propitious opportunity presented itself.[1]

Among these settlers was Francisco Gómez Robledo, rehabilitated from his unpleasant experience with the Mexican Inquisition two decades earlier. Any stigma that might have resulted from his identification as a crypto-Jew apparently had no deleterious effect on his career, as, on the eve of the Pueblo Revolt, he emerged as one of Governor Otermín's most trusted military advisers. On August 9, 1680, two days before the day selected by Pueblo leaders for the beginning of the insurrection, word of the impending revolt reached the governor's ear. He immediately dispatched Gómez Robledo, now elevated to the rank of *maese del campo*, to the pueblo of Tesuque to arrest two of the conspirators. The details revealed in their confession allowed Otermín to prepare for the defense of the capital. But word of the arrests also found its way to those planning the attack, motivating them to accelerate the timetable for their initial assault on Santa Fe and neighboring communities.[2] Hostilities began on the evening of Friday, August 9, when insurrectionists from the pueblo of Tesuque attacked and killed Spanish colonist Cristóbal de Herrera. The following morning, August 10, Indians from the various pueblos in northern New Mexico initiated simultaneous attacks on Spanish settlements throughout the Upper and Middle Río Grande Valley, resulting in the deaths of scores of civilians, soldiers, and priests.[3]

Once the attack had begun, and rumors of mass destruction of missions and settlements in Río Arriba reached Otermín's ear, the governor again turned to Gómez Robledo, sending him on a dangerous reconnaissance mission to inspect the extent of the devastation in the areas of the Tewa pueblos around Santa Cruz de la Cañada. On August 12, two days into the revolt, Gómez Robledo reported that thirty Spanish had been killed and that the rebels had fortified themselves at the pueblo of Santa Clara and the hills surrounding the pueblo of Tesuque. The next day, the governor ordered a futile counterattack, in which Gómez Robledo and fifteen other soldiers were wounded. The Spanish dug in to withstand the siege by the attackers, which commenced on August 15 and continued for five days. Driven to desperation by the cutoff of their water supply, Governor Otermín ordered a surprise attack on August 20, breaking the offensive lines of the Indians. Realizing that their situation was hopeless, the governor bowed to the inevitable, and the decision was made on August 21 to abandon the capital. Gómez Robledo served as one of four *maeses del campo*, along with extended-family members Thomé and Juan Domínguez de Mendoza and Diego de Trujillo, who directed the withdrawal.[4]

During the exile in El Paso, the structure of the New Mexican government remained much the same as it had been before the revolt. Governor Otermín was replaced in 1683 by Domingo Jironza Petríz de Cruzate. Among the officials who joined Jironza's retinue that year, as notary of government and war, was a twenty-two-year-old man who was to play an extremely significant role in post-reconquest New Mexico, holding almost every major office, from secretary to the governors of New Mexico to mayor of Santa Fe to protector of the Indians. Moreover, he was to serve as the progenitor for several families whom, three hundred years later, would assert a Jewish heritage.

THE *CONVERSO* ORIGINS OF THE RAEL DE AGUILAR FAMILY

Alonso (or Alfonso) Rael de Aguilar was born in Lorca, in the southeastern Spanish province of Murcia, in early February 1661, the son of Juan de Osca Alzamora and Juliana Rael de Aguilar.[5] A family legend among some of the twenty-first-century Rael descendants holds that the name Rael evolved from the name Israel.[6] Indeed, it appears that the story may well have some basis in fact. Alonso's granddaughter María Manuela Rael de Aguilar, a resident of the Río Abajo town of Tomé, is mentioned three times in the baptismal records for 1756 of the nearby mission church of the pueblo of Isleta, as María Manuela *Ysrael* de Aguilar,[7] an indication that the parish priests, and likely the entire community, were aware of the family's ethnicity. But the connection between the surnames Rael and Israel may be traced back almost three hundred years earlier, to the fifteenth-century frontier between the Christian province of Murcia and the Muslim kingdom of Granada, in the decades immediately before the defeat of Granada in 1492.

As in many other parts of Christian Spain, Jews played a significant role in the development of the province of Murcia and, specifically, the town of Lorca for centuries before the expulsion and forced conversions of 1492. With the exception of a decade-long period of violent anti-Jewish persecution in the early fifteenth century, Jews and Christians generally enjoyed a cordial relationship. The dominant community utilized the services provided by the Jews, who not only served as merchants, physicians, surgeons, apothecaries, tailors, and municipal officials, but also engaged in farming and ranching.[8]

But, due to the strategic geographic situation of the region on the frontier between Christian- and Muslim-held territories, certain Jews also featured prominently in the campaigns that characterized the final phase of the eight-hundred-year *reconquista*, which culminated in the defeat of the southernmost Muslim kingdom, Granada, at the conclusion of the fifteenth century. It appears that the ancestors of seventeenth-century New Mexican colonist Alonso Rael de Aguilar could be found among these Jewish, and later *converso*, players. Jacob Israel, a Jew from Granada, sufficiently earned the trust of King Alfonso el Magnánimo, of Castilla, Queen María of Aragón, and Muhammad VIII el Pequeño, of Granada, to carry messages and negotiate sensitive diplomatic issues among the three rulers in the late 1420s. Although it is unknown where Israel eventually settled, it is clear that in December 1428, near the end of his mission, he sojourned in Lorca, where he became embroiled in a jurisdictional dispute with local officials.[9] Several decades later, in 1476, King Fernando and Queen Isabel appointed Gabriel Yrrahel, a Jew from Murcia, as official interpreter of the Arab language for the province.[10]

Also known for his knowledge of Arabic and Spanish, as well as for his familiarity with the lands on both sides of the frontier, was Juan Rael, fifth great-grandfather of Alonso. Rael exemplifies the "colonist-warrior" who, according to historian Juan Francisco Jiménez Alcázar, typified the Murcia–Granada borderlands in the late fifteenth century. Jiménez identified the caballero as the dominant figure of the Middle Ages in the region. But, in contrast to the orders of knights that figured so prominently in other parts of Spain, which emphasized nobility and social standing, Jiménez noted the importance of the *adalíd*, a unique brand of caballero forged by the exigencies of that frontier region. A true caudillo, the *adalíd* possessed traits of leadership, charisma,

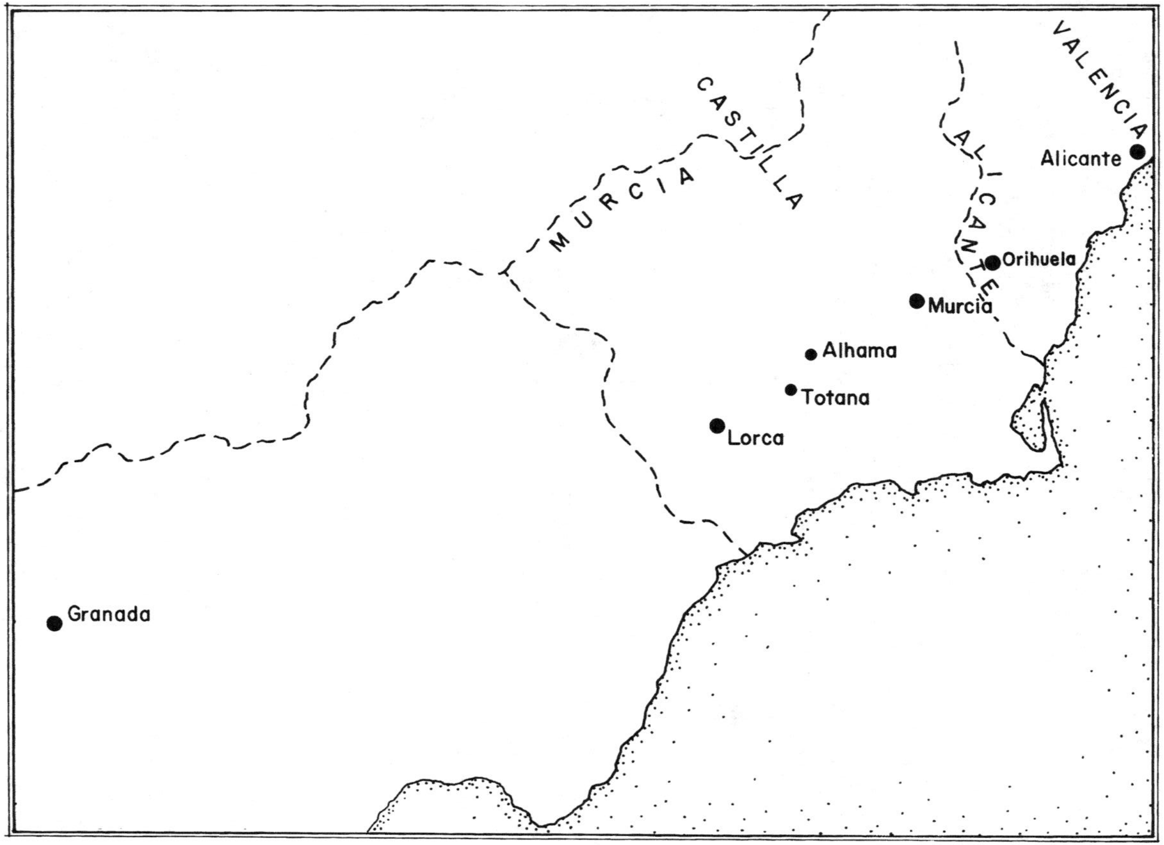

Southeastern Spain.

and valor on the battlefield. Citing *Las Siete Partidas*, the famous thirteenth-century legal code developed by King Alfonso X el Sabio, Jiménez listed the four virtues necessary for holding the title of *adalíd*: wisdom, force, natural intelligence, and loyalty. It is interesting to note that such traits as faith, piety, noble birth, and Old Christian background, so important in other orders of knights, were notably absent from the standards required of an *adalíd*. The position of *adalíd* was the highest level that a commoner could attain through military service. And although of common birth, an *adalíd* could pass on his status of nobility to future generations.[11]

In recognition of his skills on the battlefield, Juan Rael was invested as an *adalíd* by King Fernando of Aragón in 1477. Little is known of Rael's background, but Jiménez hypothesized that he was not an Old Christian, but a *converso*. To substantiate this belief, he pointed to Rael's intimate knowledge of the frontier with Granada, his ability to translate the Arabic language, and his death in the "most Christian" state, according to the testimony of witnesses. While Jiménez acknowledged the status of Rael as a New Christian, he assumed that he was a convert from Islam, apparently without considering the possibility that he had been a Jew.[12]

The likelihood that the Rael family of Lorca had converted to Christianity from Judaism, rather than from Islam, is supported by an examination of contemporary records. Francisco de Asís Veas Arteseros, in his volume on the history of the Jews of Lorca, offered a detailed account of the commercial life of the Jewish community and, based on notarial records from the 1470s, placed one of the *converso* Raeles clearly within this context:

> Representing the commercial guild was the shopkeeper Rabbi Mosé, who maintained a perfect knowledge of both the Talmud and the art of buying and selling; whose opinions held much weight, not only within the environment of the *judería*; and was a man respected by all, as evidenced by a reading of the notices that referred to him. A man of no small means, he earned his living trading in fabrics and related fields, such as dyeing. Rabbi Mosé, along with a man named Baeça, operated a dyeing shop near the oil mill that pertained to the heirs of Juan Giner. . . .
>
> In the commercial operations of this notable member of the Lorca Jewish community, one can find all classes of fabrics and threads, capable of satisfying the most demanding of clientele, to the extent that, when the Council ordered the *mayordomo* to purchase clothes for *the son of Rael "who had turned to become a*

> *Christian,*" the council official did not hesitate for a moment in recommending Don Mosé to comply with the mandate of his colleagues in clothing the New Christian with all that was necessary, and with splendor [emphasis added].[13]

The recognition of Juan Rael as a convert to Christianity; the connection between "the son of Rael" and Rabbi Mosé of Lorca; the existence of Jews with the name Israel or Yrrahel in the decades before the birth of Juan Rael; the similarity among the names Rael, Yrrahel, and Israel; and the unusual, infrequently used nature of the name itself all suggest a Jewish origin of the Rael family. The assertion that Juan Rael, *el adalíd*, must have been Muslim, rather than Jewish, was based on nothing more than the unsupported assumption that Jews did not engage in military activities. Veas Arteseros argued this position, relying on the premise that "Jews were never soldiers."[14] To the contrary, the record is replete with references to Jews and *conversos* serving in the military, fighting side by side with Old Christians against the Muslims.[15] Records of the Murcia Inquisition from seven decades after the Edict of Expulsion of 1492 refer to the wife of Lope Adalíd, of Lorca, "of a generation of Jews," penanced for observing ceremonies of the Law of Moses and for anticipating the coming of the Messiah.[16] No documentation has been found linking any of the Rael family with Muslims in the fifteenth or sixteenth century. Nor can the surname be found connected to an Arab origin in any of the standard etymological dictionaries.[17]

An analysis of notarial and sacramental records genealogically ties the *converso* Juan Rael, *el adalíd*, directly to Alonso Rael de Aguilar, who, in the early 1680s, left his native Lorca for New Spain and, ultimately, New Mexico. The intervening six generations witnessed migrations by the family from Lorca across the border between the provinces of Murcia and Alicante to the town of Orihuela, and back again to Lorca. The coincidence of the timing of the departures of the Raeles and their extended family from the two towns with periods of activity of the Holy Office of the Inquisition against the crypto-Jews of these communities warrants a close examination of the clan's evolution from the fifteenth to the seventeenth century.

Juan Rael married into the Fernández de Ribavellosa family, and the union produced three children: Juan, María, and Lucía. Juan II became a royal notary in Granada and appears to have died without issue.[18] The succession from Juan Rael, *el adalíd*, to Alonso Rael de Aguilar, colonist in New Mexico, passed through Juan's daughter María. María appears to have been married twice, first to a cousin, Juan Rael, and later to Miguel de Morata.[19] The offspring of María produced at least six males with the name Juan Rael, one of whom was the great-great-great grandfather of Alonso. Around 1550, Juan's wife gave birth to Diego Rael, who in 1571 married Catalina García.[20] Among the children of this union were Cristóbal (b. ca. 1575) and Jaume (b. 1581).[21] Cristóbal Rael married Anna Arróniz, who gave birth to Juan in 1598.[22] Juan Rael married Ana Enriques in 1619,[23] and among their children was Juliana Rael de Aguilar, born in 1625,[24] who married Juan de Osca Alzamora in 1651,[25] and produced Alonso Rael de Aguilar ten years later.

The sacramental records indicate that Diego Rael and Catalina García moved from Lorca to Orihuela between 1571 and 1581, and that their descendants moved back to Lorca between 1651 (the date of the marriage of Juan de Osca Alzamora and Juliana Rael de Aguilar) and 1655 (the date of birth of Alonso's brother, Juan).[26] The departure of this branch of the Rael family from Lorca in the 1570s immediately followed the most concentrated campaign against the *judaizantes* of Lorca ever carried out by the Murcian tribunal of the Holy Office of the Inquisition, in which dozens of individuals were penanced for the secret practice of Judaism.[27] Among those arrested and convicted during this era for observing the Law of Moses was Theresa de Morata, a likely relative of the Rael family.[28] Orihuela was located just a short distance to the east, across the provincial border separating the Castilian province of Murcia from the Valencian province of Alicante. Although Orihuela was nominally subject to the tribunal of Murcia in the mid-sixteenth century, no resident of the town is recorded as having been arrested for the practice of *judaizante*.[29] But while the town was "foreign," it was also familiar. Orihuela had a long history of Jewish and, later, *converso* settlement, dating back to the twelfth century, so crypto-Jews would not have felt out of place there.[30] In his book on the history of the Jews of Lorca, Veas Arteseros described the trading relationships that had taken place between the two communities, indicating that "the presence of Lorcans was not unusual."[31] The remigration of the Rael–Osca family to Lorca in the early 1650s likely was due less to inquisitorial activity, than to the epidemic that devastated Orihuela and the social unrest that characterized the ensuing years.[32]

Little is known about the early years of Alonso Rael de Aguilar. That he later served as secretary to the governors of New Mexico, as well as in other professional capacities, suggests strongly that he had a formal education, although the source of that training is not known.[33] His father, Juan de Osca Alzamora, who, interestingly enough, did not know how to sign his own name, appears to have been a man of no small means. He was a master tailor,[34] a profession identified earlier with Jews and, after the expulsion, with *conversos*, but also owned a hacienda on the outskirts of Lorca, portions of which he rented to tenants.[35] He also owned at least three houses in Lorca, located in the parish of San Mateo.[36] Significantly, among Osca's business dealings was a partnership in a hacienda with Pedro Núñez Chacón, who was penanced by the Inquisition in 1666 for secretly practicing Judaism.[37]

Circumstances similar to those that possibly stimulated Alonso's great-great-grandfather to leave his native Lorca in the 1570s could well have served as a catalyst for the twenty-two-year-old Alonso to flee across the Atlantic to the New World. Just as the inquisitorial persecutions of the mid-sixteenth century coincided with the abandonment of Lorca by Diego Rael and his family for Orihuela, Alonso Rael de Aguilar's departure for the Indies came on the heels of a renewed campaign against crypto-Jews by the Holy Office of Murcia in the early 1680s. It was in June 1680 that word first leaked out that a "conspiracy of Judaism" was being hatched in the region.[38] By June 1681, the inquisitors expressed the fear that the plot had reached dangerous proportions and that their infrastructure was not adequate to deal with it:

> In this Holy Office, the conspiracy of Judaism continues. It began with two general testimonies and reports, one from a witness who was in Livorno [Leghorn], where he had *judaizante* relatives who tried to persuade him to observe the Law of Moses, and the other from a woman of this city [Murcia], whose mother and other relatives claimed to coerce her to the same end. And in order to convince both witnesses, they told them that many other kinfolk were also observers [of Judaism], and that other persons of this kingdom were known as Portuguese, because of their reputation as descendants of Jews. Some of the witnesses having come forward, and because of other indications, they were arrested. Some have confessed, while others deny the charges, and others sent to prison, . . . and some have fled. . . . We find ourselves having difficulty with these people, as they are many in number, and we have only twenty-eight jail cells, and they are in poor condition, and look even worse, and in the rest it is impossible to stop communication with the construction of some thin walls.[39]

The inquisitors identified Lorca as one of three towns riddled with crypto-Jews, reporting that "fifteen arrests were made, five here in

Murcia, and the rest in Totana, Alhama, and Lorca, because each one of these places is a synagogue."[40]

By 1683, thirty-two people had been arrested and convicted for the heresy of *judaizante*, from Lorca alone.[41] Among those penanced by the Inquisition in 1681 for the secret practice of Judaism were two members of the Alcaráz family, who quite possibly were related to the Rael de Aguilars: Leonor Fernández, wife of Pedro de Alcaráz, and María Fernández, who was married to Diego López de Alcaráz.[42] The date of Alonso Rael de Aguilar's departure from Lorca for Sevilla, and thence to New Spain and New Mexico, is not known, but, based on the earliest record of his presence in El Paso in September 1683, he most likely left in 1681 or 1682.[43]

It is interesting to note that during his service in El Paso, Alonso always signed his name as Alphonso (or Alfonso/Alonso) de Aguilar, omitting the potentially suspicious Rael. It was only in 1693, on the eve of the reconquest of New Mexico by the Spanish, that his signature began to include the full name Rael de Aguilar.[44]

In 1691, after eleven miserable years of exile in El Paso, a new and dynamic young *madrileño* nobleman took the reigns as governor of New Mexico: Diego José de Vargas Zapata y Lujan Ponce de León Contreras (known to historians as simply Diego de Vargas). After dealing with hostilities against the Indians of the Sonoran Desert, Vargas turned his attention to the reconquest of New Mexico the following summer. Leading a small expedition northward in August 1692, the governor found the Pueblo Indians leaderless and in disarray. Taking advantage of the chaotic situation, Vargas was able to effect a promise of peace from the Pueblo forces who had held Santa Fe for so long. That, during this phase of the reconquest, the Spanish forces achieved a symbolic victory without firing a shot contributed to the popular myth, still prevalent, of a "bloodless" reconquest. But when Vargas returned in December 1693 with a full complement of troops to recapture the capital, he encountered stiff resistance, and, according to Vargas's biographer, John L. Kessell, "the snow ran red with [the] blood" of the Pueblo people.[45] Eighty-one Indians were either killed in the battle or executed afterward.[46]

THE ARRIVAL OF NEW COLONISTS

The complete pacification of the province would not be accomplished for several years. Diego de Vargas knew that in order to achieve the effective reestablishment of royal sovereignty, he would need the participation of a large number of colonists—no easy task, in view of the reputation earned by New Mexico as a remote and inhospitable place, inhabited by a people who deeply resented their presence. News of Vargas's initial success in 1692 enticed about eight hundred people from Mexico City and Zacatecas, led by Cristóbal de Velasco and Fray Francisco Farfán, including one hundred soldiers and seventeen priests, to join several of the pre-revolt New Mexican families in the governor's first effort to resettle the province the following year.[47] Realizing that these numbers were not adequate to effectively repopulate the region, Vargas turned to one of his most trusted military officers, Juan Páez Hurtado, in 1694, and directed him to initiate efforts to recruit additional colonists from the mining towns of Parral, Llerena, Sombrerete, and Zacatecas. In May 1695, Páez Hurtado arrived in Santa Fe with some two hundred more people, mostly families, to reinforce the settlement. Drought, lack of food, and recurrent hostilities with the Pueblo Indians continued to plague the young colony, resulting in extreme deprivation and civil unrest for the first decade or so after Vargas's reconquest.[48]

Among the colonists who arrived in New Mexico in 1693 were several with probable New Christian backgrounds. Two brothers, Miguel Mathías and José de Quintana, were among the reinforcements recruited from Mexico City by Velasco and Farfán. José Antonio Esquibel has been able to trace these individuals to sixteenth-century Sevilla and, eventually, to the *converso* Álvarez de Toledo family in the late fourteenth century.[49]

José de Atienza Alcalá y Escobar, who was the progenitor of the Atencio family, another of the colonists who arrived in 1693, can also be traced to possible Jewish roots in the region of Guadalajara, northeast of Madrid. Atienza's father and grandfather were from the town of Brihuega, located about eighteen miles northeast of Guadalajara. Sacramental records for Brihuega were destroyed during the Spanish Civil War, rendering it impossible to trace the family history beyond José's grandparents: Cristóbal de Atienza, María San Baptista, Francisco de Alcalá, and María de Escobar.[50] A search of the records of the Inquisition tribunal of Cuenca, to which the region was subject, however, turned up several Atienzas convicted of the secret practice of Judaism. Two of them were from the neighboring town of Cifuentes: Alonso Sánchez de Atienza, son of Rui Sánchez de Atienza, who confessed his heresy on July 19, 1492, and Juan de Atienza, sentenced to be burned at the stake in 1494. And from Brihuega was Pedro de Alcalá, a weaver, the son of Pedro de Alcalá, whose brother Juan de Alcalá was convicted of *judaizante* in 1558.[51]

Also of possible Jewish origin was José Bernardo Mascareñas, who, along with his wife and children, also formed part of the Velasco–Farfán party. Mascareñas traced his paternal line to his great-grandparents Antonio Mascarenhas and Catalina Suares, residents of Lisboa, who were born around the turn of the seventeenth century.[52] At least eleven persons, either with the name or married to a Mascarenhas, were tried and convicted for practicing Judaism in the various tribunals of the Portuguese Inquisition, mostly from Coimbra.[53] One of José Bernardo's uncles, Juan de Quiñones Mascareñas, was a silversmith in Mexico City in the 1650s.[54]

Juan de Góngora died shortly before his departure for New Mexico in 1693. Undeterred by her husband's untimely death, María Petronila de la Cueva, now head of her household, braved the odds and made the trek northward with her seven children. According to José Antonio Esquibel and John B. Colligan, Góngora's family could be traced to *converso* roots on at least one branch. His grandmother María de Triceño Palomeque descended from the famous Pulgar family, among whose members was Fernando de Pulgar, secretary to and chronicler of the Catholic Monarchs, Fernando and Isabel, at the end of the fifteenth century. Over one hundred years later, Triceño's husband, Bartolomé de Góngora, would comment on this element of the family's genealogy in a publication on colonial government.[55] Indeed, Fernando de Pulgar not only was well known as a New Christian at court (the two other secretaries who served with him were of similar background), but served as a forceful advocate on behalf of his fellow *conversos*. He protested against marriage and occupational restrictions imposed on New Christians and argued against harsh treatment of crypto-Jews by the Holy Office, believing the policy of persecution to be unjust and ineffective and recommending, instead, a kinder and gentler program of religious education.[56]

Three of the more curious additions to Velasco and Farfán's enterprise were Frenchmen who had survived a disastrous expedition to Texas in 1684 to 1687, during which its leader, René-Robert Cavelier, sieur de La Salle, and almost all the other participants lost their lives. Jean l'Archivèque, Jacques Grolet, and Pierre Meusnier wandered about the northern frontier of New Spain until they were rescued, arrested, taken to Spain, returned to Mexico, and, ultimately, recruited forcibly for duty in New Mexico.[57] Two of them, l'Archivèque and Grolet, Hispanicizing their names to Juan Archibeque and Santiago Gurulé, married Spanish women who had joined Velasco and Farfán's expedition and served as the progenitors of generations of New Mexicans with surnames not found anywhere else in the world.

Research conducted in the archives of Bayonne and La Rochelle, the birthplaces of l'Archivèque and Grolet, respectively, as well as in Bordeaux, offer hints that the ancestors of both may have included converts from Judaism to Christianity.[58] After the declaration by King Henri II in 1551, allowing merchants and other New Christians to settle in France legally, Portuguese *conversos* flocked to major commercial centers, including the Atlantic ports of Bayonne, Bordeaux, and La Rochelle. While some New Christians returned to Judaism, many others remained Catholic, and still others, the most successful and well integrated of the mercantile families, converted to Protestantism.[59]

Born in Bayonne in 1665, Jean l'Archivèque was the son of Claude l'Archivèque and Marie D'Armanac.[60] His father, paternal grandparents, and paternal great-grandparents were merchants from Bordeaux who relocated to Bayonne in the 1650s. Before the conversion to Catholicism of his paternal grandfather, Pierre l'Archivèque, in the mid-seventeenth century, the family had been Protestant. One of Jean's uncles, also named Jean, had married a Portuguese immigrant to Bordeaux, Marie de San Andres, alias Marie D'Allenet, daughter of Abel D'Allenet, presumably also Portuguese. In addition, Jean's great aunt was named Esther. On his mother's side, his uncle Pierre Tendron served as a master surgeon and master apothecary in Bayonne.[61] The occupational patterns, geographic origins, connection with Portuguese families, and presence of Jewish biblical first names in the family all suggest that l'Archivèque was descended from New Christians.

Considerably less is known about the family background of Jacques Grolet. He was born around 1664 or 1665 in the Atlantic port town of La Rochelle, the son of cooper Yvon Grolet and Marie Odon.[62] La Rochelle was the focus of settlement for a large number of *conversos* in the sixteenth century, with many settling in the parish of Saint-Jean-du-Perot, the residence of Grolet and Odon and the birthplace of Jacques. Parish records include a marriage register for François Grolet (or Grelet), son of Aaron Grolet, and Marie Gautier.[63] Given the date of their marriage, they were likely the uncle and aunt of Jacques Grolet. Like Jacques, François was a sailor and a resident of St. Saint-Jean-du-Perot. The paucity of information about the family, due largely to gaps in the contemporary record, makes it difficult to ascertain the ethnic background of the Grolet family with any degree of probability. That the Grolet family lived in the parish inhabited by *conversos* and a member of the family had a Jewish biblical name, however, raise the possibility of a New Christian origin for the family.

Another of the colonists of 1693 who would have a major impact on New Mexico in the post-reconquest era was Ignacio Roybal y

Galicia.

Torrado. Born in 1671 in Caldas de Reies, Galicia, to Pedro Roybal y Torrado and Elena da Cruz, Ignacio married Francisca Gómez Robledo, niece of pre-revolt New Christian settler Francisco Gómez Robledo, within just months of his arrival in Santa Fe.[64] Roybal traced his origins back at least three generations in Caldas de Reies, located about halfway between Santiago de Compostela and Pontevedra.[65] On his mother's side, the family was linked with the Paz family, his maternal aunt María da Cruz having married Pedro Paz around 1647.[66]

Among the many *judaizantes* tried and convicted by the Holy Office of the Inquisition of Galicia were several who had that surname, including

- Hernando de Paz, lawyer of Bayona; his wife, Beatríz; and their children, Ana, Guiomar, and Tomás, arrested in 1609.
- Violante de Paz and Miguel de Paz, children of Ysabel Méndez and Diego Lorenzo, keeper of the salt supply for the Villa de Redondela, located just south of Pontevedra, also arrested in 1609.
- Felipa de Paz, wife of Duarte de León; and Ysabel Coronel, wife of Antonio de Paz, of Tui, and their daughter, Mencía de Paz, of Bayona, all taken in 1609.
- Another Felipa de Paz, married to Duarte de Acosta, of Pontevedra, reconciled in 1624.
- Beatríz de Paz, wife of Ensign Alonso de Medina, of Bayona, penanced in 1629.
- María de Paz, widow of Geronimo López, of Betanzos; and Mencía de Paz y Salzedo, also of Betanzos, apprehended in 1680 for practicing Judaism.[67]

The large number of Paz family members identified by the Holy Office as crypto-Jews in the seventeenth century, combined with the relatively uncommon character of the name in the region and the presence of a Jewish community of note in Caldas de Reies before the expulsion in 1492,[68] suggest a link between the Roybales of Caldas and the *judaizantes* of southern Galicia.

Mercantile Occupations

Among the ancestors of the nine individuals who, by the late twentieth century, either claimed a Jewish heritage or demonstrated family customs or genetic traits associated with Jewish populations, there could be found progenitors who were pursuing characteristically Jewish occupations in the eighteenth and early nineteenth centuries. Jews and, later, *conversos* throughout the ages tended to gravitate toward mercantile professions. Those in Spain, Portugal, and Mexico were no exception to this inclination, nor, it appears, were those in the far northern frontier of New Mexico during the Spanish and Mexican periods of its history. Tracing commercial occupational patterns in the early eighteenth century proves a very difficult task, given the remote character of New Mexico in the decades following the reconquest in 1693. The first few years of the reestablished settlement were characterized by lingering Pueblo resistance to Spanish control, drought, disease, and starvation; products for local consumption, to say nothing of exports, were scarce. Once the colony had achieved a degree of self-sufficiency, commerce was, for the most part, limited to barter trade between the inhabitants of the Río Grande Valley—Spanish and Pueblo alike—and the nomadic Indians: Navajos, Apaches, Utes, and Comanches. Grain, livestock, and a small number of European wares were exchanged for skins, captives, and buffalo meat. A few woven goods made their way to Chihuahua, but extensive trade to the south would not develop for decades.[69]

Events thousands of miles away, both at the Bourbon court in Madrid and in the viceregal seat in Mexico City, were to have a profound impact on the lives of the colonists in New Mexico in the late eighteenth century, expanding their commercial opportunities and creating, for the first time in the history of the colony, an identifiable class of merchants. In his groundbreaking book, *From Settler to Citizen*, Ross Frank detailed the effects of royal political and economic reforms, and of climatic devastation in New Spain, on commercial life in New Mexico.

Realizing the tremendous potential of his holdings on the North American continent, ranging from California to Florida, King Carlos III of Spain embarked on a series of administrative and military reorganizations designed to integrate the isolated northern provinces and to effect a lasting peace with the nomadic Indians, whose hostility not only mitigated against such an integration, but also stifled the internal economic development of each region. In 1776, he created a separate administrative unit, the Provincias Internas, which united, on paper at least, the frontier provinces of Texas, New Mexico, Arizona, and California. If only these colonies could trade with one another, according to royal authorities, the economy of each would be enhanced, and, more important to the Crown, a prosperous, integrated, and more secure frontier would emerge.[70]

The establishment of a system of safe and well-protected roads linking the eastern and western regions of the provinces was not to be accomplished for another hundred years. Nevertheless, the investment in military personnel and infrastructure contributed greatly to the conclusion of a lasting peace with the Comanches, commencing in 1786, and the reduction of tensions with other Indian groups. This, in turn, stimulated the expansion of Spanish settlement southward and eastward from the Río Grande Valley into the Pecos and Mora River Valleys, northward beyond Taos and Abiquiú, and southward and westward from Albuquerque. But of equal importance was the effect that the government's military spending had on the economy of New Mexico. The infusion of hard currency—an estimated 2 million pesos between 1770 and 1811—made it possible for settlers to purchase goods coming up from Mexico City and Chihuahua.[71]

Coincidental with the enhanced ability to pay for imports with specie and the opening up of new lands for agricultural production, a devastating series of droughts ravaged much of New Spain in the 1780s. The famine that resulted from this catastrophe, and the consequent increase in the price of food, stimulated an unprecedented demand for New Mexican grains and livestock, as well as textiles and hides. Within a decade or two, the merchants participating in the trade with Chihuahua and points south numbered in the hundreds. The prosperity enjoyed by the northern province was accompanied by a new occupational diversity, linked very closely to the production and marketing of goods for both export and domestic consumption.[72]

But during this transitional period, in which may be seen the beginnings of the formation of a mercantile class in New Mexico, it was not always easy to identify who these merchants were or to distinguish them from those who produced the goods or transported them to market. As Frank recorded the observation of Governor Fernando de Chacón in 1797:

> Those who call themselves merchants, according to the governor, "are not, in so much as they have no license and what they really practice is the occupation of traveler. They must tour all of the province to sell their merchandise, and in this they invest four or six months of the year, and the rest in tilling the land that they possess. [Then] they make the trip to this capital in order to take their fruits and return to provide themselves newly, since without doing this it would be impossible to subsist."[73]

The invisibility of merchants as an identifiable group is dramatically illustrated by the fact that although, by Frank's estimation, there were "hundreds of people who participated in the annual trade with Chihuahua,"[74] only two individuals were noted as such on the rolls of the New Mexico census of 1790: Don José Mariano de la Peña, born in Mexico City, and Chihuahua native Don José Rafael Sarracino.[75] Conspicuous by its absence is the name of Don Antonio José Ortiz, who Frank described as a "wealthy merchant" at the time of his death a decade and a half later, but was referenced in the census by his military rank of general.[76] Similarly, the census taken in 1823, two years after Mexico achieved its independence from Spain, when trade not only was flourishing with the south, but had just opened up with the

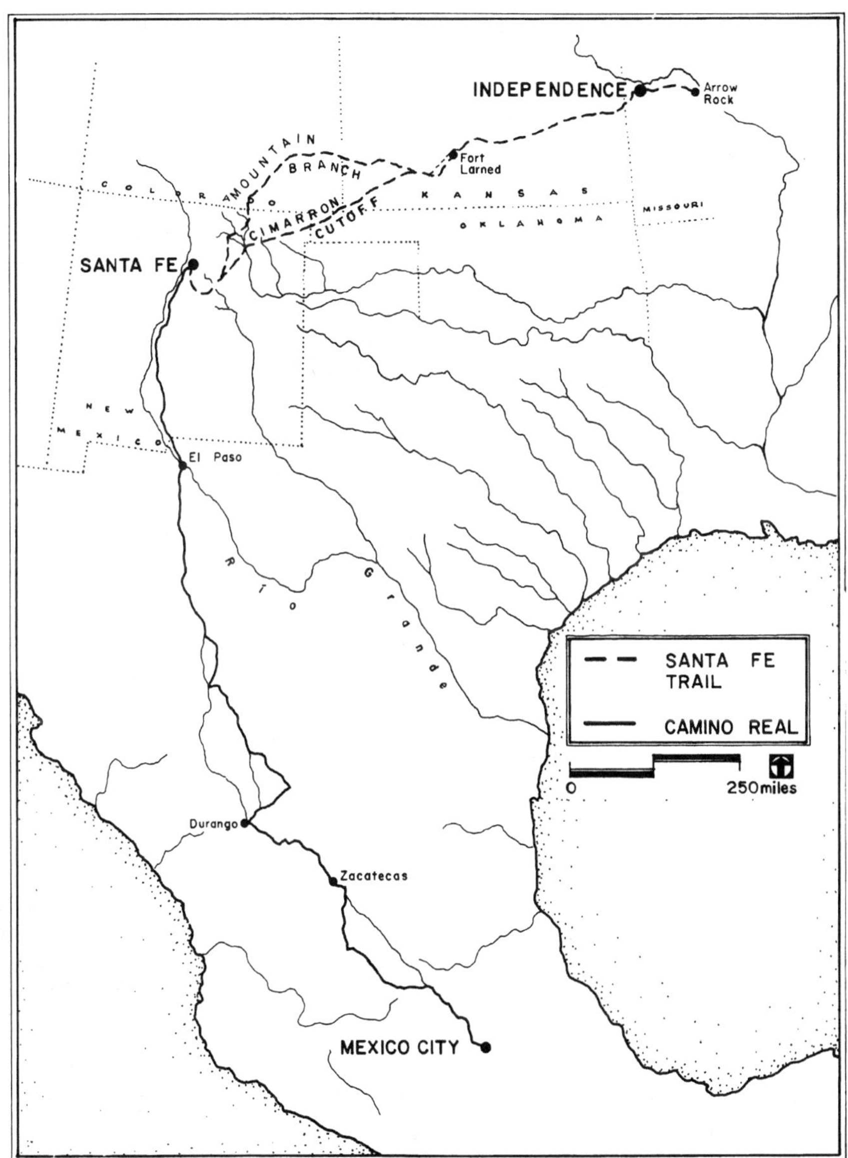

Camino Real and Santa Fe Trail.

United States by way of the Santa Fe Trail east to Independence, Missouri, counted just three merchants: Don Juan Esteban Pino, Don Atanacio Domingo, and Don José Francisco Baca.[77]

While census records obscure the identity of many of those New Mexicans engaged in mercantile activities in the eighteenth and early nineteenth centuries, other contemporary documents proved helpful in clarifying the role of *comerciantes* involved in trade along both the Chihuahua Trail and the Santa Fe Trail.[78] Among these individuals could be found merchants who were both the descendants of the *converso* settlers in New Mexico and the ancestors of five of the nine families featured in this study, including those of Anna and Celina Rael and Josefa Dolores Gonzales Groff.

Antonio José Ortiz, the fifth great-grandfather of Anna and Celina Rael, was one of the most influential political, military, cultural, and commercial figures of his day. Born in Santa Fe in 1734, Ortiz traced his roots both to original settlers of New Mexico in the sixteenth century and to colonists who had accompanied Diego Vargas in his reconquest in the late seventeenth century. In addition to serving as a prominent trader along the Chihuahua Trail, Ortiz held several key military posts in Santa Fe and used his wealth and influence to sponsor important artistic and architectural projects in and around the capital.[79] His son, Antonio José Ortiz II, married Micaela Baca, daughter of Baltasar Baca and Rafaela Baca,[80] and followed in his father's footsteps, as did grandson Ignacio Ortiz, who in addition to holding the position of mayor of Santa Fe, became one of the most active players in the trade along the Chihuahua and Santa Fe Trails by the 1840s.[81] Several extended-family members—including Antonio, Antonio Matías, Fernando María, Francisco, Gaspar, Ignacio Ricardo, Isidro, Jesús María, José, José Francisco, José María, Juan Rafael, Mateo, Miguel, and Tomás—were involved in east–west and north–south commerce as well.[82]

Also included in Anna and Celina Rael's genealogy are

- Vicente Troncoso, a Mexico City–born military officer who, while on duty in the northwestern part of New Mexico, realized the potential for marketing in Chihuahua and other parts of New Spain textiles and pottery made by the Navajos. Troncoso had started to sell some of the Navajo vessels in Mexico, but he died in 1792, before he had the opportunity to realize the potential of his ideas. But, as Frank pointed out, "Troncoso's natural reaction to Navajo material culture exhibited the heightened spirit of enterprise that characterized the new commercial foundation of the New Mexican economy" at the end of the eighteenth century.[83] His son-in-law, also an ancestor of Anna and Celina Rael, Ramón Alaríd, followed the family tradition, carrying goods between Santa Fe and El Paso in the 1830s.[84]
- Felipe Romero, born in Santa Fe in 1785 to Juan Diego Ro-

mero and María Gertrudis de la Luz Padilla, and married to Juana Baca, daughter of Manuel Baca and María Roybal, who carried New Mexican goods to Chihuahua and Durango.[85]

- Don Ygnacio Baca, married to María Bitalia Tafoya, who directed freight from Santa Fe to Sonora and engaged in trade in livestock and agricultural products in the early nineteenth century.[86]
- José Luis Baca, born in 1808 to Ygnacio Baca and María Bitalia Tafoya, and married to María Luisa Serafina Abeitia, daughter of Diego Abeitia and Josefa Armijo, who also traded between Santa Fe and Sonora.[87]

Perhaps the most successful merchant family in New Mexico from the late eighteenth century, through the Mexican republican government, and through the American territorial administration were the ancestors of Josefa Dolores Gonzales Groff: the Pereas of Bernalillo. By the end of the Mexican period in 1846, the Pereas were one of five families (along with the Armijos, Chaveses, Oteros, and Yrizarris) who not only controlled the sheep trade, but also monopolized the importation of goods from the United States.[88] Born in Bernalillo in 1782, Pedro José de los Dolores Perea (great-great grandfather of Josefa Dolores) was the first in a line of prominent merchants whose success would carry over into the twentieth century. One of his lines can be traced to Bartolomé Romero, who enlisted as an officer in the expedition of Juan de Oñate and who likely had *converso* roots. He was also married to a Romero, Bárbara, daughter of Andrés Francisco Romero and María Manuela Gutierres.[89]

Like many in his family, Pedro José raised and transported sheep to markets in Mexico. On one trip in 1837, he drove 3,000 sheep, valued at 1,175 pesos, for sale in Durango. Three years later, he took another 3,480 sheep, worth 1,740 pesos, to Chihuahua and Durango.[90] By 1860, he had amassed a fortune of $40,000 in personal estate, making him among the most wealthy people in the territory.[91] Pedro José's sons, Juan and José Leandro,[92] were also invested in trading activities both east to Missouri and south to Chihuahua. Susan Calafate Boyle, in her impressive study of the participation of Hispano merchants in the trade along the Santa Fe and Chihuahua Trails, reported that in 1842, Juan brought "30,129.5 yards of fabrics, different types of sewing threads, ribbons, cotton socks, and a hundred hats," as well as 26,589 yards of linen, west to New Mexico.[93] In 1844, the two brothers sent more than $40,000 worth of imported merchandise to Chihuahua, Zacatecas, and Aguascalientes; fifteen years later, they shipped thirty-five tons in fourteen wagons, along with 162 head of cattle, from Missouri to Santa Fe. José Leandro would become, like his father, "one of the wealthiest men in New Mexico."[94]

In addition to Josefa Dolores Gonzales Groff and Anna and Celina Rael, others of the group under consideration in this study trace their roots to active merchants in the eighteenth and early nineteenth centuries: Ramón Salas to Antonio José Chávez, Diego Antonio Montoya, and José Manuel Sánchez, all traders along the Chihuahua Trail; Fabiola Rivera Valdéz to Jesús Luján and Francisco Quintana; and Gerald González to Santiago de Jesús González.[95] As with the Pereas, these mercantile connections would be continued and expanded after the assumption of sovereignty of New Mexico by the United States in 1846.

In her work on the history of New Mexican merchants, Boyle made repeated references to the similarity between the German Jewish traders who dominated commercial life in the territory in the decades after the United States annexed New Mexico and the Hispano merchants of the Mexican period, pointing out that "wealthy New Mexicans shared many of the characteristics of their German counterparts, and, like them, did not enter the trade for speculative reasons, but sought to build a thriving and permanent business enterprise."[96] Moreover, she pointed out,

> Hispano merchants pioneered many of the activities that [William] Parish associated with the German Jews. They were particularly successful in securing and arranging deliveries of merchandise from eastern markets, such as Baltimore, Pittsburgh, Philadelphia, New York, and—for bulkier goods; Independence and St. Louis. . . .
>
> Years before the Jewish merchant Charles Ilfeld moved to Taos in 1865, New Mexican merchants had put in practice an economic system based on the model Parish so aptly described. Several wealthy entrepreneurs participated in the evolution of a form of mercantile capitalism that allowed them to control the economic life of the province. Their commercial activities foreshadowed those that German Jews would carry out during the last decades of the nineteenth century.[97]

She concluded: "An examination of their commercial activities clearly reveals that many Hispanos possessed a strong drive for 'the material productiveness' Parish found only among the German Jews. This drive allowed them to take advantage of the opportunities that Santa Fe trade offered to consolidate the comfortable economic conditions they had inherited."[98]

Whether or not Boyle's observations concerning the similarities between the Hispano merchants in early-nineteenth-century New Mexico and their Ashkenazic successors implied a Sephardic ethnic heritage for the New Mexicans is an intriguing question, but one that cannot be resolved with any degree of certainty. What is clear is that several of these *comerciantes* can be traced to noted sixteenth- and seventeenth-century *converso* families, and at least some of their twentieth-century descendants were to demonstrate an awareness of a secret Jewish heritage.

Reflecting patterns similar to those demonstrated by the descendants of *conversos* in the sixteenth and seventeenth centuries, members of these mercantile families tended to marry among themselves and serve as godparents and witnesses for one another's life-cycle events. Juan Perea, for example, son of Pedro José de los Dolores Perea and Bárbara Romero, married Josefa Chaves, daughter of Francisco Xavier Chaves and Ana María Álvarez del Castillo. Serving as godparents at the baptism of their son, Julián, in 1830 were uncle José Chaves and his wife, Manuela Armijo, both representing leading New Mexican merchant families.[99] The Ortizes and Bacas show several points of intersection during this period, as they had since the early colonial period, when Cristóbal Baca and his wife, Ana Ortiz, accompanied Juan de Oñate to New Mexico in 1598, and their grandson Antonio Baca married María de Aragón, daughter of Sebastiana Ortiz, in Bernalillo in 1706.[100] Three of the children of prominent Santa Fe merchant Don Antonio José Ortiz married into the Baca family. Don Antonio José Ortiz II wed Doña Micaela Baca, daughter of Baltasar Baca and Rafaela Baca, around 1784,[101] while Don Miguel Ortiz married Doña María Ysabel Baca, of Belén, daughter of Miguel Baca and Juana María Baca,[102] and, in 1782, Doña Getrudis Ortiz married Don Juan Domingo Baca.[103] And in 1790, a cousin, Antonio Matías Ortiz, son of Don Juan Ortiz and Doña María Rivera, married María Francisca Baca.[104]

Books in the Library of Manuel Delgado

One of the wealthiest individuals in New Mexico on the eve of Mexican independence was Don Manuel Delgado, who operated an extensive mercantile operation based in Santa Fe. The grandson of a merchant from Pachuca, a mining area northeast of Mexico City,

Delgado had an estate valued at almost 25,000 pesos at the time of his death in 1815. Among his possessions were the contents of his store; *ranchos* in Pojoaque, Cerrillos, Cuyamungué, and San Miguel del Vado; and other property in Los Palacios and Santa Cruz de la Cañada. But it was the items of little monetary value, rather than his extensive wares and land, that may provide the key to achieving a greater understanding of Delgado's position within the Santa Fe community.

Manuel Delgado died intestate, and in the partition of his estate among his heirs, the valuators created an inventory of his holdings. Included among his household effects were nineteen nonfiction books on various topics, ranging from history to law, religion, military codes, and agriculture, as well as seventeen novels. Four of the nineteen nonfiction works dealt with Old Testament themes, three exclusively: *Flos sanctorum* (The Flowering of the Saints), *Davíd perseguido* (David Persecuted), *Salomón coronado* (Solomon Crowned), and *Monarquía hebrea* (Hebrew Monarchy).[105] David Gitlitz discussed at length the *conversos'* use of Christian sources to reconstruct traditional Jewish holy books, observing that they used such works as substitutes for reading the Hebrew Bible, which would have been prohibited.[106] Two of the books in the inventory of Delgado's estate were among those described by Gitlitz as commonly found in the possession of Mexican crypto-Jews:

> *Conversos* used a wide range of other religious and literary materials as a source of inspiration and information about the Old Testament. The favorites were books that dealt in any way with Old Testament subjects, whether or not they were overtly Christian in their orientation. Among the books most commonly mentioned in [Inquisition] trial testimony . . . were
>
> > *Davíd perseguido* (Lozano?). This book was most likely the long, moralizing work by the Doctor of Theology Cristóbal Lozano, published serially between 1652 and 1663. In recounting the Old Testament story of David, the book engages in a variety of novelesque, historical and philosophical digressions. The book was extremely popular in the late seventeenth century and went through several editions. When threatened by the Inquisition in Majorca, Raphael Valls burned his copy of this book in 1677. . . .
> >
> > *Flos sanctorum* (Villegas). This enormously popular five-volume compendium of saints' lives, the *Flowering of the Saints*, was published by Alonso de Villegas Selvago between 1580 and 1603. Among other things, it provided biographical ma-

> terial on a number of Old Testament figures. An amplified book with the same title was published by the Jesuit historian Fray Pedro de Ribadeneyra in 1599–1604. The Portuguese *converso* Duarte Rodríguez [Veracruz, Mexico, 1646] "used to read *Flos Sanctorum* of Villegas and the lives of the Patriarchs and prophets, Judith and Esther." Gonzalo Vaez, burned in the Mexican *auto* of 1649, also prayed from the *Flos Sanctorum*, which he called "the missals in the vernacular." . . . Pedro Onofre confessed in Majorca in 1678 that the *Flos Sanctorum* was popular among Judaizers because it contained "chapters which dealt with the favors God had done for the people of Israel and the Patriarchs of the old Law."[107]

The two other works cited in the inventory of Delgado's library can also be interpreted as a means of gaining access to Jewish biblical sources. The narrative found in *Monarquía hebrea* (1719), written by Vicente Bacallar y Sanna, marqués de San Felipe, followed closely that of the books of Judges and Kings in the Bible,[108] while *El hijo de David, Salomón coronado* (1672), written by Spanish author Juan Baños de Velasco y Acevedo, tells the story of King Solomon.[109]

FRAGMENTARY INDICATIONS OF CRYPTO-JUDAISM IN CHURCH DOCUMENTS

The paucity of documentation reflecting official concern on the part of the Spanish or Mexican authorities—civil or religious—about the observance of secret Judaism after the 1660s renders it most difficult to assess the nature and extent of such practices in the eighteenth and early nineteenth centuries. One of the few fragments of paper that did survive may shed a unique light on this phenomenon, if only by implication. Over the years, historians have been able to glean valuable information about social activity in a given culture by analyzing the efforts of those in positions of authority to curtail this behavior. Repeated laws prohibiting the possession of mind-altering drugs, for example, may superficially appear as an indication of the strength of a society's intolerance of drug use. But in reality, such injunctions often reflect just the opposite—that is, the widespread incidence of such drug abuse, which necessitates constant—and unsuccessful—attempts to eliminate the vice.

A manuscript that surfaced in the early 1980s among a collection of religious papers donated to the New Mexico State Records Center and Archives—a mid-nineteenth-century handwritten copy of a fragment of a colonial-era sermon—may well serve as an illustration of how the Church's condemnation of Jewish practices reflected a recognition that such practices were prevalent in the community.[110] The sermon, ascribed by Father Thomas Steele to a Franciscan priest in the late eighteenth or early nineteenth century, begins by admonishing the flock for various manifestations of superstition, including the impersonation of priests, sale of relics of saints, faking of miracles, and practice of Jewish observances:

> What ease I see in introducing novelties with a veneer of piety, so heedless that even in performing their devotions people want to make innovations. O Lord deliver us!
>
> I will first treat what superstition is according to its *manner*, then speak of what superstition is according to its *object*. I speak for our great joy in being among Catholics. We adore our true God in Himself, and we adore Him in His saints. In this we never run the risk of being misled by *what* we adore, but we can run a danger of being misled according to the *manner* in which we offer these devotions, that is, the danger that by the mode of our performing them we make them superstitious.
>
> Now we can do this in two ways. The first comes about if we reverence God but give Him a false and lying worship—for example, *if someone was to observe today one or more of those Jewish ceremonies that were once part of the true religion because we prophesied the Messiah who was to come. They are now false ceremonies and a lying worship, now that we adore him who has already come and saved us, and they are a most serious mortal sin, if anyone does them openly.*[111] Further, he also is guilty of superstition and a most grave sacrilege for false cult who without being a priest or ordained in any way either says mass or performs with the sacred vestments any ceremony of the sort that can only be performed by those who are already consecrated by Holy Orders to be ministers of the church. There's nobody who doesn't know this, but I do remind you that whoever knows of someone doing this is obliged under pain of excommunication to denounce the guilty party right away to the Holy Tribunal of the Inquisition [emphasis added].[112]

In his learned and comprehensive analysis of this sermon, Steele concluded that it was a generic, off-the-shelf piece, reflecting what he called "textbook theology" and originating purely from authoritative texts, not from any clerical reaction to what its author perceived as heresy being practiced in his parish.[113] But, accepting the validity of this theory, it is certainly conceivable that generations of parish priests in New Mexico would have chosen this sermon, from among the dozens at their disposal, to reflect their concern about what they regarded as a particular heresy in their midst. Records from the Mexican Holy Office throughout the colonial period are replete with indictments for such crimes as administering the sacraments without being an ordained priest, imitating miracles, and selling indulgences. And, despite the relative inattention of the Inquisition to heresy on the far northern frontier, it would not be surprising to find New Mexicans engaged in these activities as well.

That the practice of Judaism was included among the litany of sins regarded as mortal is interesting enough. What is even more intriguing is the sermon's emphasis on the evils of the *open* practice of Jewish customs. That is to say, if Judaizers engaged in these practices secretly and discretely, then the clergy would turn a blind eye. But "if anyone does them openly," he or she is guilty of "a most serious mortal sin." It seems plausible that despite the generic nature of the original intent of the sermon, those priests who chose to pull it off the shelf used its message to condemn the heresies that they encountered in their communities.

Another, less ambiguous articulation by Church officials of the existence of the practice of secret Judaism in colonial New Mexico can be found almost parenthetically in a report on an inspection of mission churches undertaken in the late eighteenth century. In 1795, five Franciscan friars conducted a census of thirteen Indian and Spanish communities. In their description of the pueblos, they discussed such issues as the physical condition of the structures, items produced in each of the villages, languages spoken, and hostile relations with the nomadic Indians. The priests devoted a page of their report to the problem of apostasy among the Pueblo people, lamenting how many of them showed disrespect for Catholic feast days. In castigating the Pueblos for their backsliding into their ancient religious practices, the clerics compared the native ceremonies with the Sabbath observances of contemporary crypto-Jews: "Very much to the contrary [referring to the Pueblos' disrespect for Christian holy days] they proceed to practice some Gentile rites, celebrated either in the kivas (which should be destroyed), or in the countryside, such that *in these days they are as observant as the Jews are of the Sabbath [sabado], which they keep, and which they order to be kept inviolably secret* [emphasis added]."[114]

In August 1846, Brigadier General Stephen Watts Kearney led some 1,700 troops across the Santa Fe Trail, spearheading an invasion by the United States into the territory of New Mexico. By the time the

Mexican War was concluded a year and a half later, approximately one-half of Mexico's national territory had been ceded to the Americans. With the extension of the United States Constitution to the new territory and the conferment of American citizenship on Hispanic New Mexicans by the Treaty of Guadalupe Hidalgo, freedom of religion reigned in New Mexico for the first time since the *entrada* of Juan de Oñate 250 years earlier. No longer would the descendants of crypto-Jews be forced to practice their ancestral religion in secret—according to the law, at least.

NOTES

1. John L. Kessell, *Kiva, Cross, and Crown: The Pecos Indians and New Mexico, 1540–1840* (Washington, D.C.: National Park Service, 1979), p. 243; Charles W. Hackett, ed., and Charmion Clair Shelby, trans., *Revolt of the Pueblo Indians of New Mexico and Otermín's Attempted Reconquest, 1680–1682* (Albuquerque: University of New Mexico Press, 1942), vol. 1, pp. cxviii–cxix.
2. Hackett, ed., *Revolt of the Pueblo Indians*, vol. 1, pp. xxvii–xxviii, 4.
3. Ibid., pp. xxxi–li.
4. Ibid., pp. lvii–lxviii, xc, cii, 9–10, 100.
5. Baptism of Alonso Rael de Aguilar, February 12, 1661, Libro quarto de bautismos, fol. 131, Parroquia de San Mateo, Lorca.
6. Rita Rael Anderson, Tijeras, telephone interview with author, October 2003; Leroy Rael, Santa Fe, telephone interview with author, October 2003; Anita Rael Saiz, Los Lunas, telephone interview with author, October 2003; Fred Rael, Tijeras, telephone interview with author, October 2003.
7. Fray Pasqual Sospedra, who served at the mission of Isleta from August 1755 to May 1759, referred to María Manuela Rael de Aguilar using the surname Israel, while Fray Carlos Delgado (1730–1734, 1736–1745), Fray Juan José de Oronzoro (1737, 1749–1755), and Fray Joachín Rodríguez Xeres (1757) cited her as Rael. Baptism of Juana María Padilla, *padrinos*: Don Baltasar Baca and Doña María Manuela Ysrral de Aguilar, January 21, 1756, microfilm, reel 5, frame 227; baptism of Juana Rita de la Luz, daughter of Don Baltasar Baca and Doña Manuela Ysrrael, March 14, 1756, reel 5, frame 229; baptism of Juana Petra, Indian, *padrinos*: Don Baltasar Baca and Doña María Manuela Ysrrael de Aguilar, July 10, 1756, reel 5, frame 231; baptism of Joseph Antonio Chaves, *padrinos*: Baltasar Baca and Doña Manuela Rael, March 28, 1748, reel 5, frame 172; baptism of Dionicia Baca, *padrinos*: Balthasar Baca and Doña Manuela Rael de Aguilar, January 19, 1755, reel 5, frame 217; baptism of María Ysabel Agerra, *padrinos*: Balthasar Baca and María Manuela Rael de Aguilar, March 10, 1757, reel 5, frame 239, all in Mission of Isleta, Archives of the Archdiocese of Santa Fe (hereafter cited as AASF). For data pertaining to the tenure of the priests at the mission of Isleta, see Fray Angelico Chávez, comp., *Archives of the Archdiocese of Santa Fe, 1678–1900* (Washington, D.C.: Academy of American Franciscan History, 1957), pp. 245, 252, 255, 256.

8. Francisco de Asís Veas Arteseros, *Los judíos de Lorca en la baja edad media* (Murcia: Real Academia Alfonso X el Sabio, 1992), pp. 61–105; José Luis González Ortiz, Francisco Chacón Jiménez, and Antonio Segado del Olmo, *Historia de la región murciana* (Murcia: Ediciones Mediterraneo, 1980), pp. 51–65; María de los Llanos Martínez Carrillo, *Revolución urbana y autoridad monárquica en Murcia durante la baja edad media (1395–1420)* (Murcia: Universidad de Murcia, 1980), pp. 51–61.
9. Roser Salicrú i Lluch, "La Corona de Aragón y los Nazaritas en el segundo reinado de Muhamad el Pequeño (1427–1429)," in *Actas del Congreso la frontera oriental nazarí como sujeto histórico (S. XIII—XVI)* (Almería: Instituto de Estudios Almerenses, 1997), pp. 199–211.
10. "Carta de los Reyes Católicos por la que nombran su interprete y escribano de letra arábica en el reyno de Murcia a Gabriel Yrrahel, judío, Madrigal, April 18, 1476" (no. 909) and "Presentación de la carta por la que los Reyes Católicos nombran a Gabriel Yrrahel su traductor e interprete de árabe en el reino de Murcia, December 7, 1476" (no. 923), in Luis Rubio García, ed., *Los judíos de Murcia en la baja edad media (1350–1500): Colección documental* (Murcia: Universidad de Murcia, 1994), vol. 2, pp. 94–96, 107–108, citing Cartas Reales, 1453–1468, fols. 255v–256r, and Libro de actas, 1476–1477, fols. 65r–v, 66v, Archivo Municipal de Murcia.
11. Juan Francisco Jiménez Alcázar, "Modelos sociales en la Lorca bajomedieval: Apuntes de la vida cotidiana," *Murgetana* 95 (1997): 112–114. See also *Las Siete Partidas del sabio rey Don Alonso el X, glosadas por el Lic. Gregorio López* (Madrid: Amarita, 1829), pt. 2, title 22, pp. 600–604.
12. Jiménez Alcázar, "Modelos sociales en la Lorca bajomedieval," pp. 114–115.
13. Veas Arteseros, *Judíos de Lorca en la baja edad media*, pp. 63–64, citing Libro de propios, 1473–1474, November 8, 1474 [September 8, 1473], Archivo Histórico de Lorca (hereafter cited as AHML).
14. Francisco de Asís Veas Arteseros, personal communication, Murcia, July 2000.
15. See, for example, Yitzhak Baer, *A History of the Jews in Christian Spain* (Philadelphia: Jewish Publication Society of America, 1971), vol. 1, pp. 59–60, 89, 113–114, 175, 204, 359, 368, 389, 397; vol. 2, p. 370.
16. Relación de las personas que salieron al auto que se celebró en la inquisición de Murcia. [D]omingo día de nra. señora que se contaron ocho de setienbre de mill y quinientos y sesenta años, citing the appearance of Ginesa Sánchez, wife of Lope Adalíd, in the auto de fe of 1560, Sección de Inquisición, legajo 2797, pt. 1, Archivo Histórico Nacional, Madrid (hereafter cited as AHN).
17. Juan Bernal Segura, *Topónimos árabes de la provincia de Murcia* (Murcia: Patronato de Cultura de la Excma. Diputación de Murcia, 1952), for example, contains no reference to the name Rael as either an Arabic place-name or a surname.
18. Jiménez Alcázar, "Modelos sociales en la Lorca bajomedieval," pp. 114, 120; Pleito, testimonios y otras diligencias judiciales sobre la partición de bienes y herencia de Lucía Rael, Lorca, August 17, 1592, statement of Estevan Martínez, Lorca, September 30, 1589, that Juan Rael, *vecino* of Granada, in his will, named his siblings, María and Lucía Rael, as his heirs, A° 1590,

AHML; Melchior de Caizedo, 1603–1611, will of Catalina de Vas, muger de Simón Navarro, Lorca, June 27, 1601, fols. 178r–180v, [Protocolos], tomo 234, AHML. Vas, the granddaughter of Lucía Rael, indicated that she was the successor of her great-uncle Juan Rael, native of Lorca and *escribano* of Granada.

19. Diego de Lisbona, 1508–1587, will of Marí Rael, February 21, 1518, [Protocolos], tomo 4, AHML. Her husband, Juan Rael, was cited as deceased. Children from this union included Pedro, Miguel, Marí, Mencía, and Juan Rael, the last two having died before 1518. María married a second time, to Miguel de Morata, and had five more children: Juan Rael de Morata, and Martín, Hernando, Diego, and Agostanza Morata (Ejecutoria de nobleza de los Morata de Tajuña, probanza que hizo Diego de Morata, 1555 [copy, April 28, 1766], fols. 6v–7r, 1-2-4, Fondo Cultural Espín, Lorca [hereafter cited as FCE]).
20. Nuptial benediction of Diego Rael, hijo de Juan Rael, difunto, con Catalina García, hija de Cristóbal Coleto, difunto, May 30, 1571, Libro primero de belaciones, fol. 26, Parroquia de San Mateo, Lorca.
21. Baptism of Jaume, hijo de Diego Rael y Catharina García, December 13, 1581, Libro segundo de bautismos, fol. 118v, Parroquia del Salvador, Archivo del Catedral de Orihuela.
22. Baptism of Juan Diego Luch, hijo de Christóval Rael y Anna Arrónis, October 21, 1598, Libro quinto de bautismos, fols. 11v–12r, Iglesia de Santiago, Orihuela.
23. Betrothal of Joan Rael y Anna Enriques, February 26, 1619, Libro de desposorios, 1618–1664, fol. 5r, Parroquia del Salvador, Archivo del Catedral de Orihuela.
24. Baptism of Honorata Juliana, hija de Juan Rael y Agna Anrique, January 9, 1625, Libro quinto de bautismos, fols. 207r–v, Parroquia del Salvador, Archivo del Catedral de Orihuela.
25. Betrothal of Joan de Osca, viudo de Agustina Gomes, y Juliana Rael, viuda de Joachim Alcocer, February 2, 1651, Libro de desposorios, 1618–1664, fols. 194v–195r, Parroquia del Salvador, Archivo del Catedral de Orihuela.
26. Baptism of Joan, hijo de Joan Osca y de Juliana Rael, December 1, 1655, Libro primero de bautismos, fol. 114r, Parroquia de San Patricio, Lorca.
27. Juan Carlos Domínguez Nafria, *La Inquisición de Murcia en el siglo XVI: El licenciado Cascales* (Murcia: Real Academia Alfonso X el Sabio, 1991), pp. 112–146; Juan Blázquez Miguel, *El tribunal de la Inquisición en Murcia* (Murcia: Real Academia Alfonso X el Sabio, 1986), pp. 131–138, and "Catálogo de los procesos inquisitoriales del Tribunal del Santo Oficio de Murcia," *Murgetana* 74 (1987): 7–109; Relación de las personas que salieron al auto que se celebró en la inquisición de Murcia, Sección de Inquisición, legajo 2797, pt. 1, AHN; Noticias curiosas sobre diferentes materias, recopiladas y anotadas por el Licenciado Sebastian de Orozco, MS. 9175: no. 49, Relación del aucto de la fee celebrado en la cibdad de murcia por los ss. inquisidores día de la ascensión que fue a xx de mayo de 1563 años; and no. 60, Relación de las personas que salieron al aucto que hizo el Sancto Oficio

de la inquisición en Murcia domingo día de nra. señora ocho días de setiembre de mill y quinentos y sesenta años, Biblioteca Nacional, Madrid.

28. Relación de las personas que salieron al auto que se celebró en la inquisición de Murcia. Segunto domingo del adviento que se contaron nuebe dias del mes de diciembre de mill quinientos y sesenta y cinco Años, citing Theresa de Morata, *vecina* of Lorca, wife of Rodrigo López, Sección de Inquisición, legajo 2797, pt. 1, AHN. This may have been the same Theresa de Morata, cited as the widow of Sancho Rael and a *vecina* of Lorca, who left a will in 1588 (Thomas Giner, 1558, [Protocolos], tomo 40, AHML). Another Theresa de Morata was included among the in-laws of Juan Rael, *el adalíd* (Ejecutoria de nobleza de los Morata de Tajuña, fols. 4r–v, 1-2-4, FCE).

29. Henry Kamen, *The Spanish Inquisition: A Historical Revision* (New Haven, Conn.: Yale University Press, 1998), p. 144; Blázquez Miguel, *Tribunal de la Inquisición en Murcia*, p. 151.

30. Yom Tov Assis, "Jaime II y los judíos en la Corona de Aragón," *Anales de la Universidad de Alicante: Historia Medieval* 11 (1997): 331–342.

31. Veas Arteseros, *Judíos de Lorca en la baja edad media*, p. 62.

32. Davíd Bernabé Gil, *Monarquía y patriciado urbano en Orihuela, 1445–1707* (Alicante: Caja de Ahorros Provincial de Alicante, 1989), pp. 129–151.

33. A search of the student records at the Universidad de Salamanca resulted in no mention of Alonso Rael de Aguilar.

34. Jerónimo Resalt, 1667–1669, Lic. Agustín Trujillo, carta de obligación contra Juan de Osca, May 22, 1669, fols. 185r–v, [Protocolos], tomo 470, AHML; Lucas Hernando de Quiros, 1669–1671, Don Juan Perezmonte contra Juan Osca, February 13, 1670, fols. 41r–v, [Protocolos], tomo 479, sec. 1, AHML.

35. Andrés de Ateguí Mula, 1672–1675, Juan Osca venda a Juan Antonio Chipori, November 24, 1672, fols. 19r–20v, [Protocolos], tomo 489, sec. 1, AHML.

36. Jerónimo Resalt, 1667–1669, Lic. Agustín Trujillo, carta de obligación contra Juan de Osca, fols. 185r–v, [Protocolos], tomo 470, AHML; Padrones de Santiago, San Mateo, San Juan y Santa María, 1660, Lorca, AHML.

37. Andrés de Ateguí Mula, 1672–1675, Antonio Pinilla Velazques y Juan Osca, poder a Manuel Fernández de Ruedas, November 24, 1672, fols. 13r–v, [Protocolos], tomo 489, sec. 1, AHML; Blázquez Miguel, "Catálogo de los procesos inquisitoriales del Tribunal del Santo Oficio de Murcia."

38. Ynquisición de Murcia, cartas, espedientes y memoriales del año de 1680, instructions by Juan Martínez de Figueroa, Murcia, June 18, 1680, Sección de Inquisición, legajo 2835, AHN.

39. Correspondencia, Inquisición de Murcia al Consejo Supremo de la Inquisición, Lic. D. Baltasar de Prado to Consejo Supremo de la Inquisición, Murcia, August 12, 1681, Sección de Inquisición, legajo 2836, AHN.

40. Correspondencia, Inquisición de Murcia al Consejo Supremo de la Inquisición, Lic. Francisco Esteban del Vado [inquisitor of Murcia] to Exmo.

Obpo. Ynquisidor General, Murcia, February 3, 1681, Sección de Inquisición, legajo 2837, AHN.

41. Blázquez Miguel, "Catálogo de los procesos inquisitoriales del Tribunal del Santo Oficio de Murcia" Relación de los reos que salieron en el auto particular de fee que celebró el Santo Oficio de la Ynquisición de Murcia en el conbento de San Francisco Domingo 15 de Marco de 1682, and Memoria de los Reos que salieron en el Auto particular de fee que se celebró en el Conbento de St. Francisco desta Ciudad de Murcia el dia 10 de Mayo de 1682, Sección de Inquisición, legajo 2819, pt. 1, AHN; Ynquisición de Murcia, cartas, espedientes y memoriales del año de 1680, Sección de Inquisición, legajo 2835, AHN; Correspondencia, Inquisición de Murcia al Consejo Supremo de la Inquisición, Lic. D. Baltasar de Prado to Consejo Supremo de la Inquisición, en 3 de Junio de 1681 se remitieron a los Señores deel Consejo las informaciones de Miguel Villar y su muger con los papeles y processos acumulados que son los siguientes: . . . Procesos de relaxados: . . . el de Leonor Fernández, muger de Pedro de Alcaráz en 23 . . . Penitenciados: . . . el de María Fernández, muger de Diego López de Alcaráz en 47, Sección de Inquisición, legajo 2836, AHN; Relación de los reos que salieron al Auto Público de fe que celebró el Tribunal del Santo Oficio de la Inquisición de Murcia en el Convento de San Francisco el Domingo 15 de Marzo de 1682, Sección de Inquisición, legajo 2022, exp. 117, AHN; Relación de causas de fe pendientes y despachadas en este Santo Officio desde 23 de Noviembre de 1683 hasta oi día de la fecha [16 de mayo de 1684], Sección de Inquisición, legajo 2838, AHN; Correspondencia, Inquisición de Murcia al Consejo Supremo de la Inquisición, carta de los inquisidores de Murcia, Dr. D. Gerónimo de Escobar Sobremonte y Cisneros and Dor. Don Joseph González, al Consejo, Murcia, November 3, 1682, Sección de Inquisición, legajo 2837, AHN.

42. Correspondencia, Inquisición de Murcia al Consejo Supremo de la Inquisición, June 3, 1681, Sección de Inquisición, legajo 2836, AHN. Francisco García de Alcaráz y Mula, *regidor* of Lorca, was married to Francisca Rael de Aguilar. Juan, Alonso, and Pedro Rael de Aguilar were the sons of Alonso de Alcaráz and Catalina Palacio Rael, who were married in 1638. Juan Alcaráz del Soto served as witness for the marriage in 1619 of Juan Rael and Ana Enriques, Alonso's maternal grandparents. See Gerónimo Ferrer, 1660, will of Doña Francisca Rael de Aguilar, muger de Don Francisco Garzía de Alcaráz y Mula, Lorca, September 17, 1659, fols. 164r–167r, [Protocolos], tomo 440; Alonso del Pozo Gamboa, 1655–1662, will of Pedro Rael de Aguilar, February 3, 1656, [Protocolos], tomo 435; will of Alonso García de Alcaráz, July 3, 1667, fols. 274v–277r, [Protocolos], tomo 469; and will of Alonso García de Alcaráz y Chabes, June 12, 1668, fols. 229r–231v, [Protocolos], tomo 474, all in AHML; baptism of Alonso, hijo de Alonso García de Alcaráz y de Catalina Rael, 1647, Libro quarto de bautismos, fol. 75v; baptism of Juan, hijo de Alonso García Alcaráz y Catalina Saravia Rael, Libro quarto de bautismos, fol. 195; and marriage of Don Alonso García de Alcaráz con Doña Catalina Rael de Aguilar, July 2, 1638, Libro segundo de belaciones, fol. 22v, all in Parroquia de San Mateo, Lorca; and betrothal of Joan Rael y Anna Enriques, February 26, 1619, Libro de desposorios, 1618–1664, fol. 5r, Parroquia del Salvador, Archivo del Catedral de Orihuela.

43. Gobernadores. Don Domingo Petris Gironza es nobrado para nuevo México: pide seis años de pagos adelantados y armas y municiones para llevar a su provincia y ponerla en estado de defensa [pronouncement by Governor Domingo Jironza Petríz de Cruzate, signed by "Alphonsso de Aguilar, escribano de govierno y guerra"], Pueblo de Nra. Sra. de Guadalupe del Paso del Río del Norte, September 26, 1683, fols. 84r–85v [also 81 and 37, 82 and 38], Ramo de Provincias Internas, tomo 35, exp. 2, Archivo General de la Nación, Mexico City.

44. Ibid.; Don Domingo Jironza Petríz de Cruzat [*sic*], Pueblo del Paso, October 15, 1683, Vault MS. 1509, box 1, folder 12, Collection of Spanish Manuscripts, Archives and Manuscripts, Brigham Young University Library, Provo, Utah.

45. John L. Kessell, lecture to the Santa Fe Fiesta Council, in *Gathering Up Again: Fiesta in Santa Fe*, dir. Jeanette DeBouzek and Diane Reyna (Albuquerque: Quotidian Independent Documentary Research, 1992), videocassette.

46. *To the Royal Crown Restored: The Journals of Don Diego de Vargas, 1692–94*, ed. John L. Kessell, Rick Hendricks, and Meredith D. Dodge (Albuquerque: University of New Mexico Press, 1995), pp. 527–534. For an exhaustive account of the history of the reconquest of New Mexico by Vargas and his troops, see also the other volumes in the splendid series of Vargas's journals: *Remote Beyond Compare: Letters of Don Diego de Vargas to His Family from New Spain and New Mexico, 1675–1706*, ed. John L. Kessell (Albuquerque: University of New Mexico Press, 1989); *By Force of Arms: The Journals of Don Diego de Vargas, New Mexico, 1691–1693*, ed. John L. Kessell and Rick Hendricks (Albuquerque: University of New Mexico Press, 1992); *Blood on the Boulders: The Journals of Don Diego de Vargas, New Mexico, 1694–97*, 2 vols., ed. John L. Kessell, Rick Hendricks, and Meredith D. Dodge (Albuquerque: University of New Mexico Press, 1998); *That Disturbances Cease: The Journals of Don Diego de Vargas, 1697–1700*, ed. John L. Kessell, Rick Hendricks, Meredith D. Dodge, and Larry D. Miller (Albuquerque: University of New Mexico Press, 2000); and *A Settling of Accounts: The Journals of Don Diego de Vargas, New Mexico, 1700–1704*, ed. John L. Kessell, Rick Hendricks, Meredith D. Dodge, and Larry D. Miller (Albuquerque: University of New Mexico Press, 2002).

47. José Antonio Esquibel and John B. Colligan, *The Spanish Recolonization of New Mexico: An Account of the Families Recruited in Mexico City in 1693* (Albuquerque: Hispanic Genealogical Society of New Mexico, 1999), pp. 1–5.

48. John B. Colligan, *The Juan Páez Hurtado Expedition of 1695: Fraud in Recruiting Colonists for New Mexico* (Albuquerque: University of New Mexico Press, 1995), pp. 13–19. Colligan postulated that Páez Hurtado padded the number of colonists in order to defraud the Crown of unjustified subsidies.

49. José Antonio Esquibel, "The Ancestral Iberian Roots of the Quintana Family of New Mexico" (manuscript, Hispanic Genealogical Research Center of New Mexico, Albuquerque). For more on the Álvarez de Toledo family, see chap. 4.

50. Esquibel and Colligan, *Spanish Recolonization of New Mexico*, pp. 112–114; sacristan of the parish church of Brihuega, personal communication, November 1, 2000.

51. Confesiones. Série Sexta, legajo 749, exp. 7; Proceso de Juan de Atienza, Cifuentes, judaismo, relajado, incompleto, 1494, legajo 14, exp. 278; Proceso de Juan de Alcalá, natural de Medinaceli, 1558, legajo 212, exp. 2448, all in Archivo Diocesano de Cuenca.

52. Esquibel and Colligan, *Spanish Recolonization of New Mexico*, pp. 257–261.

53. Processo de Gaspar de Carvalho, 1636, Coimbra, no. 4347; Processo de Ana Mascarenhas, 1633, Coimbra, no. 5044; Processo de Francisco Mascarenhas, 1625, Coimbra, no. 6807; Processo de Jorge de Almeida Mascarenhas, 1625, Coimbra, no. 4101; Processo de Manoel de Mascarenhas, 1671, Coimbra, no. 356; Processo de Tristão Soares Mascarenhas, 1626, Coimbra, no. 3919; Processo de Isabel Mascarenhas, 1639, Evora, no. 8220; Processo de Ines Mascarenhas, 1626, Coimbra, no. 9515; Processo de Antonia Mascarenhas, 1624, Coimbra, no. 9753; Processo de Antonio Mascarenhas, 1673, Lisboa, no. 5704; Processo de Manoel de Mascarenhas, 1671, Coimbra, no. 8171, all in Secção de Inquisição, Arquivo Nacional da Torre do Tombo, Lisbon. Certainly not all persons with the surname Mascarenhas were crypto-Jews or even descendants of *conversos*. That the surname is not particularly common in Portugal and that it appears in the records of so many Inquisition trials raises the possibility of a connection between the Mascareñas of New Mexico and New Christians.

54. Carta de dote, Juan de Quiñones Mascareñas y Mariana del Río, México, February 2, 1654, Notaría 110, Toribio Cobian, tomo 727 bis, 1654, Archivo General de Notarías, Mexico City.

55. Esquibel and Colligan, *Spanish Recolonization of New Mexico*, pp. 213–223.

56. Haim Beinart, *Los conversos ante el tribunal de la inquisición* (Barcelona: Riopiedras Ediciones, 1983), pp. 47–54.

57. For details on the odyssey of these individuals, their role in the death of La Salle, their sojourn among the Indians of northern New Spain, their incarceration in Mexico and Spain, and the circumstances surrounding their enlistment with Cristóbal de Velasco and Francisco Farfán, see Esquibel and Colligan, *Spanish Recolonization of New Mexico*, pp. 53–64.

58. I am indebted to the work of Marcel Douyrou, of Bordeaux, for providing important documentation relating to the history of the l'Archivèque family.

59. Pascal Rambaud, "Juifs et protestants portugais a La Rochelle: Les marranes face a la Réforme (1550–1570)," *Écrits d'Ouest: Cahiers Rochelais d'Histoire Régionale d'Art et de Littérature* 7 (1998): 1–2, 18–22; Jean-Claude Bonnin-LaRochelle, *Histoire des juifs de La Rochelle* (La Rochelle: Bonnin-LaRochelle, 1999), pp. 25–28.

60. Esquibel and Colligan, *Spanish Recolonization of New Mexico*, p. 53.

61. Paul-Louis Coÿne, *Dictionnaire des familles protestantes de Bordeaux aux XVIIe siècle*, fasc. 4 (Bordeaux: Coÿne, 1994); baptism of Claude larcheveque, July 20, 1634, Registre des baptêmes de Saint-André de Bordeaux, Archives Municipal, GG 28, acte no. 2419, Archives Departmentales annex, Bordeaux.

62. Esquibel and Colligan, *Spanish Recolonization of New Mexico*, p. 54.

63. Marriage of François Grolet (or Grelet) and Marie Gauthier, May 11, 1670, Les Archives de mariage, La Paroisse de Saint-Jean-du-Perot, La Rochelle.

64. Fray Angelico Chávez, *Origins of New Mexico Families in the Spanish Colonial Period* (Santa Fe: Gannon, 1975), p. 273.

65. This family history is based on research conducted in the sacramental records of the parish church of Santo Tomé, Caldas de Reies, and of the Archivo Histórico Diocesano, Santiago de Compostela.

66. Baptism of Pedro, hijo de Pedro Paz y de su muger, María da Cruz, padrinos: Bartolomé de Requejo y Catalina de Pino, April 9, 1649; baptism of Antonia, hija de Pedro de Paz y de su mujer, Dominga [probably María] da Cruz, padrinos: Andrés de Santa Cruz y su muger, Ana da Cruz, March 11, 1648, both in Libros sacramentales, bautizados, Parroquia de Santo Tomé, Caldas de Reies.

67. Relación de las causas que resultaron de la visita que el inquisidor Lic. Joan Ochoa hico en el obispado de Tui y Villa de Pontevedra, arcobispado de Sanctiago, este año de mill y seiscientos y nueve, Sección de Inquisición, legajo 2042, exp. 48, nos. 44–51, 133–136, 172, 209, 211, AHN; Relación de las causas despachadas en el Santo Oficio de la inquisición de Galicia desde primero de septiembre de 1623 asta primero de septiembre de 1624, fols. 20v–22r, Sección de Inquisición, legajo 2042, exp. 62, AHN; Relación de las causas despachadas en este sancto oficio del Reyno de Galicia entre año desde primero de setiembre del pasado de 1631, hasta fin del agosto deste de 1632 y las que se despacharon en auto particular en la catedral deste ciudad, fols. 21v–22v, Sección de Inquisición, legajo 2042, exp. 71, no. 31, AHN; Relación de causas de fe pendientes en la ynquisición de Galicia y del estado en que se hallan desde 1 de setiembre hasta fin del año de 1681, fols. 6v–8r, Sección de Inquisición, legajo 2042, exp. 100, nos. 19, 23, AHN.

68. José Ramón Onega, *Los judíos en el reino de Galicia* (Madrid: Editora Nacional, 1981), p. 579.

69. Ross Frank, *From Settler to Citizen: New Mexican Economic Development and the Creation of Vecino Society, 1750–1820* (Berkeley: University of California Press, 2000), pp. 14–21.

70. Ibid., pp. 76–77, 101.

71. Ibid., pp. 82–101.

72. Ibid., pp. 119–122.

73. Ibid., pp. 120–121, citing Fernando de Chacón to Comandante General Pedro de Nava, Santa Fe, July 16, 1797, microfilm, reel 14, frames 68–69, Spanish Archives of New Mexico, ser. 2, New Mexico State Records Center and Archives, Santa Fe (hereafter cited as NMSRCA).

74. Frank, *From Settler to Citizen*, p. 120.

75. Virginia Langham Olmsted, trans. and comp., *New Mexico Spanish and Mexican Colonial Censuses, 1790, 1823, 1845* (Albuquerque: New Mexico Genealogical Society, 1975), referencing census of the jurisdiction of Santa Fe, 1790, microfilm, reel 12, frames 319–502, Spanish Archives of New Mexico, ser. 2, no. 1096a, NMSRCA.

76. Frank, *From Settler to Citizen*, p. 153; Olmsted, *New Mexico Spanish and Mexican Colonial Censuses*, referencing census of the jurisdiction of Santa Fe, 1790,

household 1, microfilm, reel 12, frame 373, Spanish Archives of New Mexico, ser. 2, no. 1096a, NMSRCA.

77. Olmsted, *New Mexico Spanish and Mexican Colonial Censuses*, referencing census of 1823, microfilm, reel 3, frames 219–285, Mexican Archives of New Mexico, NMSRCA.

78. The identification of merchants was accomplished by a search through the Spanish Archives of New Mexico and other collections of papers at the New Mexico State Records Center and Archives, as well as major secondary works on the history of commerce in New Mexico during the Spanish and Mexican periods, including Frank, *From Settler to Citizen*; and Susan Calafate Boyle, *Los Capitalistas: Hispano Merchants and the Santa Fe Trade* (Albuquerque: University of New Mexico Press, 1997). I am particularly indebted to the editors and compilers of "Documentary Relations of the Southwest" (http://saint-denis.library.arizona.edu), the database prepared by the Arizona State Museum, University of Arizona, Tucson..

79. Frank, *From Settler to Citizen*, pp. 183–188.

80. Olmsted, *New Mexico Spanish and Mexican Colonial Censuses*, referencing census of the jurisdiction of Santa Fe, 1790, household 2, microfilm, reel 12, frame 373, Spanish Archives of New Mexico, ser. 2, no. 1096a, NMSRCA.

81. Boyle, *Capitalistas*, pp. 59, 131, citing a list, compiled in 1845, of those holding *guias* (commercial passports) to carry goods to Chihuahua.

82. Boyle, *Capitalistas*, pp. 26, 41, 59, 61, 64, 130–131; Frank, *From Settler to Citizen*, pp. 126, 150, 212, 214.

83. Frank, *From Settler to Citizen*, pp. 131–132; Governor Fernando de la Concha, requesting pension for the family of the late Lieutenant Vicente Troncoso, Santa Fe, April 20, 1793, microfilm, reel 13, frames 224–225, Spanish Archives of New Mexico, ser. 2, no. 1230, NMSRCA; Olmsted, *New Mexico Spanish and Mexican Colonial Censuses*, referencing census of the Presidio of Santa Fe, 1790, household 3, microfilm, reel 21, frame 508, Spanish Archives of New Mexico, ser. 2, NMSRCA.

84. Boyle, *Capitalistas*, p. 115.

85. Ibid., p. 136; baptism of Felipe Romero, *padrinos*: José María Montoya and Antonia Gómez, February 9, 1785, microfilm, reel 15, frame 568; marriage of Felipe Romero and Juana Baca, *padrinos*: Juan Baca and Juana Baca; witnesses: Domingo Fernández and Miguel Flores, May 20, 1809, microfilm, reel 31, frame 470, both in Parish of San Francisco, Santa Fe, AASF.

86. Baca Family Papers, box 1, folders 12–24, NMSRCA.

87. Baptism of José Luis Baca, *padrinos*: Pedro Baca and Gertrudis Jaramillo, June 23, 1808, microfilm, reel 15, frame 1014, Parish of San Francisco, Santa Fe, AASF; Bureau of the Census, *Population Schedules of the Seventh Census of the United States, 1850, New Mexico*, Santa Fe County, microcopy no. 432, sheet 327, NMSRCA; marriage of Don Luis Baca and Doña María Luisa Seferina Abeitia, witnesses: Antonio Valdéz and Vicente García, December 8, 1842, microfilm, reel 31, frames 879–880, Parish of San Francisco, Santa Fe, AASF; Boyle, *Capitalistas*, p. 119.

88. Boyle, *Capitalistas*, p. 43.

89. Marriage of Pedro José de los Dolores Perea and Bárbara Romero, Sandía, June 28, 1802, microfilm, reel 28, frame 613, Parish of Nuestra Señora de los Dolores, Sandía, AASF.

90. Boyle, *Capitalistas*, p. 134.

91. Ibid., p. 93.

92. Luis Gilberto Padilla y Baca, *New Mexico Baptisms, Sandía Mission, Nuestra Señora de los Dolores, 1771–1851* (Albuquerque: Hispanic Genealogical Research Center, 1998), pp. 144–145.

93. Boyle, *Capitalistas*, p. 63.

94. Ibid., p. 92.

95. Ibid., pp. 121, 126, 127, 129, 134, 136.

96. Ibid., p. 68.

97. Ibid., pp. 71–72.

98. Ibid., p. 88.

99. Baptism of Julian Perea, *padrinos*: José Chaves and Manuela Armijo, Isleta, February 13, 1830, microfilm, reel 5, frame 401, Mission of Isleta, AASF; Lila Armijo Pfeufer and Margaret Buxton, transcribers, and Margaret Leonard Windham and Evelyn Lujan Baca, comps., *New Mexico Marriages and Baptisms, San Augustín de la Isleta Church* (Albuquerque: New Mexico Genealogical Society, 1996), p. 83, citing marriage of José Chaves and María Manuela Armijo, April 11, 1830, microfilm, reel 37, frame 688, AASF.

100. Chávez, *Origins of New Mexico Families*, pp. 9, 141.

101. Olmsted, *New Mexico Spanish and Mexican Colonial Censuses*, referencing census of the jurisdiction of Santa Fe, 1790, microfilm, reel 12, frame 373, Spanish Archives of New Mexico, ser. 2, no. 1096a, NMSRCA.

102. Pfeufer and Buxton, transcribers, *New Mexico Marriages and Baptisms*, p. 40, citing marriage of Miguel Ortiz and María Ysabel Baca, August 29, 1786, microfilm, reel 37, frame 526, AASF.

103. Marie J. Roybal and Lila Armijo Pfeufer, extractors, and Margaret Leonard Windham and Evelyn Lujan Baca, comps., *New Mexico Marriages: Santa Fe—St. Francis Parish and Military Chapel of Our Lady of Light (La Castrense), 1728–1857* (Albuquerque: New Mexico Genealogical Society, 1997), p. 58, citing marriage of Juan Domingo Baca and Getrudis Ortiz, 1782, microfilm, reel 31, frame 205, Parish of San Francisco, Santa Fe, AASF.

104. Ibid., p. 102, citing marriage of Antonio Matías Ortiz and María Francisca Baca, April 11, 1790, microfilm, reel 31, frame 379, Parish of San Francisco, Santa Fe, AASF; Olmsted, *New Mexico Spanish and Mexican Colonial Censuses*, referencing census of the jurisdiction of Santa Fe, 1790, microfilm, reel 12, frame 391, Spanish Archives of New Mexico, ser. 2, no. 1096a, NMSRCA.

105. Manuel Delgado, settlement of estate, Santa Fe, 1815, microfilm, reel 2, frames 365–387, Spanish Archives of New Mexico, ser. 1, no. 252 [copy examined in History File, no. 42, Wills and Estates], NMSRCA. *Flos sanctorum* appears to have been transcribed as *Flor santuorum*.

106. David M. Gitlitz, *Secrecy and Deceit: The Religion of the Crypto-Jews* (Philadelphia: Jewish Publication Society of America, 1996), pp. 425–441.

107. Ibid., pp. 429–430. It is also possible that the *David perseguido* cited in the inventory of Delgado's estate could have referred to a play by that name written by Lope de Vega.

108. This book was published in various editions, including *La monarchía hebrea* (Madrid: Rabirez, 1761–1776), and *Monarchía hebrea* (Madrid: Manuel Martín, 1771).

109. Juan Rafael de la Cuadra Blanco, "El Escorial como nuevo templo de Salamón en la literatura de la época (II)" (available at: http://sapiens.ya.com/jrcuadra/jrfuent3.htm); Joseph L. Laurenti, *Spanish Rare Books of the Golden Age: Guide to the Microfilm Collection* (Woodbridge, Conn.: Research Publications, 1987), reel 21, no. 96.

110. "Sermon denouncing the superstitious and evil usages which have infiltrated the form of Catholic worship, n.d.," in Thomas J. Steele, ed., *New Mexican Spanish Religious Oratory, 1800–1900* (Albuquerque: University of New Mexico Press, 1997), "Anonymous Franciscan," pp. 8–17, citing Cesarita Sandoval Martínez–Alonso C. Martínez Family Papers, acc. no. 1982.001, NMSRCA.

111. Steele preferred the translation "with full knowledge," instead of "openly," for "con advertencia."

112. Steele, ed., *New Mexican Spanish Religious Oratory*, p. 11. Steele translated the original Spanish, with the exception of the phrase "con advertencia." In a footnote, he acknowledged the ambiguity of the term, as well as the possibility that it could be translated as "openly" (p. 10).

113. According to Steele, "Unfortunately, then, we do not learn anything trustworthy about New Mexican life during the period of the sermon. None of the superstitions attacked can on the basis of this sermon be asserted to have been practiced in New Mexico—or, for that manner, in the France of Thomas Aquinas, the Portugal of Fagúndez, the Spain of Sánchez, the Germany of Laymann, or the Italy of Tamburelli. They belong to that never-never land of Titius and Bertha, the John Doe and Mary Roe of moral theology; they belong to the la-la land of textbook theology" (*New Mexico Spanish Religious Oratory*, pp. 8–9).

114. Census and Report on Missions of New Mexico of the Custody of Conversion of San Pablo for the Years 1793 and 1794, October 30, 1795, pp. 5–6, microfilm, reel 21, frames 539–530, Benjamin M. Read Collection, Spanish Archives of New Mexico, ser. 2, NMSRCA. See also Frank, *From Settler to Citizen*, pp. 200–201.

CHAPTER 7

Adjustments to Anglo-American Society, 1846–1950

Despite the removal of legal barriers to the open practice of Judaism with the transfer of sovereignty of New Mexico from the Republic of Mexico to the United States, long-standing cultural taboos remained strongly in force. Thus most of the descendants of New Mexican crypto-Jews who retained a sense of their heritage, and wished to express it, continued to do so within the privacy of their homes, families, and small communities. The new climate, however, permitted some to venture out of the shadows, if only a few steps, and articulate the Jewish part of their lives in a slightly more public manner.

Many of the methodological challenges cited for the seventeenth through the early nineteenth century remained in effect during the late nineteenth and early twentieth centuries with respect to the absence of records to document the behavior of these individuals. The arrival in New Mexico of new groups of people from western Europe and the United States, in the wake of the Anglo-American annexation of the territory, might have provided new lenses through which historians could examine crypto-Jewish activities, but it appears that most of these newcomers were more concerned with conducting their own lives and businesses than with leaving behind any anthropological observations. Nevertheless, hints of *converso* identity may be gleaned from marriage and occupational patterns, as well from the names that parents gave to their children. The affiliation of many Hispano families with a number of the new Protestant denominations that arrived with the Anglos may also have indicated crypto-Jewish tendencies. Moreover, information derived from oral histories of twentieth-century descendants of crypto-Jews provides key insights into the behavior of their grandparents and great-grandparents, extending back to the nineteenth century.

THE CONVERSION OF *CONVERSOS* TO PROTESTANTISM

With the annexation of the territory of New Mexico by the United States, the Hispano and Native American people, whose roots penetrated deeply into New Mexican soil, had to adjust themselves to a new legal system, a new language, new concepts regarding land tenure, and a new array of religious ideas. The Treaty of Guadalupe Hidalgo, signed on February 2, 1848, by which sovereignty was transferred from Mexico to the United States, guaranteed to Mexican citizens the rights to their property and the "free exercise of their religion without restriction."[1] But to many, the decision of the Church hierarchy in 1850 to appoint French cleric Jean Baptiste Lamy as apostolic bishop of Santa Fe, thus passing over native clergy, represented to many Hispano New Mexicans the imposition of a new and foreign brand of Catholicism. Lamy imported priests and nuns from Germany, Italy, and France, as well as from Kentucky, Louisiana, and other parts of the United States. These clerics established schools for young men and women and filled pulpits that had remained vacant for years. Within a short time, however, friction developed between the new Church leaders and the native clergy, whom the newcomers regarded as undisciplined, lax in morals, and too tolerant of what they regarded as "superstition" among their parishioners.[2]

Although many New Mexican Catholics tried to cope with these changes, others became attracted to the various Protestant denominations that had filtered into New Mexico during the late nineteenth and early twentieth centuries. The impact of Protestantism on the Hispano community was not felt significantly until the late 1870s, three decades into the American administration of the territory. The first to make inroads into the spiritual monopoly formerly held by the Catholic Church were the more traditional groups, such as Presbyterians and Methodists.

The chasm between the values of the New Mexico Hispano Cath-

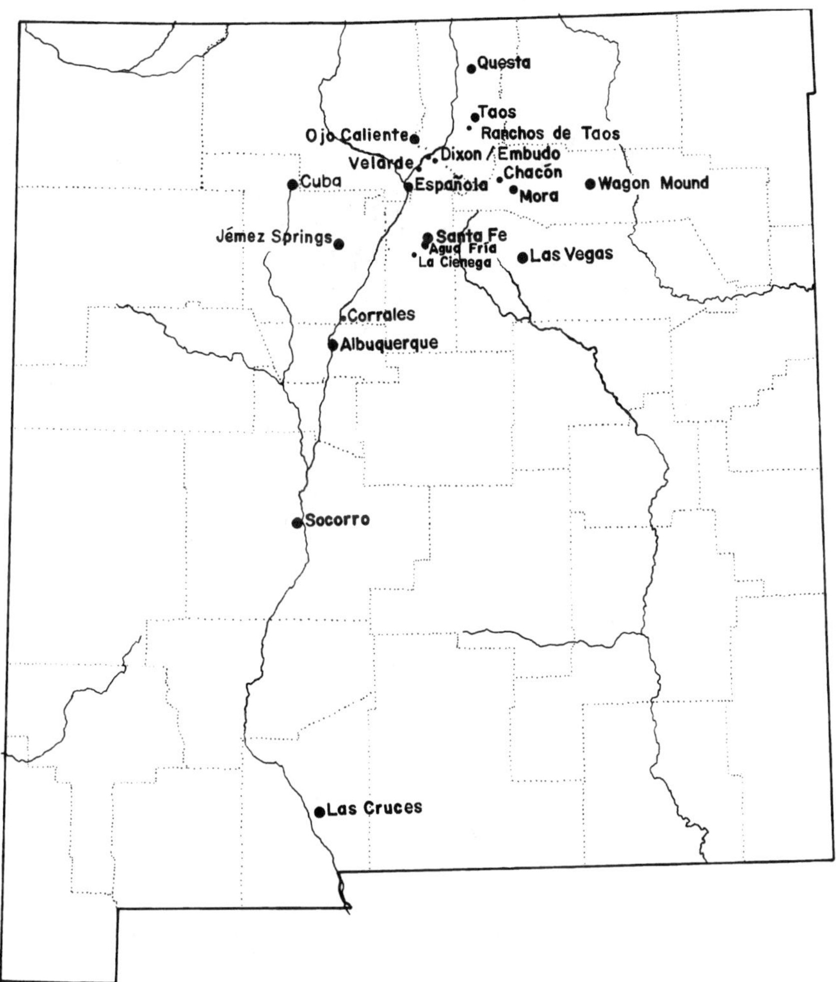

New Mexico, nineteenth and twentieth centuries.

olics and the culture imported by the newcomers could not have been more profound. In the first place, the Protestant missionaries represented the culture of the conqueror, bearing all the disdain and prejudice of the new dominant order toward people who were perceived as being backward and superstitious. As Randi Jones Walker commented in her work on the history of Protestantism in the American Southwest:

> The Protestants felt that the Church had kept the people in ignorance, did not allow the people to read the Bible, and did not provide schools. . . . The Protestant remedy for what they per-

> ceived to be the spiritual darkness and superstition of Roman Catholics was to convert them to Protestantism. . . . It began with reading the Bible, whether out of curiosity or already aroused dissatisfactions with Catholicism. The next step was recognition of certain specific errors of the Roman Church and the Protestant truths concerning these matters. Especially important was the repudiation of the authority of the priests with regard to confession, penance, and forgiveness of sins. Of equal importance was the repudiation of the mediation of Mary and the saints between the believer and God.[3]

It was precisely these distinctions between the two Christian faiths that stimulated sociologist Tomás Atencio to hypothesize that descendants of crypto-Jews may well have been some of the early converts to Protestantism in New Mexico. Growing up in Dixon, located about halfway between Santa Fe and Taos, in the mid-twentieth century, Atencio was the son of one of the first Hispano Presbyterian ministers in the state. He was aware of the Jewish heritage maintained by his family, as well as by other residents of the area, whose roots can be traced back many generations in Mexico and the borderlands. On the basis of both his family background and his sociological analysis of New Mexican culture, Atencio argued that a link existed between crypto-Judaism and early Hispano converts to Protestantism.[4]

Access to the Hebrew Bible, Atencio concluded, was the principal reason that *conversos* sought out the Protestant faiths. The Catholic Church in New Mexico had proscribed parishioners from interpreting the Bible for themselves. It was the responsibility of the priests to explain biblical texts for their flock. As Bishop Lamy stated in his Pastoral Letter of 1854:

> The Catholic Church does not wish to, nor has ever wished to, deprive its children of the divine treasures of the word of God; indeed, it orders its ministers to explain to you the divine Scripture every Sunday and on all solemn occasions. It is well known from history that the first versions of Scripture that were published in the common language much earlier than the birth of Protestantism were published by the [Catholic] Church. *What our religion does not permit with regard to the holy Scripture is for anyone using his own judgment to interpret the sense of the word of God*; indeed, it is [the responsibility of] the Church, which knows that the Scripture is the word of God. Our Lord ordered the Church to "teach all the peoples," Matt. xxviii.19, 20, "to ob-

> serve all things that had been ordered" he promised to be with the ministers of his Church all the days until the Consummation. This very Church, founded by the Son of God, is, according to St. Paul, 1 Tim. iii.15, "the support and approval of the truth." She is the living tribunal, the authority that has to explain to us the true sense of revelation. What does St. Peter say? Epla. 2.i.20, "understanding first this, that none of the prophesy of Scripture can be accomplished by one's own interpretation." And elsewhere, 2. iii. 16, we are told that in the letters of St. Paul . . . "there are certain things that are difficult to understand, those which will be falsified by the ignorant and the fickle, as well as the other writings, to their ruin" [emphasis added].[5]

Prohibited by the Catholic priests from interpreting the Bible, Hispanos who had held on to their Jewish traditions were drawn to Presbyterianism because it afforded them access to sacred texts.[6] One might also surmise that they were attracted to a faith—like Judaism—that emphasizes a direct relationship with God, eliminating the need for intercession by either priests or saints.

On the basis of interviews conducted with New Mexican Hispanos, Atencio cited numerous examples of links between crypto-Jewish families and early converts to Protestantism:

> José de la Luz Salazar . . . of southern Colorado turned his family toward Protestantism because they were Jewish. From José de la Luz' granddaughter, Josephine, we hear the following: José de la Luz called the family together when a Methodist mission came to their village in the late 1800s and announced that they were becoming Methodist, for they had never been truly Catholic; they were Jewish. Toribio Zacarias, a son, and Josephine's father, became a Methodist missionary in Colorado. . . . Josephine says she grew up in Denver knowing she was Jewish and considered herself different from the majority of Hispanos. . . .
>
> Estanislados González was born around 1876 in a village on the Río Grande south of Socorro. His great granddaughter, Lorraine, says that the family converted to Methodist because they were Jewish. Estanislados read the Bible with a shawl around his shoulder and a small "cap" on his head. He knew and observed all dietary rules which he learned from the Book of Leviticus made available by his conversion to Methodist.
>
> John Hernández from Las Cruces, New Mexico, [says] . . . that his great grandfather, a Catholic of Jewish background, im-

> migrated from Mexico to Taos, New Mexico around the mid nineteenth century. Longing for the Bible where it was unavailable to him, Hernández became a Presbyterian.[7]

From this, Atencio concluded:

> In the New Mexico experience, protest, opportunity and spiritual transformation have offered an adequate framework for understanding and explaining religious conversions. Recent scholarship has added the notion of continuity, or the search for a subjugated legacy, and the assumption that conversions come from the margins of society. Both of these, along with protest, are central to our understanding of Protestant conversions in New Mexico. They link to the Converso heritage accordingly: Conversos and their heirs who remained secretly loyal to their heritage but were deprived of Judaic knowledge, would find in Protestantism the Bible. It would provide part of the missing sacred knowledge and link them to their religious roots. . . . Moreover, Conversos historically have been strangers, at the margins, and psychologically poised for protest when the conditions became amenable. . . .
>
> José M. Benardete offers another insight for Protestant conversion: "Catholicism . . . had transformed the Marranos so radically that Judaism seemed . . . insubstantial to many of the Marranos who went abroad. . . . Still many who had difficulty assenting to the symbolism and mystery of Catholicism found Protestantism nearer to the Hebraic tradition and readily accepted the new form of Christianity."[8]

The Reverend Andrew McComb, of Embudo Presbyterian Church in Dixon, confirmed Atencio's observations. In an interview with anthropologist Seth Kunin, McComb indicated his belief that many families in his congregation traced their ancestry to colonial crypto-Jews. Because of their Jewish past, he continued, they were uncomfortable with Catholicism and sought to find a place in the Presbyterian faith.[9] Similarly, Juan Durán, a lay leader of the Presbyterian community in Chacón, across the Sangre de Cristo Mountains from Dixon, reported to Kunin that he was of Jewish origin, as were many other longstanding members of the Presbyterian church in his town.[10]

The conversion of José Ynes Perea to the Presbyterian faith in the mid-nineteenth century appears to support the historical link between crypto-Judaism and early New Mexican Protestantism. Perea, according to his biographer, Mark T. Banker, was the "heir to one of

New Mexico's wealthiest families."[11] The Pereas were one of the most prominent mercantile families in the region, from the late eighteenth century through the early American territorial period. Several descendants of the Pereas have asserted the Jewish heritage of the family, including José Ynes's grand-nieces Elizabeth Valdéz Romero, of Ranchos de Taos,[12] and Josefa Dolores Gonzales Groff, born in San Diego de Jémez.[13]

José Ynes Perea's early life demonstrated indications of alienation from the Catholic Church, including his shooting an arrow at an image of the Virgin Mary when he was a child. After the takeover of New Mexico by the United States, José Ynes's father, Juan Perea, sent the youth to a Catholic school in New York City. There, he "joined a group of students who secretly read from the Bible in defiance of school rules—and official Vatican policy. Impressed by his scriptural discoveries, José soon refused to attend confession and became known by his teachers as 'that Mexican heretic.'"[14] His spiritual path took him to St. Louis, where he underwent a formal conversion to the Presbyterian Church, and eventually back to New Mexico, where he arrived home just a year before his father's death in 1865. The old man appears not only to have approved of José Ynes's "new" faith, but also to have participated in its observances, often reading from the Spanish Bible that his son had given him.[15]

José Ynes married Victoria Armijo, a member of one of the prominent *rico* Río Abajo families with possible crypto-Jewish origins. According to Banker, Victoria "apparently tolerated, but never fully accepted José's Protestantism." Perea spent the next several years operating the family ranching enterprises, taking every opportunity to proselytize and distribute Spanish Bibles throughout the territory. In 1870, he participated in the formation of the first Presbyterian church in Las Vegas, which succeeded in attracting converts from San Miguel and Mora Counties. He continued to preach from pulpits around central and western New Mexico until his retirement in 1905. He died five years later.[16]

Folklorist Judith S. Neulander, who has dismissed any crypto-Jewish presence in New Mexico, either historical or contemporary, also noted a relationship between what seemed to be Jewish practices and Protestantism in New Mexico. But she contended that rather than the crypto-Jews being drawn to the Protestant faiths because of their theological concepts, it was Protestantism that served as the basis for what appeared to be, but were decidedly not, Jewish observances.[17]

Certain Jewish biblical first names given to Hispano children, she maintained, had no connection to crypto-Judaism. Instead, she believed that they emanated from Seventh-Day Adventists and from Pentecostal churches, such as the Church of God. In regard to the frequent use of the given name Adonay (one of the Hebrew terms for God), Neulander cited the "global Jewish aversion against humanizing the God-name" as evidence against any possible crypto-Jewish association. Rather, she argued, such names "enter[ed] Hispano tradition in the first half of the 20th century, precisely when babies were being born by the first generation proselytized by the Church of God." As an example, she cited a headstone that she found in the Catholic cemetery of Corrales, bearing the name Adonay P. Gutiérrez.[18] But had Neulander made the effort to conduct research into Gutiérrez's family history, and that of the community in which he lived, she would have found that he had been born and raised in the Cuba area, and, according to his brother Moisés, the Pentecostal church did not appear in that region until long after his birth. Moreover, Moisés Gutiérrez indicated that his family were practicing Catholics. They never had any association with Protestants, Pentecostal or otherwise, after the arrival of these churches in the region.[19] Thus any causal link between fundamentalist Protestantism and the name Adonay, at least in this example, could not have been possible.

JEWISH BIBLICAL FIRST NAMES IN NEW MEXICO

Jewish biblical given names more common than Adonay can be traced even farther back in New Mexico. Not only did these names appear in the record long before the arrival of the Pentecostal sects, but they were found among the Catholic population several decades before the establishment of any Hispano mainstream Protestant community.

It was quite common for Iberian Jews to give Jewish biblical names to their children before the expulsion and forced conversions of the late fifteenth century. But New Christians, in their attempt to disguise their former ethnicity and assimilate into the larger community, often abandoned this tradition in favor of more normative New Testament naming patterns. Nonetheless, within the privacy of their homes and small communities, many crypto-Jews maintained the practice of assuming first names from the Hebrew Bible. David M. Gitlitz described the behavior of the first generation of converts to Catholicism:

> Most Judaizing *conversos* had at least two "first" names. One, given at baptism, established the child's Christian—which is to say official—identity. Normally, but not universally, this would

> be the name of the Christian saint on whose day the child was born or baptized or a name of some member of the Holy Family and their close associates. . . . Still, as the earliest observers of crypto-Jewish customs pointed out, even those *conversos* who wanted to hide their Judaizing frequently gave their children a Jewish name as well as a Christian one.[20]

The tradition of maintaining two given names—one for external appearance and the other known only within the religious community—continued among practicing crypto-Jews in Spain and Mexico throughout the sixteenth and seventeenth centuries. Recall that in the Rodríguez Nieto family, linked to the colony of Nuevo León, founded by Luis de Carvajal y de la Cueva, in the late sixteenth century, *conversos* Manuel Díaz and Francisca Rodríguez, while living openly as Jews in Ferrara, assumed the names Yitzhak and Rivkah (Isaac and Rebecca) Nieto. Ruy Díaz had taken the name Yaacov (Jacob), and his sister, Beatríz, had become Esther.[21] Similarly, in Mexico during the 1630s and early 1640s, merchant Juan Pacheco de León and his father, Antonio de Narváez Farfán, were known inside the crypto-Jewish community in Querétaro as Salomón Machorro de León and Davíd Machorro, respectively.[22]

If the crypto-Jews of seventeenth-century New Mexico surreptitiously passed on Jewish biblical first names to their children, this practice was not recorded in the trials of the Holy Office of the Inquisition. Indeed, such names are almost totally absent from the historical documentation emanating from the entire Spanish colonial period of New Mexican history. A review of baptismal, military, and census records from the establishment of the first permanent Spanish colony in 1598 until the independence of Mexico from Spain in 1821 reveals only a handful of names that may be interpreted as indicating a Jewish heritage.[23]

Baptismal records from Santa Cruz de la Cañada in 1735 cite two male children with the first name Salatiel: one born to Juan de Archuleta and María Martín Valerio, and the other to Miguel de Salazar and Francisca Álvarez de Luna.[24] Saltiel (also spelled Salatiel, Sealtiel, Shealtiel, Saltel, and Shaltiel) was one of the four archangels not cited specifically by name in the Bible.[25] In Hebrew, the name means "asked of God."[26] While both Jews and Christians acknowledge Saltiel as a revered biblical figure (Ezra 3:2, 8; Nehemiah 12:1; Matthew 1:12; Luke 3:27),[27] the name very seldom appears among Spanish Catholics. By contrast, Saltiel was the name of a very prominent Jewish family of rabbis, physicians, courtiers, and merchants who lived throughout

Cataluña and Aragón from the eleventh through the fifteenth century, all descended from Mar Saltiel, according to family tradition, the first exilarch in the sixth century B.C.E., son of Yehoyachin (or Jehoiachin), the last king of Judah (598/597 B.C.E.). Anyone bearing the name in this region was assuredly known as a Jew.[28] Curiously, neither Salatiel Salazar nor Salatiel Archuleta surfaced in the documentary record after his baptism, suggesting that they either died early in life or assumed less conspicuous first names.

Nor do the other sources of documentation for New Mexico during this period contain evidence of Jewish biblical names. A search of the comprehensive database "Documentary Relations of the Southwest" revealed no males with the name Abrán (or Abrahán), Davíd, Isác, Leví, Rubén, Salomón, Samuél, or Zacarías living in New Mexico between 1598 and 1821. Similarly, no citation could be found among these records for females named Debora, Esther, Lea, Raquel, Rebeca, Rut, or Sara.[29]

The scarcity of such names during this era reflected the general trend exhibited farther south in Mexico. A study of given names in Mexico City over four centuries, from 1540 to 1950, conducted by historian Peter Boyd-Bowman revealed that throughout the Spanish colonial period, and through the first five decades of independence, no names exclusively from the Hebrew Bible appeared among his sample of baptismal records from the cathedral of Mexico City.[30] It must be remembered that the tribunal of the Holy Office of the Inquisition of Mexico was not formally disbanded until the independence of Mexico from Spain in 1821, and that Roman Catholicism remained the only tolerated religion in the new nation until 1857. The constitution that was promulgated that year, while not formally proclaiming freedom of worship, failed to establish Catholicism as the official faith, thus tacitly permitting the practice of other faiths. The War of Reform and the intervention of France in the 1850s and 1860s delayed the implementation of these constitutional provisions, however, and true freedom of religion did not begin in Mexico until after 1867. Although Boyd-Bowman made no observations about any cause-and-effect relationship, he did note that given names from the Hebrew Bible began to appear in the Mexico City records only in 1869 (with five Esthers, five Saras, and one Rebeca, out of a sample of four hundred names). By 1890, this number had increased to twenty male and twenty-four female names, representing a minuscule 5 percent of the sample population.[31]

By contrast, these Jewish biblical names made their appearance in New Mexico considerably earlier. Their use began in the late 1820s, just after Mexican independence, and accelerated significantly after 1846, the year that the United States assumed control of the territory. Based on census records from 1850 and 1860 of a sample of six counties (Bernalillo, Doña Ana, Río Arriba, Santa Ana, Santa Fe, and Socorro), only a handful of people with such names appear to have been born before independence in 1821 (five males, all named Benjamín). Only one was born in the 1820s, ten in the 1830s (an average of one a year), and thirty-five between 1840 and 1846 (an average of five a year). Ninety-eight were born between 1846 and 1859 (an average of 7.5 a year).

While most of the names in question are generally associated with the Hebrew Bible, there did exist within Catholic iconography a number of relatively obscure saints who had the same appellations. While some of the children who were given these names were born or baptized on dates in close proximity to the corresponding saints' days, most were not, and this suggests an identification by the parents and godparents more in touch with the original Jewish biblical figures.

According to *The Book of Saints*, eight saints are named Abraham, whose days of devotion fall on February 5, February 14, March 16, June 15, October 9, October 27, October 28, and December 6, respectively.[32] A sample of sacramental records from parishes in Albuquerque, Tomé, and Santa Fe shows that of the twenty children baptized with the name Abrán between 1830 and 1854, twelve of the dates corresponded with the Day of St. Abraham the Hermit, on March 16, while eight appear to have been random.[33] The baptism of Ynacio Benjamín Aragón, on February 1, 1859, in Tomé, bore no correlation to the Day of St. Benjamin, which falls on March 31.[34] In the case of Daniél (and Daniela), none of the three children with that name were born close to the dates of any of the twelve St. Daniels cited in *The Book of Saints*.[35] Of the eight Days of St. David, only three of twenty children given that name were born near the dates in question.[36] The baptisms of two Albuquerque boys named José Eliseo fell months away from the Day of St. Elisha.[37] In the case of José Moisés Baca, of Tomé, his birth date of November 13, 1857, occurred two weeks before the day of one of six St. Moseses.[38] Samuél Valdonado's birth on June 27, 1858, bore no association with any of the four Days of St. Samuel.[39] And while none of the three Albuquerque boys baptized Salomón between 1845 and 1850 had birthdays close to any of the four Days of St. Solomon,[40] the three Ysács and three Zacaríases from Tomé were born near their respective saints' days.[41] Rebecca, the biblical namesake for Ana María Rebeca Aragón, born in Valencia in 1847, was not considered a saint by the Catholic Church.[42]

Whether the use of these Jewish biblical names can be correlated with corresponding saints' days or they occurred by chance, the important point is that their appearance in the historical record coincided with two watershed developments in New Mexican history: the independence of Mexico from Spain in 1821, and the transfer of sovereignty of New Mexico from the Republic of Mexico to the United States in 1846.

The break from Spain was accompanied by the severing of ties with all elements of the Spanish royal hierarchy, including the Holy Office of the Inquisition. Although the days of large-scale inquisitorial campaigns against crypto-Jews had long passed, the symbolic presence of the Holy Office in New Spain still represented a menacing force that served to discourage any open display of ethnic identity by the descendants of *conversos*. As part of the royal retribution in 1812 against Father Miguel Hidalgo, a leader in the fight for Mexican independence, the secular authorities enlisted the services of the Inquisition, which accused him, among the other charges of heresy, of the crime of practicing secret Judaism.[43] After independence was finally achieved in 1821, the specter of the Holy Office was lifted from Mexican—and New Mexican—society. To be sure, legal, social, and cultural pressures for religious conformity still remained. The Mexican constitutions that were in force until the American invasion ensured that Roman Catholicism would reign as the only tolerated religion. But it appears that the less repressive climate generated by the departure of the Inquisition encouraged a small number of descendants of crypto-Jews living in New Mexico to express their ethnic identity by choosing Jewish biblical first names for some of their children. And once it was no longer illegal to practice a faith other than Catholicism after 1846, this trend toward more openness appears to have accelerated throughout the late 1840s and the 1850s.

Could the appearance of these Hebrew names in New Mexico at this time be explained by factors unrelated to crypto-Judaism? The question of the impact of Protestantism on naming patterns during this period is not convincing, as the missionaries did not begin to make inroads into the Hispano community until the late 1870s and the 1880s. Was it possible that these families were so impressed by Anglo traders on the Santa Fe Trail and, later, by American soldiers, lawyers, and administrators that they started to name their children after these newcomers? Not likely. Even if they did, one would expect to find among the documentary record a broader array of more representative Anglo names, such as Josiah, Charles, Stephen, James, Kirby, and Christopher.

Might there have been some directive from the Catholic Church—emanating from the Vatican, Mexico City, or the diocese in Durango—that encouraged local priests to select baptismal names from the Hebrew Bible? Nothing appears in the record to so indicate. Earlier tradition suggested that Catholics in Europe tended not to give such names to their children, and, according to *The Encyclopedia of Religion*, "during the Reformation, Protestants began using Old Testament names for their children, *to distinguish themselves from Roman Catholics.* The Council of Trent decreed that all baptized infants must be given a saint's name [emphasis added]."[44]

Canon law is silent on the question of giving such names. Canon-law expert Nelson H. Minnich, of the Catholic University of America, explained:

> According to the footnotes to canon 761 of the 1917 code of canon law edited by Pietro Gasparri that requires the assigning of a "Christian name" at baptism, the earlier rulings which created this obligation are: Clement XII's apostolic letters "Compertum" of 24 August 1734, doubt II, and "Concredita Nobis" of 13 May 1739; Benedict XIV's encyclical "Inter omnigenas" of 2 February 1744, paragraph 3, and his constitutions "Omnium sollicitudinum" of 12 September 1744, paragraph 14, doubt II, paragraph 40, and "Quod provinciale" of 1 August 1754.[45]

The code cited no rulings issued in the nineteenth century that would have led parish priests to begin baptizing children with names from the Hebrew Bible.

Nor does there appear to be any pronouncement from the Mexican Church hierarchy, in either Mexico City or Durango, that would have resulted in any change in naming patterns. According to Manuel J. Rodríguez, who served as vice chancellor and chancellor of the Archdiocese of Santa Fe from 1954 to 1970:

> My opinion is that, without a doubt, there was never any directive promulgated (i) for the universal church, or (ii) for the diocese of Durango, forbidding, allowing, encouraging, or discouraging the use of Old Testament names as baptismal names. I think that the explanation for the phenomenon you discovered is a very simple one, based on the instinct of self-preservation. As you know, in New Mexico the Inquisition reigned supreme until 1820. I would think that the *anusim* would bend over backward in order not to be accused of judaizing. It is a very stubborn fact that people changed their names as and when neces-

> sary, just as they were forced to hide this or that aspect of their lives. . . . I can see how a Crypto-Jewish parent would not want to tempt reality by imposing Isaac or Rebecca on their offspring [during the time of the Inquisition]. But when 1846 came along, why not?[46]

Considering the coincidence of the appearance of Jewish biblical names in New Mexico following the disbandment of the Holy Office of the Inquisition, plus the increase in the use of such names following the 1846 invasion by the United States (and the concomitant lifting of religious restrictions), as well as the absence of any other plausible causal factors, it is logical to conclude that this phenomenon was an early attempt on the part of descendants of crypto-Jews subtly to express their ethnic identity in a public manner, for the first time since the forced conversions of 1492.

CIRCUMCISION

Another way in which crypto-Jewish identity surfaced in the late nineteenth and early twentieth centuries came through the practice of circumcision of male infants. The ritual of circumcision is one of the oldest commandments in the Jewish faith, mandated in Genesis 17:9–14, in which the act represents the external manifestation of God's covenant with the Jewish people:

> 9. And God said unto Abraham: "And as for thee, thou shalt keep My covenant, thou and thy seed after thee throughout their generations. 10. This is My covenant, which ye shall keep, between Me and you, and thy seed after thee: every male among you shall be circumcised. 11. And ye shall be circumcised in the flesh of your foreskin; and it shall be a token of a covenant betwixt me and you. 12. And he that is eight days old shall be circumcised among you, every male throughout your generations, he that is born in the house, or bought with money of any foreigner, that is not of thy seed. 13. He that is born in thy house, and he that is bought with thy money, must needs be circumcised; and My covenant shall be in your flesh for an everlasting covenant. 14. And the uncircumcised male who is not circumcised in the flesh of his foreskin, that soul shall be cut off from his people; he hath broken My covenant."[47]

While circumcision continued to be practiced among Jews, it was rejected by founders of the Christian faith. In the early years of the development of Christianity, an intense debate raged between those who advocated adherence to ancient Jewish traditions and those who rejected most of these rites. The former, led by the apostles Peter and James, considered the new movement to be one of several sects that were evolving contemporaneously within Judaism. Consequently, they believed that converts to Christianity had to fulfill all the Jewish commandments, including circumcision. The latter faction, whose principal advocate was Paul, considered Christianity to be a faith separate and distinct from Judaism, and viewed Jewish Law and the Gospel to be in contradiction to each other. The imperfection of humans prevented them from observing the Law completely, he believed, and thus salvation would result from belief in Jesus, rather than from obedience to the old commandments.

Consistent with this position, Paul argued for the elimination of the requirement of circumcision in the conversion of the gentiles to Christianity. He contended that in the age of the new faith, circumcision was now irrelevant. Circumcision of the heart, in Paul's view, was more important than circumcision of the flesh. Moreover, the conversion of the gentiles could be accomplished far more effectively with the elimination of this exclusivist requirement.[48]

At the Council of Jerusalem, the apostolic assembly that convened to determine the matter, the position advocated by Paul triumphed over that propounded by Peter. Those Christians who continued to cling to the ritual were regarded as "enemies of the cross of Christ."[49] From that point on, circumcision was no longer to be practiced by Christians.[50] The thirteenth-century Catholic Spanish legal code, *Las Siete Partidas*, was quite specific about the identification of circumcision with Judaism. *Partida* 7, title 24, law 1, states: "A party who believes in, and adheres to the law of Moses is called a Jew, according to the strict signification of the term, as well as one who is circumcised, and observes the other precepts commanded by his religion."[51]

So sharp was the difference between those who performed this ritual and those who did not that centuries later the discovery of circumcision among defendants accused of practicing secret Judaism in Spain, Portugal, and Mexico was cited as compelling evidence of guilt by the Holy Office of the Inquisition. And while, according to David Gitlitz, it was not widely observed by *conversos* in Spain or in most parts of the colonies, due precisely to the high risk of detection, among Mexican crypto-Jews circumcision was quite common.[52] Recall that the circumcision of Francisco, Juan, and Andrés Gómez Robledo in seventeenth-century New Mexico served to mark them as Judaizers.[53]

From the end of the persecutions against crypto-Jews in the 1660s until the late nineteenth century, the record is silent on whether the descendants of New Mexican *conversos* continued the practice of circumcision. New Mexicans followed the general pattern throughout the United States in the late nineteenth and early twentieth centuries, whereby gentiles—Hispano and Anglo alike—did not observe this custom. Not until the late 1930s was the practice introduced into the general community in the American Southwest, when doctors, newly arrived from the east coast, began advising parents to circumcise their male infants for hygienic reasons. But among certain segments of traditional Hispano culture, resistance to this new development remained strong. In her analysis of medical practices in the region, medical anthropologist Margarita Artschwager Kay observed: "Practitioners of Western medicine urge that baby boys be circumcised, but most families do not consent. The results are considered disfiguring to the baby's *cosita* or *weenito*. The older women are firmly opposed to the practice because they believe that when the child grows up and gets married, he will inflict pain to his wife if he is circumcised."[54] But oral-history interviews conducted with other elderly Hispanos in New Mexico in the late twentieth century reveal that circumcision was performed not only among their generation. These informants also reported that their fathers and grandfathers had undergone the process as well, thus placing the practice of circumcision well back to the late nineteenth century in certain families.

Septuagenarian brothers J. B. and Eugenio Rael, of Questa, located to the north of Taos, for example, reported that circumcision was common in their community, not only in the early twentieth century, but earlier as well. The procedure was performed by *parteras* (midwives):

> A: I believe that here they say that it [circumcision] is practiced. I recall that it has been practiced.
> Q: Do you have any idea who performed the circumcisions?
> A: . . . the midwives.
> Q: The midwives performed the circumcisions?
> A: Yes, they did it.
> Q: For all the people, or only for certain families?
> A: No, I believe for everyone that was born in this time.
> Q: In this time? What about before, in your generation?
> A: And earlier . . . much more. It was done more. In our time, I know that it was so, and I tell you that earlier than those days it occurred even more often.[55]

Josefa Dolores Gonzales Groff, one of the nine sample individuals selected for this study, indicated that three of her uncles had been taken from Jémez Springs to Albuquerque to be circumcised. As Gonzales Groff was born in 1898, these circumcisions would have been performed as early as the 1870s.[56] Similarly, Emilio Coca, also one of the sample individuals and born in 1933 in Ranchos de Taos, stated that he was informed by his mother that he had been circumcised by his paternal grandfather, Abél Coca, and that his father, José Demetrio Coca, born in 1903, had been similarly circumcised.[57] Francisco Elojio Tercero, born in the 1940s in Agua Fría, just a few miles downstream from Santa Fe, related that both his father and his grandfather had been circumcised and that the practice was common in Agua Fría, always performed by local *parteras*.[58] Seventy-two-year-old Elvira May Stanton recollected that she had been told of her family's Judaism by her maternal grandmother, Elvira Getrudis Gallegos, whose brothers, born in Las Vegas in the 1870s, had undergone the procedure. Moreover, Stanton continued, Gallegos saw to it that her sons were circumcised as well. The tongue-lashing that Gallegos received from the local priest for performing this rite served as a motivation for her to leave the Catholic Church.[59] And Paula Randal Smith recounted the family story of the circumcision of her maternal grandfather, Lizardo Quintana, born in Wagon Mound in 1900.[60] In each of these cases, knowledge of the family's Jewish background was either passed down directly or strongly suspected by the informant.

In at least one instance, circumcision appears to have been performed on the one son "chosen" to carry on the Jewish tradition. Fidel Gutiérrez, another of the sample individuals in this study, was born in 1929 in Velarde, located approximately ten miles to the north of Española. As a teenager, Fidel was told of the family's Jewish heritage by his grandfather. He, alone of his four brothers, was circumcised.[61]

Knowledge of the religious significance of circumcising male infants appears to have continued into the late twentieth century. The founder of the Northern New Mexico Women's Health and Birth Center in Taos indicated that in the early 1990s, 64 percent of her patients were Hispana, and of that group, almost all the mothers asked that circumcision be performed on their sons. While most of them could not articulate the reason for their request, she related that the mother of one of her patients, a woman in her seventies, told her that she knew that her ancestors had been forced to convert from Judaism to Catholicism. Circumcision, the woman continued, represented a "secret covenant" with God and simply had to be performed.[62]

INTERMARRIAGE WITH ASHKENAZIM

These manifestations of a Jewish heritage among New Mexican Hispanos, which began to appear after the assumption of government by the United States in the mid-nineteenth century, seem to have escaped the notice of the Ashkenazic Jews who arrived in the region, first from Germany and later from Poland and other countries in eastern Europe.[63] That the diaries and letters of these immigrants that have survived to the present do not include any reference to the *conversos* may well reflect the paucity of these accounts. A more likely explanation may relate to the absence of a contextual knowledge of or interest in crypto-Judaism on the part of the eastern European Jews. Most of the correspondence left behind by these individuals deals with family and commercial matters, with very few of the accounts containing observations of social and cultural aspects of their new community. It is doubtful that many of them would have even known about the existence of Spanish Jews, given the limited knowledge of the topic in Europe when they received their formal education. Moreover, the interaction between the Ashkenazim and the local Hispano population, in general, tended to be restricted to business and commerce, which would hardly have fostered intimate contact between the two groups.

An exception to this absence of intimacy was reflected in the handful of marriages between Ashkenazic Jewish men and New Mexican Hispanas in the early territorial period. Henry J. Tobias has pointed out that Ashkenazim with the means to do so married women from either Germany or the eastern United States. He concluded that "religious affiliation remained an important condition for the New Mexican Jewish men in their selection of mates and that they sought to maintain their identity even as their direct ties with Germany slowly began to decline."[64] The two dozen or so Jewish men who were not in a position to afford the luxury of importing brides married local Hispana women, thus violating the generations-old stricture against marrying out of the faith.

Or did they? Could they have known about the Jewish background maintained by their brides' families? Perhaps even more compelling is the question of why traditional Hispano Catholic fathers would have permitted their daughters to marry not only Anglos, but Jews, considered by the nineteenth-century Church as the killers of Christ. Only two of these cross-cultural marriages appear to have been celebrated by Catholic priests.[65] Two other couples were wed in civil ceremonies.[66] How many of the other approximately twenty unions were officially sanctioned and how many were common-law marriages remains unknown, as the majority of the county civil marriage records from the early territorial period have not survived.

The extent to which the Hispano families into which these Ashkenazic Jewish men married can be traced to *converso* origins awaits further genealogical analysis. At least one of the women, however, can be linked to descendants of crypto-Jews. Guadalupe Abeyta, who married Aaron Gold at St. Francis Cathedral in Santa Fe on November 12, 1862, was the sister of María Luisa Serafina Abeyta, the great-great grandmother of Anna and Celina Rael, who comprise one of the nine sample families selected for this study.[67]

OBSERVATIONS BY MARY AUSTIN

If the newly arrived Ashkenazic Jews failed to recognize the crypto-Jews within their midst, the presence of the descendants of *conversos* did not escape the attention of the prominent southwestern writer Mary Austin. Born in Illinois in 1868 and raised in California, Austin moved to New Mexico in 1924. Collaborating with journalist Charles Fletcher Lummis and folklorist Arthur León Campa, she steeped herself in Hispano folk traditions, collecting stories and ensuring their preservation in written form.[68] She also participated in the identification, interpretation, and photographing of *retablos*, *bultos*, and other sacred images created by Hispano artists.[69] Even before she made New Mexico her residence, Austin had prepared a description of social life in northern New Mexico: "Social Survey of Taos County, New Mexico." Among her Anglo-centric observations of Hispano and Native American life in the Taos area is a cryptic reference to the presence of Jews in the Hispano community:

> The Spanish settlers of Taos were of two classes. Grants of land were made to representatives of old families and occasionally to officers in the army which had been recruited from somewhat lower social strata in Spain.
>
> These brought with them some hereditary followers, farmers and handcraftsmen, and numbers of Indians from Old Mexico, chiefly Thalascans [Tlaxcalans]. Later they brought Indian slaves principally Navajos who also became incorporated in the population.
>
> There does not appear to be any of the Spanish Jew among these old settlers, such as may be traced further south in New Mexico.[70]

This non sequitur begs an obvious question: If "Spanish" Jews, "such as may be traced further south in New Mexico," were not to be found in the area around Taos, then where, farther south, did she encounter these people? Unfortunately, nowhere in the thousands of pages of her personal papers can there be found any further mention of "Spanish" Jews elsewhere in New Mexico.[71] She did, however, cite the presence of Jewish biblical images, such as St. Moses and St. Job, among the carved and painted objects of devotion among Hispano people in the state.[72]

ASSIMILATION

Although the transfer of sovereignty from Mexico to the United States had a profound impact on the cultural landscape of New Mexico in 1846, its full effect would not be felt until well into the twentieth century. The early years of American rule witnessed the superimposition of Anglo-American influence over the territory. New Mexicans had to adjust to a new political elite (governors, administrators, and judges), a new religious elite (archbishops, priests, and missionaries), and a new economic elite (merchants and lawyers), all of whom spoke a different language and represented an alien culture. But, for the most part, the internal affairs of Hispano rural communities throughout New Mexico remained much the same as they had been before the Mexican War. Spanish remained the dominant language, facilitating the passing down of cultural traditions from one generation to the next.

But in the early and middle decades of the twentieth century, this superimposition slowly and almost imperceptibly transformed itself into a true imposition of Anglo-American culture. The arrival of movies, radio, and television, plus the participation of New Mexicans in World Wars I and II, exposed the inhabitants of this remote frontier region to a far greater range of ideas and influences than they had known before. Moreover, the development and expansion of public schools throughout the state resulted in an influx of teachers from the East, most of whom were neither familiar with Hispano culture nor fluent in the Spanish language. Many of the newcomers were committed to the concept of "Americanization," the doctrine that had worked successfully to break down ethnic traditions among southern and eastern European immigrants in the large cities of the eastern United States and assimilate them into mainstream American society. In an effort to impose English as the dominant language, educators punished Hispano students in New Mexico, both physically and psychologically, for speaking Spanish in class and on the playground.[73]

The combination of positive and negative pressures proved effective. Beginning in the metropolitan areas, and spreading to the rural communities, English began to supplant Spanish as the primary language spoken at home and in school. Traditional Spanish given names gave way to Anglicized forms. Francisco was replaced by Frank; María was superseded by Mary; Mercedes became Mercy. Distance, too, became a factor in the breakdown of traditional culture. The decline of the rural economy precipitated a migration from small, rural villages to larger population centers, such as Albuquerque, Santa Fe, and Las Cruces. In this environment, the manner in which culture was transmitted changed radically as well. Grandchildren, separated by distance and language from their grandparents, were not able to learn the traditions and values that had been passed down from their ancestors in the same manner as had their immediate forebears. In just a couple of decades, many centuries-old traditions were lost.[74]

Linguist Eduardo Hernández-Chávez aptly observed this connection between the loss of language and the loss of culture:

> A shared language embodies peoplehood—and in this we can agree with the proponents of official English. It encodes the customs and traditions of ethnicity; it is the means of social interaction in the family and community; it carries with it the emotional attachments of upbringing and the values that give meaning to a shared existence; in short, it is crucial to the notion of culture.
>
> Language loss threatens to destroy these relationships. Communication between different-language community members is weakened; the sense of a shared destiny is lost; intra-ethnic conflicts arise; historical knowledge fails to be passed on; and individuals suffer feelings of alienation from their historical ethnicity. These are some of the consequences, at least in part, of language loss. There are possibly others. Cultural alienation can have as its products poor educational performance, socioeconomic marginalization, and a host of other ills.[75]

Among the cultural casualties in New Mexico was the phenomenon of crypto-Judaism. On the basis of the interviews conducted with descendants of the *conversos*, it appears that, in many families, specific knowledge of their Jewish heritage ceased being transmitted in the mid-twentieth century. While certain customs continued to be passed down—such as circumcision, dietary laws, and naming patterns—they became disconnected from a larger cultural context. Children growing up in the 1940s, 1950s, and 1960s witnessed their parents lighting candles on Friday night, refraining from eating pork, or slaughtering their meat with special care not to consume the blood, but were not told the reason for these observances. It was only when their suspicions were aroused decades later that they asked their elders, who reluctantly answered "Eramos judíos"(We were Jews).

To social psychologist Janet Liebman Jacobs, the cultural losses suffered by the descendants of crypto-Jews in the twentieth century were added to the continuum of those produced by centuries of forced assimilation into mainstream Catholic society:

> Throughout this study of hidden ancestry and the recovery of Sephardic roots, accounts of loss and deprivation characterize descendant narratives as the respondents speak with regret of an unknown family history, a forgotten cultural past, or the absence of an ancestral religious tradition. Their expressions of loss highlight the effects of cultural destruction and forced assimilation on ethnic and racial communities that, although learning to adapt, nonetheless bear the consequences of a cultural genocide that leaves its own deep and lasting impression on the collective psyche of the once-colonized group.[76]

But Jacobs observed another, more pernicious, twentieth-century influence that mitigated against the passing down of crypto-Jewish traditions:

> As family narratives kept alive the memory of Jewish suffering and the need for secrecy, the advent of the Holocaust reinforced the fear that the dangers of Jewishness were neither imagined nor historical. According to a number of descendants, the genocide of World War II, coupled with the periodic resurgence of antisemitic attacks on Jews or suspected Jews living in Latin America and the Southwest of the United States, renewed the desire for secrecy and denial among surviving crypto-Jewish populations.[77]

The questions posed by the descendants of crypto-Jews around the turn of the twenty-first century and the answers received from their elders, as well as from their family histories, have stimulated a series of vigorous discussions, both inside and outside the crypto-Jewish community. This discourse, sometimes civil and sometimes not, has shed light on important issues of religion, identity, and ethnic politics. It has caused tension within families, while reconciling contradictions long held by family members. It has forged productive collaborations among scholars, while touching off a firestorm of controversy within the academic community.

NOTES

1. Richard Griswold del Castillo, *The Treaty of Guadalupe Hidalgo: A Legacy of Conflict* (Norman: University of Oklahoma Press, 1990), app. 2, "The Treaty of Guadalupe Hidalgo as Ratified by the United States and Mexican Governments, 1848," article 9, p. 190.
2. Jean Baptiste Lamy, *Archbishop Lamy: In His Own Words*, ed. and trans. Thomas J. Steele (Albuquerque: LPD Press, 2000); Fray Angelico Chávez, *But Time and Chance: The Story of Padre Martínez of Taos* (Santa Fe: Sunshine Press, 1981); John Ray de Aragón, *Padre Martínez and Bishop Lamy* (Las Vegas, N.M.: Pan-American, 1978).
3. Randi Jones Walker, *Protestantism in the Sangre de Cristos, 1850–1920* (Albuquerque: University of New Mexico Press, 1991), pp. 30–31.
4. Tomás Atencio, "The Converso Legacy in New Mexico Hispano Protestantism," *El Caminante*, no. 2 (2003): 10–15.
5. Carta Pastoral del Ilmo. Señor Don Juan Lamy al clero y a los fieles de este obispado, Santa Fe, fiesta de Epifanía, 1854, microfilm, reel 56, frames 320–321, Archives of the Archdiocese of Santa Fe (hereafter cited as AASF).
6. Atencio, "Converso Legacy," p. 11.
7. Ibid., p. 14.
8. Ibid., pp. 14–15.
9. Reverend Andrew McCone, Dixon, interview with Seth Kunin, August 2001.
10. Juan Durán, Mora, interview with Seth Kunin and author, August 2001.
11. Mark T. Banker, "Missionary to His Own People: José Ynes Perea and Hispanic Presbyterianism in New Mexico," in Carl Guarneri and David Álvarez, eds., *Religion and Society in the American West* (Lanham, Md.: University Press of America, 1987), p. 79.
12. Atencio, "Converso Legacy," p. 15.
13. Josefa Dolores Gonzales Groff, Santa Fe, interview with author, June 1990.
14. Banker, "Missionary to His Own People," p. 83.
15. Ibid., p. 84.
16. Ibid., pp. 84–114.
17. Judith S. Neulander, "The New Mexican Crypto-Jewish Canon: Choosing to Be 'Chosen' in Millennial Tradition," *Jewish Folklore and Ethnology Review* 18 (1996): 33–43, and "Cannibals, Castes and Crypto-Jews: Premillennial Cosmology in Postcolonial New Mexico" (Ph.D. diss., Indiana University, 2001), pp. 52–68, 247–278.
18. Neulander, "New Mexican Crypto-Jewish Canon," p. 41, and "Cannibals, Castes and Crypto-Jews," p. 273.
19. Moisés Gutiérrez, La Jara, interview with Seth Kunin and author, August 2001.
20. David M. Gitlitz, *Secrecy and Deceit: The Religion of the Crypto-Jews* (Philadelphia: Jewish Publication Society of America, 1996), p. 201.

21. For more on the Rodríguez Nieto family, see chap. 3.

22. Proceso y causa criminal contra Juan Pacheco de León, alias Salomón Machorro, natural de la ciudad de Antequera en España, vezino y mercader de pueblo de Querétaro, Primera y segunda audiencias, México, June 12–14, 1642, fols. 581r–585v, Ramo de Inquisición, tomo 400, no. 2, Archivo General de la Nación, Mexico City (hereafter cited as AGN); Proceso y causa criminal contra Antonio de Narbáez Farfán, alias Davíd Machorro, difunto, natural de Antequera, padre de Juan Pacheco de León, que murió en la mar, viniendo a este reyno, 1649, Ramo de Inquisición, tomo 503, exp. 7, AGN. The family of Juan Pacheco de León/Salomón Machorro de León was living in Amsterdam and Leghorn. His mother was known alternatively as María, Beatríz, and Luna; his maternal aunts and uncles had taken the names Ysác, Jacob, Sara, and Judit; his siblings had assumed the names Ysác and Raquel; and his father, Antonio de Narváez Farfán/Davíd Machorro, had died on his voyage to New Spain.

23. This analysis excludes names from the Hebrew Bible that have obvious and prominent New Testament connotations, such as José (both the son of the patriarch Jacob and the father of Jesus), Simón (another son of Jacob, but also a prominent Catholic saint), Jacobo (one of the patriarchs, but also San Jacobo [also known as San Diego or Santiago], the patron saint of Spain), and Salomé (both the feminine form of Salomon and the dancer who, in the Gospel of Mark, asked Herod for the head of St. John the Baptist). Considered as "Jewish" names for purposes of consideration in this discussion are those that are prominent in the Hebrew Bible, but have no or only marginal connection to Christianity. I acknowledge that such figures as Abrán/Abrahám, Ysác, Moisés, Sara, Raquel, and Ester were granted the status of sainthood within the Catholic Church, but their position was not equal to that of the New Testament saints. I also recognize the existence of Christian saints, for the most part obscure, who have the names of certain Jewish biblical figures. Traditional Spanish Catholic baptismal patterns, however, generally did not include the use of such names.

24. Baptism of Salatiel Archuleta, *padrinos*: Joseph Romero and Juana Teresa Romero, March 28, 1735, microfilm, reel 13, frame 36; baptism of Salatiel Salazar, *padrinos*: Bartolomé Fernández de la Pedrera and Ysabel Montolla, October 6, 1735, reel 13, frame 38, both in Parish of Santa Cruz de la Cañada, AASF.

25. Gutierre Tibón, *Diccionario etimológico comparado de los apellidos españoles, hispanoamericanos y filipinos* (Mexico City: Fondo de Cultura Económica, 1992), p. 214.

26. Vibeke Sealtiel Olsen, "Our Family Name" (available at: http://www.maxpages.com/donadeli/Famname).

27. "Shealtiel," *Easton's Bible Dictionary* (available at: http://www.ccel.org/e/easton/ebd/ebd.html).

28. Moshe Shaltiel-Gracian, "Family History," *The Shealtiel Family Worldwide* (available at: http://homepage.interaccess.com/~ssalt/home.html). Among the surnames assumed by the Saltiel family was חן, the Hebrew word for "grace." Many of the Saltiels left Spain for Salonika in the wake of the anti-

Jewish riots of 1391. Others stayed and ultimately converted to Catholicism, with כהן Hispanicized to Gracián. Thus the Gracián family of Cataluña and Aragón traces its roots to the Saltiel family, likely including the famous seventeenth-century Jesuit theologian Baltasar Gracián. See Guillermo Díaz-Plaja, *Espíritu del barroco: Tres interpretaciones* (Barcelona: Editorial Apolo, 1940), pp. 86–87; and *Baltasar Gracián: Obras completas*, ed. Arturo del Hoyo (Madrid: Aguilar, 1960), p. xi n.3.

29. Arizona State Museum, "Documentary Relations of the Southwest" (available at: http://saint-denis.library.arizona.edu). The search was conducted throughout the Master Database and Biofile.

30. Peter Boyd-Bowman, "Los nombres de pila en México desde 1540 hasta 1950," *Nueva Revista de Filología Hispánica* 19 (1970): 12–48.

31. Ibid., pp. 27–30.

32. Benedictine Monks of St. Augustine's Abbey, Ramsgate, comps., *The Book of Saints: A Dictionary of Persons Canonized or Beatified by the Catholic Church*, 5th ed. (New York: Crowell, 1966), pp. 3–4.

33. The calculations are based on an analysis of baptisms extracted in *Albuquerque Baptisms, 1706–1850* (Albuquerque: New Mexico Genealogical Society, 1983); Margaret L. Buxton, Donald S. Dreeson, Felipe Mirabal, and Lila Armijo Pfeufer, extractors, and Margaret Leonard Windham and Evelyn Luján Baca, comps., *New Mexico Baptisms, Nuestra Señora de la Inmaculada Concepción de Tomé*, vol. 1, *22 March 1793–8 May 1853* (Albuquerque: New Mexico Genealogical Society, 1998); Donald S. Dreeson and Lila Armijo Pfeufer, extractors, and Margaret Leonard Windham and Evelyn Luján Baca, comps., *New Mexico Baptisms, Nuestra Señora de la Inmaculada Concepción de Tomé*, vol. 2, *11 February 1847–12 June 1881* (Albuquerque: New Mexico Genealogical Society, 1998); and Thomas D. Martínez, Benito Estevan Montoya, and Rosina LaSalle, comps., *Santa Fe Baptisms, 1747–1848* (San Jose, Calif.: Martínez, 1993).

34. Benedictine Monks, comps., *Book of Saints*, p. 115.

35. Ibid., pp. 193–194.

36. Ibid., pp. 195–196.

37. Ibid., p. 231.

38. Ibid., pp. 511–512.

39. Ibid., p. 625.

40. Ibid., p. 652.

41. Ibid., pp. 362, 737.

42. St. Rebecca was not found in *The Book of Saints*, nor is Rebecca cited as a saint in the *New Catholic Encyclopedia* (New York: McGraw-Hill, 1967).

43. Seymour B. Liebman, *The Inquisitors and the Jews in the New World: Summaries of Procesos, 1500–1810, and Bibliographic Guide* (Coral Gables, Fla.: University of Miami Press, 1974), p. 86. Liebman misidentified Hidalgo's name as José María Hidalgo y Costilla.

44. Frederick Mathewson Denny, "Names and Naming," in *The Encyclopedia of Religion*, ed. Mircea Eliade (New York: Macmillan, 1987), vol. 10, p. 304.

45. Nelson H. Minnich, e-mail message to author, August 23, 2002.

46. Manuel J. Rodríguez, e-mail message to author, August 27, 2002.

47. *The Pentateuch and Haftorahs*, ed. J. H. Hertz, 2nd ed. (London: Soncino Press, 1961), pp. 58–59.

48. See, for example, *The Writings of St. Paul*, ed. Wayne A. Meeks (New York: Norton, 1972), pp. 11–12, 20–22, 33, 72–75; Lucien Cerfaux, *The Spiritual Journey of Saint Paul* (New York: Sheed and Ward, 1968), p. 165; Günter Bornkamm, *Paul*, trans. D. M. G. Stalker (New York: Harper & Row, 1971), pp. 10, 32–34, 38; Benjamin W. Robinson, *The Life of Paul* (Chicago: University of Illinois Press, 1918), pp. 95–101; and Giuseppe Ricciotti, *Paul the Apostle* (Milwaukee: Bruce, 1953), pp. 272–277.

49. S. M. Polan, "Circumcision," in *New Catholic Encyclopedia*, vol. 3, pp. 878–879, citing Philippians 3:18.

50. David L. Gollaher, *Circumcision: A History of the World's Most Controversial Surgery* (New York: Basic Books, 2000), pp. 31–43.

51. *Las Siete Partidas*, trans. and ed. Samuel Parsons Scott (Chicago: Comparative Law Bureau, American Bar Association, 1931), p. 1433.

52. Gitlitz, *Secrecy and Deceit*, pp. 202–207. See also chap. 2. In Aragón, it appears, circumcision was practiced among *conversos* with greater frequency than in other parts of Spain. See Encarnación Marín Padilla, "Relación judeoconversa durante la segunda mitad del siglo XV en Aragón: Nacimientos, hadas, circuncisiones," *Sefarád* 41 (1981): 273–300, and 42 (1982): 59–77.

53. For more on the Gómez Robledo brothers, see chap. 5.

54. Margarita Artschwager Kay, "Health and Illness in a Mexican American Barrio," in Edward H. Spicer, ed., *Ethnic Medicine in the Southwest* (Tucson: University of Arizona Press, 1977), pp. 156–157.

55. J. B. Rael and Eugenio Rael, Questa, interview with author, February 1991, translation from Spanish by the author.

56. Josefa Dolores Gonzales Groff, Santa Fe, interview with author, June 1990.

57. Emilio Coca, Santa Fe, interviews with author, February 1988 and September 2002.

58. Francisco Elojio Tercero, Santa Fe, interview with author, January 1994.

59. Elvira May Stanton, Rio Rancho, interview with Seth Kunin and author, September 2003.

60. Paula Randal Smith, Santa Fe, interview with author, April 2000.

61. Fidel Gutiérrez, Velarde, interview with Seth Kunin and author, August 2001.

62. Elizabeth Gilmore, Taos, telephone interview with author, September 2002. The Northern New Mexico Women's Health and Birth Center was founded in 1980 as the Northern New Mexico Midwifery Center.

63. For a comprehensive account of the history of the Ashkenazic Jews in New Mexico, see Henry J. Tobias, *A History of the Jews in New Mexico* (Albuquerque: University of New Mexico Press, 1990).

64. Ibid., pp. 57–58.

65. Marriage of Aaron Gold and Guadalupe Abeyta, November 12, 1862; marriage of William Rosenthall and Josefa Sandoval, May 25, 1871, both in microfilm box 160, Marriages, St. Francis Cathedral, Church of Jesus Christ of Latter-Day Saints, New Mexico State Records Center and Archives, Santa Fe (hereafter cited as NMSRCA). In her divorce proceedings against Simon Rosenstein, undertaken in 1866, Altagracia Armijo asserted that the two had been married in the Catholic Church in 1857, but no record of the marriage could be found in the Archives of the Archdiocese of Santa Fe (Records of the United States Territorial and New Mexico District Court for Bernalillo County, acc. no. 1959-124, Civil Case File, no. 350, box 22, NMSRCA).

66. Arthur Bibo, "Genealogy of the Bibo Family" (manuscript, Center for Southwest Research, Zimmerman Library, University of New Mexico, Albuquerque, 1968), citing marriage of Simon Bibo and María Ramona Candelaria, September 23, 1871, Valencia County Records [no vol.], pp. 56–57; marriage of Albert Gusdorf and Margarita Valdes y Simpson, July 1, 1901, Taos County Records, Probate/Marriage Register, 1865–1905, p. 295, NMSRCA.

67. Marriage of Aaron Gold and Guadalupe Abeyta, November 12, 1862, microfilm box 160, Marriages, St. Francis Cathedral, Church of Jesus Christ of Latter-Day Saints, NMSRCA .

68. For a detailed discussion of Mary Austin's career in New Mexico, see T. M. Pearce, *Mary Hunter Austin* (New York: Twayne, 1965); and Augusta Fink, *I-Mary: A Biography of Mary Austin* (Tucson: University of Arizona Press, 1983). The correspondence between Mary Austin and Campa, Lummis, and Frank Applegate, housed at the Henry E. Huntington Library, also sheds light on her role in the preservation of Hispano culture.

69. Mary Austin, miscellaneous notes on Spanish Mexico and New Mexico, AU 361, box 24, Austin (Mary Hunter) Collection, Henry E. Huntington Library, San Marino, Calif. (hereafter cited as Austin Collection).

70. Mary Austin, "Social Survey of Taos County, New Mexico" (1919), pp. 9–10, AU 543, Austin Collection. See also Tobias, *History of the Jews in New Mexico*, pp. 20–21.

71. Later in the same report, Austin cited "a hotel here [Ojo Caliente] kept by a Spanish Jew," referring to Antonio F. Joseph, the son of Antonio Joseph (who had been the territorial delegate to the United States Congress from 1885 to 1895) and the owner of the hot springs and resort at Ojo Caliente ("Social Survey of Taos County, New Mexico," p. 29). The elder Joseph was the son of Peter Joseph de Tevis, a Portuguese merchant who had emigrated to Taos in the 1840s. It does not appear that the Josephs were related to any of the old New Mexican Hispano families. See *New Mexico State Business Directory* (Denver: Gazetteer, 1919), p. 409; *Biographical Directory of the American Congress, 1774–1989* (Washington, D.C.: Government Printing Office, 1989), p. 1284; Bureau of the Census, *Twelfth Census of Population, 1900, New Mexico*, Taos County, dwelling 337, family 353, and *Thirteenth Census of Population, 1910, New Mexico*, Taos County, dwelling 258, family 282, both microfilm, NMSRCA; and Myra Ellen Jenkins, chief, Historical Services Division, to Anne Lucero, Santa Fe, September 29, 1976, Historical File, no. 103, NMSRCA.

72. Austin, miscellaneous notes on Spanish Mexico and New Mexico: photographs for "Spanish Colonial Arts in the U.S." "List of photographs given to Mr. [Frank] Applegate" and "Local *santos* of New Mexico, their symbols and the powers imputed to them by the Spanish Colonials and the Pueblo Indians" (typescript), AU 361, box 24, folder 1, Austin Collection. For more on figures from the Hebrew Bible depicted on objects of devotion, see chap. 8.

73. Eduardo Hernández-Chávez, "Native Language Loss and Its Implications for Revitalization of Spanish in Chicano Communities," in Barbara J. Merino, Henry T. Trueba, and Fabian A. Samaniego, eds., *Language and Culture in Learning: Teaching Spanish to Native Speakers of Spanish* (Washington, D.C.: Falmer Press, 1993), pp. 64–66; Sarah Deutsch, *No Separate Refuge: Culture, Class, and Gender on an Anglo-Hispanic Frontier in the American Southwest, 1880–1940* (New York: Oxford University Press, 1987), pp. 63–86; Lynne Marie Getz, *Schools of Their Own: The Education of Hispanos in New Mexico, 1850–1940* (Albuquerque: University of New Mexico Press, 1997), pp. 34–37; Thomas P. Carter, *Mexican Americans in School: A History of Educational Neglect* (New York: College Entrance Examination Board, 1970), pp. 97–111.

74. For a general discussion of the impact of cultural assimilation on the Hispano community in New Mexico and the Southwest, see Shelly Roberts, *Remaining and Becoming: Cultural Crosscurrents in an Hispano School* (Mahwah, N.J.: Erlbaum, 2001).

75. Hernández-Chávez, "Native Language Loss," p. 66.

76. Janet Liebman Jacobs, *Hidden Heritage: The Legacy of the Crypto-Jews* (Berkeley: University of California Press, 2002), p. 149.

77. Ibid., p. 28.

CHAPTER 8

Vestiges of Crypto-Judaism in New Mexico at the Turn of the Twenty-first Century

Having traced the history of crypto-Judaism in New Mexico from its origins to the mid-twentieth century, the logical question to be asked is: To what extent has this phenomenon survived into the twenty-first century? This issue has captivated the attention of social scientists over the past two decades. Beginning in the 1980s, scholars from the fields of sociology, anthropology, social psychology, material culture, and folklore began to collect and analyze data, and to develop conclusions about the nature and extent of *converso* culture in contemporary society. A consensus has developed among the majority of those who have conducted fieldwork in New Mexico that confirms the persistence of a crypto-Jewish legacy in the region. The historical plausibility of such a survival is supported not only by the documentary record, but by genetic and genealogical research as well.

ANALYSIS BY SOCIAL SCIENTISTS

Sociologist Tomás Atencio was the first social scientist to examine the question, initiating his fieldwork in the late 1980s. Having grown up in northern New Mexico, Atencio was aware of a *converso* heritage in the state and noted a historical connection between crypto-Judaism and conversion to Protestantism in the late nineteenth century. In his analysis of contemporary society, Atencio disavowed any intent to verify a crypto-Jewish presence in the area.[1] Nevertheless, he proceeded to describe what he believed were *converso* influences on Hispano culture at the turn of the twenty-first century. Adopting what he called a phenomenological and hermeneutic approach to his research, Atencio discerned an evolution of Sephardic tradition from colonial times to the present:

> New Mexico *manitos* are experiencing a crypto-Jewish regeneration. Almost every *manito* family has a member who has examined the family's genealogy, has interpreted diaries and listened to family stories to discern crypto-Jewish links. A few have appropriated the Converso legacy as theirs and are now observing Jews; others recognize that crypto-Judaism is one among other forces which have shaped the Hispano mind and soul, but do not embrace the Faith. Some scholars view the trend as a form of collective behavior, a social movement, of Hispanos' search for identity. In this search for identity, crypto-Judaism is another layer of the influences which have shaped the *manito*.[2]

Atencio identified a number of themes from a Spanish and Mexican *converso* past, lenses through which he was able to view twentieth-century practices in New Mexico relating to life-cycle events—patterns of endogamy, food customs, and Sabbath observances—and concluded that, indeed, contemporary New Mexican society was influenced by its crypto-Jewish history.[3]

Complementing Atencio's research, Israeli ethnographer and historian Schulamith C. Halevy began her investigations in 1992, making several visits to the American Southwest and interviewing dozens of informants. An expert in rabbinic studies and comparative religion, Halevy searched for

> family customs that can only be reasonably explained as of Jewish origin. If such customs are combined with a sense of separate cultural identity, then that could buttress a claim of Sephardic descent. I looked for practices that were traceable either to Rabbinic law or Sephardic custom, and which were not shared by other Catholics. . . . Practices that appear as evidence of Judaizing in Edicts of Faith and Inquisition dossiers—especially those from Mexico—were considered important indicators.[4]

On the basis of her fieldwork, Halevy was able to identify an aggregation of practices in New Mexico—such as celebrating the Jewish

Sabbath, ritually slaughtering animals, salting meat, refraining from consuming meat and dairy products at the same meal, fasting on Monday and Thursday, observing Jewish burial customs, and sweeping floors inward from the walls to the middle of rooms to avoid desecrating the mezuzah (small parchment scroll inscribed with prayers and enclosed in a case affixed to a doorpost)—and thus confirmed, in her judgment, the existence of a crypto-Jewish presence in modern times.[5]

Seth D. Kunin was the first anthropologist to apply a sophisticated theoretical construct to the study of crypto-Jewish society in New Mexico. Like Atencio, Kunin stated that it was not his purpose to either deny or demonstrate the historical validity of the community, but to examine the dynamic nature of the group made up of those who assert a *converso* heritage at the turn of the twenty-first century.[6] But, also like Atencio and despite this expressed intention, Kunin appeared to confirm the presence of customs, practices, and belief structures among New Mexican Hispanos consistent with a historical evolution of these traditions from earlier generations. He also recognized influences on crypto-Jewish culture from other sources, including Protestantism, Catholicism, Ashkenazic Judaism, and general Anglo-American culture.

On the basis of his fieldwork, which spanned nine summers, Kunin posited four basic types of crypto-Jewish identity manifested in New Mexico in the late twentieth century. The first category included those who possessed four traits: (1) self-identification as Jews; (2) observance of Jewish practices; (3) ability to trace their genealogy to *converso* populations in Spain, Portugal, or Mexico; and (4) acceptance of Jewish beliefs. Those who fell into this group also tended to reject both the New Testament and the concept of Jesus as the Messiah. Kunin's second category was made up of people who maintained a Jewish identity, but whose expressions of Judaism were more ambiguous than those of the members of the first group. They typically practiced Jewish customs, but did so without knowledge of the origins of their observances. The third group, the largest in Kunin's estimation, consisted of those who maintained Jewish practices, but had no Jewish identity. They might abstain from eating pork or might build *jacales* (temporary structures) in their fields during the Jewish holiday of Sukkot (Feast of Tabernacles), but remain steadfast in their identity as Catholics or Protestants. The last designation constituted those who had no documented genealogy or traditions indicating Jewish origins and who did not observe Jewish practices, but merely *felt* themselves to be Jewish. This group often included messianic Christians, Christians who celebrated the Jewishness of Jesus, and

Christians who wished to live their lives according to the same values and traditions that he did.[7]

In the mid-1990s, social psychologist Janet Liebman Jacobs became intrigued with stories that she had read in the popular literature. Employing the ethnographic methodologies of in-depth interviews and participant observation, Jacobs set out to study "the effects of hidden ancestry on the construction of religious and ethnic identity" and to "explore how the descendants of medieval crypto-Jews responded to the discovery of their Jewish heritage and to the secrecy that surrounds this ancestral history." She established three criteria for the confirmation of a crypto-Jewish identity: (1) practice of Jewish-based rituals; (2) identification of family names in Inquisition records; and (3) transmission of knowledge of Jewish ancestry within the family.[8]

Jacobs conducted interviews with fifty individuals—twenty-five men and twenty-five women—84 percent of whom were from the American Southwest. Approaching her research from "feminist, social, psychoanalytic and post-colonial perspectives," she focused on the themes of the role of women as agents in the transmission of culture, the conflict between diversity and conformity in rural culture, the image of the Jew in Western and New Mexican culture, and the manner in which time and geographic space affected crypto-Jewish identity.[9]

Among those social science scholars who have conducted fieldwork into the question of crypto-Judaism in contemporary New Mexico, the lone dismissive voice is that of folklorist Judith S. Neulander. Beginning in 1994, Neulander published a series of articles, leading up to her doctoral dissertation,[10] in which she sharply criticized what she referred to as a spurious "'crypto-Jewish canon,' or a body of demonstrably unfounded beliefs about the cultural past."[11]

Customs perceived by others as suggestive or indicative of crypto-Judaism Neulander dismissed as either irrelevant or attributable to other origins. For example, the Jewish practice of *shechitah*, or the ritual slaughtering of animals, she claimed, was "neither practiced nor valued by secretly professing Jews who left Spain in 1492," and "Mexican colonial crypto-Jews had relinquished *shechitah*."[12] Rather than representing a Jewish observance, Neulander maintained, the butchering of meat by hanging the animal upside down, slitting its throat, and letting the blood drain from the carcass was a common practice among Hispanos in New Mexico, having no connection with *converso* practices. She drew the distinction between "the Old Testament mandate that distinguishes crypto-Jewish blood-draining [and] its antithetical Hispano twin. That is, while crypto-Jews carefully drained and spilled the blood in order to prevent its consumption, Hispanos carefully drain and collect the blood, in order to consume it."[13]

It is unclear how long Neulander spent doing her fieldwork in New Mexico or how many people she interviewed. This information was not presented in either her articles or her dissertation. The only informant whom she cited as having testified to his grandfather's draining of blood on the ground, she dismissed as having contradicted his mother's account in an attempt to "reshape a family history, conforming more and more closely to popular crypto-Jewish motifs in each generation."[14]

Halevy, Atencio, and Kunin did not share Neulander's opinion about the mutual exclusivity of Hispano and *converso* slaughtering practices. Nor did they appear to accept the notion that their informants had "reshaped" their observations to fit a preconceived set of expectations. To the contrary, all of them, on the basis of their field research, noted such customs among Hispano crypto-Jews in New Mexico. Halevy detailed the care that had to be taken during and after butchering meat, including using a sharp knife, porging (removal of the sciatic nerve), discarding the blood, and salting the meat to ensure the total removal of blood.[15] Atencio concurred with Halevy's observations, noting: "Some New Mexicans still remove the nerve on the upper thigh, but do not know why they do it. In crypto-Judaism, blood was never eaten but was drained to the ground and then covered up. Some *matanzeros* [designated slaughterers] still let blood drain on the ground and cover it with dirt and do not eat the blood, because, according to one informant, it was against the Bible."[16] Kunin, in referring to his designation of Hispanos most strongly identified with crypto-Judaism, reported: "All individuals in this category told stories of their not being allowed to eat pork. Most also described taking animals to particular butchers for slaughter. They suggested that the butchers had a particular place where 'Jewish' meat was killed. They also emphasised that, in accordance with traditional Jewish practice, the blood was removed and poured away. It was never used as food."[17]

Among the other elements that Neulander rejected as bearing any connection to crypto-Judaism in New Mexico is a four-sided gambling top, known commonly as the *pon y saca* (put in and take out), analogous to the Ashkenazic dreidel. Neulander cited numerous authorities who pointed out the cultural universality of such a toy, emphasizing the many differences between the Iberian/New Mexican teetotum and the eastern European Jewish dreidel. Such differences include the shape, construction materials, and use of the New Mexican *pon y saca* throughout the year, whereas use of the dreidel is confined to the winter months.[18] While Halevy concurred with this analysis,[19] Kunin viewed the *pon y saca* in New Mexico from a different perspective.

Kunin believed that the toy may well exemplify the anthropological concept of bricolage, or the borrowing by one culture of elements from others to help define itself. According to Kunin, bricolage "suggests that all culture is created from materials at hand as long as the elements can be made to fit or exemplify the underlying structure. The *bricoleur* unconsciously uses what is available in both the natural and the contextual environment to build elements that fit into his own cultural pattern or structure."[20] He held that the identification of the *pon y saca* with crypto-Jewish culture was

> clearly explicable within *bricolage*. The model suggests that it is possible that when individuals identifying themselves as Crypto-Jews . . . came into contact with other aspects of the Jewish community, especially the Ashkenazim who settled in the Southwest after the conquest by the United States, they selected elements of Jewish culture which fit their own structure and enhanced their cultural opposition to the Christian Hispanic aspects of their identity and that of the wider Hispanic community. Jewish cultural elements would be particularly appropriate in emphasising the A not B structure because of their clear and perhaps public association with Jewish identity. Inclusion of these elements into Crypto-Judaic culture would thereby strengthen Crypto-Judaic identity.[21]

According to the interviews conducted by Kunin, many informants related that the top is played with during the late fall or early winter, close to the holidays of Christmas and Hanukkah, and they directly associated it with Hanukkah. "Thus," concluded Kunin, "the presence of the 'dreidel,' far from weakening the identification of Crypto-Judaic culture, may be understood as part of the natural process of cultural development."[22]

Neulander also dismissed any association between the six-pointed star, or hexagram, and crypto-Judaism in New Mexico, explaining at great length how this symbol has been used by many different cultures over time and had no particular tie to Jewish culture until the late nineteenth century.[23] Certain uses of the hexagram in New Mexico and other parts of the Americas can, however, be linked to Jewish and crypto-Jewish associations. Although Halevy conceded that "the six-pointed star is not by any means a uniquely Jewish symbol," she pointed out that "it has been used in recent times as an 'insider's' sign of

Judaism in a number of regions from Mexico to Brazil,"[24] suggesting that the hexagram is another element of Kunin's concept of bricolage.

Having dismissed these as well as other indications as spurious, Neulander then proceeded to her principal argument: that practices and symbols perceived by other scholars as signs of crypto-Judaism represent, in fact, manifestations of fundamentalist Protestantism. Pentecostals and Adventists, she maintained, believe that *they* were the "true Jews" and would be rewarded with immortality on Judgment Day. "'Fleshy' non-believing Jews," though, would be exterminated. Thus such customs as observance of the Jewish Sabbath, dietary laws, feast days, and circumcision, rather than representing any vestiges of crypto-Judaism in New Mexico, are merely expressions of faith by followers of these Pentecostal and Adventist sects.[25]

Responding to this contention, Kunin pointed out that while a small number of those who assert a crypto-Jewish heritage might fall into this category, the majority do not. During the interviews that he conducted with dozens of informants, he found that very few of them knew of any Pentecostal or Adventist family background.[26] Considering the relatively recent arrival of these sects in New Mexico, in the 1930s and 1940s, if such an influence had been present, these informants would certainly have so recalled.

Halevy also took strong issue with Neulander's theory. She drew a distinction between laws possibly learned by the Pentecostals and Adventists from reading the Hebrew Bible and "Jewish rabbinic practices that clearly distinguish their practitioners from members of any Christian sect." These include lighting candles on Friday evening, ritually slaughtering animals, salting meat, separating meat and dairy products, discarding eggs with blood spots, and following certain mourning practices. Responding to Neulander's work, Halevy contended:

> Her thesis does nothing to explain any of the Rabbinic practices I have repeatedly found in families asserting Jewish descent. Nor does it explain why these people do not abstain from wine or tobacco. The alternative scenario, whereby interest in the Seventh-Day sects arose, at least to some extent, from a desire to get closer to Judaism without actually risking a crossover, remains considerably more likely. This is exactly the explanation given me by the son of an Adventist from Recife [Brazil] who was told of his Jewish descent and whose family maintains some Jewish practices. People who secretly rested and worshiped on Saturday would provide a fertile ground for Seventh-Day missionary ac-

> tivities. It has also been suggested [by Atencio] that a catalyst for Protestant inroads in New Mexico was provided by anusim who were eager to be permitted access to the Old Testament. These explanations are eminently more plausible than the notion that some Church of God members simply forgot who they were in the course of a few decades.[27]

This logical progression from crypto-Judaism to Adventism was echoed by Jacobs, who placed this transition in the context of religious syncretism:

> In turning to the syncretic beliefs of modern-day descendants, messianic themes of salvation are found in diverse religious orientations that have developed out of the descendants' recovery of their Sephardic roots. The family history of one Mexican descendant in particular illuminates the relationship between crypto-Jewish descent and the adoption of a spiritual worldview that incorporates messianic themes from both the Hebrew Bible and the New Testament.[28]

The subject to which Jacobs referred was the only one of her fifty informants to have affiliated with the Adventist Church of God and lived in Arizona, not New Mexico.

Having dismissed all indications of crypto-Judaism noted by other scholars as spurious, Neulander concluded that those Hispanos who assert a *converso* heritage must be inventing a past that they never had in order advance themselves socially. In a culture dominated by "an Anglo ruling class," she continued, proof of Jewish racial origins demonstrates "whiteness," allowing Hispanos to distinguish themselves from their mestizo and mulatto neighbors.[29]

Jacobs discussed the development in the late-twentieth-century United States of "an image of an idealized Jewish culture that is associated with European origins," reflecting the growing self-identification of American Jews as "white." And while she conceded that some descendants of crypto-Jews followed this pattern, she emphasized that many did not:

> In contrast to this European emphasis, however, a sizable number of descendants have taken a more multicultural view of their Jewish lineage. These respondents, who identify as mestiza/o or as mixed-race Latinas/os, have voiced concerns about the preoccupation with European heritage and a white cultural bias within the contemporary descendant movement. . . . Descendants from Texas and New Mexico also express a strong connection to

Chicana/o ancestry and to Native American heritage, a multiethnic background in which they take a great deal of pride.[30]

During my research into the family history of a man who asserted a crypto-Jewish heritage, the informant related that one of his maternal great-grandmothers had been a Navajo. He had been told by her that she had been a *cautiva*, a captive taken as a young girl from her tribe by a raiding party, in the mid-nineteenth century and had been raised in a Hispano home.[31] Subsequent archival research revealed that, to the contrary, the woman appears not to have been a *cautiva* or even a Native American. She had been born into a Hispano (predominantly European) family and baptized as an infant.[32] When I shared this material with the informant, he demonstrated dismay and disbelief, insisting that the document to which I referred must have been forged, that his ancestor certainly must have been an Indian. This is hardly the sort of reaction one would expect from someone seeking to invent a mythical European past.

Finally, Neulander complained that, due to the presence of untrained ethnographers, "the New Mexican field has become too contaminated to take any crypto-Jewish report at face value."[33] This lament notwithstanding, other social scientists have not regarded any such "contamination" as presenting a barrier to their research into the manifestations of crypto-Judaism in New Mexican society. To the contrary, they not only have confirmed the presence of a *converso* heritage in the region, but have developed thought-provoking ideas about the dynamics both within the community and between the community and the outside world.

INDICATIONS OF CRYPTO-JUDAISM IN MATERIAL CULTURE

The survival of a crypto-Jewish heritage into the twentieth century is also suggested by possible expressions of *converso* identity in material culture.[34] It appears that descendants of New Mexican crypto-Jews may have articulated this cultural expression through the creation of altar screens, *retablos*, and *bultos* (two- and three-dimensional images of religious figures); the placement of mezuzot on doorposts; and the use of Jewish imagery in churches and on headstones. Extrapolating such cultural expressions from objects is tentative at best, due to the ambiguous interpretations that may be ascribed to the symbols. Symbols that may seem to impart a Jewish connection may well derive from other, unrelated cultural contexts. Thus determining the specific circumstances in which these items were created or placed is an important element in achieving an accurate assessment of their relevance. In the absence of such context, one can only raise questions about such connections, in the hopes that further research and scholarship will shed more light on the issue.

Headstones may offer important clues to possible expressions of *converso* identity on the part of Hispano families in New Mexico. In various *camposantos* (cemeteries) throughout the state are markers adorned with six-pointed stars, Hebrew writing, seven-branched candelabra, and other symbols suggestive of a Jewish heritage. Sephardic Jews have been marking the graves of their deceased with stones engraved with such designs since the fifth century. In the Portuguese town of Mértola, archaeologists unearthed a Jewish headstone dated October 4, 482, displaying a Latin inscription and adorned with a seven-branched menorah. The menorah is considered by scholars to have been "the principal symbol of Judaism" since the destruction of the Second Temple in 70 C.E., found on sarcophagi, on facades and doorways of early synagogues and in inlaid mosaic floors.[35] Historically, Jewish tombstones, both Sephardic and Ashkenazic, carried the names of the deceased and of their fathers. They also traditionally included certain formulaic inscriptions, such as the Hebrew letters פנ, for *po nikbar* or *po nitman*, meaning "here lies," or תנצבה, an acronym for "May his soul be bound up in the bond of eternal life," taken from 1 Samuel 25:29.[36]

Although the six-pointed star, recognized since the late nineteenth century as the Magen David, or Star of David, was not Judaic in origin and was not unique to Jewish culture historically,[37] the symbol often could be found in association with Jewish communities, from antiquity to modern times.[38] The hexagram began to appear on Jewish headstones, both Ashkenazic and Sephardic, in southern Italy; Tortosa, Spain; and Prague in the sixteenth century.[39] A ledger stone dating from 1728 and marking the grave of Isaac Bravo, a Sephardic merchant in Kingston, Jamaica, bore a prominent Magen David, incised with Hebrew inscriptions describing the virtues of the deceased.

Early burial rituals in New Mexico included the internment of corpses under the floor of the local parish or mission church. When this ceased to be a common practice in the early nineteenth century for reasons of health and sanitation, cemeteries began to develop, some adjacent to the parish church, and others in locations more remote from the village. While some of these *camposantos* maintained a formal association with the Catholic Church, many by the late nine-

Fragments of a headstone, featuring an epitaph in Latin and a menorah, Mértola, Portugal, 482 C.E. (From *Os judeos portugueses entre os descobrimentos e a diáspora* [Lisbon: Associação Portuguesa de Estudos Judaicos, 1994], p. 22, ill. 8)

teenth century were only family or community graveyards.[40] Permanent tombstones did not appear until the late nineteenth century. Early markers were simple wooden crosses, followed by monuments fashioned from sandstone or limestone by local craftspeople.[41]

Headstones decorated with Jewish symbols and inscribed with Hebrew letters can be found in cemeteries across New Mexico, dating from the early twentieth century to the recent past. In some instances,

Leger stone marking the grave of Isaac Bravo, Shaare Shalom Synagogue, Kingston, Jamaica, died 1723. (From David Mayer Gradwohl, "*Benditcha Sea Vuestra Memoria*: Sephardic Jewish Cemeteries in the Caribbean and Eastern North America," *Markers: Journal of the Association of Gravestone Studies* 15 [1998]: 7, fig. 5)

Headstone marking the grave of Juan D. Martínez, eastern New Mexico, died 1911. (© Cary Herz Photography)

no direct contextual link can be established to definitively connect the symbolism to a crypto-Jewish heritage. A marker dating from 1911 found in the eastern part of the state, for example, adorned with a large, boldly engraved cross, three five-pointed stars, and two doves, also contains two delicately etched seven-branched candelabra flanking the cross. The contrast between the bold lines of the cross and the light strokes of the candelabra suggests that the image of a menorah was placed on the stone in such an inconspicuous manner to express a Jewish identity recognizable to those in the community, while avoiding the suspicions of outsiders. The village in which the cemetery is located is very sparsely populated, and the identity of the individual whose grave was marked with this stone is unknown to some local residents, although one person who traced his roots to the small settlement expressed a strong awareness of his family's crypto-Jewish heritage, as well as a kinship to the deceased.[42]

Dozens of headstones featuring six-pointed stars have been recorded in Hispano *camposantos* throughout the state. While many of these markers still await the necessary contextual research, others can be reasonably considered as expressions of Jewish identity. One such stone, dating from 1971 and located in a cemetery in northern New Mexico, features both the six-pointed star and the first name of the deceased, Esther, written not only in English, but also in Hebrew as אסתר בת יוסף (Esther bat Yosef, or Esther, daughter of Joseph). Also on the stone are carved the acronyms פנ and תנצבה, the inscriptions traditionally found on a Jewish monument. Such a quintessentially Jewish stone appears quite out of place among hundreds of markers bearing images of Jesus, the Virgin Mary, and other, more normative, Catholic symbols.

The brother of the deceased reported that their mother, at the approximate time that she chose the headstone, announced to him that they were "Sephardic Jews." He expressed the belief that her awareness of the family's Jewish heritage served as the motivation for her selection of the cemetery marker. During an interview, he produced a pendant belonging to his mother, a handcrafted silver six-pointed star, one of two that she owned. According to him, the mother was aware of the symbol's association with Judaism:

> Interviewer: Do you know whether she ever talked about this as being a symbol of Judaism?
>
> Brother: She knew what it symbolized. There was no question in her mind about this. She knew her history and everything. She just never talked about it much.
>
> Interviewer: So this just wasn't something that was a nice shape.
>
> Brother: She knew what she was getting. Because she bought that other one in gold.[43]

Another example of the contextual relationship between six-pointed stars and possible expressions of Jewish identity may be found on military headstones from 1975 and 1983 marking the graves of

Headstone marking the grave of Esther Ramona Solano, northern New Mexico, died 1971. (© Cary Herz Photography)

veterans of the United States armed forces. All such monuments were required to be ordered from the Veterans Administration (now the Department of Veterans Affairs). The order forms issued by the Veterans Administration unambiguously identified the six-pointed star with Judaism. The application for the marker from 1975, found in a Catholic cemetery in a small Hispano village in northern New Mexico, offered the veteran's family, as the "Religious Emblem," the choice of "Latin Cross (Christian)," "Star of David (Hebrew)," or "No Emblem." The widow of the deceased, who prepared the form, typed a double X in the box indicating the Star of David.[44] Although she was not available to be interviewed, her brother reported that other relatives had spoken of the presence of "Jewish blood" in the family. He further speculated about a connection between the choice of the Star of David and the middle name of his departed brother-in-law, David.[45]

The headstone from 1983 suggests a more ambiguous circumstance, in that the grave is marked by not one, but two military headstones: one with a cross and the other with a Star of David. A brother ordered the Christian marker from the Veterans Administration, and almost simultaneously a sister ordered a stone designated on the order form as "Star of David (Jewish)." Inadvertently, the Veterans Admin-

Headstone marking the grave of Gabriel David Maes, northern New Mexico, died 1975. (Photo by Seth Kunin)

istration shipped both stones, and the family elected to install both at the gravesite.[46] Both siblings are deceased, and the surviving family members could offer no explanation for the choice of the Jewish marker. The sister who ordered the headstone with the six-pointed star belonged to a Pentecostal sect, the Church of the Living Word, which might account for the selection. But the deceased and the rest of his family were practicing Catholics. The presence of names from the Hebrew Bible among his relatives suggests a possible Jewish origin for

Headstones marking the grave of Alisandro Moises Padilla, central New Mexico, died 1983. (© Cary Herz Photography)

the family. The deceased was named Alisandro Moises, and his cousins included Sarah and Esther.[47] The cousins are buried in the same cemetery, and their headstones were adorned with small pebbles, quite possibly an indication of Jewish observance.

This custom of placing small stones on top of the markers of relatives or friends is practiced by Ashkenazim, as well as by some Sephardim. The origin of this observance is obscure and is the subject of several interpretations. Some authors express the view that it is merely a sign of respect for the departed or an indication that someone visited the site.[48] Eastern European Jews, according to Alfred J. Kolach, place the stones "in order to bridge the absence of direct communication between the living and the dead . . . as a way of reminding the dead that the living have not forgotten them."[49] In Egypt, Sephardic Jews regarded the ritual as symbolic of atoning for the sins of the deceased, for which punishment would have been stoning.[50] Evidence of this practice may be seen in Hispano cemeteries in various parts of New Mexico, such as the pebble left on a headstone decorated with a six-petaled lily with an exaggerated stamen. The headstone is located in the family cemetery of Dennis Durán, who asserts a crypto-Jewish family heritage. Durán indicated his belief that the flower represents the Star of David and that the stamen stands for the Hebrew letter ש

Headstone marking the grave of Maclovia Roybal, northern New Mexico, died 1975. (Photo by Emilio Coca)

(*shin*), the first letter of שדי (Shaddai), or the Almighty.[51] While these symbols convey a Jewish meaning to certain families in New Mexico, it is important to note that six-petaled flowers can also be found on tombstones in other parts of the United States and Europe that have no connection with Judaism.[52]

Similarly, while generic hexagrams adorn the doors, domes, and windows of churches in many parts of the world, in at least one church in New Mexico the six-pointed stars over the altar are a symbol of the Jewish faith to some of the parishioners. When the interior of the Church of San Felipe de Neri, in Old Town, Albuquerque, was renovated around the turn of the twentieth century, artisans placed six-pointed stars in the cornices of the arch over the altar.[53] A century later, local residents reported that the stars represent the Jewish heritage of the Hispano community. María Lucero de Sánchez, who was born in 1894, indicated that her father, Federico Lucero, had passed on to her an awareness that "the stars were a reminder of a previous homeland" for Sephardim expelled from Spain.[54] Similarly, retired church volunteer Richard Chávez expressed the belief that "a lot of people who came here [from Spain] were Jews." His aunt, who engaged in Jewish observances until her death in the late 1940s, had

Altar of the Church of San Felipe de Neri, Albuquerque, 1903. (Albuquerque Museum, photograph no. 80.152/4)

related to him that his family descended from early Jewish settlers in New Mexico and that the Stars of David at the Church of San Felipe symbolize the Jewish faith.[55]

Judith Neulander dismissed the connection between the hexagrams of San Felipe de Neri and any expression of crypto-Judaism on the part of the community of Old Town, Albuquerque, citing not only the routine presence of the symbol on Christian religious structures, but the placement of the decidedly non-Jewish Sacred Heart of Jesus in the center of each star.[56] Photographic evidence, however, demonstrates clearly that when the stars were originally placed over the altar before 1903, and for decades afterward, they were devoid of such a Christian image, the Sacred Heart of Jesus and Immaculate Heart of Mary not being added until the 1930s or 1940s.[57]

Another possible indication of the expression of Jewish identity through material culture may be found in a document recently unearthed from the Archives of the Archdiocese of Santa Fe by anthropologist and *santero* Charles M. Carrillo that describes the *altar mayor*, or main altar, of the parish church on the plaza of Santa Fe around the turn of the nineteenth century. In contrast to other reredoses in colonial New Mexico—which depicted images of the Holy Trinity, Jesus, Mary, Joseph, and various saints, as well as several Franciscan devotions—the Santa Fe altar screen, probably painted elsewhere in New Spain and imported to the north, featured exclusively the Hebrew Bible figures of Aaron, Moses, Samson, and David, as well as Holy Faith. "These [representations]," Carrillo maintained, "are the only known examples of 'Old Testament' paintings to ever grace a New Mexican colonial church. What is more unusual is the fact that the main parish church in Santa Fe had such images, and this very fact awaits explanation."

Carrillo offered several possible explanations for the origin of the altar screen and the incorporation of figures from the Hebrew Bible, to the exclusion of those from the New Testament:

> The answer may be as simple as the fact that the city was named the "Royal Villa of the Holy Faith of Saint Francis," and the altar screen reflected the name of the Villa with allegorical figures alluding to Holy Faith. Colonial altar screens from New Spain often incorporated "Old Testament" figures, that prefigured other saints, although never exclusively so. The presence of Aaron, Moses, Samson and David conceivably alluded to the triumph of faith over paganism. Or there was always the possibility that the absence of New Testament images may have reflected a crypto-Jewish influence on part of the artist.[58]

Similarly, among the thousands of painted *retablos* and carved *bultos* produced during the eighteenth, nineteenth, and early twentieth centuries by New Mexican *santeros*, there are rarely any images other than those of New Testament figures. Two interesting exceptions to this generalization were representations of St. Job and St. Moses. Ross Frank analyzed the creation and evolution of two *bultos*, both depicting a forlorn man in a seated position, originally conceived in the 1880s as Christ, Man of Sorrows (also known as Ecce Homo, or Christ Seated in His Passion). By the 1930s, however, these images had lost their identification with Jesus and had been transformed by their subsequent owners into Santo Jo', or St. Job.[59] How can this transfiguration be explained? Frank reconciled the apparent contradiction by noting a strong connection between the two biblical characters:

> The parallels between Job and Christ were part of the general devotional repertoire in New Spain during the 18th century. As New Mexico came out of the 1770–1790 period, vecinos came to see this parallel in devotional works that centered on Christ

> created as part of the Santo/santero tradition. New Mexico is somewhat unique in the breadth of the treatment of Christ iconographically, and the Penitente connection between the suffering of Christ and the devotion of the brother also seems to mirror the parable posed by Job (suffering as mortal penance = future reward). This scenario would infer that the Christ part of the parallel dropped out of the identification of the bultos as a conscious effort to retain the significance of the parallel precisely because the earlier historical period had such an impact on the creation of vecino identity—it was retained as part of the cultural-historical memory of the people in the region.[60]

But Frank also held out the possibility that "the *Santo Jo*' Man of Sorrows was connected through crypto-Jewish underground iconography, and that during the 19th century the feigned iconography related to Christ faded as family memories privileged the significant hidden meaning."[61] This scenario was echoed by New Mexican *santero* scholar Paul Rhetts, who hypothesized that

> 1) either the concept of Ecce Homo was too confusing or too obscure that people confused Christ with Job and over time . . . forgot the connection with Christ in his Passion, or 2) some other significant religious reason came into play to purposely change the devotion. One explanation of the purposeful religious transformation could be the need to hide one's religious beliefs. Changing this image into an Old Testament image might make some sense for someone who was trying to hide their own true religious beliefs.[62]

It is curious to note that although there existed a strong cult of St. Job in the Low Countries,[63] there were "no santos in New Mexico that are directly identified as Job."[64] By contrast, David M. Gitlitz pointed out that, during the persecutions of crypto-Jews in Nuevo León by the Mexican Inquisition in the 1580s and 1590s, the Carvajal family invoked "various saints of the Old Testament, such as Tobit and many other prophets, Isaiah, Job and others," and Luis de Carvajal's brother Gaspar referred to "Saints Moses, Susanna, Abraham, Job and Jeremiah."[65]

St. Job was also found in an inventory of photographs of New Mexican *santos* taken by Ansel Adams and compiled by writer Mary Austin for artist Frank Applegate in the early 1920s, along with a *retablo* and *bulto* of "*San Moses*, or *San Moise*." Both Austin and Applegate played instrumental roles in the founding of the Spanish Colonial

Arts Society, which fostered the revival of Hispano arts in the 1920s and 1930s. St. Job was described as "Seated nude. Covered with boils. Helps those with boils and smallpox."[66] Austin offered St. Moses as an example of how "the santeros did not confine themselves to the saints of the New Testament and those later elevated to sainthood by the catholic church." The anonymous *santero* who created Moses represented him "in elaborate oriental robes and with his rod and serpent chasing rats and mice."[67]

The tradition of carving images of Moses extended into the late twentieth century, as exemplified by the Salazar family of Taos. Leo Salazar (1933–1991) descended from a long line of *santeros*, including Tomás José Salazar, a noted carver in the 1840s. He learned his craft by observing his mentor, Patrocino Barela, who epitomized the Hispano craft revival of the 1930s.[68] Salazar described how he first came to create his signature piece: "I picked up a small log one day and thought I saw an outstretched hand in it. The hand was holding the tablets—the Ten Commandments. I knew that it had to be Moses, so I started carving him."[69] If there was any Judaism in Salazar's background, it was not apparent to his wife or to his son, Leonardo, who continued his father's passion for carving images of Moses. The elder Salazar's mother died young, and his father never conveyed any information about the family's heritage. According to Leonardo, Leo's passion for Moses (as well as for other religious figures) emanated from his devotion to reading the Bible, both the Old and New Testaments.[70]

While Salazar was not aware of any crypto-Jewish connection to his work, other New Mexican *santeros* who include figures from the Hebrew Bible or other symbols of Judaism in their work maintain a strong sense of their *converso* heritage. Charles Sánchez, of Tomé, expressed the belief that his family has a crypto-Jewish heritage and that his town is "one of the truly Judaic communities of Sephardic background." Although professing Catholics, Sánchez's parents and grandparents practiced what he considered to be Jewish observances, such as avoiding the consumption of pork, family bathing on Fridays, lighting candles on Friday night, and observing the Jewish Sabbath. He described a relative's closed, windowless room as a "*sinagogue*, a little synagogue," where religious rites were carried out.

Sánchez recognized the six-pointed star as a sign of Judaism and has included it in his work. His monstrance incorporates the Star of David as a conscious Jewish symbol. Another carving features "three stars on the top, a Star of David in the middle, and a menorah on the bottom, and I title those crosses, '*Cruz de los Judíos de Nuestra Tierra Sagrada*' [Cross of the Jews of Our Sacred Land]." Other pieces contain only

Charles Sánchez holding his monstrance, 2001. (© Mercedes López-Wooten)

the top half of the hexagram, revealing three points, which Sánchez regarded as a cryptic homage to the Magen David. While Sánchez deliberately has used the Star of David and menorah to symbolize his culture's crypto-Jewish heritage, he also articulated his belief that they also represent Jesus and the Seven Sorrows, reflecting the artist's dual religious self-perception. Asked what he thought of his work's having been favorably received within the Hispano community, Sánchez responded, "It represents the fact that people need to recognize that, like our family, we have Sephardic blood, we have Jewish heritage, background, that's what it represents. Very simple. And if you're gonna go down 'denial river,' you're going the wrong way."[71]

Artist Bernadette Pino, of Taos, also cited her Jewish family background as the motivation for the themes, inspired by the Hebrew Bible, in her paintings. A family legend holds that one set of maternal ancestors hid their Judaism by masquerading as a priest and a nun living in a convent in Spain before migrating to New Mexico. Once there, they converted from their nominal Catholicism to Methodism, but, according to Pino's mother, Naomi Baca Pino, her great-grandfather continued to practice such Jewish customs as ritual circumcision of male infants, recitation of prayers on Friday night, and abstinence from consuming either pork or animal blood. Naomi Pino also reported that her father recognized the six-pointed star as a Jewish symbol and displayed a framed embroidered Star of David in the family's living room.[72] Jacobo de la Serna began creating images from the Hebrew Bible in the early 1990s, stimulated by what he regarded as a "feeling of Jewishness." Although he never received confirmation of any Jewish heritage from his Catholic family, he reported that his parents abstained from eating pork (they claimed that they were allergic); that his mother, following the slaughtering of animals, poured the blood from the carcass into a hole in the ground; and that his maternal grandfather, from the Abiquiú area, had been circumcised.[73]

Not all *santeros* who created images from the Hebrew Bible ascribed their inspiration to a *converso* heritage. Orlando Romero, a devout Catholic from Nambé, despite acknowledging crypto-Jewish roots, insisted that his *converso* background provided no motivation for his creation of *retablos* reflecting Jewish biblical themes, such as David and Goliath, Noah and his wife, Adam and Eve, and the Exodus of the Jews from Egypt.[74]

The appearance of mezuzot in the homes of New Mexican Hispanos also raises questions about the possible identification of those families with crypto-Jewish culture. In 1992, an elderly Hispano man sold his adobe house in Old Town, Albuquerque. When the new owner began to renovate the old house, he found two mezuzot, one affixed to the doorpost of the rear entrance, and the other fastened to the frame of an opening in the ceiling of a bedroom closet that led to a very small storage space. Inside the compartment were found several pairs of white cotton gloves.[75] The first mezuzah case was painted brown, matching the color of the doorpost. The surface of the second was left intact. Both appeared to be of 1960s origin, of the type manufactured in Israel and sold in synagogue gift shops. Within each was found a small, rolled-up piece of paper on which was printed the Shema, a Hebrew prayer proclaiming the oneness of God and outlining the daily obligations of observant Jews.

An interview with the pre-1992 owner of the house and his daugh-

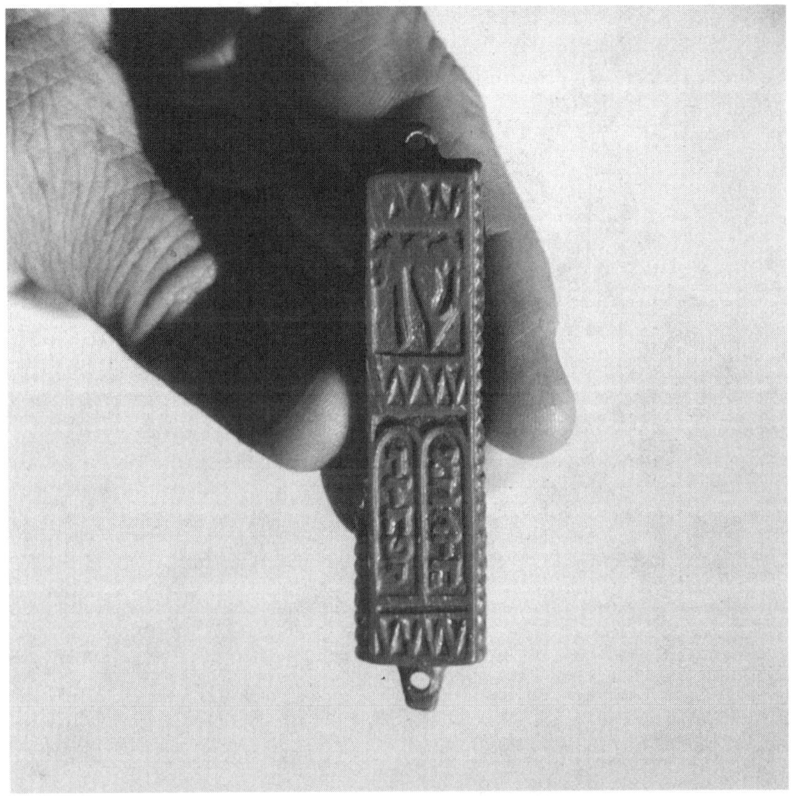

Mezuzah case from the doorpost of house, Albuquerque. (Photo by author)

ter proved inconclusive. Although they had lived in the home for more than forty years, they claimed not to have ever seen the objects. The daughter recalled that the house had been rented to "a young Jewish couple from Israel" in the late 1980s, which ostensibly would have explained the presence of such artifacts.[76] Subsequent research through editions of the *Albuquerque City Directory*, dating from 1949 to 1992, however, revealed no resident listed at the address in question, other than the family who had sold the house.[77]

Did these mezuzot represent an expression of Jewish identity on the part of this Hispano family? Was the mezuzah on the back door painted over in order to camouflage it? Was the storage space inside the ceiling in the bedroom closet a place to keep sacred objects? Or did these mezuzot simply represent generic amulets, designed to bring good luck to the home, without any connection to the Jewish faith? Or could there, indeed, have been a young Jewish couple living in the

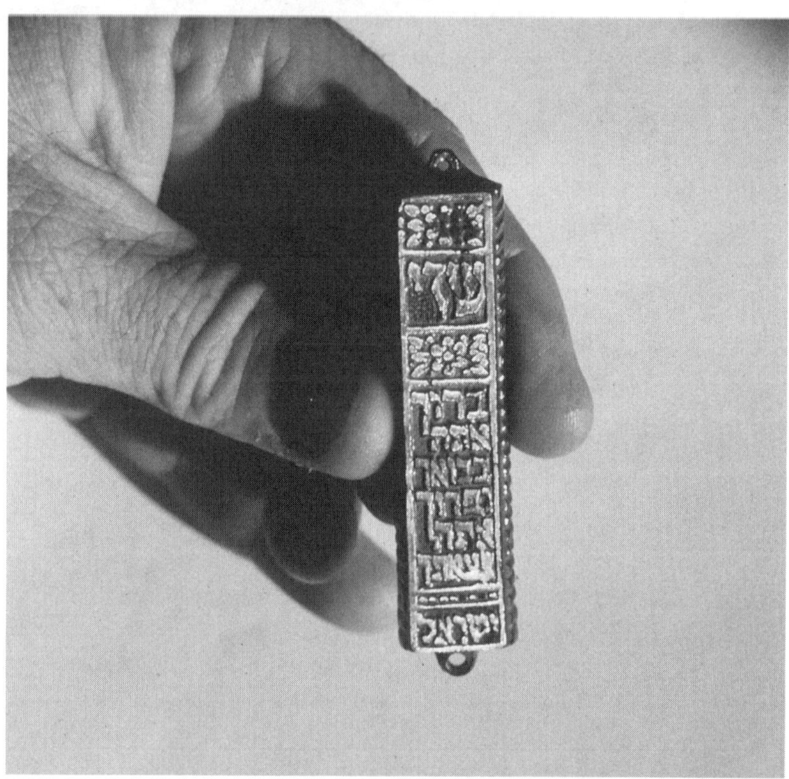

Mezuzah case from the frame in the ceiling of a bedroom closet, Albuquerque. (Photo by author)

house for a short time, whose tenancy escaped the notice of neighbors or inclusion in the historical record? Absent more specific information, one is left only to speculate.

Another mezuzah was reported in the 1990s by an elderly Hispana, since deceased, who lived in Las Vegas, New Mexico. This mezuzah appeared to be considerably older than those in the house in Albuquerque, and, rather than gracing her doorpost, it was nailed to the wall in her kitchen. In her bedroom could be found a nine-branched *hanukkiah*, or Hanukkah menorah, of recent origin, complete with candles, standing next to a bag of holy dirt from the Catholic Santuario de Chimayó. The owner of these artifacts professed no awareness of a Jewish background of the family, and attempts to contact her relatives have proved unsuccessful.[78]

Can material culture, a repertoire of objects, be considered as an indicator of a hidden Jewish identity among populations in New Mexico? No Judaica, Jewish ritual objects, that can be traced to the

Scroll inscribed with a biblical passage found inside case, Albuquerque. (Photo by author)

Iberian Peninsula have survived among the people who have identified themselves with this origin. After all, they are at least two dozen generations removed from active, open Jewish practice. The heritage that their ancestors left behind was a hidden observance, stripped of objects used for ritual purposes. The presence of particular objects among today's descendants may not speak *directly* of this heritage.

Nonetheless, is it possible that headstones adorned with six-pointed stars, menorahs, and Hebrew inscriptions represent modern manifestations of crypto-Jewish identity? Could the depiction of figures from the Hebrew Bible in *retablos*, *bultos*, and church altar screens reflect an expression of devotion to Jewish themes and a subtle rejection of Christian icons? Could the placement of a mezuzah on a doorpost have meant to designate a Jewish home? If one accepts Kunin's concept of bricolage, then it is conceivable that through contact with Jews whose roots can be traced to Germany and eastern Europe, Hispano descendants of crypto-Jews borrowed symbols from the Ashkenazic newcomers and appropriated them as their own.

Mezuzah case on a kitchen wall, Las Vegas. (© Cary Herz Photography)

Objects do not speak for themselves. Absent proper contextual examination, one is left only to speculate about the cultural significance of material culture that appears to be suggestive of a crypto-Jewish past. In certain cases, links can be established between the artifacts and a Jewish context. In others, such connections have yet to be made. Considerably more research has to be undertaken by scholars from the social sciences in order to ascertain the nature and extent of the manifestation of crypto-Jewish symbolism in New Mexican Hispano society.

INDICATIONS OF CRYPTO-JUDAISM IN MEDICAL AND GENETIC RESEARCH

Investigating links between present-day Hispanos and historical crypto-Jewish populations is being facilitated by other, more scientific, means as well. Experts from the fields of medicine, genetics, and history have collaborated to study the correlation between descendants of *conversos* and certain diseases that have appeared among New Mexican Hispanos, illnesses that have a high incidence among Jews. One of these is a rare autoimmune dermatological disease, pemphigus vulgaris (PV), which recently has come to light in the state.

Pemphigus has been diagnosed in eighteen people in New Mexico, thirteen of them Hispanos. This disorder—characterized by painful skin blisters, scaling, and loss of protection against infection—usually occurs in about one in every million people and is found more frequently in Jews than in the general population. The presence of such a high number of pemphigus patients, concentrated among Hispanos, stimulated interest in both the medical and academic communities. Human leukocyte antigens (HLA) testing was performed on the thirteen Hispano patients. The results showed that a very high percentage of them carry the identical genome and protein sequencing as Jews afflicted with the disease. Interviews with seven of the Hispano pemphigus patients suggest a cultural, as well as genetic, connection with a Jewish family past. A detailed analysis of the medical, genetic, and ethnographic study may be found in the appendix.

While a considerable amount of interdisciplinary research has been conducted establishing a relationship between PV and descendants of crypto-Jews in New Mexico, medical and genetic scientists have suggested links with other diseases as well. Bloom syndrome (BS), "a rare autosomal recessive disorder resulting in short stature, a sun-sensitive facial erythema and immunodeficiency," like PV, appears with considerably greater frequency in Ashkenazic Jewish populations than in the general community. The predominant mutation, blm^{ash}, was found in fifty-eight of sixty chromosomes among Ashkenazic Jews, compared with five of ninety-one among non-Ashkenazic BS patients.[79] Curiously, these five patients were gentile Hispanos with long roots in New Mexico–southern Colorado, Mexico, and El Salvador. The geneticists who studied this phenomenon concluded that "the blm^{ash} chromosomes discovered in both the Ashkenazic and the non-Ashkenazic Spanish American population ultimately trace to a common ancestor." They discounted the theory that each of the five families had a recent Ashkenazic ancestor, citing the small number of Ashkenazim in these regions before the late nineteenth century and the knowledge in two of the families that no such ancestors existed. Among the more plausible explanations they offered was that "the blm^{ash} mutation was present in the Sephardic population in Spain" and was brought to Mexico, El Salvador, and New Mexico–southern Colorado by descendants of *conversos*, supporting the concept that all Ashkenazim and Sephardim descended from the same gene pool: "Thus, it is conceivable that a 16th- or 17th-century Sephardic immigrant to the New World who had converted to Christianity and who carried blm^{ash} could have been the ancestor of Spanish American Christians carrying blm^{ash} chromosomes today."[80]

Geneticists and physicians are also currently examining possible links between crypto-Jewish populations and other autoimmune diseases, including Kaposi's sarcoma, female breast and ovarian cancer, and pseudocholinesterase deficiency. All these disorders have occurred with greater frequency in Hispano populations in northern New Mexico and southern Colorado than in the general community, and are associated with Jewish populations.[81] Considerably more interdisciplinary research must be completed before any definitive conclusions can be reached.

In addition to the investigation into diseases, geneticists are beginning to explore the possibility of ascertaining the ancestry of Jews among New Mexican Hispanos by means of DNA testing. In 1997, Michael F. Hammer, of the University of Arizona, initiated an investigation to determine paternal descent from *cohanim*, those Jews who maintain an oral tradition of tracing their biblical roots to Aaron, brother of Moses and the first high priest of Israel.[82] In the wake of this analysis, Hammer initiated a collaboration with a company in Houston to conduct genetic tests on a small number of New Mexican Hispanos who suspected a Jewish family background. Hammer and his colleagues believe that the DNA tests establish a connection between these New Mexicans and historic Semitic populations. While these studies are only tentative first steps, geneticists anticipate that new advances in technology will permit them to more precisely investigate the nature of the link between Hispano populations in the American Southwest and possible *converso* ancestors.[83]

INDICATIONS OF CRYPTO-JUDAISM IN GENEALOGY

As medical and genetic investigations contribute to the historical plausibility of a survival of crypto-Judaism in New Mexico, so can genealogical research provide connections between Hispanos who today assert a *converso* heritage and a Jewish past. Family histories were compiled for nine individuals who either expressed an awareness of Jewish roots or suffered from pemphigus vulgaris, in order to ascertain the extent to which their roots could be traced to Jews and *conversos* in Mexico, Spain, Portugal, or other parts of Europe. The nine were selected on the basis of diversity of age, gender, and geographic origin, and care was taken to ensure that there was no known consanguinity among the people in the pool. Seven members of the group had been told about the Judaism in their families by relatives. One had only a vague impression of *converso* roots, and another, one of the PV patients, knew of no ties to Jewish ancestors.

Emilio Coca, a seventy-year-old retired high-school history teacher from the Taos area, reported that he had been aware of his family's Jewish heritage since childhood, having been informed by his paternal grandfather that they were "judíos españoles y indios" (Spanish Jews and Indians, referring to a Navajo great-great-grandmother). Coca did not regard himself as a Christian—neither he nor his siblings had been baptized—but as a Jew. Among the religious observances recalled by Coca were Friday-night lighting of candles and Saturday-morning family meetings during which the group would read and discuss passages from the Old Testament. In late July or early August, he reported, he and his male relatives would commemorate the destruction of the Temple in Jerusalem by gathering outside their house. They would cover their heads with a serape while his grandfather sprinkled them with ashes from cedarwood. His family refrained from eating pork, and they slaughtered their meat by stunning the animal, slitting the jugular vein, and draining the carcass completely, never consuming the blood. The carcass would be rubbed with salt water, and the sciatic nerve removed. Around Christmas, he and his family would spin a *pon y saca*, or four-sided top. During an interview, Coca produced a *trompito* carved out of Bakelite, with which he recalled playing when he was a child in the 1930s.[84]

Josefa Dolores Gonzales Groff, born in the Jémez Valley in 1898, was told of her Judaism by her mother at a young age. Her family refrained from eating pork or shellfish, separated milk products from meat products, cooked only with olive oil instead of lard, observed the Sabbath on Saturday, and ate only unleavened bread during Passover. She recalled that her paternal grandfather would not eat meat unless the carcass of the animal had been drained of blood and the meat salted. She had been taught that the life of the animal was in the blood, which thus should not be consumed, and recounted how others in her community had eaten *morcilla* (blood pudding), but never her family. Circumcision was practiced among her relatives, her uncles having been taken to Albuquerque to have the rite performed. Although outwardly Catholic, she never went to confession, but confessed her sins directly to God, rejecting the necessity of the priest as intermediary. She regarded Jesus as a prophet, but not the son of God, and could not understand the concept of the Virgin Mary. She identified other extended-family members as Jews, indicating that they all took pains to hide their identity. The Pereas, Sánchezes, and Chaveses—all prominent New Mexico mercantile families in the eighteenth and nineteenth centuries—according to her, were identified as Jewish.[85]

Fidel Gutiérrez, born in 1929 in Velarde, in the Río Grande Valley of northern New Mexico, had also known about his family's background since his youth, having been told by his father, "No somos cristianos, somos judíos" (We are not Christians; we are Jews). His family converted from Catholicism to Presbyterianism shortly before his birth. Gutiérrez recalled the household's elaborate preparation for the observance of the Sabbath on Friday night and Saturday. On Friday afternoon, the house would be cleaned and the children given baths and haircuts. Elaborate meals were prepared on both Friday and Saturday night, and no work would be performed until Sunday. The family read the Bible every night, but only the Old Testament, never the New.[86]

While Coca, Groff, and Gutiérrez were informed about the Jewish heritage in their families at a young age, four others in the sample did not learn of their background until adulthood. Both thirty-eight-year-old Ramón Salas and seventy-three-year-old PV patient Román Romero, of the South Valley of Albuquerque, learned of their crypto-Jewish origins later in life from their cousin, who had assumed a leadership role in what she preferred to call the "Sephardic" community. Salas was raised as a Catholic, and in his late twenties attended Mass regularly and sang in the church choir. But after being told of his

Dennis Durán visiting his family cemetery, northern New Mexico. (© Cary Herz Photography)

Jewish heritage by family members, he became intrigued with Judaism as a faith. He agonized over the difficult choice between two important components of his religious heritage. Ultimately, he decided to undergo a formal conversion, and he celebrated his Bar Mitzvah in April 1992, coinciding with the quincentenary of the Edict of Expulsion of the Jews from Spain.[87]

Romero and his sister, Frances Herrera, too, were raised as Catholics. Herrera had learned about the Jewish background in her family two decades earlier from her cousin, who had left Catholicism to practice Judaism openly. Herrera's husband, also related to the cousin, had been told of his Jewish family roots as well. Although they were raised in separate households due to the early deaths of their parents, both Romero and Herrera recalled lighting candles on Friday night as the family said the Rosary. Moreover, Herrera would place small rocks on the headstones of loved ones, "Just to remember that I was there, to let them know I was there. . . . A lot of people do that."[88]

Similarly, Dennis Durán and Gerald González discovered their *converso* heritage as adults. Durán, forty-nine, traced much of his family to the Pojoaque Valley, north of Santa Fe. Raised in a combination Catholic and Mormon household, Durán converted to Judaism in his early twenties, following his completion of an undergraduate course

Gerald González sitting on the steps of the Inquisition building, Monsaráz, Portugal. (© Cary Herz Photography)

in comparative religion, attracted partly by the antiquity of the religion and partly by his familiarity with several of the customs. A decade or so later, he questioned his relatives about the possibility that the family had Jewish roots. Initially they vehemently denied any such knowledge, but ultimately conceded that his suspicions were correct.[89]

González, fifty-nine, whose roots extend to southern New Mexico, the Pecos River Valley, and the Bernalillo area, had speculated about possible Jewish family origins for several years before receiving positive confirmation from his elderly paternal aunts. They passed on to him the story that the Gonzálezes had left Spain for Portugal many generations earlier to flee inquisitorial persecution, and eventually migrated back to Spain, across the Atlantic Ocean to Mexico, and from there to New Mexico. They recalled family stories relating that their ancestors had practiced the Jewish religion, although later generations were Catholics. Yet in response to González's question about when the family stopped practicing Judaism, one of the aunts replied, "I think that my dad [González's grandfather], in his heart there was a little part of him that was Jewish."[90]

In contrast to those who received direct confirmation of their Jewish heritage, sisters Celina and Anna Rael, fifty-four and fifty-six, respectively, had only a vague notion of their family's Jewish background when they were growing up in Santa Fe during the 1950s and 1960s. They often were told by outsiders that they were Jews, and as teenagers they began to explore the connections between suspicious family dietary customs and a possible *converso* past. The sisters recall the discomfort demonstrated by their mother and maternal grandmother when they expressed their intention to incorporate their newly discovered heritage into their lives and to discuss their experiences openly. Anna decided to convert formally to Judaism, while Celina opted to integrate her ancestral faith into her Catholic cultural identity.[91]

Finally, Fabiola Rivera Valdez, seventy, of Santa Fe, was one of the two PV patients among the nine sample informants. Valdez demonstrated a genome and protein-sequencing pattern indicative of a Jewish ancestry, but she had no knowledge of any *converso* family ties. Born and raised in the Catholic Church, she became a "born-again Christian" at about age fifty. She recalled no family dietary, Sabbath, or other observances that could be linked to a Jewish heritage, with the possible exception of the circumcision of her younger brother, born at home in 1937. Two of her paternal uncles had been given names from the Hebrew Bible: Daniel and Salomon.[92]

The family histories of these nine sample individuals were extensively investigated, in order to ascertain the extent to which they could be traced to Jewish antecedents. I interviewed each participant, securing the names and the approximate dates and places of birth of parents, grandparents, and great-grandparents, wherever possible. From this point, my staff and I researched through sacramental, census, civil and criminal court, land grant, notarial, and Inquisition records in cities and towns in various parts of New Mexico, Mexico, Spain, Portugal, France, and Italy, in an attempt to trace the ancestors backward in time. Inevitably, the absence of documentation (due to fire, theft, war, neglect, or other ravages of time) resulted in genealogical dead ends in certain lines of the families. In others, the records provided a clear family tree extending as far as twenty-three generations, back to the mid-fifteenth century.[93]

In each of the nine families, clear genealogical links were established with the approximately two dozen colonists identified in earlier chapters as probable or possible *conversos* who had settled in New Mexico in the sixteenth and seventeenth centuries. Some families showed a stronger link than others, ranging from a low of five crypto-

Jewish ancestors for Fidel Gutiérrez to fifty-four for Celina and Anna Rael.[94] The average number of *converso* progenitors was twenty-three. The same pattern of endogamy demonstrated by the descendants of crypto-Jews in the seventeenth century appears to have been maintained by *their* descendants through the succeeding centuries, as evidenced by the degree to which their family trees can be traced to the same ancestors multiple times. Celina and Anna Rael, for example, are connected to *converso* settler Diego de Vera no fewer than nine times; Juan de Victoria Carvajal, seven times; Simon de Abendaño, six times; and Francisco Gómez, six times. Emilio Coca descended from Juan Gonzáles Bernal on eight lines; Gerald González, from Juan Griego on three lines; and Fabiola Valdez, from Ignacio Roybal on six lines and from Juan Griego on three lines.

The tendency toward endogamy may also be seen in the pattern displayed by the ancestors of the nine sample individuals to marry predominantly people of similar European origins, and less among Indians, blacks, mulattos, and mestizos, relative to the general New Mexican population. To be sure, members of such non-European racial groups occasionally could be found among the ancestors of each of the families, especially in the seventeenth century. Juan Griego, identified in testimony from seventeenth-century Inquisition trials as a *judío*, for example, married an Indian woman, Pascuala Bernal. Their mestizo son, Juan Griego, the younger, married a mestiza, Juana de la Cruz. Isabel, the daughter of the elder Griego and Bernal, married a Portuguese man, Sebastián Gonzales.[95] But racial identity in colonial New Mexico was quite fluid. The ability of New Mexican colonists to transcend pigmentary boundaries may be seen in the metamorphosis of one of Anna and Celina Rael's maternal branches from mestizo to Spanish in just two generations. Catalina Durán, a mestiza from Zacatecas, arrived in New Mexico in 1695, with the expedition of Juan Páez Hurtado to reinforce the recolonizing expedition of Diego de Vargas.[96] Her son Vicente Ferer Durán de Armijo married a mestiza, María Magdalena de Arzate. But despite these origins, their son, Salvador Manuel de Armijo, somehow became "cleansed" of his Indian origins and was identified as "Spanish" in the marriage record of his children, and both he and his wife were accorded the honorific titles *don* and *doña*, reserved for colonial elite families.[97]

The presence of a small number of *indios* and mestizos among the early colonial New Mexican families notwithstanding, the family trees of the nine individuals selected for this study demonstrate a marked dearth of nonwhite ancestors compared with their neighbors. An analysis of the census of 1790 reveals that 52.93 percent of the population of New Mexico was Spanish, while 30.60 percent was mestizo; 14.51 percent, Indian; 0.67 percent, mulatto; and 1.21 percent, undetermined racial origin.[98] By contrast, 91.2 percent of the ancestors of the nine individuals who claimed a Jewish heritage or were afflicted by pemphigus vulgaris were counted in the census as Spanish; 7.5 percent, mestizo; 1.3 percent, Indian; and 0 percent, mulatto.[99]

Thus the genealogical and medical/genetic evidence supports the plausibility of a historical extension of crypto-Judaism into the modern era in New Mexico. The presence of Jewish-associated autoimmune diseases among the Hispano population, the similarity of genetic indicators between New Mexican Hispano patients and Jewish patients afflicted by these diseases, and the tendency of the *converso* descendants to marry within a limited pool all provide a logical basis to support the conclusions of those social scientists who perceive a crypto-Jewish survival in the American Southwest.

CONCLUSIONS

On the basis of the clues provided by the historical record, material culture, genetics, genealogy, and ethnography, it appears that crypto-Jews and their descendants have been an important component of the multiethnic mosaic that constitutes the state of New Mexico, from the initial exploration and colonization enterprises by the Spanish in the late sixteenth century down to the recent past. The participation of descendants of Iberian crypto-Jews in the early settlement endeavors in New Mexico in the seventeenth and eighteenth centuries represented the culmination of efforts by *conversos* to escape persecution by the Holy Office of the Inquisition in Spain and Portugal after the expulsions and forced conversions in the late fifteenth century. The farther they could migrate from the centers of inquisitorial activity, the greater their chance for survival and security. Escape to the New World from the Iberian Peninsula initially offered that refuge to the *conversos*, but after the establishment of the Inquisition in Mexico City, and its sporadic, yet intense campaigns against crypto-Jews, the far reaches of the northern frontier of New Spain came to be the most secure haven—one of the "ends of the earth" cited by Mexican *judaizante* María de Rivera in 1642.

Due to a combination of the successful efforts of many crypto-Jews to avoid detection by the authorities, the selective attention devoted by the Mexican Inquisition to crypto-Jews throughout the colonial period, and the remoteness and isolation of New Mexico from the capital of the viceroyalty, 1,500 miles to the south, *conversos* were able to assimilate easily into Spanish society. Thus while the Jewish origin of several of the early colonists are well known and documented, other settlers likely had similar roots, but evaded detection, either by contemporary Inquisition officials or by future historians. Many of the descendants of crypto-Jews living in New Mexico appear to have selected spouses from within the *converso* community. This pattern of endogamy could be found among the earliest settlers in the late sixteenth and early seventeenth centuries and continued, to some extent, through subsequent generations.

Documents emanating from the persecutions by the Holy Office of the Inquisition in Mexico and New Mexico in the mid-seventeenth century suggest that while some of the colonists were found to be practicing Jewish rites, few of their cohorts appear to have shown any concern or even paid any attention. Absent the politically motivated campaign of the Franciscans acting as inquisitors in the 1660s, no one in New Mexico seems to have cared about the heretical activities in which their neighbors may have been engaged.

With the waning of interest on the part of the Holy Office of the Inquisition in prosecuting *judaizantes* in Mexico and New Mexico after the mid-seventeenth century, documentation directly recording the presence of crypto-Jews on the far northern frontier diminished significantly. Nevertheless, hints of a *converso* presence in New Mexico could be discerned in the eighteenth, nineteenth, and early twentieth centuries through occupational patterns, the tendency of certain families to give their children names from the Hebrew Bible or to practice ritual circumcision of male infants, and occasional incidental references in surviving documents to the presence of crypto-Jews in the region. Moreover, some scholars believe that in the late nineteenth century, after the conquest of New Mexico by the United States, some Catholic descendants of crypto-Jews took advantage of the more religiously tolerant atmosphere to convert to Presbyterianism, Methodism, and other mainstream Protestant faiths. By doing so, they could gain access to the Bible—the interpretation of which was discouraged by the Catholic Church—and practice a faith that rejected the need for priests and saints as intermediaries between worshipers and God, while not revealing their true ethnic origins.

The survival of crypto-Judaism into the late twentieth century is suggested by analyses done by anthropologists, sociologists, and social psychologists who have conducted fieldwork and research in New Mexico among descendants of the *conversos*. Hints of this persistence are also evident in objects of material culture found in churches and cemeteries throughout the state. Genetic and genealogical research supports the historical plausibility of such a survival of crypto-Judaism. Autoimmune diseases that appear disproportionately in Jewish populations are found among Hispanos whose genome and protein sequencing and genetic mutations are comparable to those of Jews afflicted by such diseases. Genealogical research conducted among a sample of those Hispanos who suffered from one of these diseases or who alleged a Jewish heritage demonstrated that their families could be traced directly to Jewish and crypto-Jewish families in Mexico, Spain, Portugal, and other parts of Europe.

The historical presence of crypto-Jews among the Hispano population of New Mexico offers the opportunity to challenge traditionally held assumptions about Jews and Hispanos and to better appreciate and understand the complex multicultural history of the area that currently comprises the southwestern United States. Most people today would consider Jews and Hispanos to be distinct peoples, with mutually exclusive histories and cultures. The former, in the popular mind, trace their origins to the *shtetls* of eastern Europe, where their ancestors would have worn long black coats and spoken Yiddish. The latter are perceived to be exclusively Roman Catholics, not only today, but since time immemorial. Few people, save a handful of historians, are aware of the rich and dynamic interplay among Muslims, Catholics, and Sephardic Jews on the Iberian Peninsula from the eighth through the fifteenth century. During this era of *convivencia*, Iberians could be Muslim and Spanish, Catholic and Spanish, and Jewish and Spanish. Following the forced conversions of the 1490s, the descendants of this rich ethnic mix could be found in all corners of the Iberian empire, from Europe to Africa, Asia, and the Americas, carrying with them remnants of their ancestral faiths and cultures.

It is hoped that this book, focusing on the descendants of the crypto-Jews in a remote corner of the northern frontier of New Spain, will have helped to challenge the stereotypes regarding the history of Jews and Hispanos and to demonstrate in a meaningful way the complex and diverse character of the history of the American Southwest.

NOTES

1. Tomás Atencio, "Crypto-Jewish Remnants in Manito Society and Culture," *Jewish Folklore and Ethnology Review* 18 (1996): 59.
2. Tomás Atencio, "The Converso Legacy in New Mexico Hispano Protestantism," *El Caminante*, no. 2 (2003): 10–15. *Manitos* are defined by Atencio as "New Mexico's Indohispanos and Indohispanas whose historical threads are anchored in the Colonial period. Literally translated, manito is the shortened diminutive of *hermano*, brother" ("Crypto-Jewish Remnants," p. 59).

3. Atencio, "Crypto-Jewish Remnants," pp. 60–64.

4. Schulamith C. Halevy, "Manifestations of Crypto-Judaism in the American Southwest," *Jewish Folklore and Ethnology Review* 18 (1996): 69.

5. Ibid.; Schulamith C. Halevy, "Jewish Practices Among Contemporary Anusim," *Shofar* 18 (1999): 82.

6. Seth D. Kunin, "Juggling Identities Among the Crypto-Jews of the American Southwest," *Religion* 31 (2001): 44.

7. Ibid., pp. 47–51.

8. Janet Liebman Jacobs, *Hidden Heritage: The Legacy of the Crypto-Jews* (Berkeley: University of California Press, 2002), pp. 2–12.

9. Ibid., pp. 12–18, 42–66.

10. Judith S. Neulander, "Crypto-Jews of the Southwest: An Imagined Community," *Jewish Folklore and Ethnology Review* 16 (1994): 64–68; "The New Mexican Crypto-Jewish Canon: Choosing to Be 'Chosen' in Millennial Tradition," *Jewish Folklore and Ethnology Review* 18 (1996): 19–58; and "Cannibals, Castes and Crypto-Jews: Premillennial Cosmology in Postcolonial New Mexico" (Ph.D. diss., Indiana University, 2001).

11. Neulander, "New Mexican Crypto-Jewish Canon," p. 19.

12. Ibid., pp. 25–26; Neulander, "Cannibals, Castes and Crypto-Jews," pp. 76–79. Neulander conceded that some crypto-Jewish women in Mexico performed "light butchering," by which the animal's blood spilled onto the ground, but she insisted that the heavier slaughtering by men was "unremarkable" that is, it did not include any such disposal of the blood. Neulander apparently was unaware of the extensive treatment given the topic of butchering practices in David M. Gitlitz, *Secrecy and Deceit: The Religion of the Crypto-Jews* (Philadelphia: Jewish Publication Society of America, 1996), pp. 542–548. Gitlitz cited dozens of instances where crypto-Jews in Spain and the New World, including Mexico, practiced *shechitah* from the fifteenth through the seventeenth century.

13. Neulander, "New Mexican Crypto-Jewish Canon," p. 26.

14. Ibid.

15. Halevy, "Jewish Practices Among Contemporary Anusim," pp. 90–91.

16. Atencio, "Crypto-Jewish Remnants," p. 64.

17. Kunin, "Juggling Identities Among the Crypto-Jews," p. 48.

18. Neulander, "New Mexican Crypto-Jewish Canon," pp. 22–23.

19. Halevy, "Jewish Practices Among Contemporary Anusim," p. 88.

20. Kunin, "Juggling Identities Among the Crypto-Jews," p. 51.

21. Ibid., pp. 55–56.

22. Ibid., p. 56.

23. Neulander, "New Mexican Crypto-Jewish Canon," pp. 29–31. Neulander relied heavily for her analysis on Gershon Scholem, "The Star of David: History of a Symbol," in *The Messianic Idea in Judaism and Other Essays on Jewish Spirituality* (New York: Schocken Books, 1971), pp. 257–281.

24. Halevy, "Jewish Practices Among Contemporary Anusim," p. 84.

25. Neulander, "New Mexican Crypto-Jewish Canon," pp. 34–43.
26. Kunin, "Juggling Identities Among the Crypto-Jews," pp. 45, 51.
27. Halevy, "Manifestations of Crypto-Judaism in the American Southwest," p. 72. See also Halevy, "Jewish Practices Among Contemporary Anusim."
28. Jacobs, *Hidden Heritage*, p. 89.
29. Neulander, "New Mexican Crypto-Jewish Canon," p. 46.
30. Jacobs, *Hidden Heritage*, p. 145.
31. Emilio Coca, Santa Fe, interview with author, August 1998. For a detailed account of the history of *cautivos* in New Mexico, see Estevan Rael Gálvez, "Identifying Captivity and Capturing Identity: Narrative of American Indian Slavery in New Mexico and Colorado, 1776–1934" (Ph.D. diss., University of Michigan, 2002).
32. Baptism of María de la Luz Cruz, daughter of José Jacinto Cruz and María Rosalia Romero, *padrinos*: José Rafael Romero and María Juliana Córdova, both *vecinos* of El Llano del Rancho, February 24, 1857, microfilm, reel 25-A, Parish of Guadalupe, Taos, Archives of the Archdiocese of Santa Fe (hereafter cited as AASF).
33. Neulander, "New Mexican Crypto-Jewish Canon," p. 26.
34. I am greatly indebted to the work of folklorist Annette B. Fromm for her analysis of possible links between Hispano material culture and the contemporary crypto-Jewish community in New Mexico. Many of the observations outlined in the section of this chapter dealing with material culture are the result of her research and taken from her report "Material Culture as Expressive of Crypto-Jewish Identity in New Mexico" (manuscript, New Mexico State Records Center and Archives, Santa Fe, 2002).
35. Joy Ungerlieder-Mayerson, *Jewish Folk Art, from Biblical Days to Modern Times* (New York: Summit Books, 1986), p. 22.
36. Warren Blatt, "Reading Hebrew Tombstones" (available at: www.jewishgen.org/infofiles/tombstones.html).
37. Harvey Lutske, *The Book of Jewish Customs* (Northvale, N.J.: Aronson, 1995), pp. 103–104; Scholem, "Star of David," p. 259.
38. The earliest known indication of a hexagram in a uniquely Jewish context was found on the seal of Joshua ben Asaiah, dated to the seventh century B.C.E. Six-pointed stars also appeared in association with five-pointed stars and a swastika in the synagogue of Capernaum in the second or third century C.E. The symbol could also be found as the insignia on the flag of the Jewish community of Prague in the mid-fourteenth century. See Scholem, "Star of David," pp. 260, 275; and Ungerlieder-Mayerson, *Jewish Folk Art*, p. 103.
39. Scholem, "Star of David," pp. 266, 276–277.
40. Martina Will, "'God Gives and God Takes Away': Death and Dying in New Mexico, 1760–1850" (Ph.D. diss., University of New Mexico, 2000).
41. Dorothy Benrimo, *Camposantos* (Fort Worth, Tex.: Amon Carter Museum of Western Art, 1966), p. 3; Russell J. Barber, "The Agua Mansa Cemetery: An Indicator of Ethnic Identification in a Mexican-American Community,"

in Richard M. Meyer, ed., *Ethnicity and the American Cemetery* (Bowling Green, Ohio: Bowling Green State University Popular Press, 1993), p. 162.

42. Paul Marez, Santa Fe, interview with Seth Kunin and author, September 2003. Genealogical research determined that the daughter of Marez's great-great-aunt was married to the brother of the deceased. See Marriages, 1857–1946, April 2, 1872, May 26, 1879, and February 1, 1899, microfilm, reel 61-A, Parish of St. Joseph, Anton Chico, AASF; and Bureau of the Census, *Twelfth Census of Population, 1900, New Mexico*, Guadalupe County, precinct 7, dwelling 18, family 18, and dwelling 43, family 43, and *Thirteenth Census of Population, 1910, New Mexico*, Guadalupe County, precinct 5, dwelling 152, family 152, and dwellings 179–181, families 179–181, both microfilm, New Mexico State Records Center and Archives, Santa Fe (hereafter cited as NMSRCA). The deceased was not listed in the census of 1920, according to Bureau of the Census, *Fourteenth Census of Population, 1920, New Mexico*, Guadalupe County, microfilm, NMSRCA.

43. "Juan García" [actual name withheld at request of interviewee], Albuquerque, interview with Seth Kunin and author, August 2001.

44. Veterans Administration, DD Form 1330, Applications for Headstones and Markers, August 14, 1975, Record Group 15, entry 52, National Archives and Records Administration, Washington, D.C.

45. Andrés Maes, Cleveland, New Mexico, interview with Seth Kunin and author, September 2003.

46. David K. Schettler, director, Memorial Programs Service, Department of Veterans Affairs, Washington, D.C., e-mail message to author, August 5, 2003.

47. "Joaquín Villa" [actual name withheld at request of interviewee], Socorro, interview with Seth Kunin and author, September 2003; "Beatríz Arroyo" [actual name withheld at request of interviewee], Socorro, interview with Seth Kunin and author, September 2003.

48. Roberta Halporn, "American Jewish Cemeteries: A Mirror of History," in Meyer, ed., *Ethnicity and the American Jewish Cemetery*, p. 154; Lutske, *Book of Jewish Customs*, p. 83; John Gary Brown, *Soul in the Stone: Cemetery Art from America's Heartland* (Lawrence: University Press of Kansas, 1994), p. 62.

49. Alfred J. Kolach, *The Jewish Mourners Book of Why* (New York: Jonathan David, 1993), pp. 231–232.

50. Raphael Patai, *On Jewish Folklore* (Detroit: Wayne State University Press, 1983), p. 297.

51. *Expulsion and Memory: Descendants of the Hidden Jews*, dir. Simcha Jacobovici and Roger Pyke (videocassette, Toronto: Associated Producers, 1996).

52. Klaus Wust, *Folk Art in Stone, Southwest Virginia* (Edinburgh, Va.: Shenandoah History, 1970); Terry Jordan, *Texas Graveyards, a Cultural Legacy* (Austin: University of Texas Press, 1990), pp. 50, 90.

53. The stars do not appear in a photograph of the altar taken in 1881, but can be found on a photograph dated 1903 (photograph no. 80.152/4, Albuquerque Museum), reproduced in Thomas J. Steele, *Works and Days: A History of San Felipe de Neri Church, 1867–1895* (Albuquerque: Albuquerque Museum, 1983), p. 71.

54. Emma Moya, "New Mexico's Sephardim: Uncovering Jewish Roots," *La Herencia del Norte* 12 (1996): 13.

55. Richard Chávez, Albuquerque, interview with Seth Kunin and author, September 2003.

56. Neulander, "Cannibals, Castes and Crypto-Jews," pp. 124–128.

57. Manny Contreras, Albuquerque, interview with Seth Kunin and author, September 2003.

58. Charles M. Carrillo, "'Old Testament' Figures in New Mexican Colonial Art" (forthcoming). Historian Michael Perko hypothesized that the Old Testament figures represented on the altar screen derived from a New Testament source: Hebrews 11 (e-mail messages to author, November 13 and December 16, 2003). According to the *New American Bible*, "This chapter draws upon the people and events of the Old Testament to paint an inspiring portrait of religious faith, firm and unyielding in the face of any obstacles that confront it" (*New American Bible* [Washington, D.C.: Confraternity of Christian Doctrine, 1970, 1986, 1991], p. 271).

59. Ross Frank, *From Settler to Citizen: New Mexican Economic Development and the Creation of Vecino Society, 1750–1820* (Berkeley: University of California Press, 2000), pp. 228–233.

60. Ross Frank, e-mail message to author, April 3, 2002.

61. Ibid.

62. Paul Rhetts, e-mail message to author, March 19, 2002. The transformation from the seated Christ, or Ecce Homo, to Job in New Mexico was also noted by Robert L. Shallop, who observed that "in Northern New Mexico, strangely enough, the same figure was adopted as *Hiob*" (*Wooden Saints: The Santos of New Mexico* [Feldafing: Buchhein Verlas, 1967], pp. 44–45); Robert Stroessner, who described the transformation as "a mistaken concept which developed in New Mexico in the late 19th century" (*Santos of the Southwest: The Denver Art Museum Collection* [Denver: Denver Art Museum, 1971], p. 48); and Larry Frank, who explained that "since Job is not a saint, the santero adapted to the desires of the Hispanic faithful and created a 'Santo Hiob' to satisfy their needs" (*New Kingdom of the Saints* [Santa Fe: Red Crane Books, 1992], p. 157).

63. Louis Réau, *Iconographie de l'art chrétien* (Paris: Presses Universitaires de France, 1955), vol. 1, pt. 2, p. 312.

64. Paul Rhetts, e-mail message to author, March 19, 2002.

65. Gitlitz, *Secrecy and Deceit*, p. 117.

66. Mary Austin, miscellaneous notes on Spanish Mexico and New Mexico: photographs for "Spanish Colonial Arts in the U.S." "List of photographs given to Mr. [Frank] Applegate" and "Local *santos* of New Mexico, their symbols and the powers imputed to them by the Spanish Colonials and the Pueblo Indians" (typescript), AU 361, box 24, folder 1, Austin (Mary Hunter) Collection, Henry E. Huntington Library, San Marino, Calif.

67. Mary Austin, "Spanish Colonial Arts Manuscript, Santos, Particularly Transcribed by Alta Applegate, chapter XIV, 'Santos,'" p. 4, MS. 97, box 1, folder 42, Frank Applegate Collection, Center for Southwest Research, Zimmerman Library, University of New Mexico, Albuquerque; "Spanish

Colonial Arts," MS. 255, box 2, folder 20, and "Spanish Colonial Arts," MS. 255, box 2, folder 21, both in T. M Pearce Collection, Center for Southwest Research, Zimmerman Library, University of New Mexico. Neither the artifacts nor the photographs of St. Moses appear to have survived.

68. *Leon* [*sic*] *Jorge Salazar* [exhibition catalog] (Colorado Springs: Taylor Museum, 1973).

69. Jane Fahey McDonald, "Woodcarvers Hew Saints from New Mexico Cedar," *Albuquerque Tribune*, December 18, 1984, p. B1.

70. Leonardo Salazar, Albuquerque, interview with Seth Kunin and author, September 2003; Lidia Salazar, Taos, interview with Seth Kunin and author, September 2003.

71. Charles Sánchez, Tomé, interview with Seth Kunin and author, August 2001.

72. Bernadette Pino, Taos, interview with Seth Kunin and author, August 2001; Naomi Baca Pino, Albuquerque, interview with Seth Kunin and author, August 2001.

73. Jacobo de la Serna, Santa Fe, interview with author, July 2001.

74. Orlando Romero, Santa Fe, interview with author, March 2003.

75. William Robertson, Albuquerque, interview with author, September 1993.

76. "Pedro Apodaca" and "María Espinosa" [actual names withheld at request of interviewees], Albuquerque, interview with author, April 2002.

77. *Albuquerque City Directory* (El Paso, Tex.: Hudspeth, 1949–1972; Dallas: Polk, 1973–1992). The directories listed the family as having lived at that address from 1949 to 1985. Another Hispano resident was cited in 1986. From 1987 to 1992, the directories described the property as vacant.

78. "Juana Trujillo" [actual name withheld at request of interviewee], Las Vegas, New Mexico, interview with author, April 1994.

79. Nathan A. Ellis, Susan Ciocci, Maria Proytcheva, David Lennon, Joanna Groden, and James German, "The Ashkenazic Jewish Bloom Syndrome Mutation blm^{ash} Is Present in Non-Jewish Americans of Spanish Ancestry," *American Journal of Human Genetics* 63 (1998): 1685.

80. Ibid., pp. 1688, 1691–1692.

81. Dharam V. Ablashi, Louise G. Chatlynne, James E. Whitman, Jr., and Ethel Cesarman, "Spectrum of Kaposi's Sarcoma–Associated Herpesvirus, or Human Herpesvirus 8, Diseases," *Clinical Microbiology Reviews* 15 (2002): 439–464; Lisa G. Mullineaux, Teresa M. Castellano, Jeffrey Shaw, Lisen Axell, María E. Wood, Sami Diab, Catherine Klein, Mark Sitarik, Amie M. Deffenbaugh, and Sharon L. Graw, "Identification of Germline 185delAG BRCA1 Mutations in Non-Jewish Americans of Spanish Ancestry from the San Luis Valley, Colorado," *Cancer* 98 (2003): 597–602; Richard M. Goodman, *Genetic Disorders Among the Jewish People* (Baltimore: Johns Hopkins University Press, 1979), pp. 190–192; Dr. Paul Fullerton, personal communication, March 26, 1996.

82. Michael F. Hammer, Karl Skorecki, Sara Selig, Shraga Blazer, Bruce Rappaport, Robert Bradman, Neil Bradman, P. J. Waburton, and Monic Ismajlowicz, "Y Chromosomes of Jewish Priests," *Nature* 385 (1997): 32.

83. Bennett Greenspan, president, Family Tree DNA, e-mail message to author, August 13, 2003. For further details regarding DNA tests of Hispanos, see http://www.FamilyTreeDNA.com.

84. Emilio Coca, Santa Fe, interview with Seth Kunin, September 2003.

85. Josepha Dolores Gonzales Groff, Santa Fe, interview with author, June 1990.

86. Fidel Gutiérrez, Velarde, interview with author, August 1988.

87. Kathleen Teltsch, "Scholars and Descendants Uncover Hidden Legacy of Jews in Southwest," *New York Times*, November 11, 1990, p. 16; Nancy Plevin, "Secret Jews Step Out of the Shadows," *Albuquerque Journal*, March 31, 1991, pp. B1, B4; Edward R. Silverman, "Heritage Refound," *New York Newsday*, November 29, 1992, p. 13.

88. Roman Romero and Frances Herrera, Albuquerque, interview with author, April 1993; Romero and Herrera, Albuquerque, interview with Seth Kunin and author, August 1999.

89. Roger E. Hernández, "Hispanic Jews," *Vista*, April 1995, pp. 18, 29.

90. Delia González de Sánchez and Estella González de Criswell, Garfield, interview with Gerald González, November 1995; Gerald González, "Doña Teresa de Aguilera y Roche and the Inquisition of Mexico" (paper presented at the Society for Crypto-Judaic Studies Conference, San Diego, Calif., August 2003).

91. Maria Steiglitz, "New Mexico's Secret Jews: Now Is It Safe to Tell?" *Lilith* 16 (1991): 8–12.

92. Fabiola Rivera Valdez, Santa Fe, interview with author, May 1993.

93. Complete genealogical charts for these individuals may be examined at http://jewishgen.org/sefardSIG/nmcj.

94. This disparity was due largely to the limited documentation for the Gutiérrez line, in contrast to the relatively more complete genealogical record for Rael.

95. José Antonio Esquibel, "The Formative Era for New Mexico's Colonial Population: 1693–1700," in Claire Farago and Donna Pierce, eds., *Transforming Images: Locating New Mexican Santos In-between Worlds* (University Park: Pennsylvania State University Press, 2005). Esquibel noted the presence of mestizos and *castizos* among the second generation of other Spanish New Mexican families as well—including Anaya Almazán, Martín Serrano, and Montoya—suggesting Indian origins for their mothers. The term *castizo* has an ambivalent etymology, with some authorities indicating a racial designation of pure European, and others pointing to a mixture of Spanish and mestizo. See *Diccionario de autoridades* (1726–1737; facsimile, Madrid: Editorial Gredos, 1976), vol. 1, p. 225; Joan Corominas, *Diccionario crítico etimológico de la lengua castellana* (Madrid: Editorial Gredos, 1954–1957), vol. 1, pp. 722–724; Francisco de Santamaría, *Diccionario de mejicanismos* (Mexico City: Editorial Porrúa, 1983), p. 226; and Efraín Castro Morales, "Los cuadros de castas de la Nueva España," *Jahrbuch für Geschichte von Staat, Wirtschaft, und Gesellschaft Lateinamerikas* 20 (1983): 671–690.

96. John B. Colligan, *The Juan Páez Hurtado Expedition of 1695: Fraud in Recruit-*

ing Colonists for New Mexico (Albuquerque: University of New Mexico Press, 1995), pp. 40–41.

97. Marriage of Antonio José Durán de Armijo and María Guadalupe Durán y Chaves, June 16, 1774, microfilm, reel 26, frames 218–219, Parish of San Felipe de Neri, AASF. Curiously, four of Antonio José's siblings married four of María Guadalupe's brothers and sisters. See José Antonio Esquibel and John B. Colligan, *The Spanish Recolonization of New Mexico: An Account of the Families Recruited in Mexico City in 1693* (Albuquerque: Hispanic Genealogical Society of New Mexico, 1999), pp. 376–377. For a more comprehensive analysis of race and class in colonial New Mexico, see Adrian Bustamante, "'The Matter Was Never Resolved': The *Casta* System in Colonial New Mexico, 1693–1823," *New Mexico Historical Review* 66 (1991): 143–163.

98. Bustamante, "'Matter Was Never Resolved,'" p. 153, table 2.

99. Census of the jurisdiction of Santa Fe, 1790, microfilm, reel 12, frames 319–502, and reel 23, frames 255–261, Spanish Archives of New Mexico, ser. 2, no. 1096a, NMSRCA. The New Mexico census of 1790 covered the area from Belén to Alameda, as well as Santa Fe, Santa Cruz de la Cañada, Picurís, Taos, and Abiquiú. The census counted 159 ancestors of the 9 sample families, comprising 145 *españoles*, 11 mestizos, 1 *indio*, 1 *genízaro*, and 1 *coyota*. For statistical purposes, the *genízaro* was counted as an *indio*, and the *coyota* as a mestizo. Although several of the ancestors listed in the census appeared multiple times in the family trees, they were counted only once in this analysis.

APPENDIX

Pemphigus Vulgaris Among Hispanos in New Mexico and Its Possible Connection with Crypto-Jewish Populations

Kristine K. Bordenave and Stanley M. Hordes

Pemphigus vulgaris (PV) is a rare autoimmune skin disease, characterized by blisters, resulting in pain, shedding of the skin, and consequent loss of protection against infection.[1] Like other immunologic disorders, PV seems to have a predilection for certain ethnic groups. Immunogenic studies have linked disease and ethnicity through human leukocyte antigens (HLA)-typing.[2] Ashkenazic Jews have an increased incidence of PV as compared with other ethnic groups,[3] and HLA studies in the Ashkenazic Jewish patients yielded a high incidence of the following types: A10 (A25 and A26), B35, B38, DR4, and DQ3. Due to the perceived increased prevalence of PV among Hispanos in New Mexico, a study of immunogenetics, ethnicity, and culture was completed. The research team located all eighteen PV patients in the state of New Mexico. Thirteen of them were Hispano. New Mexico's ethnic distribution is approximately 40 percent Hispano of a total population of approximately 1.3 million. Forty-two percent of the Hispano PV patients carried the HLA type A10; 25 percent, B35; and 75 percent, DR4 and DQ3. In addition, of the ten DR4 alleles sequenced, 60 percent were DRB1*0407.

Recognizing a newly emerging and once secret population of Sephardic Jews in New Mexico, it should be questioned whether the predominance of Hispano patients as compared with non-Hispanos may be due to Jewish genetic influences. Sixty percent of the study's Hispano population agreed to an interview reviewing their heritage, cultural practices, and religious beliefs. Of these, half either were aware of or supplied information highly suggestive of Sephardic Jewish origins.

Pemphigus vulgaris is characterized by antibodies deposited in the skin. These antibodies are directed against proteins that connect skin cells, leading to blasta formation. Although many patients first present with oral mucosal lesions, their lesions often become more diffusely spread (scalp, trunk, feet, and hands) as the disease progresses.

The incidence of this disease varies from 0.1 to 0.5 case per 100,000 a year in the general population. However, there is a greater incidence among Jews (1.6 to 3.2 cases per 100,000 population a year). The initial presentation of PV is more common in the fourth, fifth, and sixth decades of life and tends to have an equal distribution between men and women. PV does not appear to have any geographic bias; however, pemphigus foliaceus (specialty fogo selvagum) is endemic in certain areas of Brazil. Regarding the relative distribution of this disease, extensive studies have evaluated and compared Jews and non-Jews, but there had been no studies evaluating Hispanos. Therefore, the purpose of this study was to HLA-type and compare New Mexican Hispanos with other previously studied ethnic groups.

Over the past several years, many published HLA studies have reported an increased incidence of A10 (A25 and A26), B35, B38, and DR4, DQ3(8) in PV patients of Ashkenazic Jewish descent. Although these HLA types are also seen in non-Jewish patients, the incidence of these HLA types is significantly higher in Ashkenazic Jews. For example, in one study, HLA-DR4, DQ3(8) occurred in 92.3 percent of Ashkenazic Jewish patients. Seventy-five percent of these patients carried either HLA-B35 or HLA-B38. In another study by the same researchers, HLA-DR4, DQ3(8) occurred in only 48 percent of the non-Jewish PV patients, while 60 percent displayed HLA-DR6, DQ5. Three of these twenty-five patients (12 percent) displayed either HLA-B35 or HLA-B38. It is through these two studies that A. Razzaque Ahmed and his colleagues suggest that there are two major histocompatability complex (MHC) susceptibility alleles: the "more ancient" HLA-B35 or HLA-B38, DR4, DQ3(8), arising among Jews; and the HLA-B55, DR6, DQ5, arising among people of southern European extraction.[4]

Given these studies and the perceived increase in the prevalence of PV among Hispanos in New Mexico, all Hispano PV patients in the state underwent HLA-typing by standard serological methods, polymerase chain reaction (PCR), and DNA sequencing.

All eighteen PV patients in New Mexico were contacted and interviewed about their ethnicity and willingness to participate in the study. Thirteen of these patients were of Hispanic descent and agreed to phlebotomy, but only seven agreed to undergo a detailed personal interview regarding their heritage, cultural practices, and religious beliefs.

Of the eighteen patients with PV, thirteen (72 percent) were Hispano. This is equal to a prevalence rate of PV in Hispanos of 2 per 100,000 population a year, or three times the prevalence rate of non-Hispanos in New Mexico. This confirms the suspicion that there is an increased prevalence of PV in Hispanos in New Mexico when compared with non-Hispanos and expected values.

Blood was obtained from all thirteen Hispano patients, drawn using sterile technique in (2–3) 10-milliliter Becton Dickson vacutainer tubes (2) containing 143 units of sodium heparin and (1) containing the anticoagulant ethylenediaminetetraacetic acid (EDTA).[5] This blood was stored at room temperature for up to forty-eight hours. HLA studies were then performed using standard techniques.

HLA-typing yielded the following results:

Allele	**Patients**
A25	3 of 12
A26	3 of 12
B35	3 of 12
DR4	10 of 12
DRB1*0402	6 of 10
DRB1*0404	3 of 10
DRB1*0407	1 of 10
DQ3	10 of 12

The normal frequency of HLA-DR4 in Hispano controls is 29.8 percent.[6] Earlier studies have reported a PV association with HLA-DR4 in 93 to 98 percent of Ashkenazic Jews, but only 26 to 57 percent of non-Ashkenazic Jews. Patients thought to be of southern European extraction are more likely to have HLA-DR6. If HLA-DR4 is seen less frequently than HLA-DR6 in patients of southern European extraction, it is surprising that 83 percent, or ten of twelve, of New Mexican Hispanos with PV carry HLA-DR4.

We also found in increased incidence (42 percent) of HLA-A25 and HLA-A26 among the patients. The normal frequency for HLA-A25 and HLA-A26 among Hispano controls is 11 percent (4 percent for HLA-A25, and 7 percent for HLA-A26). Three (27 percent) of the patients carried HLA-B35 (normal frequency among Hispano controls is 28 percent).

Seven of the thirteen Hispano PV patients whose HLA tests revealed a Jewish genetic pattern were interviewed to help define their ethnicity, genealogy, and cultural and religious beliefs. Each of the patients was asked questions relating to the level of consciousness of the Jewish background in his or her family and to residual observances, practiced knowingly or unknowingly, suggestive of a Jewish heritage. Only one of the seven patients maintained neither Jewish awareness nor customs. Four were not explicitly conscious of any Jewish past, but followed customs that may have represented residual Jewish practices. Two of the patients were aware of the Judaism in their families' past.

One man in his seventies, outwardly Catholic, spoke of growing up in a household where the consumption of pork products was strictly prohibited. In violation of Catholic tradition, his father read the Bible at home, stressing the importance of the Old Testament over the New. The Sabbath was observed on both Saturday and Sunday, in commemoration of the Jewish and Catholic days of rest. Although he was not himself circumcised, he articulated an awareness of infant male circumcision being performed on others in the community, sometimes by midwives using a hot safety pin as the surgical instrument. Jewish death, burial, and mourning customs were acknowledged, including the rending of clothes and the placing of small pebbles on the top of headstones when visiting the grave of a loved one.

The other patient who was aware of the Jewish heritage of his family was interviewed together with his older sister. Several years earlier, their cousin had made a decision to publicly acknowledge her Judaism and to live openly as a Jew in Albuquerque. The patient and his sister spoke of family traditions, such as refraining from eating pork, lightning candles on Friday evening, abstaining from work on Saturdays, reading from the Hebrew Bible, and placing small pebbles on the headstones of family members. Genealogical research was conducted on the family of this patient, utilizing parish baptismal, marriage, and burial records; census records; civil court records; and land records in New Mexico, Mexico, and Spain from the sixteenth through twentieth centuries.[7] The patient's ancestors include several Spanish, Portuguese, or Mexican New Christians from the early colonial period.

This research demonstrates that the increased prevalence of HLA-A10 (25 and 26) and HLA-DR4, DQ3 in New Mexican Hispanos with PV is due to the region's previously unrecognized Sephardic Jewish heritage. To further test this hypothesis, it is necessary to conduct extensive genealogical investigations. Later studies to increase the sample size would improve the statistical significance of this theory. This will be accomplished by HLA-typing and interviewing PV patients in Texas, Arizona, and Mexico. These areas have been chosen since they are known to have had secret Sephardic Jewish populations.

Jews comprise a highly conserved genetic population; however, many ethnically mixed offspring were the result of Jews' being forced into new environments around the world. This is likely to have resulted in the sharing of some genetic material that may cause diseases predominantly seen in Jewish populations. For at least two thousand years, Jews have been living in southern European countries, such as Italy, Spain, and Portugal. It is likely that the PV patients of Ashkenazic and non-Ashkenazic descent studied by Ahmed and his co-workers are of the same original ancestry. If PV originated among the Jews before their dispersal around the world, we would expect to find this disease in diverse populations. In addition, the immunogenetics would reflect increasing variation with a probable bottleneck and founder effects.

The recent medical literature indicates that immunologic disease appears to be associated with the major histocompatability complex, specifically the Type II (DR and DQ) antigens. It is likely that the increased prevalence of PV in Hispanos is related to HLA Class II phenotypes and genotypes that are associated with PV in Jewish populations and may be due to Jewish genetic influence. This will further clarify the possibility that PV had a single origin and may alter the medical community's focus of human genetic study in autoimmune disease.

NOTES

1. This appendix follows closely portions of Stanley M. Hordes and Kristine K. Bordenave, "'*Pemphigus vulgaris*' entre la población de origin hispano y su relación con el criptojudaísmo en Nuevo México," in Judit Bokser Liwerant and Alicia Gojman de Backal, eds., *Encuentro y alteridad: Vida y cultura judía en América Latina* (Mexico City: Universidad Nacional Autónoma de México, Universidad Hebrea de Jerusalén, Asociación Mexicana de Amigos de la Universidad de Tel Aviv, and Fondo de Cultura Económica, 1999), pp. 57–72. The technical portion of the article discussed in this section was prepared by Bordenave. See also Kristine K. Bordenave, Jeffrey Griffith, Stanley M. Hordes, Thomas M. Williams, and R. Steven Padilla, "The Historical and Geomedical Immunogenetics of Pemphigus Among the Descendants of Sephardic Jews in New Mexico," *Archives of Dermatology* 137 (2001): 825–826.

2. HLA-typing is the testing performed to determine compatibility for organ donation and to ascertain paternity. People with the same or similar HLA

types belong to the same or similar genetic groups. Each HLA type is identified by a letter and a number.

3. To date, these tests have been performed predominantly on Ashkenazic Jews, and, as a consequence, little is known about the frequency of pemphigus vulgaris among Sephardim. A study conducted in 1964 demonstrated that from 1949 to 1963, 27 percent of PV patients in Israel were Sephardic Jews. See Richard M. Goodman, *Genetic Disorders Among the Jewish People* (Baltimore: Johns Hopkins University Press, 1979), p. 438, citing L. Ziprkowski and M. Schewach-Millet, "A Long-Term Study of Pemphigus," *Proceedings of the Tel-Hashomer Hospital* 3 (1964): 46. Early works stressed genetic differences between Ashkenazim and Sephardim based on interbreeding by Ashkenazim with northern and eastern European non-Jewish populations. See, for example, Rafael Patai and Jennifer L. Patai-Wing, *The Myth of the Jewish Race* (New York: Scribner, 1975). More recent studies, however, have demonstrated the close genetic relationship between Ashkenazic and Sephardic Jews, allowing for the relevance of the comparisons between the pathology and genetic characteristics of Ashkenazim and of descendants of New Mexican crypto-Jews. See, for example, M. F. Hammer, A. J. Redd, E. T. Wood, M. R. Bonner, H. Jarjanazi, T. Karafet, S. Santachiara-Benerecetti, A. Oppenheim, M. A. Jobling, T. Jenkins, H. Ostrer, and B. Bonné-Tamir, "Jewish and Middle Eastern Non-Jewish Populations Share a Common Pool of Y-Chromosome Biallelic Haplotypes," *Proceedings of the National Academy of Sciences* 97 (2000): 6769–6774; S. Livshits, R. R. Sokal, and E. Kobyliansky, "Genetic Affinities of Jewish Populations," *American Journal of Human Genetics* 49 (1991): 131–146; B. Bonne-Tamir, S. Ashbel, and R. Kenett, "Genetic Markers: Benign and Normal Traits of Ashkenazi Jews," in Richard M. Goodman and Arno G. Motulsky, eds., *Genetic Diseases Among Ashkenazi Jews* (New York: Raven Press, 1979), pp. 59–76; and A. Szeinberg, "Polymorphic Evidence for a Mediterranean Origin of the Ashkenazi Community," in Goodman and Motulsky, eds., *Genetic Diseases Among Ashkenazi Jews*, pp. 77–91.

4. A. Razzaque Ahmed, E. J. Yunis, K. Khatri, R. Wagner, G. Notani, Z. Awdeh, and C. A. Alper, "Major Histocompatibility Complex Haplotypes Studies in Ashkenazi Jewish Patients with Pemphigus Vulgaris," *Proceedings of the National Academy of Sciences* 87 (1990): 7658–7662; A. Razzaque Ahmed, R. Wagner, K. Khatri, G. Notani, Z. Awdeh, C. A. Alper, and E. J. Yunis, "Major Histocompatibility Complex Haplotypes and Class II Genes in Non-Jewish Patients with Pemphigus Vulgaris," *Proceedings of the National Academy of Sciences* 88 (1991): 5056–5060.

5. Blood was obtained from all thirteen Hispano patients. One of the samples could not be included in the serological testing because of bacterial contamination. Only ten samples underwent DNA testing, due to the lack of specimens. The blood was HLA-typed by standard serological methods using both Gen Trak and Biotest trays by Dr. Kristine Bordenave under the supervision of Dr. Gary Troup's laboratory staff. DRB1 was further subtyped using PCR amplification and DNA sequencing in Dr. Jeffrey Griffith and Dr. Thomas Williams's laboratory. All results were then reviewed and compared with controls and current literature by Dr. Kenneth Friedman, Department of Internal Medicine, University of New Mexico School of Medicine.

6. Control data in this study are based on One Lamda Desktop Companion, California Hispanic cohort.

7. Complete genealogical research remains to be conducted on all seven patients who demonstrated an HLA pattern consistent with that of Jewish patients. To date, such an investigation has been performed with regard to only two of the patients.

Bibliography

PRIMARY SOURCES

Mexico

ARCHIVO GENERAL DE LA NACIÓN, MEXICO CITY

Ramo de Archivo Histórico de Hacienda

[Minutes of the *consulado* of Mexico City], August 2, 1635. Legajo 213, exp. 12.

Ramo de Civil

Pleito de hexecución de Gonzalo de las Casas contra Luis de Carabajal, 1571. Tomo 921, exp. 43.

Ramo de Concurso de Peñalosa

[Interrogatory and testimony presented by former governor Juan Manso pertaining to the suit against General Don Bernardo López de Mendizábal], August 9, 1662. Tomo 1.

Testimonio de Francisco Xavier, August 9, 1662. Tomo 1.

Testimonio de Sargento Mayor Diego Romero, July 8, 1661. Tomo 1.

Testimonio del ynforme que su ssa. el Dr. Don Bernardo López de Mendizábal, governador y capitán general de este Reyno, hace al Exmo. Señor Virrey de la Nueva España, September 8, 1660. Tomo 1.

Prisión y embargo de bienes de Doña Teresa de Aguilera y Roche, August 27, 1662. Tomo 1.

Testimonio a la letra que el Señor Capitán y Sargento Mayor D. Diego Dionísio de Peñalosa Briceño y Verdugo, Governador y Capitán General del Nuevo México mandó trasuntar de la Residencia que remitió al Exmo. Señor Virrey de la Nueva España de la que dió el Capitán D. Bernardo López de Mendizábal, Año de 1661. Tomo 1, legajo 1, no. 2.

Auto de prisión, embargo y remate de bienes del Capitán Nicolas de Aguilar, May 2, 1662. Tomo 1, legajo 1, no. 5.

Autos de prisión, embargo y remate de bienes del Sargento Mayor Diego Romero—Año de 1662, inventory of estate of Diego Romero, May 2, 1662, and May 4, 1662. Tomo 2, legajo 1, no. 7.

Autos de prisión, embargo y remate de bienes del Sargento Mayor Francisco Gómez Robledo, fecho el año de 1662, inventory of estate of Francisco Gómez Robledo, May 4, 1662, and May 18, 1662. Tomo 2, legajo 1, no. 6.

El maestre del campo Thomé Domínguez de Mendoza, vecino de las provincias del Nuevo México, en nombre del capitán Don Diego de Peñalosa y Briseño, goberndor de dichas provincias sobre los bienes que se le embargaron por el Pe. Fray Alonso de Posada . . . se depositaron. Pide se le entreguen, 1663–1694. Tomo 3.

Auto de prisión y embargo de bienes com su remate del Capitán Christóval de Anaia Almasan, May 14, 1662. Tomo 3, legajo 1, no. 22.

Ramo de Inquisición

Autos y diligencias hechas por los sanbenitos antiguos y recientes y postura de los que sean de relajados por este Santo Oficio, 1574–1632. Tomo 77, exp. 35.

Contra Diego Landín, por aver dicho que Diós por ser Diós avía dicho mas verdad que el y que dezía tanta verdad como avían dicho los santos, September 24–November 8, 1606. Tomo 171, exp. 111.

Ynformación de la limpieza del linaje del Capitán Francisco de Urdiñola, natural de la provincia de Guipúzcoa, y Leonor de Lois, su muger, vecinos del Río Grande y Mazapíl. Familiar del Santo Oficio, September 1592. Tomo 197, exp. 6.

Proceso contra Juan Núñez, balanzario de la real caja, por alumbrado y sospechoso de judaizante, 1598. Tomo 210, exp. 2.

Expediente de las raciones diarias que recibian los presos de la [*sic*] carceles secretas del Santo Oficio, 1589. Tomo 213, exp. 12.

Pedro Robledo, familiar de la Inquisición de Toledo, pide que se le admita información de su título y que se le nobre familiar en México, 1591. Tomo 213, exp. 19.

Documentos relativos al proceso contra el Capitan Francisco de Urdiñola, familiar, por homicidio de Domingo Landaverde, October 1593. Tomo 214, exp. 20.

Causa contra Cristóbal de Herrera, mercader, vecino de la ciudad de Zacatecas, 1614. Tomo 309.

Testificaciónes procedentes de diversas comisaros denuncias declaraciónes, y otros asuntos todos concernientes al Sto. Oficio con su índice alfabético y foliado particularmente del 1 a 370, deposición de Juana Bautista Conte, biuda, contra Xptóbal de Herrera, mercader, May 4, 1626. Tomo 356, exp. 6.

Genealogía del Pe. Fr. Estévan de Perea, predicador y custodio de las Provincias de México, 1628. Tomo 365, exp. 11.

Don Alonso de Oñate, impedió la visita de un navío en la Veracruz, July 2–7, 1604. Tomo 368.

Borrador de la relación de las causas que se han despachado desde principio del año del 1634 hasta fin de 1635. Tomo 381, exp. 5.

El procurador del Real Fisco contra Jorge Jacinto por quantía de 10 pesos de una arrova de vino perteneciente a Simón Váez, 1644. Tomo 392, exp. 13.

Proceso y causa criminal contra Melchor Rodríguez López, 1642. Tomo 395, exp. 3.

Proceso y causa criminal contra Thomás Núñez de Peralta, 1642. Tomo 395, exp. 5.

Proceso y causa criminal contra el Bachiller Pedro Tinoco, 1642. Tomo 396, exp. 2.

Proceso y causa criminal contra Simón Váez Sevilla, 1642. Tomo 398, exp. 1.

Proceso y causa criminal contra Juan Pacheco de León, alias Salomon Machorro, natural de la ciudad de Antequera en España, vezino y mercader de pueblo de Querétaro, Primera y segunda audiencias, June 12–14, 1642. Tomo 400, no. 2.

Proceso y causa criminal contra Pedro de Espinosa, 1642. Tomo 403, exp. 1.

Proceso y causa criminal contra María de Rivera, 1642. Tomo 403, exp. 3.

Proceso y causa criminal contra Antonio Caravallo, 1642. Tomo 409, exp. 2.

Proceso y causa criminal contra Pedro Fernández de Castro, 1642. Tomo 409, exp. 4.

Proceso y causa criminal contra Luis Núñez Pérez, 1642. Tomo 412, exp. 2.

Testificaciones de Manuel Rodríguez Núñez contra diversas personas, 1644. Tomo 414, exp. 2.

Proceso y causa criminal contra Manuel de Acosta, 1643. Tomo 418, exp. 1.

Acusación del fiscal del Santo Oficio contra Bernardo López de Mendizábal, por judaizante y otros delitos, 1663. Tomo 421, exp. 6.

Relación de causa de Sebastián Cardoso, 1642. Tomo 426, exp. 13.

Proceso y causa criminal contra Gonzalo Díaz, 1649. Tomo 431.

Proceso y causa criminal contra Jorge Duarte, 1648. Tomo 431, exp. 4.

Diligencias fechas contra algunos reconciliados, 1649. Tomo 432.

Cartas referentes al ingenio de Cristóbal de Mendizábal, 1650. Tomo 436, exp. 31.

Remisión a España de los reos penitenciados por esta Inquisición entregandolos al General de Flota quien dió recivo de ellos, 1650. Tomo 454, exp. 29.

Proceso y causa criminal contra Luis Pérez Roldán, 1642. Tomo 487, exp. 14.

Proceso y causa criminal contra Diego Rodríguez, alias Ovandaxo, 1642. Tomo 487, exp. 15.

Traslado del papel que remitió a este Santo Oficio el Sr. Obispo Don Juan de Pálafox y Mendoza, visitador general de este Reyno en veinte de noviembre de 1641 que es el original que escribió al ex^{mo} Sr. Marqués de Villena,

Duque de Escalona, Virrey de esta Nueva España segun refiere el dicho Villete, 1641. Tomo 489.

[*Cédula* of Felipe IV], January 7, 1641. Tomo 489.

Papeles del Sr. Virrey Conde de Salvatierra acerca del donativo de los portugueses, January 17, 1643. Tomo 489.

Sobre remisión de judaizantes a España, 1651. Tomo 489.

Proceso y causa criminal contra Pedro Fernández de Castro, 1642. Tomo 409, exp. 4.

Causa criminal contra Antonio Báez, 1623. Tomo 489, exp. 4.

Proceso y causa criminal contra Duarte Castaño, 1647. Tomo 497, exp. 8.

Proceso y causa criminal contra Luis de Amezquita, 1642. Tomo 499, exp. 1.

Proceso y causa criminal contra Antonio de Narbáez Farfán, alias Davíd Machorro, difunto, natural de Antequera, padre de Juan Pacheco de León, que murió en la mar, viniendo a este reyno, 1649. Tomo 503, exp. 7.

[Report of the *alcalde de las cárceles de penitencia*], 1649. Tomo 503, exp. 36.

Cabeza de proceso contra Jorge Jacinto Bazán y Miguel Tinoco, penitenciados por el Santo Tribunal, 1649. Tomo 503, exp. 76.

El Señor fiscal del Santo Oficio contra el Capitán Nicolas de Aguilar por proposiciones, 1661. Tomo 512, exp. 2.

Inventario y sequestro de bienes de Luis Pérez Roldán, vecino de esta ciudad de México, 1657. Tomo 572, exp. 10.

Proceso y causa criminal contra Cristóbal de Anaya por proposiciones heréticas, 1661. Tomo 582, exp. 1.

Proceso y causa criminal contra el sargento mayor Francisco Gómez Robledo, por sospechoso de delitos del judaismo, y haver dicho proposiciones heréticas, Primera audiencia, July 4, 1663. Tomo 583, exp. 3.

Causa contra el Capitán Diego Romero, natural de la Villa de Santa Fe en Nuevo Mexico, por hereje, 1663. Tomo 586, exp. 1

Proceso contra Bernardo López de Mendizábal, gobernador de Nuevo México, por proposiciones heréticas y sospechoso de judaizante. 1662. Tomo 593, exp. 1.

Primera audiencia de Don Bernardo López de Mendizábal, por proposiciones irreligiosas y escandalosas, April 28, 1663. Tomo 594, exp. 1.

El Señor fiscal del Santo Oficio contra Doña Teresa de Aguilera y Roche, mujer de Don Bernardo López de Mendizábal, por sospechosa de delitos de judaismo, 1663. Tomo 596, exp. 1.

Testificaciones que se an sacado a pedimiento del sr. fiscal de uno de los quadernos que se remitieron por el comisario del Nuevo México contra Juan Gómez, vezino de dicho Nuevo México, 1662–1663. Tomo 598, exp. 7.

Denunciaciones contra Juan Domínguez de Mendoza. Nuevo México, 1667. Tomo 610, exp. 7.

Quaderno primero de cédulas reales tocantes a este Santo Oficio, 1555–1776. Lote Riva Palacio, Tomo 1.

Proceso contra Luis de Carvajal, Governador del Nuevo Reino de León, natural de la Villa de Mogadorio, 1589. Lote Riva Palacio, Tomo 11, exp. 3.

Libro donde se sientan todos los presos que han entrado en esta cárcel de las casas de Picazo desde trece de julio de 1642 siendo alcaide Pedro Ximénes de Zervera, 1647. Lote Riva Palacio, Tomo 48, exp. 2.

Ramo de Provincias Internas

Gobernadores. Don Domingo Petris Gironza es nobrado para nuevo México: pide seis años de pagos adelantados y armas y municiones para llevar a su provincia y ponerla en estado de defensa, September 16, 1683. Tomo 35, exp. 2.

Ramo de Real Fisco de la Inquisición

Cartas misivas y correspondencia comercial, 1624. Tomo 13, exp. 3.

Declaraciones hechas ante el comisario del Santo Oficio en la ciudad de Los Angeles, por los bienes secuestrados a Juan Méndez de Villaviciosa, Diego Méndez de Silva, Francisco López, y Simón Baez, 1642. Tomo 15, exp. 12.

Francisco Ortuño, en nombre de la Condesa de Peñalva en contra del Real Fisco en juicio sucesorio por los bienes de Simón Váez Sevilla, 1661. Tomo 58, exp. 4.

Ynforme del hecho en el [deteriorated] los condes de Peñalba, 1661. Tomo 58, exp. 5.

Ramo de Reales Cédulas

Sobre que lo que se debe hacer con los portugueses y demas extranjeros que se encuentran radicados en la Nueva España, February 10, 1642. Tomo 1, exp. 288.

Ordenado al Virrey de la Nueva España, que cumpla las Reales Cédulas expedidas en relación a los portugueses, February 10, 1642. Tomo 1, exp. 289.

Al Virrey, sobre que remita a España a los reos judaizantes condenados por aquel Tribunal, August 31, 1648. Tomo 3, exp. 45.

Al Virrey, ordenandole nuevamente que se envien a España los reos condenados por el Tribunal del Santo Oficio, December 11, 1649. Tomo 3, exp. 88.

Ramo de Reales Cédulas Duplicadas

[*Cédulas* pertaining to the conditions in New Mexico, hostility with Apaches, resupply, etc.], September 11–October 5, 1678. Tomo 31, exp. 296.

ARCHIVO GENERAL DE NOTARÍAS, MEXICO CITY

Escribanía de Antonio de Villalobos, 1580–1603.

Escribanía de Juan Oviedo Valdivieso, 1641. Tomo 469

Notaría 110, Toribio Cobian. Tomo 726, 1650–1652; tomo 727, 1564; tomo 728, 1656; tomo 729, 1658.

ARCHIVO JUDICIAL DEL DISTRITO
Y TERRITORIOS FEDERALES, MEXICO CITY

Alonso Hernández, maestro de sastre, contra el capitán Melchor Rodríguez López por 127 pesos por que el executó, 1649. Legajo 32.

INSTITUTO NACIONAL DE ANTROPOLOGÍA
E HISTORIA, MEXICO CITY

Archivo Histórico, Colección Antigua
Libro primero del juzgado de bienes confiscados, 1661. Tomo 60.

ARCHIVO HISTÓRICO DE PARRAL

Testamento de Manuel Jorge, June 7, 1655. Microfilm, reel 1654B.

ARCHIVO PARROQUIAL DE ZACATECAS

Libro de matrimonios, 1605–1626.

Spain

ARCHIVO HISTÓRICO NACIONAL, MADRID

Sección de Inquisición
Proceso contra Diego López de Perea, vecino de la ciudad de Guadalajara, judaizante, 1543. Legajo 160, exp. 9.
Proceso contra Juan de Pastrana, mercader, vecino de Guadalajara, 1538. Legajo 173, exp. 13.
Cartas originales del Tribunal de México para el Consejo, 1640–1648. Legajo 1054.
Proceso criminal sobre competición de jurisdición con la Real Audiencia de Guadalaxara contra el Capitan Francisco de Urdiñola, familiar del Santo Oficio de la Inquisición de México, 1595. Legajo 1734, no. 5.
Diferentes autos y papeles tocantes a la visita del tribunal del Santo Oficio de México que sirven para comprovación de los cargos della y de lo demás que se obrado, 1646. Legajo 1736, exp. 4.
Resumen de los cargos que resultan asi comunes como particulares de la visita de la Inquisición de México, 1658. Legajo 1737, exp. 11.
Libro de la razón de la visita de hacienda del Santo Oficio de la Inquisición de la ciudad de México, 1657–1668. Legajo 1737, exp. 20.
Diferentes documentos para prueba de la visita que esta a cargo del Sr. Inquisidor Dr. Don Pedro de Medina Rico, 1656. Legajo 1738, exp. 1.
Relación de las causas despachadas este anno, en la inquisición de Canaria desde

primero de enero de 1609 asta fin del dicho anno, Francisco de Vera Mojíca 1609. Legajo 1829, exps. 2–20.

Relación de los reos que salieron al Auto Público de fe que celebró el Tribunal del Santo Oficio de la Inquisición de Murcia el el Convento de San Francisco el Domingo 15 de Marzo de 1682. Legajo 2022, exp. 117.

Relación de las causas que resultaron de la visita que el inquisidor Lic. Joan Ochoa hico en el obispado de Tui y Villa de Pontevedra, arcobispado de Sanctiago, este ano de mill y seiscientos y nueve. Legajo 2042, exp. 48, nos. 44–51, 133–136, 172, 209, 211.

Relación de las causas despachadas en el Santo Oficio de la inquisición de Galicia desde primero de septiembre de 1623 asta primero de septiembre de 1624. Legajo 2042, exp. 62.

Relación de las causas despachadas en este sancto oficio del Reyno de Galicia entre año desde primero de setiembre del pasado de 1631, hasta fin del agosto deste de 1632 y las que se despacharon en auto particular en la catedral deste ciudad. Legajo 2042, exp. 71, no. 31.

Relación de causas de fe pendientes en la ynquisición de Galicia y del estado en que se hallan desde 1 de setiembre hasta fin del año de 1681. Legajo 2042, exp. 100, nos. 19, 23.

Relación de las personas que salieron a el auto público de la fe que se zelebró por el Santo Oficio de la inquisición de Sevilla en la Plaza de San Francisco della día de el Glorioso Apostol San Andrés de este Presente año de 1624, judaizantes. Legajo 2075, pt. 2, exp. 31.

Relaciones de causas y autos de fe, 1559–1715. Legajo 2075, pt. 2, exps. 38, 40.

Relaciones de las causas de fe, 1622–1699. Legajo 2135, exps. 23, 24.

Relación de las personas que salieron al auto que se celebró en la inquisición de Murcia. [D]omingo dia de nra. señora que se contaron ocho de setienbre de mill y quinientos y sesenta años. Legajo 2797, pt. 1.

Relación de los reos que salieron en el auto particular de fee que celebró el Santo Oficio de la Ynquisición de Murcia en el conbento de San Francisco Domingo 15 de Marco de 1682. Legajo 2819, pt. 1.

Ynquisición de Murcia, cartas, espedientes y memoriales del año de 1680. Legajo 2835.

Correspondencia, Inquisición de Murcia al Consejo Supremo de la Inquisición, 1681. Legajo 2836.

Correspondencia, Inquisición de Murcia al Consejo Supremo de la Inquisición, 1681. Legajo 2837.

Relación de causas de fe pendientes y despachadas en este Santo Officio desde 23 de Noviembre de 1683 hasta oi día de la fecha [16 de mayo de 1684]. Legajo 2838.

[Correspondence between Supreme Council of the Inquisition and Mexican Tribunal], 1579–1594. Libro 1048.

[Correspondence between Supreme Council of the Inquisition and Mexican Tribunal], 1595–1603. Libro 1049.

México—Libro nono de cartas de la Inquisición de la Nueva España, al consejo de Inquisición desde el año de [1649] hasta el de [1653]. Libro 1055.

Corral de Almaguer

Libro primero de bautismos, 1539–1574.

Libro tercero de bautismos, 1580–1599.

ARCHIVO GENERAL DE INDIAS, SEVILLE

Sección de Audiencia de Guadalajara

Ynformación resibida de officio en la audiencia real del nuevo reyno de galicia contra lo que hiso de parte Luis de Caravajal de la Cueva, governador y capitán general del nuevo reyno de León va al real consejo de las yndias, 1587. Legajo 47, N. 47.

Sección de Audiencia de México

[Correspondence], 1591–1593. Legajo 22.

[Correspondence], 1595–. Legajo 23.

[Report of the people who remained in New Mexico], 1601. Legajo 26.

Fray Pedro de San Luis a Felipe II, March 12, 1578. Legajo 103, R. 2.

Traslado de las ynformaciones, autos y otras diligencias que se hizieron contra el Capitán Gaspar Castaño de Sosa y sus soldados sobre aver ydo al nuevo méxico, 1592. Legajo 220.

Informaciones de oficio y parte, Domingo Martínez de Zearrata y Pedro de Zearrata, participación en la jornada a Nuevo México en busca de Capitán Gaspar Castaño, 1592. Legajo 220, N. 24.

[Instructions to Captain Juan Morlete for an expedition to New Mexico in pursuit of Gaspar Castaño de Sosa and his companions], October 1, 1590. Legajo 220, exp. 30-A.

Sección de Contratación

Ante los oidores de la Contratación . . . en Cádiz y Sevilla para embargar perteneciente a portugueses que venia en los galeones y flotas del aquel año; varios autos y diligencias, 1641–1642. Legajo 102B.

Expediente de concesión de licencia para pasar a Nueva España a favor de Pedro Robledo, vecino de Carmena, con su muger, Catalina López y a sus hijos, Ana, Diego, Luis y Lucía, y a su sobrino Luis, a vivir con sus primos, Miguel de Sandoval y Catalina Sandoval, vecinos de México, 1574. Legajo 2055, no. 77.

Relación de pasajeros a Nueva España encabezada por Alonso de Oñate, encargado de llevar refuerzos para la jornada de Nuevo México, dirigida por su hermano Juan de Oñate y el maestre de campo Vicente de Saldívar; le acompañan los siguientes pilotos, mosqueteros y carpinteros de ribera, March 20, 1604. Legajo 5281, no. 45.

Sección de Indiferente

Asiento y capitulación con el Capitan Luys de Carvajal sobre el descubrimiento y población del Nuevo Reyno de León, May 31, 1579. Legajo 416, L. 7.

Orden del rey a la Casa de Contratación, June 14, 1579. Legajo 416, L. 7.

Sección de Patronato

Asiento y capitulación que hizo la Audiencia de México con Cristóbal Martín, sobre ir, en persona, al descubrimiento, pacificación y población de Nuevo México, bajo las condiciónes que expone, October 26, 1583. Legajo 22, R. 6.

Asiento y capitulación que el virrey de Nueva España, Marqués de Villamanrique, hizo con Juan Bautista de Lomas Colmenares, sobre el descubrimiento y población de las provincias del Nuevo México, March 11, 1589. Legajo 22, R. 8.

Capitulaciónes hechas por Juan Baptista de Lomas Colmenares con el virrey de Nueva España, Marques de Villamanrique, sobre el descubrimiento de Nuevo México, February 15, 1589. Legajo 22, R. 9.

BIBLIOTECA NACIONAL, MADRID

Noticias curiosas sobre diferentes materias, recopiladas y anotadas por el Licenciado Sebastian de Orozco: no. 49, Relación del aucto de la fee celebrado en la cibdad de murcia por los ss. inquisidores dia de la ascensión que fue a xx de mayo de 1563 años. MS. 9175.

Noticias curiosas sobre diferentes materias, recopiladas y anotadas por el Licenciado Sebastian de Orozco: no. 60, Relación de las personas que salieron al aucto que hizo el Sancto Oficio de la inquisición en Murcia domingo dia de nra. señora ocho dias de setiembre de mill y quinentos y sesenta años. MS. 9175.

Relación de las operaciones del Duque de Escalona, Marques de Villena, desde su arribo a Nueva España hasta que fue dispuesto, y copia del manifesto del Conde de Santiesteban, hijo del dicho Sr. Duque, a favor de su padre y la respuesta a este de . . . Don Juan de Pálafox y Mendoza, 1643. MS. 12054.

MUSEO CANARIO, LAS PALMAS, CANARY ISLANDS

Proceso seguido en el S.O. contra Estévan de Jerez, por declarar en cierta información que Francisco de Vera Muxíca era cristiano viejo siendo como era, descendiente de judíos, conversos, etc., 1609. Fondo Antiguo, XCIV-10.

Proceso seguido en el S.O. contra Francisco Rodríguez, vecino de Garachico, porque en cierta información de limpieza de sangre que para pasar Indias con cierta cantidad de vino hizo Juan Núñez Jaimez, declaro ser este cristiano viejo, siendo notorio descendiente de los Almonte, naturales de Lepe, reconciliados por el Tribunal, 1584. Fondo Antiguo, CXXXIII-20.

Libro primero de genealogías, 1528. Fondo Antiguo, CLII-1.

Libro segundo de genealogías, 1628. Fondo Antiguo, CLII-2.

ARCHIVO PROVINCIAL DE TOLEDO

[Juan Robledo, apothecary of Toledo, rents shops in the Plaza de San Salvador from Domingo Pérez], June 11, 1567. Notarías, Bernardino de Navarra. Legajo 1973.

ARCHIVO HISTÓRICO MUNICIPAL DE LORCA

Libro de propios, 1473–1474.

Padrones de Santiago, San Mateo, San Juan, y Santa María, 1660.

Pleito, testimonios y otras diligencias judiciales sobre la partición de bienes y herencia de Lucía Rael, August 17, 1592. A° 1590.

[Protocolos], tomo 4, Diego de Lisbona, 1508–1587.

[Protocolos], tomo 40, Thomas Giner, 1558.

[Protocolos], tomo 234, Melchior de Caizedo, 1603–1611.

[Protocolos], tomo 435, Alonso del Pozo Gamboa, 1655–1662.

[Protocolos], tomo 440, Gerónimo Ferrer, 1660.

[Protocolos], tomo 469, 1667.

[Protocolos], tomo 470, Jerónimo Resalt, 1667–1669.

[Protocolos], tomo 474, 1668.

[Protocolos], tomo 479, Lucas Hernando de Quiros, 1669–1671.

[Protocolos], tomo 489, sección 1, Andrés de Ateguí Mula, 1672–1675.

FONDO CULTURAL ESPÍN, LORCA

Ejecutoria de nobleza de los Morata de Tajuña, Probanza que hizo Diego de Morata, 1555 [copy, April 28, 1766], 1-2-4.

ARCHIVO DIOCESANO DE CUENCA, ARCHIVO DE LA INQUISICIÓN

Proceso de Juan de Atienza, Cifuentes, judaismo, relajado, incompleto, 1494. Legajo 14, exp. 278.

Proceso de Diego Hernández, cristiano nuevo del Corral de Almaguer, judaismo, relajado, 1518. Legajo 71, exp. 1044.

Proceso de Juan de Alcalá, natural de Medinaceli, 1558. Legajo 212, exp. 2448.

Proceso de Isabel Romero, muger de Alonso del Campo, Quintinar de la Orden, judaismo, reconciliada, 1589. Legajo 323, exp. 4642.

Confesiones. Série Sexta. Legajo 749, exp. 7.

PARROQUIA DE SANTO TOMÉ, TOLEDO

Libro de bautismos, 1563–1572.
Libro de matrimonios, 1574–1641.

IGLESIA DEL SALVADOR, SANTA CRUZ DE LA PALMA, CANARY ISLANDS

Libro primero de bautismos, 1569.

ARCHIVO DIOCESANO DE CIUDAD RODRIGO

Padrones, 1598, 1612–1615, 1617–1623, 1625, 1629.
Parroquia de San Juan Bautista, matrimonios y bautismos, ca. 1596–ca. 1623. Libro 219.

ARCHIVO HISTÓRICO DIOCESANO DE LA LAGUNA DE TENERIFE, CANARY ISLANDS

Nuestra Señora de la Concepción, Libro segundo de bautismos, ca. 1589–ca. 1596.

ARCHIVO HISTÓRICO DIOCESANO DE CANARIAS, LAS PALMAS, CANARY ISLANDS

Libros 2–5 de bautismos, 1529–1587.

PARROQUIA DE SAN MATEO, LORCA

Libro quarto de bautismos.
Libro primero de belaciones.
Libro segundo de belaciones.

PARROQUIA DE SAN PATRICIO, LORCA

Libro primero de bautismos.

ARCHIVO DEL CATEDRAL DE ORIHUELA

Parroquia del Salvador
Libro segundo de bautismos.
Libro quinto de bautismos.
Libro de desposorios, 1618–1664.

IGLESIA DE SANTIAGO, ORIHUELA

Libro quinto de bautismos.

PARROQUIA DE SANTO TOMÉ, CALDAS DE REIES

Libros sacramentales, bautizados.

Portugal

ARQUIVO NACIONAL DA TORRE DO TOMBO, LISBON

Secção de Inquisição

Processo de Manoel de Mascarenhas, 1671. Coimbra, no. 356.

Processo de Jorge Castanho, 1629. Coimbra, no. 1939.

Processo de Francisco Lobo, 1604. Coimbra, no. 2838.

Processo de Tristão Soares Mascarenhas, 1626. Coimbra, no. 3919.

Processo de Jorge de Almeida Mascarenhas, 1625. Coimbra, no. 4101.

Processo de Francisca Fernandes, 1535. Coimbra, no. 4345.

Processo de Gaspar de Carvalho, 1636. Coimbra, no. 4347.

Processo de Manoel Castanho, 1626. Coimbra, no. 5040.

Processo de Ana Mascarenhas, 1633. Coimbra, no. 5044.

Processo de Francisco Mascarenhas, 1625. Coimbra, no. 6807.

Processo de Briolana de Sousa, 1599. Coimbra, no. 7994.

Processo de Manoel de Mascarenhas, 1671. Coimbra, no. 8171.

Processo de Ines Mascarenhas, 1626. Coimbra, no. 9515.

Processo de Antonia Mascarenhas, 1624. Coimbra, no. 9753.

Processo de Isabel Castanho, 1591. Evora, no. 1641.

Processo de Diogo Castanho, 1589. Evora, no. 3649.

Processo de Isabel Mascarenhas, 1639. Evora, no. 8220.

Processo de Alvaro Fernandes Castanho, 1635. Evora, no. 10531.

Processo de Alvaro Gomes, 1547. Lisboa, no. 191.

Processo de Joana de Sousa, 1618. Lisboa, no. 2743.

Processo de Antonio Mascarenhas, 1673. Lisboa, no. 5704.

Processo de Nicalou Castanho, 1554. Lisboa, no. 5944.

Processo de Gaspar de Sousa, 1621. Lisboa, no. 8485.

Processo de Gaspar Afonso Castanho, 1592. Lisboa, no. 12839.

Culpas de Judaismo: Culpas vindas das inquisições espanholas contra judaiçantes de Portugal; correspondencia das referidas inquisições; listas dos acusados por culpas diversas, 1587–1635. Coimbra, livro 70.

France

ARCHIVES DEPARTMENTALES ANNEX, BORDEAUX

Registre des baptêmes de Saint-André de Bordeaux. Archives Municipal, GG28, acte no. 2419.

LA PAROISSE DE SAINT-JEAN-DU-PEROT, LA ROCHELLE

Les Archives de mariage.

United States

NATIONAL ARCHIVES AND RECORDS ADMINISTRATION, WASHINGTON, D.C.

Veterans Administration. Applications for Headstones and Markers, 1975. Record Group 15, entry 52.

NEW MEXICO STATE RECORDS CENTER AND ARCHIVES, SANTA FE

Spanish Archives of New Mexico, Series 1

Manuel Delgado, settlement of estate, 1815. No. 252, microfilm, reel 2, frames 365–387.

Spanish Archives of New Mexico, Series 2

Census of the jurisdiction of Santa Fe, 1790. No. 1096a, microfilm, reel 12.

Governor Fernando de la Concha, requesting pension for the family of the late Lieutenant Vicente Troncoso, April 20, 1793. No. 1230, microfilm, reel 13, frames 224–225.

Benjamin M. Read Collection

Census and Report on Missions of New Mexico of the Custody of Conversion of San Pablo for the Years 1793 and 1794, October 30, 1795. Microfilm, reel 21, frames 535–541.

Mexican Archives of New Mexico

Census of 1823, microfilm, reel 3, frames 219–285.

Baca Family Papers

Box 1, folders 12–24. Acc. no. 1963-002.

Cesarita Sandoval Martínez–Alonso C. Martínez Family Papers

Sermon denouncing the superstitious and evil usages which have infiltrated the form of Catholic worship, n.d. Acc. no. 1982-001.

Church of Jesus Christ of Latter-Day Saints

Sacramental records. Microfilm.

Miscellaneous

Bureau of the Census. *Population Schedules of the Seventh Census of the United States, 1850, New Mexico*. Microcopy no. 432.

———. *Population Schedules of the Eighth Census of the United States, 1860, New Mexico, Schedule 1, Free Inhabitants*. Microfilm.

———. *Population Schedules of the Ninth Census of the United States, 1870, New Mexico, Schedule 1, Inhabitants*. Microfilm.

———. *Tenth Census of Population, 1880, New Mexico*. Microfilm.

———. *Twelfth Census of Population, 1900, New Mexico.* Microfilm.
———. *Thirteenth Census of Population, 1910, New Mexico.* Microfilm.
———. *Fourteenth Census of Population, 1920, New Mexico.* Microfilm.
Myra Ellen Jenkins, chief, Historical Services Division, to Anne Lucero, Santa Fe, September 29, 1976. Historical File, no. 103.
Records of the United States Territorial and New Mexico District Court for Bernalillo County. Acc. no. 1959-124. Civil Case File, box 22, no. 350.
Taos County Records, Probate/Marriage Register, 1865–1905.

CENTER FOR SOUTHWEST RESEARCH, ZIMMERMAN LIBRARY, UNIVERSITY OF NEW MEXICO, ALBUQUERQUE

Bibo, Arthur. "Genealogy of the Bibo Family." Manuscript, 1968.

Frank Applegate Collection
Austin, Mary. "Spanish Colonial Arts." MS. 97. Box 1, folder 42.
Austin, Mary. "Spanish Colonial Arts Manuscript, Santos, Particularly Transcribed by Alta Applegate, chapter XIV, 'Santos.'" MS. 97. Box 1, folder 42.

T. M. Pearce Collection
Austin, Mary. "Spanish Colonial Arts." MS. 255. Box 2, folder 20.
Austin, Mary. "Spanish Colonial Arts." MS. 255. Box 2, folder 21.

ALBUQUERQUE MUSEUM

Photograph no. 80.152/4, 1903.

ARCHIVES OF THE ARCHDIOCESE OF SANTA FE, NEW MEXICO

Carta Pastoral del Ilmo. Señor Don Juan Lamy al clero y a los fieles de este obispado, Santa Fe, fiesta de Epifanía, 1854. Microfilm, reel 56, frames 320–321.
Mission of Isleta. Baptisms. Microfilm, reel 5.
Parish of Guadalupe, Taos. Baptisms. Microfilm, reel 25-A.
Parish of Nuestra Señora de los Dolores, Sandía. Marriages. Microfilm, reel 28.
Parish of St. Joseph, Anton Chico. Marriages. Microfilm, reel 61-A.
Parish of San Felipe de Neri, Albuquerque. Marriages. Microfilm, reel 26.
Parish of San Francisco, Santa Fe. Baptisms. Microfilm, reel 15.
Parish of San Francisco, Santa Fe. Marriages. Microfilm, reel 31.
Parish of Santa Cruz de la Cañada. Baptisms. Microfilm, reel 13.

BRIGHAM YOUNG UNIVERSITY LIBRARY, PROVO, UTAH

Don Domingo Jironza Petríz de Cruzat [*sic*], Pueblo del Paso, October 15, 1683. Vault MS. 1509. Box 1, folder 12, Collection of Spanish Manuscripts, Archives and Manuscripts.

HENRY E. HUNTINGTON LIBRARY, SAN MARINO, CALIFORNIA

Austin (Mary Hunter) Collection

Miscellaneous notes on Spanish Mexico and New Mexico. AU 361, box 24.

"Social Survey of Taos County, New Mexico." Manuscript, 1919. AU 543.

SECONDARY SOURCES

Ablashi, Dharam V., Louise G. Chatlynne, James E. Whitman, Jr., and Ethel Cesarman. "Spectrum of Kaposi's Sarcoma–Associated Herpesvirus, or Human Herpesvirus 8, Diseases." *Clinical Microbiology Reviews* 15 (2002): 439–464.

Ahmed, A. Razzaque, R. Wagner, K. Khatri, G. Notani, Z. Awdeh, C. A. Alper, and E. J. Yunis. "Major Histocompatibility Complex Haplotypes and Class II Genes in Non-Jewish Patients with Pemphigus Vulgaris." *Proceedings of the National Academy of Sciences* 88 (1991): 5056–5060.

Ahmed, A. Razzaque, E. J. Yunis, K. Khatri, R. Wagner, G. Notani, Z. Awdeh, and C. A. Alper. "Major Histocompatibility Complex Haplotypes Studies in Ashkenazi Jewish Patients with Pemphigus Vulgaris." *Proceedings of the National Academy of Sciences* 87 (1990): 7658–7662.

Alberro, Solange. *Inquisición y sociedad en México, 1571–1700*. Mexico City: Fondo de Cultura Económica, 1988.

Albuquerque City Directory. El Paso, Tex.: Hudspeth, 1949–1972.

Albuquerque City Directory. Dallas: Polk, 1973–1992.

Alessio Robles, Vito. *Francisco de Urdiñola y el norte de la Nueva España*. Mexico City: Imprenta Mundial, 1931.

Almond, Steven. "Hispanics Rediscover Jewish Identity." *New Mexico Magazine*, June 1991, pp. 26, 31.

Alpert, Michael. *Crypto-Judaism and the Spanish Inquisition*. Houndsmills, Eng.: Palgrave, 2001.

Anaya Hernández, Luis Alberto. *Judeoconversos e Inquisición en las Islas Canarias, 1402–1605*. Las Palmas: Cabildo Insular de Gran Canaria, 1996.

Aragón, John Ray de. *Padre Martínez and Bishop Lamy*. Las Vegas, N.M.: Pan-American, 1978.

Assis, Yom Tov. "Jaime II y los judíos en la Corona de Aragón." *Anales de la Universidad de Alicante: Historia Medieval* 11 (1997): 331–371.

Atencio, Tomás. "The Converso Legacy in New Mexico Hispano Protestantism." *El Caminante*, no. 2 (2003): 10–15.

———. "Crypto-Jewish Remnants in Manito Society and Culture." *Jewish Folklore and Ethnology Review* 18 (1996): 59–68.

Azevedo, J. Lúcio de. *História dos cristãos-novos portugueses*. 3rd ed. Lisbon: Clássica Editora, 1989.

Baer, Yitzhak. *A History of the Jews in Christian Spain*. 2 vols. Philadelphia: Jewish Publication Society of America, 1971.

Bakewell, Peter J. *Silver Mining and Society in Colonial Mexico: Zacatecas, 1546–1700*. Cambridge: Cambridge University Press, 1971.

Banker, Mark T. "Missionary to His Own People: José Ynes Perea and Hispanic Presbyterianism in New Mexico." In Carl Guarneri and David Álvarez, eds., *Religion and Society in the American West*, pp. 79–104. Lanham, Md.: University Press of America, 1987.

Barber, Russell J. "The Agua Mansa Cemetery: An Indicator of Ethnic Identification in a Mexican-American Community." In Richard M. Meyer, ed., *Ethnicity and the American Cemetery*, pp. 156–172. Bowling Green, Ohio: Bowling Green State University Popular Press, 1993.

Beinart, Haim. *The Expulsion of the Jews from Spain*. Translated by Jeffrey M. Green. Oxford: Littman Library of Jewish Civilization, 2002.

———. *Los conversos ante el tribunal de la Inquisición*. Barcelona: Riopiedras Ediciones, 1983.

———. *Los judíos en España*. Madrid: Editorial Mapfre, 1992.

Benrimo, Dorothy. *Camposantos*. Fort Worth, Tex.: Amon Carter Museum of Western Art, 1966.

Bernal, Daniel Mesa. *De los judíos en la historia de Colombia*. Santa Fe de Bogotá: Planeta, 1996.

Bernal Estévez, Ángel. *El consejo de Ciudad Rodrigo y su tierra durante el siglo XV*. Salamanca: Ediciones de la Diputación de Salamanca, 1989.

Bernal Segura, Juan. *Topónimos árabes de la provincia de Murcia*. Murcia: Patronato de Cultura de la Excma. Diputación de Murcia, 1952.

Biographical Directory of the American Congress, 1774–1989. Washington, D.C.: Government Printing Office, 1989.

Blake, Fay Forman. "The Hidden Jews of New Mexico." *Journal of Progressive Judaism* 8 (1997): 5–26.

Blatt, Warren. "Reading Hebrew Headstones." Available at: http://www.jewishgen.org/infofiles/tombstones.html.

Blázquez Miguel, Juan. "Catálogo de los procesos inquisitoriales del Tribunal del Santo Oficio de Murcia." *Murgetana* 74 (1987): 7–109.

———. *El tribunal de la Inquisición en Murcia*. Murcia: Real Academia Alfonso X el Sabio, 1986.

Bocanegra, Mathías de. *Jews and the Inquisition of Mexico: The Great Auto de Fe of 1649 as Related by Mathías de Bocanegra*. Translated and edited by Seymour B. Liebman. Lawrence, Kans.: Coronado Press, 1974.

Bodian, Miriam. *Hebrews of the Portuguese Nation: Conversos and Community in Early Modern Amsterdam*. Bloomington: Indiana University Press, 1997.

Böhm, Günther. *Historia de los judíos en Chile*. Vol. 1, *Periódo colonial: El bachiller Francisco Maldonado de Silva, 1592–1639*. Santiago: Editorial Andrés Bello, 1984.

Bokser Liwerant, Judit, and Alicia Gojman de Backal, eds. *Encuentro y alteridad: Vida y cultura judía en América Latina.* Mexico City: Universidad Nacional Autónoma de México, Universidad Hebrea de Jerusalén, Asociación Mexicana de Amigos de la Universidad de Tel Aviv, and Fondo de Cultura Económica, 1999.

Bolton, Herbert Eugene. *Coronado: Knight of Pueblos and Plains.* New York: Whittlesey House, 1949.

Bonne-Tamir, B., S. Ashbel, and R. Kenett. "Genetic Markers: Benign and Normal Traits of Ashkenazi Jews." In Richard M. Goodman and Arno G. Motulsky, eds., *Genetic Diseases Among Ashkenazi Jews*, pp. 59–76. New York: Raven Press, 1979.

Bonnin-LaRochelle, Jean-Claude. *Histoire des juifs de La Rochelle.* La Rochelle: Bonnin-LaRochelle, 1999.

Borah, Woodrow. "The Portuguese of Tulancingo and the Special *Donativo* of 1642–1643." *Jahrbuch für Geschichte von Staat, Wirthchaft und Gessellschaft Lateinamerikas* 1 (1964): 386–398.

Bordenave, Kristine K., Jeffrey Griffith, Stanley M. Hordes, Thomas M. Williams, and R. Steven Padilla. "The Historical and Geomedical Immunogenetics of Pemphigus Among the Descendants of Sephardic Jews in New Mexico." *Archives of Dermatology* 137 (2001): 825–826.

Bornkamm, Günter. *Paul.* Translated by D. M. G. Stalker. New York: Harper & Row, 1971.

Boxer, Charles. *The Dutch in Brazil: 1624–1654.* Oxford: Clarendon Press, 1957.

Boyajian, James C. *Portuguese Bankers at the Court of Spain, 1626–1650.* New Brunswick, N.J.: Rutgers University Press, 1983.

Boyd-Bowman, Peter. "Los nombres de pila en México desde 1540 hasta 1950." *Nueva Revista de Filología Hispánica* 19 (1970): 12–48.

Boyle, Susan Calafate. *Los Capitalistas: Hispano Merchants and the Santa Fe Trade.* Albuquerque: University of New Mexico Press, 1997.

Brown, John Gary. *Soul in the Stone: Cemetery Art from America's Heartland.* Lawrence: University Press of Kansas, 1994.

Bustamante, Adrian. "'The Matter Was Never Resolved': The *Casta* System in Colonial New Mexico, 1693–1823." *New Mexico Historical Review* 66 (1991): 143–163.

Calero, Luis F. *Chiefdoms Under Siege: Spain's Rule and Native Adaption in the Southern Colombian Andes, 1535–1700.* Albuquerque: University of New Mexico Press, 1997.

Caro Baroja, Julio. *Los judíos en la España moderna y contemporánea.* 3 vols. Madrid: Ediciones ISTMO, 1978.

———. *La sociedad criptojudía en la corte de Felipe IV.* Madrid: Imprenta y Editorial Maestre, 1963.

Carrete Parrondo, Carlos. *Provincia de Salamanca.* Salamanca: Universidad Pontificia de Salamanca, 1981.

Carroll, Michael P. "The Debate over a Crypto-Jewish Presence in New Mexico: The Role of Ethnographic Allegory and Orientalism." *Sociology of Religion* 63 (2002): 1–19.

Carter, Thomas P. *Mexican Americans in School: A History of Educational Neglect.* New York: College Entrance Examination Board, 1970.

Carvajal, Luis de. *The Enlightened: The Writings of Luis de Carvajal, el Mozo.* Translated and edited by Seymour B. Liebman. Coral Gables, Fla.: University of Miami Press, 1967.

Castaño de Sosa, Gaspar. *A Colony on the Move: Gaspar Castaño de Sosa's Journal, 1590–1591.* Annotated by Albert H. Schroeder and translated by Don S. Matson. Santa Fe: School of American Research, 1965.

Castro, Américo. *The Structure of Spanish History.* Princeton, N.J.: Princeton University Press, 1954.

Castro Morales, Efraín. "Los cuadros de castas de la Nueva España." *Jahrbuch für Geschichte von Staat, Wirtschaft, und Gesellschaft Lateinamerikas* 20 (1983): 671–690.

Cerfaux, Lucien. *The Spiritual Journey of Saint Paul.* New York: Sheed and Ward, 1968.

Chávez, Fray Angelico. *But Time and Chance: The Story of Padre Martínez of Taos.* Santa Fe: Sunshine Press, 1981.

———. *Origins of New Mexico Families in the Spanish Colonial Period.* Santa Fe: Gannon, 1975.

———, comp. *Archives of the Archdiocese of Santa Fe, 1678–1900.* Washington, D.C.: Academy of American Franciscan History, 1957.

Chipman, Donald. "The Oñate-Moctezuma-Zaldivar Families of Northern New Spain." *New Mexico Historical Review* 52 (1977): 297–310.

Chua-Eoan, Howard G. "Plight of the Conversos." *Time* [international edition], March 4, 1991, p. 7.

Cohen, Martin A. *The Martyr: Luis de Carvajal, a Secret Jew in Sixteenth-Century Mexico.* Philadelphia: Jewish Publication Society of America, 1973. Reprint, Albuquerque: University of New Mexico Press, 2001.

Colligan, John B. *The Juan Páez Hurtado Expedition of 1695: Fraud in Recruiting Colonists for New Mexico.* Albuquerque: University of New Mexico Press, 1995.

———. "More About Diego de Vera Perdomo." *Herencia: Quarterly Journal of the Hispanic Genealogical Research Center of New Mexico* 7 (1999): 1–8.

Contreras Contreras, Jaime. *Sotos contra Riquelmes: Regidores, inquisidores y criptojudíos.* Madrid: Muchnik, 1992.

Corominas, Joan. *Diccionario crítico etimológico de la lengua castellana.* 4 vols. Madrid: Editorial Gredos, 1954–1957.

Cossío, David Albert. *Historia de Nuevo León.* 6 vols. Monterrey: Cantú Leal, 1925–1933.

Coÿne, Paul-Louis. *Dictionnaire des familles protestantes de Bordeaux aux XVIIe siècle.* Fasc. 4. Bordeaux: Coÿne, 1994.

Cross, Harry. "Commerce and Orthodoxy: A Spanish Response to Portuguese Commercial Penetration in the Viceroyalty of Peru, 1580–1640." *Americas* 35 (1978): 151–167.

de la Cuadra Blanco, Juan Rafael. "El Escorial como nuevo templo de Salamón en la literatura de la época (II)." Available at: http://sapiens.ya.com/jrcuadra/jrfuent3.htm.

de la Mota y Escobar, Alonso. *Descripción geográfica de los reinos de Nueva Galicia, Nueva Vizcaya, y Nuevo León.* Guadalajara: Robredo, 1966.

Deutsch, Sarah. *No Separate Refuge: Culture, Class, and Gender on an Anglo-Hispanic Frontier in the American Southwest, 1880–1940.* New York: Oxford University Press, 1987.

Diccionario de Autoridades. 3 vols. 1726–1737. Facsimile, Madrid: Editorial Gredos, 1976.

Domínguez Nafria, Juan Carlos. *La Inquisición de Murcia en el siglo XVI: El licenciado Cascales.* Murcia: Real Academia Alfonso X el Sabio, 1991.

Domínguez Ortíz, Antonio. "Historical Research on Spanish Conversos in the Last Fifteen Years." In M. P. Hornik, ed., *Collected Studies in Honour of Américo Castro's Eightieth Year*, pp. 63–82. Oxford: Lincombe Lodge Research Library, 1965.

———. *La clase social de los conversos en Castilla en la edad moderna.* 1955. Facsimile, Granada: Universidad de Granada, 1991.

———. *Los conversos de orígin judío despues de la expulsión.* Madrid, 1955.

———. *Los judeoconversos en la España moderna.* Madrid: Editorial Mapfre, 1992

Eimeric, Nicolau. *Manual de inquisidores, para uso de las inquisiciones de España y Portugal, o compendio de la obra titulada Directorio de inquisidores.* Mompelier, 1821.

Eliade, Mircea, ed. *The Encyclopedia of Religion.* 16 vols. New York: Macmillan, 1987.

Ellis, Nathan A., Susan Ciocci, Maria Proytcheva, David Lennon, Joanna Groden, and James German. "The Ashkenazic Jewish Bloom Syndrome Mutation blm^{ash} Is Present in Non-Jewish Americans of Spanish Ancestry." *American Journal of Human Genetics* 63 (1998): 1685–1693.

Esquibel, José Antonio. "The Álvarez de Toledo Family." Manuscript, Hispanic Genealogical Research Center of New Mexico, Albuquerque.

———. "The Ancestral Iberian Roots of the Quintana Family of New Mexico." Manuscript, Hispanic Genealogical Research Center of New Mexico, Albuquerque.

———. "The Formative Era for New Mexico's Colonial Population: 1693–

1700." In Claire Farago and Donna Pierce, eds., *Transforming Images: Locating New Mexico Santos In-between Worlds*. University Park: Pennsylvania State University Press, 2005.

———. "The Jewish-Converso Ancestry of Doña Beatriz de Estrada, Wife of Don Francisco Vásquez de Coronado." *Nuestras Raíces* 9 (1997): 134–143.

———. "New Light on the Jewish-Converso Ancestry of Don Juan de Oñate: A Research Note." *Colonial Latin American Historical Review* 7 (1998): 175–190.

———. "The Romero Family of Seventeenth-Century New Mexico," part 1. *Herencia: Quarterly Journal of the Hispanic Genealogical Research Center of New Mexico* 11, no. 1 (2003): 1–30.

———. "The Romero Family of Seventeenth-Century New Mexico," part 2. *Herencia: Quarterly Journal of the Hispanic Genealogical Research Center of New Mexico* 11, no. 3 (2003): 2–20.

Esquibel, José Antonio, and John B. Colligan. *The Spanish Recolonization of New Mexico: An Account of the Families Recruited in Mexico City in 1693*. Albuquerque: Hispanic Genealogical Society of New Mexico, 1999.

Expulsion and Memory: Descendants of the Hidden Jews. Directed by Simcha Jacobovici and Roger Pyke. Toronto: Associated Producers, 1996. Videocassette.

Ferry, Barbara, and Debbie Nathan. "Mistaken Identity? The Case of New Mexico's 'Hidden Jews.'" *Atlantic Monthly*, December 2000, pp. 85–96.

Ferry, Robert. "The Blancas: Women, Honor, and the Jewish Community in Seventeenth-Century Mexico." Paper presented at the Fourteenth Annual Conference of the New Mexico Jewish Historical Society, Albuquerque, November 10, 2001.

Fink, Augusta. *I-Mary: A Biography of Mary Austin*. Tucson: University of Arizona Press, 1983.

Flint, Richard, and Shirley Cushing Flint, eds. *The Coronado Expedition to Tierra Nueva: The 1540–1542 Route Across the Southwest*. Boulder: University of Colorado Press, 1997.

Frank, Larry. *New Kingdom of the Saints*. Santa Fe: Red Crane Books, 1992.

Frank, Ross. *From Settler to Citizen: New Mexican Economic Development and the Creation of Vecino Society, 1750–1820*. Berkeley: University of California Press, 2000.

Fromm, Annette. "Material Culture as Expressive of Crypto-Jewish Identity in New Mexico." Manuscript, 2002. New Mexico State Records Center and Archives, Santa Fe.

Galbis Díaz, María del Carmen, ed. *Archivo General de Indias: Catálogo de pasajeros a Indias, siglos XVI, XVII y XVIII*. Vol. 6, *1578–1585*. Seville: Ministerio de Cultura, 1986.

Gallegos, Bernardo P. *Literacy, Education, and Society in New Mexico, 1693–1821*. Albuquerque: University of New Mexico Press, 1992.

Garate, Donald T. "Juan de Oñate's *Prueba de Caballero*, 1625: A Look at His Ancestral Heritage." *Colonial Latin American Historical Review* 7 (1998): 129–173.

García César, María Fuencisla. *El pasado judío de Ciudad Rodrigo*. Salamanca: Universidad Pontificia de Salamanca, 1992.

García-Abásalo, Antonio F. *Martín Enríquez y la reforma de 1568 en Nueva España*. Seville: Diputación Provincial de Sevilla, 1983.

Gathering Up Again: Fiesta in Santa Fe. Directed by Jeanette DeBouzek and Diane Reyna. Albuquerque: Quotidian Independent Documentary Research, 1992. Videocassette.

Gerber, Jane S. *The Jews of Spain: A History of the Sephardic Experience*. New York: Free Press, 1992.

Gerhard, Peter. *The Northern Frontier of New Spain*. Princeton, N.J.: Princeton University Press, 1982.

Getz, Lynne Marie. *Schools of Their Own: The Education of Hispanos in New Mexico, 1850–1940*. Albuquerque: University of New Mexico Press, 1997.

Gibson, Charles. *Spain in America*. New York: Harper & Row, 1967.

Gil, Davíd Bernabé. *Monarquía y patriciado urbano en Orihuela, 1445–1707*. Alicante: Caja de Ahorros Provincial de Alicante, 1989.

Gil, Juan. *Los conversos y la Inquisición sevillana*. 2 vols. Seville: Universidad de Sevilla, 2000.

Gitlitz, David M. *Secrecy and Deceit: The Religion of the Crypto-Jews*. Philadelphia: Jewish Publication Society of America, 1996. Reprint, Albuquerque: University of New Mexico Press, 2002.

Glaser, Edward. "Referencias antisemitas en la literatura peninsular de la Edad de Oro." *Nueva Revista de Filología Hispánica* 8 (1954): 39–62.

Gollaher, David L. *Circumcision: A History of the World's Most Controversial Surgery*. New York: Basic Books, 2000.

González Ortiz, José Luis, Francisco Chacón Jiménez, and Antonio Segado del Olmo. *Historia de la región murciana*. Murcia: Ediciones Mediterraneo, 1980.

Goodman, Richard M. *Genetic Disorders Among the Jewish People*. Baltimore: Johns Hopkins University Press, 1979.

Gradwohl, David Meyer. "*Benditcha Sea Vuestra Memoria*: Sephardic Jewish Cemeteries in the Caribbean and Eastern North America." *Markers: Journal of the Association of Gravestone Studies* 15 (1998): 1–25.

Gran diccionario de la lengua castellana (de autoridades). Barcelona: Fomento Comercial del Libro, 1932.

Greenleaf, Richard E. "France V. Scholes: Historian's Historian, 1897–1979." *New Mexico Historical Review* 75 (2000): 321–333.

———. "The Little War of Guadalajara—1587–1590." *New Mexico Historical Review* 43 (1968): 119–135.

———. *The Mexican Inquisition of the Sixteenth Century*. Albuquerque: University of New Mexico Press, 1969.

———. *Zumárraga and the Mexican Inquisition, 1536–1543*. Washington, D.C.: Academy of American Franciscan History, 1961.

Griswold del Castillo, Richard. *The Treaty of Guadalupe Hidalgo: A Legacy of Conflict*. Norman: University of Oklahoma Press, 1990.

Guerrero Navarette, Yolanda. *Organización y gobierno en Burgos durante el reinado de Enrique IV de Castilla, 1453–1476*. Madrid: Universidad Autónoma, 1986.

Gutiérrez, Ramón. *When Jesus Came, the Corn Mothers Went Away: Marriage, Sexuality, and Power in New Mexico, 1500–1846*. Stanford, Calif.: Stanford University Press, 1991.

Hackett, Charles Wilson, ed. *Historical Documents Relating to New Mexico, Nueva Vizcaya, and Approaches Thereto, to 1773, Collected by Adolph F. A. Bandelier and Fanny R. Bandelier*. 3 vols. Washington, D.C.: Carnegie Institution, 1937.

Hackett, Charles Wilson, ed., and Charmion Clair Shelby, trans. *Revolt of the Pueblo Indians of New Mexico and Otermín's Attempted Reconquest, 1680–1682*. 2 vols. Albuquerque: University of New Mexico Press, 1942.

Haederle, Michael. "The Hidden Jews of the Southwest." *El Palacio* 98 (1992–1993): 38–43, 56–57.

Halevy, Schulamith C. "Jewish Practices Among Contemporary Anusim." *Shofar* 18 (1999): 80–99.

———. "Manifestations of Crypto-Judaism in the American Southwest." *Jewish Folklore and Ethnology Review* 18 (1996): 68–76.

Halporn, Roberta. "American Jewish Cemeteries: A Mirror of History." In Richard M. Meyer, ed., *Ethnicity and the American Jewish Cemetery*, pp. 131–155. Bowling Green, Ohio: Bowling Green University Popular Press, 1993.

Hammer, Michael F., A. J. Redd, E. T. Wood, M. R. Bonner, H. Jarjanazi, T. Karafet, S.Santachiara-Benerecetti, A.Oppenheim, M. A. Jobling, T. Jenkins, H. Ostrer, and B. Bonné-Tamir. "Jewish and Middle Eastern Non-Jewish Populations Share a Common Pool of Y-chromosome Biallelic Haplotypes." *Proceedings of the National Academy of Sciences* 97 (2000): 6769–6774.

Hammond, George P. *Don Juan de Oñate and the Founding of New Mexico*. Santa Fe: El Palacio Press, 1927.

Hammond, George P., and Agapito Rey. *Don Juan de Oñate, Colonizer of New Mexico, 1595–1628*. Albuquerque: University of New Mexico Press, 1953.

———. *Expedition into New Mexico Made by Antonio de Espejo, 1582–1583*. Los Angeles: Quivira Society, 1929.

———. *The Rediscovery of New Mexico: The Expeditions of Chamuscado, Espejo, Castaño de Sosa, Morlete, and Leyva de Bonilla and Humaña*. Albuquerque: University of New Mexico Press, 1966.

Haring, Clarence H. *The Spanish Empire in America*. New York: Harcourt, Brace & World, 1947.

Hendricks, Rick, and Gerald J. Mandell. "Francisco de Lima, Portuguese Merchants of Parral, and the New Mexico Trade, 1638–1675." *New Mexico Historical Review* 77 (2002): 261–293.

———. "Juan Manso, Frontier Entrepreneur." *New Mexico Historical Review* 75 (2000): 339–367.

Henningsen, Gustav. "El 'Banco de Datos' del Santo Oficio: Las relaciones de causas de la inquisición española (1550–1700)." *Boletín de la Real Academia de la Historia* 174 (1977): 547–570.

———. "The Database of the Spanish Inquisition: The 'Relaciones de Causas' Project Revisited." In Heinz Mohnhaupt and Dieter Simon, eds., *Vorträge zur Justizforschung: Geschichte und Theorie,* vol. 2, pp. 43–85. Frankfurt am Main: Klostermann, 1993.

Hernández, Frances. "The Secret Jews of the Southwest." In Martin A. Cohen and Abraham J. Peck, eds., *Sephardim in the Americas: Studies in Culture and History*, pp. 411–454. Tuscaloosa: University of Alabama Press, 1993.

Hernández, Marie Theresa. *Delirio: The Fantastic, the Demonic, and the Réel.* Austin: University of Texas Press, 2002.

Hernández, Roger E. "Hispanic Jews." *Vista*, April 1995, pp. 18, 29

Hernández Martín, Luis Agustín. *Protocolos de Domingo Pérez, escribano público de La Palma (1546–1533)*. Santa Cruz de la Palma: Caja General de Ahorros de Canarias, 1999.

Hernández-Chávez, Eduardo. "Native Language Loss and Its Implications for Revitalization of Spanish in Chicano Communities." In Barbara J. Merino, Henry T. Trueba, and Fabian A. Samaniego, eds. *Language and Culture in Learning: Teaching Spanish to Native Speakers of Spanish*, pp. 58–74. Washington, D.C.: Falmer Press, 1993.

Himmerich y Valencia, Robert. *The Encomenderos of New Spain, 1521–1555*. Austin: University of Texas Press, 1991.

Hitti, Philip K. *History of the Arabs*. London: Macmillan, 1937.

Hoberman, Louisa Schell. *Mexico's Merchant Elite, 1590–1660: Silver, State, and Society*. Durham, N.C.: Duke University Press, 1991.

Hordes, Stanley M. "The Crypto-Jewish Community of New Spain, 1620–1649: A Collective Biography." Ph.D. diss., Tulane University, 1980.

———. "The Historical Context of LA 54347." In Bradley J. Vierra, *A Sixteenth-Century Spanish Campsite in the Tiguex Province*, pp. 207–221. Santa Fe: Museum of New Mexico, Laboratory of Anthropology, 1989.

———. "Historiographical Problems in the Study of the Inquisition and the Mexican Crypto-Jews in the Seventeenth Century." *American Jewish Archives* 34 (1982): 138–152.

———. "Irrigation at the Confluence of the Río Grande and Río Chama:

The Acequias de Chamita, Salazar and Hernández, 1600–1680." Report, State of New Mexico, on the relation of *S. E. Reynolds, State Engineer, Plaintiff,* v. *Roman Aragon, et al.*, Defendants, no. 7941—Civil, Río Chama Mainstream Section, Río Chama Ditches, June 24, 1996.

———. "'The Sephardic Legacy in the Southwest: The Crypto-Jews of New Mexico,' Historical Research Project Sponsored by the Latin American Institute, University of New Mexico." *Jewish Folklore and Ethnology Review* 15 (1993): 137–138.

Howell, James. *Epistolae Ho-Eliane, Familiar Letters, Domestic and Foreign.* London, 1645.

Hoyo, Eugenio del. *Historia del Nuevo Reino de León (1577–1723).* Monterrey: Instituto Tecnológico y de Estudios Superiores de Monterrey, 1972.

———. "Notas y comentarios a la 'Relación' de las personas nombradas por Luis de Carvajal y de la Cueva para llevar al descubrimiento, pacificación y población del Nuevo Reino de León, 1580." *Humánitas* 19 (1978): 251–281.

———. "¿Sefarditas en el Nuevo Reino de León?" *Humánitas* 12 (1971): 247–254.

Hume, Martin A. S. *The Spanish People: Their Origin, Growth and Influence.* London: Heinemann, 1901.

Israel, Jonathan. *Race, Class and Politics in Colonial Mexico.* Oxford: Oxford University Press, 1975.

Jackson, Gabriel. *The Making of Medieval Spain.* New York: Harcourt Brace Jovanovich, 1972.

Jacobs, Janet Liebman. *Hidden Heritage: The Legacy of the Crypto-Jews.* Berkeley: University of California Press, 2002.

Jiménez Alcázar, Juan Francisco. "Modelos sociales en la Lorca bajomedieval: Apuntes de la vida cotidiana." *Murgetana* 95 (1997): 103–120.

Jordan Terry. *Texas Graveyards, a Cultural Legacy.* Austin: University of Texas Press, 1990.

Kamen, Henry. *Inquisition and Society in Spain in the Sixteenth and Seventeenth Centuries.* Bloomington: Indiana University Press, 1985.

———. *The Spanish Inquisition.* London: Weidenfeld and Nicolson, 1965.

———. *The Spanish Inquisition: A Historical Revision.* New Haven, Conn.: Yale University Press, 1998.

Kay, Margarita Artschwager. "Health and Illness in a Mexican American Barrio." In Edward H. Spicer, ed., *Ethnic Medicine in the Southwest,* pp. 99–166. Tucson: University of Arizona Press, 1977.

Kayserling, Meyer. "The First Jew in America." In Herbert B. Adams, ed., *Columbus and His Discovery of America,* pp. 45–50. Baltimore: Johns Hopkins Press, 1892.

Kessell, John L. *Kiva, Cross, and Crown: The Pecos Indians and New Mexico, 1540–1840*. Washington, D.C.: National Park Service, 1979.

Kohut, George Alexander. "The Martyrdom of the Carabajal Family in Mexico, 1590–1601." *Jewish Tribune* (Portland, Ore.), March 25, 1904.

Kolach, Alfred J. *The Jewish Mourners Book of Why*. New York: Jonathan David, 1993.

Kramer, Wendy. *Encomienda Politics in Early Colonial Guatemala, 1524–1554: Dividing the Spoils*. Boulder, Colo.: Westview Press, 1994.

Krieger, Judith Gale. "Pablo de Santa María: His Epoch, Life, and Hebrew and Spanish Literary Production." Ph.D. diss., University of California, Los Angeles, 1988.

Kunin, Seth D. "Juggling Identities Among the Crypto-Jews of the American Southwest." *Religion* 31 (2001): 41–61.

Lacave, José Luis. *Juderías y sinagogas españolas*. Madrid: Editorial Mapfre, 1992.

Lamy, Jean Baptiste. *Archbishop Lamy: In His Own Words*. Edited and translated by Thomas J. Steele. Albuquerque: LPD Press, 2000.

Las Siete Partidas. Translated and edited by Samuel Parsons Scott. Chicago: Comparative Law Bureau, American Bar Association, 1931.

Las Siete Partidas del sabio rey Don Alonso el X, glosadas por el Lic. Gregorio López. Madrid: Amarita, 1829.

Laurenti, Joseph L. *Spanish Rare Books of the Golden Age: Guide to the Microfilm Collection*. Woodbridge, Conn.: Research Publications, 1987.

Lea, Henry Charles. *A History of the Inquisition in Spain*. 4 vols. New York: Macmillan, 1908.

León, Alonso de. *Historia de Nuevo León, con noticias sobre Coahuila, Tamaulipas, Texas y Nuevo México, escrita en el siglo XVII*. Monterrey: Universidad de Nuevo León, 1961.

León Tello, Pilar. *Los judíos de Toledo*. Madrid: Consejo Superior de Investigaciones Científicas, 1979.

Liebman, Seymour B. "The Great Conspiracy in New Spain." *Americas* 30 (1973): 18–31.

———. "The Great Conspiracy in Peru." *Americas* 28 (1971): 176–190.

———. *The Inquisitors and the Jews in the New World: Summaries of Procesos, 1500–1810, and Bibliographic Guide*. Coral Gables, Fla.: University of Miami Press, 1974.

———. *The Jews in New Spain: Faith, Flame, and the Inquisition*. Coral Gables, Fla.: University of Miami Press, 1970.

Livshits, S., R. R. Sokal, and E. Kobyliansky. "Genetic Affinities of Jewish Populations." *American Journal of Human Genetics* 49 (1991): 131–146.

Llorca, Bernardino. *La Inquisición en España*. Barcelona: Editorial Labor, 1954.

Llorente, Juan Antonio. *The History of the Inquisition of Spain*. London: Whittaker, 1826.

Lockhart, James. "Encomienda and Hacienda: The Evolution of the Great Estate in the Spanish Indies." *Hispanic American Historical Review* 49 (1969): 411–429.

Lockhart, James, and Enrique Otte, trans. and ed. *Letters and People of the Spanish Indies: The Sixteenth Century*. Cambridge: Cambridge University Press, 1976.

Loeb, Isidro. "Le Nombre des juifs de Castille et d'Espagne au moyen âge." *Revue d'Études Juives* 14 (1887): 161–183.

Lutske, Harvey. *The Book of Jewish Customs*. Northvale, N.J.: Aronson, 1995.

Malkiel, Yakov. "Hispano-Arabic *Marrano* and Its Hispano-Latin Homophone." *Journal of the American Oriental Society* 68 (1948): 175–184.

Mann, Vivian B., Thomas F. Glick, and Jerrilynn D. Dodds, eds. *Convivencia: Jews, Muslims and Christians in Medieval Spain*. New York: Jewish Museum, 1992.

Marín Padilla, Encarnación. "Relación judeoconversa durante la segunda mitad del siglo XV en Aragón: Nacimientos, hadas, circuncisiones." *Sefarád* 41 (1981): 273–300.

———. "Relación judeoconversa durante la segunda mitad del siglo XV en Aragón: Nacimientos, hadas, circuncisiones." *Sefarád* 42 (1982): 59–77.

Márquez Villanueva, Francisco. "The Converso Problem: An Assessment." In M. P. Hornik, ed., *Collected Studies in Honour of Américo Castro's Eightieth Year*, pp. 317–333. Oxford: Lincombe Lodge Research Library, 1965.

———. "Conversos y cargas consejiles en el siglo XV." *Revista de Archivos, Bibliotecas y Museos* 63 (1957): 503–540.

———. *Investigaciones sobre Juan Álvarez Gato*. Madrid: Real Academia Española 1960.

Martínez, Thomas D., Benito Estevan Montoya, and Rosina LaSalle, comps. *Santa Fe Baptisms, 1747–1848*. San Jose, Calif.: Martínez, 1993.

Martínez Carrillo, María de los Llanos. *Revolución urbana y autoridad monárquica en Murcia durante la baja edad media (1395–1420)*. Murcia: Universidad de Murcia, 1980.

Martínez Liébana, Evelio. *Los judíos de Sahagún en la transición del siglo XIV y XV*. Valladolid: Junta de Castilla y León, Consejería de Cultura y Turismo, 1993.

Martz, Linda. "Relaciones entre conversos y cristianos viejos en Toledo en la edad moderna: Unas perspectivas distintas." *Toletum* 37 (1997): 45–70.

Martz, Linda, and Julio Porres. *Toledo y los toledanos en 1561*. Toledo: Patronato "José María Cuadrado," del Consejo Superior de Investigaciones Científicas, 1974.

McDonald, Jane Fahey. "Woodcarvers Hew Saints from New Mexico Cedar." *Albuquerque Tribune*, December 18, 1984, p. B1.

Medina, José Toribio. *Historia de la Inquisición en México.* Mexico City: Ediciones Fuente Cultural, 1905.

———. *Historia del tribunal de la Inquisición de Lima, 1569–1820.* 2 vols. Santiago: Fondo Histórico y Bibliográfico J. T. Medina, 1956.

Metz, Leon. "El Paso Can Take Pride in First Thanksgiving." *El Paso Times,* March 29, 1998, p. 15.

Montenegro Duque, Ángel, José Luis Moreno Peña, and Sabino Nebreda Pérez. *Historia de Burgos: Edad media.* Burgos: Caja de Ahorros Municipal de Burgos, 1987.

Moya, Emma. "New Mexico's Sephardim: Uncovering Jewish Roots." *La Herencia del Norte* 12 (1996): 9–13.

———. "Sephardim." *La Herencia del Norte* 16 (1998): 64–65.

———. "Sephardim." *La Herencia del Norte* 18 (1998): 72.

———. "Sephardim." *La Herencia del Norte* 19 (1998): 61.

———. "Sephardim." *La Herencia del Norte* 20 (1998): 56.

———. "Sephardim." *La Herencia del Norte* 26 (2000): 54–55.

———. "Sephardim." *La Herencia del Norte* 27 (2000): 96.

———. "Sephardim." *La Herencia del Norte* 28 (2000): 56.

———. "Sephardim." *La Herencia del Norte* 29 (2001): 47.

———. "Sephardim." *La Herencia del Norte* 30 (2001): 56.

———. "Sephardim." *La Herencia del Norte* 32 (2001): 45.

Mullineaux, Lisa G., Teresa M. Castellano, Jeffrey Shaw, Lisen Axell, María E. Wood, Sami Diab, Catherine Klein, Mark Sitarik, Amie M. Deffenbaugh, and Sharon L. Graw. "Identification of Germline 185delAG BRCA1 Mutations in Non-Jewish Americans of Spanish Ancestry from the San Luis Valley, Colorado." *Cancer.* Forthcoming.

Netanyahu, Benzion. *The Marranos of Spain from the Late XIVth to the Early XVIth Century According to Contemporary Hebrew Sources.* New York: American Academy for Jewish Research, 1966.

———. *The Origins of the Inquisition in Fifteenth Century Spain.* New York: Random House, 1995.

Neulander, Judith S. "Cannibals, Castes and Crypto-Jews: Premillennial Cosmology in Postcolonial New Mexico." Ph.D. diss., Indiana University, 2001.

———. "Crypto-Jews of the Southwest: An Imagined Community." *Jewish Folklore and Ethnology Review* 16 (1994): 64–68.

———. "The New Mexican Crypto-Jewish Canon: Choosing to be 'Chosen' in Millennial Tradition." *Jewish Folklore and Ethnology Review* 18 (1996): 19–58.

New American Bible. Washington, D.C.: Confraternity of Christian Doctrine, 1991.

New Catholic Encyclopedia. New York: McGraw-Hill, 1967.

New Mexico State Business Directory. Denver: Gazetteer, 1919.

Nidel, David S. "Modern Descendants of Conversos in New Mexico." *Western States Jewish History* 16 (1984): 249–262.

Olmsted, Virginia Langham, trans. and comp. *New Mexico Spanish and Mexican Colonial Censuses, 1790, 1823, 1845*. Albuquerque: New Mexico Genealogical Society, 1975.

Os judeus portugueses entre os descobrimentos e a diáspora. Lisbon: Associação Portuguesa de Estudos Judaicos, 1994.

Pacheco, Joaquín Francisco, and Francisco de Cárdenas y Espejo, eds. *Colección de documentos inéditos relativos al descubrimiento, conquista y organización de las antiguas posesiones españoles*. 42 vols. Madrid: Imprenta de Hospicio, 1871.

Padilla y Baca, Luis Gilberto. *New Mexico Baptisms, Sandía Mission, Nuestra Señora de los Dolores, 1771–1851*. Albuquerque: Hispanic Genealogical Research Center of New Mexico, 1998.

Patai, Raphael. *On Jewish Folklore*. Detroit: Wayne State University Press, 1983.

Patai, Rafael, and Jennifer L. Patai-Wing. *The Myth of the Jewish Race*. New York: Scribner, 1975.

Paul. *The Writings of St. Paul*. Edited by Wayne A. Meeks. New York: Norton, 1972.

Payne, Stanley. *A History of Spain and Portugal*. 2 vols. Madison: University of Wisconsin Press, 1973.

Pearce, T. M. *Mary Hunter Austin*. New York: Twayne, 1965.

The Pentateuch and Haftorahs. Edited by J. H. Hertz. 2nd ed. London: Soncino Press, 1961.

Pfeufer, Lila Armijo, and Margaret Buxton, transcribers, and Margaret Leonard Windham and Evelyn Lujan Baca, comps. *New Mexico Marriages and Baptisms, San Augustín de la Isleta Church*. Albuquerque: New Mexico Genealogical Society, 1996.

Pires Gonçalves, José. *Monsaráz: Vida, morte e ressurreição de uma vila alentejana*. Lisbon: Edição de Casa do Alentejo, 1966.

Plevin, Nancy. "Conversos' Straddle Two Lives." *Albuquerque Journal*, March 31, 1991, pp. B1, B4.

———. "Secret Jews Step Out of the Shadows." *Albuquerque Journal*, March 31, 1991, pp. B1, B4.

Poole, Stafford. "The Politics of *Limpieza de Sangre*: Juan de Ovando and His Circle in the Reign of Philip II." *Americas* 55 (1999): 359–389.

Rael Gálvez, Estevan. "Identifying Captivity and Capturing Identity: Narrative of American Indian Slavery in New Mexico and Colorado, 1776–1934." Ph.D. diss., University of Michigan, 2002.

Rambaud, Pascal. "Juifs et protestants portugais a La Rochelle: Les marranes face a la Réforme (1550–1570)." *Écrits d'Ouest: Cahiers Rochelais d'Histoire Régionale d'Art et de Littérature* 7 (1998): 9–24.

Raphael, David T. *The Conquistadores and Crypto-Jews of Monterrey*. Valley Village, Calif.: Carmi House, 2001.

Réau, Louis. *Iconographie de l'art chrétien*. 2 vols. Paris: Presses Universitaires de France, 1955–1959.

Relaciones de pueblos del obispado de Cuenca. Cuenca: Diputación Provincial de Cuenca, 1983.

Ricard, Robert. *The Spiritual Conquest of Mexico: An Essay on the Apostolate and the Evangelizing Methods of the Mendicant Orders in New Spain, 1523–1572*. Translated by Lesley Byrd Simpson. Berkeley: University of California Press, 1966.

Ricciotti, Giuseppe. *Paul the Apostle*. Milwaukee: Bruce, 1953.

Riva Palacio, Vicente. *México a traves de los siglos*. 5 vols. Barcelona: Establecimiento Tipo, 1888–1889.

Roberts, Shelly. *Remaining and Becoming: Cultural Crosscurrents in an Hispano School*. Mahwah, N.J.: Erlbaum, 2001.

Robinson, Benjamin W. *The Life of Paul*. Chicago: University of Illinois Press, 1918.

Romera Iruela, Luis, and María del Carmen Galbis Díez. *Catálogo de pasajeros a Indias durante los siglos XVI, XVII y XVIII*. 7 vols. Seville: Archivo General de Indias, 1980–.

Roth, Cecil. *A History of the Marranos*. Philadelphia: Jewish Publication Society of America, 1932.

———. *A Life of Menasseh Ben Israel: Rabbi, Printer, and Diplomat*. Philadelphia: Jewish Publication Society of America, 1934.

Roth, Cecil, and Geoffrey Wigoder, eds., *Encyclopedia Judaica*. Jerusalem: Keter, 1972.

Roth, Norman. *Conversos, Inquisition, and the Expulsion of the Jews from Spain*. Madison: University of Wisconsin Press, 1995.

Roybal, Marie J., and Lila Armijo Pfeufer, extrators, and Margaret Leonard Windham and Evelyn Lujan Baca, comps. *New Mexico Marriages: Santa Fe—St. Francis Parish and Military Chapel of Our Lady of Light (La Castrense), 1728–1857*. Albuquerque: New Mexico Genealogical Society, 1997.

Rubio García, Luis, ed. *Los judíos de Murcia en la baja edad media (1350–1500), Colección documental*. 3 vols. Murcia: Universidad de Murcia, 1994.

Sabán, Mario Javier. *Judíos conversos: Los antepasados judíos de las familias tradicionales argentinas*. Buenos Aires: Editorial Distal, 1990.

Salicrú i Lluch, Roser. "La Corona de Aragón y los Nazaritas en el segundo reinado de Muhamad el Pequeño (1427–1429)." In *Actas del Congreso la frontera oriental nazarí como sujeto histórico (S. XIII–XVI)*, pp. 199–211. Almería: Instituto de Estudios Almerenses, 1997.

Sánchez, Joseph P. *The Río Abajo Frontier, 1540–1692: A History of Early Colonial New Mexico.* Albuquerque: Albuquerque Museum, 1987.

Santamaría, Francisco de. *Diccionario de mejicanismos.* Mexico City: Editorial Porrúa, 1983.

Santos, Richard. *Silent Heritage: The Sephardim and the Colonization of the Spanish North American Frontier.* San Antonio, Tex.: New Sepharad Press, 2000.

Sarávia, Antonio José. *Inquisição e cristãos-novos.* 6th ed. Lisbon: Editorial Estampa, 1994.

Sarna, Jonathan D. "The Mythical Jewish Columbus and the History of America's Jews." In Bryan F. Le Beau and Menahem Mor, eds., *Religion in the Age of Exploration: The Case of Spain and New Spain,* pp. 81–95. Omaha, Neb.: Creighton University Press, 1996.

Scholem, Gershom. "The Star of David: History of a Symbol." In *The Messianic Idea in Judaism,* pp. 257–281. New York: Schocken Books, 1971.

Scholes, France V. *Church and State in New Mexico.* Albuquerque: University of New Mexico Press, 1937.

———. "The First Decade of the Inquisition in New Mexico." *New Mexico Historical Review* 10 (1935): 195–241.

———. "Problems in the Early Ecclesiastical History of New Mexico." *New Mexico Historical Review* 7 (1932): 32–74.

———. *Troublous Times in New Mexico, 1659–1670.* Albuquerque: University of New Mexico Press, 1942.

Serrano y Sanz, Manuel. *Origines de la dominación española en América.* Madrid: Veilly-Bailliere, 1918.

Shallop, Robert L. *Wooden Saints: The Santos of New Mexico.* Feldafing: Buchhein Verlas, 1967.

Shapiro, Benjamin, and Nan Rubin. "The Hidden Jews of New Mexico Radio Project" (National Public Radio): Program One: "Search for the Buried Past" (1988); Program Two: "Rekindling the Spirit" (1992); Program Three: "Return to Iberia" (1995).

Sicroff, Albert. *Los estatuos de limpieza de sangre: Controversias entre los siglos XV y XVII.* Madrid: Taurus, 1979.

Sierro Malmierca, Feliciano. *Judíos, moriscos e inquisición en Ciudad Rodrigo.* Salamanca: Diputación de Salamanca, 1990.

Silverman, Edward R. "Heritage Refound." *New York Newsday,* November 29, 1992, p. 13.

Simmons, Marc. *The Last Conquistador: Juan de Oñate and the Settling of the Far Southwest.* Norman: University of Oklahoma Press, 1991.

Simpson, Leslie Byrd. *The Encomienda in New Spain: The Beginning of Spanish Mexico.* Rev. ed. Berkeley: University of California Press, 1982.

Snow, David H., comp. *New Mexico's First Colonists: The 1597–1600 Enlistments for New Mexico Under Juan de Oñate, Adelante [Adelantado] and Gobernador.*

Albuquerque: Hispanic Genealogical Research Center of New Mexico, 1996.

Snyder, Patricia Giniger. "America's Secret Jews." *B'nai Brith International Jewish Monthly*, October 1991, pp. 26–30, 38.

Steele, Thomas J. *Works and Days: A History of San Felipe de Neri Church, 1867–1895*. Albuquerque: Albuquerque Museum, 1983.

———, ed. *New Mexican Spanish Religious Oratory, 1800–1900*. Albuquerque: University of New Mexico Press, 1997.

Steiglitz, Maria. "New Mexico's Secret Jews: Now Is It Safe to Tell?" *Lilith* 16 (1991): 8–12.

Stroessner, Robert. *Santos of the Southwest: The Denver Art Museum Collection*. Denver: Denver Art Museum, 1971.

Suárez Fernández, Luis, ed. *Documentos acerca de la expulsión de los judíos*. Valladolid: Consejo Superior de Investigaciones Científicas, 1964.

Szeinberg, A. "Polymorphic Evidence for a Mediterranean Origin of the Ashkenazi Community." In Richard M. Goodman and Arno G. Motulsky, eds., *Genetic Diseases Among Ashkenazi Jews*, pp. 77–91. New York: Raven Press, 1979.

Teltsch, Kathleen. "After 500 Years, Discovering Jewish Ties that Bind." *New York Times*, November 29, 1992, p. 28.

———. "Scholars and Descendants Uncover Hidden Legacy of Jews in Southwest." *New York Times*, November 11, 1990, p. 16.

Tibón, Gutierre. *Diccionario etimológico comparado de los apellidos españoles, hispanoamericanos y filipinos*. Mexico City: Fondo de Cultura Económica, 1992.

Tobias, Henry J. *A History of the Jews in New Mexico*. Albuquerque: University of New Mexico Press, 1990.

Toro, Alfonso. *La familia Carvajal*. Mexico City: Editorial Patria, 1944.

———, ed. *Los judíos en la Nueva España: Documentos del siglo XVI correspondientes al ramo de Inquisición*. Mexico City: Archivo General de la Nación y Fondo de Cultura Económica, 1932, 1993.

Uchmany, Eva A. *La vida entre el judaísmo y el cristianismo en la Nueva España, 1580–1606*. Mexico City: Archivo General de la Nación and Fondo de Cultura Económica, 1992.

Ungerlieder-Mayerson, Joy. *Jewish Folk Art, from Biblical Days to Modern Times*. New York: Summit Books, 1986.

Vargas, Diego de. *Blood on the Boulders: The Journals of Don Diego de Vargas, New Mexico, 1694–97*. Edited by John L. Kessell, Rick Hendricks, and Meredith D. Dodge. 2 vols. Albuquerque: University of New Mexico Press, 1998.

———. *By Force of Arms: The Journals of Don Diego de Vargas, New Mexico, 1691–1693*. Edited by John L. Kessell and Rick Hendricks. Albuquerque: University of New Mexico Press, 1992.

———. *Remote Beyond Compare: Letters of Don Diego de Vargas to His Family from New Spain and New Mexico, 1675–1706*. Edited by John L. Kessell. Albuquerque: University of New Mexico Press, 1989.

———. *A Settling of Accounts: The Journals of Don Diego de Vargas, New Mexico, 1700–1704*. Edited by John L. Kessell, Rick Hendricks, Meredith D. Dodge, and Larry D. Miller. Albuquerque: University of New Mexico Press, 2002.

———. *That Disturbances Cease: The Journals of Don Diego de Vargas, 1697–1700*. Edited by John L. Kessell, Rick Hendricks, Meredith D. Dodge, and Larry D. Miller. Albuquerque: University of New Mexico Press, 2000.

———. *To the Royal Crown Restored: The Journals of Don Diego de Vargas, 1692–94*. Edited by John L. Kessell, Rick Hendricks, and Meredith D. Dodge. Albuquerque: University of New Mexico Press, 1995.

Veas Arteseros, Francisco de Asís. *Los judíos de Lorca en la baja edad media*. Murcia: Real Academia Alfonso X el Sabio, 1992.

Vieira, António. *Obras escolhidas*. 12 vols. Lisbon: Livraria Sá da Costa, 1951–1954.

Villagrá, Gaspar Pérez de. *Historia de la Nueva México*. 2 vols. Mexico City: Museo Nacional, 1900.

———. *History of New Mexico by Gaspar Pérez de Villagrá, Alcalá, 1610*. Translated by Gilberto Espinosa. Los Angeles: Quivira Society, 1933.

Walker, Randi Jones. *Protestantism in the Sangre de Cristos, 1850–1920*. Albuquerque: University of New Mexico Press, 1991.

West, Robert C. *The Mining Community in Northern New Spain: The Parral Mining District*. Berkeley: University of California Press, 1949.

Wiesenthal, Simon. *Sails of Hope: The Secret Mission of Christopher Columbus*. Translated by Richard Winston and Clara Winston. New York: Macmillan, 1973.

Will, Martina. "'God Gives and God Takes Away': Death and Dying in New Mexico, 1760–1850." Ph.D. diss., University of New Mexico, 2000.

Williams, Florence. "Keeping the Faith." *New Republic*, October 26, 1998, p. 12.

Wiznitzer, Arnold. "Crypto-Jews in Mexico During the Sixteenth Century." *American Jewish Historical Quarterly* 51 (1962): 168–214.

Wolf, Lucien. "Crypto-Jews Under the Commonwealth." *Transactions of the Jewish Historical Society of England* 1 (1893): 55–75.

———, ed. and trans. *Jews in the Canary Islands: Being a Calendar of Jewish Cases Extracted from the Records of the Canariote Inquisition in the Collection of the Marquess of Bute*. 1926. Reprint, Toronto: University of Toronto Press, 2001.

———, ed. *Judíos en las Islas Canarias: Calendario de los casos extraídos de los Archivos de la Inquisición canaria de la colección del Marqués de Bute*. Tenerife: Editorial J.A.D.L., 1988.

Wust, Klaus. *Folk Art in Stone, Southwest Virginia*. Edinburgh, Va.: Shenandoah History, 1970.

Zavala, Silvio. *La encomienda indiana*. Mexico City: Editorial Porrúa, 1992.

Ziprkowski, L., and M. Schewach-Millet. "A Long-Term Study of Pemphigus." *Proceedings of the Tel-Hashomer Hospital* 3 (1964): 46.

Index